A _Yankee_ CENTURY

Harvey Frommer

A *Yankee* CENTURY

INTRODUCTION BY PAUL O'NEILL

Berkley Books, New York

A Berkley Book
Published by The Berkley Publishing Group
A division of Penguin Putnam Inc.
375 Hudson Street
New York, New York 10014

This book is an original publication of The Berkley Publishing Group.

Photographs on the following pages are provided by Photofest: 13, 18, 19, 21, 22, 23, 24, 26, 29, 32, 34, 36, 37, 38, 44–45, 48, 49, 50, 51, 61, 62, 68, 71, 83, 95, 105, 107, 112, 115, 121, 123, 135, 136, 137, 144, 149, 154, 159, 164, 169, 171, 183, 186, 191, 192, 193, 195, 197, 199, 204, 211, 222, 223, 227, 232, 236, 241, 249, 250, 253, 254, 260, 283, 291, 293, 296, 312, 315, 318, 325, 328, 331, 333, 334, 337, 338, 355, 371, 373, 376, 379, 380, 384, 394, 395, 399, 401

Photographs on the following pages are provided by Photofest/Icon: ii, v, xv, 1, 3, 6, 9, 10, 16, 41, 47, 53, 54, 55, 60, 64–65, 74–75, 77, 80, 85, 96–97, 129, 131, 132, 133, 138, 140, 146, 147, 155, 158, 161, 173, 177, 181, 184, 185, 187, 188–189, 201, 206, 207, 213, 215, 224, 225, 230, 235, 246, 265, 271, 275, 278, 281, 301, 302, 305, 306–307, 308, 309, 311, 313, 327, 339, 351, 357, 365, 368, 382, 386, 389, 390–391

PRINTING HISTORY
Berkley hardcover / October 2002

Visit our website at
www.penguinputnam.com

Library of Congress Cataloging-in-Publication Data

Frommer, Harvey.
A Yankee century : a celebration of the first hundred years
of baseball's greatest team / Harvey Frommer.
p. cm.
Includes index.
ISBN 0-425-18617-2
1. New York Yankees (Baseball team)—History. I. Title.

GV875.N4 F74 2002
796.357'64'097471—dc21   2002074443

PRINTED IN THE UNITED STATES OF AMERICA
10 9 8 7 6 5 4 3 2 1

For Irv Kaze, who gave me my start in publishing,
and
For my family . . .
Myrna, Jennifer and Jeff, Fred, Ian

CONTENTS

■ PART 1 ■

CHAPTER ONE

MARCH OF YANKEE TIME

A day-by-day, month-by-month, year-by-year,
decade-by-decade look at one hundred years of Yankee baseball

3

CHAPTER TWO

STADIUM

From Hilltop Park to the Polo Grounds to Yankee Stadium
(old and new) and even the two-year stop at Shea

41

CHAPTER SEVEN

WHAT'S IN A NAME

Noms de plume, aliases, sobriquets, catchwords—nicknames, all time,
all ways for Yanks

313

CHAPTER EIGHT

BY THE NUMBERS

We've got your number, from 0 to $189 million—the ten-year
deal Jeter signed in 2001

327

CHAPTER NINE

100 QUESTION YANKEE QUIZ

From the ridiculous to the sublime, one hundred questions
(and answers) about all things Yankee—test your knowledge

357

CHAPTER TEN

FOR THE RECORD

List, charts, firsts, lasts, sidebars, argument starters and enders . . .

373

ACKNOWLEDGMENTS

ALWAYS AT THE top of any list is Myrna Katz Frommer, whose unerring eye and sensitive touches are reflected all over this book. Fred Frommer, young journalist extraordinaire, did some yeoman proofing. Thank you.

Although I did not have the opportunity to interview all of the people quoted in these pages, to all of the interviewees and "coaches" who gave of themselves with time and memories—thanks so much. Hopefully, I have not left anyone out: Mel Allen, Sparky Anderson, Yogi Berra, Dale Berra, Clay Bellinger, Scott Brosius, Bobby Brown, Andy Carey, Chris Chambliss, Jerry Coleman, Barry Deutsch, Dom DiMaggio, Bob Feller, Howard Elson, Red Foley, Tommy Henrich, Monte Irvin, Irv Kaze, Ralph Kiner, Tony Kubek, Don Larsen, Jack Lang, Eddie Layton, Robert Merrill, Tracy Nieporent, Drew Nieporent, Irv Noren, Mel Parnell, Pedro Ramos, Willie Randolph, Al Rosen, Bob Sheppard, Ron Straci, Bob Tewksbury, Jerry Vale, Bill Valentine, David Vigliano, Dave Winfield, Don Zimmer.

Thanks to my editor, the ebullient Martha Bushko, for her enthusiastic support and attention. Thanks also to all the folks at Berkley for their interest and help.

For the great photos—Ron and Howard Mandelbaum of Photofest.

INTRODUCTION

by Paul O'Neill

WHEN I WAS traded to the New York Yankees by the Reds in 1992, I was devastated. I had grown up in Cincinnati and was signed by the Reds right out of high school. The city and the team were places I was comfortable with. New York City and the Yankees were foreign to me.

But my father said: "Being a Yankee will turn out to be the best thing that ever happened to you." He turned out to be right.

Yet, at the start I didn't think so. The Yankees back then were a struggling, sub-par team, and the Bronx was a place I had heard negative things about. In fact, early on my car was stolen—twice. But I stuck with the Yankees, the Bronx, the fans, and learned pretty quickly that there was something very special about all of them.

I went on to make nine consecutive Opening Day starts for the Yankees and was fortunate enough to hit .300 or better in each of my first six seasons with the team, to win a batting title, and to play on four Yankee world-championship teams. It was extraordinary to be in that supercharged environment, to play under pressure day after day, season after season.

But even more significant was my realization that I was becoming part of the history of the most famous, celebrated, and glamorous sports team ever.

I had the honor of playing right field—the same position that had been held down by such greats as Babe Ruth, Tommy Henrich, Hank Bauer, Roger Maris, Reggie Jackson, and Dave Winfield.

I'll always remember running out onto the field with my teammates at Yankee Stadium at the start of a game. I'll always remember listening to Frank Sinatra sing at the end of a game: "If I can make it there, I'll make it anywhere." I'll always remember the fans calling out my name, "O'Neill, O'Neill, O'Neill," chanting, "Paul-ie, Paul-ie, Paul-ie."

My time as a New York Yankee was nine years and one day, and it came to an end after the 2001 season. I am just one of about twelve hundred players who have performed in pinstripes, and I feel a connection in one way or another with all of them. I hit the jackpot being a member of the New York Yankees.

That is what Harvey Frommer's *A Yankee Century* is about—the connections, the Yankee tradition, the culture passed down through the decades.

This definitive book captures the sweep and the scope of the team from the Bronx. It is about super talents, guys who willed themselves to succeed. It is about the high moments in franchise history and also about the disappointments. It is about the magic, the aura. It is all about celebrating one hundred years of Yankee baseball.

If you love baseball, if you love the New York Yankees—you will love this book.

—PAUL O'NEILL

Team

OF THE CENTURY

THE BEGINNING FOR the franchise was muted.

In their first two decades the New York Yankees won no pennants and managed just two second-place finishes. But then over the next forty-four years the team dominated the American League, winning nearly two of every three pennants and twenty World Series.

After that came another pennant drought of a dozen years, followed by years of plenty. Between 1976 and 1980, the Yankees won four division titles, three pennants, and two more world championships. For the next fourteen years, once again there were no pennants. And then came the world championships in 1996, 1998, 1999, and 2000.

From an inauspicious start back in 1903, once the New York Yankees got going, the world of baseball was never the same. The team from the Bronx has won more regular season games than any other franchise in the history of baseball, thirty-eight American League championships in an eighty-year period, and just about one World Series for every three played, twenty-six in all. The Yankees have been in more World Series and won more world championships and league championships than any other team in history.

They own bragging rights to the top five players of all time in World Series runs scored, RBIs, and total bases; the top three players of all time in World Series home runs, slugging percentages, and pitching; the most players inducted into the Baseball Hall of Fame in Cooperstown.

No matter what prism Yankee baseball history is viewed through, the image is supreme. The owners have been ambitious and aggressive, the managers prepared and innovative, the players talented and driven, and the regal home field commands respect.

The Yankees have actually played on four different home fields: Hilltop Park (1903–1912), the Polo Grounds (1913–1922), Yankee Stadium (1923 to the present); there were also a couple of odd seasons spent at Shea Stadium (1974–1975) while the old Yankee Stadium underwent a massive facelift.

But the big ballpark, the House that Ruth Built, powerful, historic, helped create and maintain the Yankee tradition right from the start. Through the years players from other teams have come into Yankee Stadium before a game, gawking, awed, and intrigued by the fabled monuments and plaques.

Different owners have put their stamp on the franchise, but Colonel Jacob Ruppert and George Steinbrenner have had the greatest impact.

The aristocratic and arrogant Ruppert held sway over Yankee fortunes from 1915 to 1939, a time of mostly great glory for the Bronx Bombers. One of the richest individuals in America in his time, Ruppert spent a good deal of his treasure on the Yankees. It was Ruppert who was responsible for Yankee Stadium and for the building blocks of the Yankee mystique. He truly earned his nickname, Master Builder in Baseball.

George Michael Steinbrenner III—who has owned the Yankees longer than any other owner—has been on the Yankee scene since 1973, a scene marked by turbulent issues, through stormy and down times to dramatic and thrilling successes. The man they call the Boss has been as devoted and driven about all things Yankee as anyone ever associated with the team. A big spender and poor loser like Ruppert, Steinbrenner remains totally immersed in the affairs of his team.

From the first manager, Clark Griffith (1903–1908), through Joe Torre (1996 to the present), there have been a total of forty-two Yankee pilots. They have ranged from indolent to driven, from brilliant to slow-witted, from cautious to carefree. A few, like Billy Martin, Yogi Berra, and Lou Piniella, have served multiple managing terms.

The self-effacing Miller Huggins (1918–1929) was the franchise's first great Yankee manager. Just five feet four inches and 140 pounds, the man they called

Hug was an unlikely Yankee. The eighth manager in the sixteen-year history of the franchise, Huggins initially was dwarfed by Babe Ruth and other Yankees in reputation and physical stature. But his tenacity and brilliance overcame his size and image handicaps. The first monument ever at Yankee Stadium was dedicated to the odd little man, "the greatest manager who ever lived," in Pitcher Waite Hoyt's phrase—who moved the Yankees from mediocrity to greatness.

Joe McCarthy came to the Yankees from the Cubs in 1931 and stayed on the scene as manager until 1946. A minor-leaguer for fifteen seasons, "Marse Joe" never played in the major leagues, yet he is the winningest manager of all time. Dedication to craft was one of McCarthy's most outstanding traits, and he passed this on so that it has become part of Yankee culture. The square-jawed pilot spent sixteen years in pinstripes, a time in which his teams won 1,460 games and recorded a superb .627 winning percentage. His 1936–1939 teams won four consecutive world championships.

Outlandish, unorthodox, a true baseball lifer, Charles Dillon Stengel was on the scene as manager from 1949 to 1960, a time of legendary accomplishments for the New York Yankees. Out of Kansas City, Missouri, Casey was a master of the pun, the one-liner; he scrambled verbs and adverbs and mangled other parts of speech. But oh, could he manage a ball club. His Yankees won ten pennants and seven World Series, including a record five straight world championships, 1949 through 1953. Only once in his dozen seasons as Yankee manager did a Stengel team win fewer than ninety games. Casey's Yankee career managing record was 1,149–696, a winning percentage of .623.

Pugnacious, disagreeable, driven, Billy Martin had five stints managing the Yankees: 1975–1978, 1979, 1983, 1985, and 1988. Number One's comings and goings were grist for New York City newspaper gossip and a source of endless fascination for fans. His record as a Yankee manager was 556 wins, 385 losses. His teams won two American League titles and one world championship. He died too soon at age sixty-one in a tragic automobile accident.

Joe Torre came to the New York Yankees in 1996. His previous record as a manager was undistinguished. He began the 1996 season with more than a thousand career losses, never having finished higher than fourth. But with the Yankees he turned himself and the franchise around. A communicator, a calm presence, a skilled handler of players (and owners), Joseph Paul Torre promptly showed the stuff that may qualify him as one of the top Yankee managers ever. The first manager in franchise history to be born in the New York City area, the sixth manager to reach the 500-victory plateau (582 wins through 2001), Torre's glittering record includes four World Series titles and five American League championships in just six Yankee seasons.

Owners and managers notwithstanding, it is the players who have truly given the Yankees their magic, their aura, their identity. More than twelve hundred have worn pinstripes.

There have been Babe Ruth's Yankees, Joe DiMaggio's Yankees, Mickey Mantle's Yankees, Reggie Jackson's Yankees, Derek Jeter's Yankees. There have been players with unique talents and standout personas whose images linger down the decades:

The tiny Wee Willie Keeler, hitting 'em where they ain't.

The sturdy Yogi Berra rushing to leap into Don Larsen's arms after the perfect game.

The determined Ryne Duren, wearing the coke-bottle eyeglasses, throwing the fastball to the backstop.

The solid Lou Gehrig playing on and on through the hurt and the pain.

The adroit Phil Rizzuto deftly bunting the ball.

The zoned-in Eddie Lopat tossing the junk balls.

The multitalented Mick busting it down the first-base line, head down after bashing one of his monster home runs.

The peripatetic Thurman Munson in the dirty uniform, blocking home plate.

The composed and collected Mariano Rivera, always ready for the pressure.

Yankee fans have thrilled to the quiet class and dignity of Joe DiMaggio, Earle Combs, Elston Howard, Don Mattingly, Willie Randolph, Lou Gehrig, Roy White, Bobby Murcer, Mariano Rivera, Derek Jeter, Bernie Williams.

They have tuned in to and sometimes been turned off by feisty, fiery, moody ones like Bob Meusel, Joe Page, Roger Maris, Thurman Munson, Billy Martin, Paul O'Neill.

They have admired the gifted ones like Mickey Mantle, Whitey Ford, Dave Winfield, Jim "Catfish" Hunter, Red Ruffing, Joe Gordon, Graig Nettles, Herb Pennock, Ron Guidry.

They have been entertained and also annoyed by characters like Lefty Gomez, Mickey Rivers, Phil Linz, Sparky Lyle, Reggie Jackson, Goose Gossage, Joe Pepitone.

They have felt a special affection for the tough and dependable ones like Bill Skowron, Chris Chambliss, Hank Bauer, Tommy Henrich, Ralph Houk, Allie Reynolds, Bill Dickey, Tony Lazzeri.

And they have marveled at the Babe, bigger and better than them all, swinging from the heels, connecting with the crowd, lit up by power and personality.

So come, let us celebrate one hundred years of New York Yankees baseball.

PART

1

CHAPTER ONE

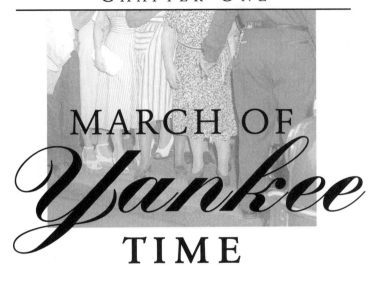

MARCH OF
Yankee
TIME

1890s

FEBRUARY 6, 1895   Babe Ruth is born at 216 Emory Street, Baltimore, Maryland.

JULY 12, 1899   Jack Chesbro makes his major-league pitching debut.

1903

JANUARY 9   Frank Farrell and Bill Devery purchase the defunct American League Baltimore franchise for $18,000. The team is moved to Manhattan.

MARCH 12   The New York team is approved as a member of the American League. They will play baseball in a quickly constructed, all-wood park at 168th Street and Broadway.

APRIL 22 The Highlanders play their first game in Washington before 11,950. The Senators defeat them 3–1.

APRIL 23 The Highlanders win their first game, trimming Washington 7–2.

APRIL 30 The Highlanders win their home opener at Hilltop Park, defeating Washington 6–2.

JULY 14 Clark Griffith, a player-manager, is the first Yankee pitcher to hit a home run.

1904

JULY 4 Pitcher Jack Chesbro wins his fourteenth game in a row for the Highlanders.

AUGUST 24 Outfielder Wee Willie Keeler hits two inside-the-park home runs against the St. Louis Browns in a 9–1 win at New York.

OCTOBER 7 Jack Chesbro pitches the Highlanders to a 3–2 win over Boston, his forty-first victory. Chesbro's 41–12 record will top the American League in wins and winning percentage.

1905

AUGUST 4 A unique battery works a game for the Highlanders: Doc Newton pitches and Mike "Doc" Powers catches. Powers is a physician.

AUGUST 5 First baseman Hal Chase has a record thirty-eight putouts in a doubleheader against the St. Louis Browns.

1906

MAY 7 Manager Clark Griffith is struck in the mouth while arguing a call by umpire Tim Hurst. Hurst is suspended for five days.

SEPTEMBER 1 The New York Highlanders win their sixth game in three days, sweeping their third straight doubleheader from Washington, an American League record.

SEPTEMBER 4 The New Yorkers move into first place, sweeping Boston 7–0 and 1–0, their fifth doubleheader sweep in a row, a major-league record.

1907

MAY 31 Shortstop Kid Elberfeld steals home twice against Boston.

JUNE 28 A Highlander utility player named Branch Rickey has thirteen bases stolen on him by the Washington Senators. The young man, who will go on to greater moments in baseball, appears that season in fifty-two games and bats .182.

1908

SEPTEMBER 7 The Highlanders lose a 4–0 two-hitter to Walter Johnson, his third straight shutout in four days.

1909

SEPTEMBER 11 Jack Chesbro is traded to Boston, where he will pitch only one game before retiring from baseball.

1912

APRIL 11 Pinstripes appear on the uniforms of the New York Highlanders for the first time.

APRIL 20 After being rained out the previous two days, the Red Sox defeat the New York Highlanders 7–6 in eleven innings before a crowd of twenty-seven thousand in the first game ever played at Fenway. That same day the *Titanic* sinks.

APRIL 21 A benefit game for the survivors of the *Titanic* disaster is staged at Hilltop Park. The New York Giants trounce the Highlanders 11–2.

OCTOBER 5 The final game is played at Hilltop Park as the Highlanders nip the Senators 8–6.

1913

APRIL After becoming tenants of the New York Giants at the Polo Grounds, the Highlanders are officially renamed the Yankees.

1914

AUGUST 3 Les Nunamaker of the Yankees becomes the only twentieth-century catcher to throw out three runners attempting to steal in one inning.

1915

JANUARY 11   The Yankees are purchased for $460,000 by Colonel Jacob Ruppert and Colonel Tillinghast L'Hommedieu Huston.

FEBRUARY 10   Allie Reynolds is born in Bethany, Oklahoma.

MAY 6   Babe Ruth, playing for the Boston Red Sox, hits his first major-league home run. Yankee pitcher Jack Warhop yields the historic homer.

1917

APRIL 24   George Mogridge hurls a no-hitter in a 2–1 triumph at Fenway Park. He becomes the first Yankee pitcher to accomplish the feat.

JUNE 17   The Yankees and Giants play the first Sunday baseball game before twenty-one thousand fans for World War I charity.

1918

Miller Huggins begins his first year as manager of the Yankees. He will manage the Yankees from 1918 until 1929.

Colonel Jake Ruppert, Miller Huggins, and Babe Ruth

1919

SEPTEMBER 24   Babe Ruth of the Boston Red Sox hits his twenty-eighth home run, breaking Ned Williamson's single-season home-run mark set in 1884. Ruth's drive, against the New York Yankees, clears the right-field *roof* of the Polo Grounds. Ruth will finish the season with twenty-nine homers.

1920

JANUARY 3   Babe Ruth's contract is purchased from the Boston Red Sox by the Yankees for $125,000 and a $350,000 loan against the Fenway Park mortgage.

MAY 1   Babe Ruth hits his first home run as a Yankee, propelling the Yankees to a 6–0 victory over the Red Sox.

JUNE 26   Lou Gehrig, a junior at New York City's School of Commerce, smashes a grand-slam home run, giving his team a 12–8 victory in a high school championship game in Chicago.

JULY 16   Babe Ruth hits his thirtieth home run, breaking his single-season record of twenty-nine. He will finish the season with fifty-four homers.

AUGUST 16   Yankees pitcher Carl Mays beans Indians shortstop Ray Chapman. The Cleveland infielder dies the next day, becoming the first and only death in the history of major-league baseball.

OCTOBER 1   The Yankees become the first team to draw one million people to their games, ending the season with a total attendance of 1,289,422.

OCTOBER 29   Ed Barrow, former Red Sox manager, is appointed general manager of the Yankees.

1922

MAY 5   Construction work on Yankee Stadium is under way.

MAY 21   Colonel Ruppert pays $1.5 million for Colonel Huston's share of the Yankees.

SEPTEMBER 5   Babe Ruth hits his last home run at the Polo Grounds. Boston's Herb Pennock, who gave up the Babe's first Polo Grounds dinger as a Yankee on May 1, 1920, gives up Ruth's last one there.

SEPTEMBER 11   An estimated overflow crowd of forty thousand shows up for the farewell home games of the Yankees at the Polo Grounds. More than twenty-five thousand are turned away. The Yankees sweep a doubleheader from the A's.

SEPTEMBER 30   The Yankees clinch their second AL pennant with a 3–1 win over the Red Sox at Fenway.

1923

JANUARY 30   The Red Sox trade pitcher Herb Pennock to New York for infielder Norm McMillan, pitcher George Murray, outfielder Camp Skinner, and $50,000.

APRIL 18   Yankee Stadium opens before an estimated crowd of 74,200. Babe Ruth hits the stadium's first home run; the Yankees defeat the Boston Red Sox, 4–1.

Lou Gehrig, that same day, pitching for Columbia University, strikes out seventeen Williams College batters in a 5–1 loss.

SEPTEMBER 4   Sam Jones no-hits the Athletics 2–0.

SEPTEMBER 23   Signed in June for a $1,500 bonus, Lou Gehrig records the first of his 493 career home runs as a Yankee.

SEPTEMBER 28   En route to a 24–4 victory, the Yankees pound out thirty hits against Boston, an American League record.

OCTOBER 10   Yankee Stadium hosts its first World Series game. With two out in the top of the ninth inning of game one and the score 4–4, a thirty-four-year-old New York Giants outfielder named Casey Stengel lines a pitch from Joe Bush into the left-center-field gap and comes home with an inside-the-park home run, giving the Giants a 5–4 victory over the Yankees.

OCTOBER 15   The Yankees defeat the New York Giants to win their first world championship in the first all–New York World Series. They take the series four games to two.

1925

JUNE 1   Lou Gehrig pinch-hits for Pee-Wee Wanninger and begins his record streak of 2,130 consecutive games played.

JUNE 2   First baseman Wally Pipp is hit on the side of the head during batting practice and as a result is replaced at first base by Lou Gehrig.

JULY 23   Lou Gehrig hits the first of what will be his major-league-record twenty-three grand-slam home runs as the Yankees defeat the Washington Senators, 11–7.

AUGUST 1   The Yankees purchase Tony Lazzeri's contract from Salt Lake City of the Pacific Coast League. Lazzeri will begin playing for the Yankees the following spring.

SEPTEMBER 8   Red Sox pitcher Buster Ross gives up Babe Ruth's three hundredth career home run.

SEPTEMBER 10   Babe Ruth and Lou Gehrig homer in the same game for the first time.

Jimmie Foxx, Babe Ruth, Lou
Gehrig, and Al Simmons

SEPTEMBER 22   Ben Paschal of the New York Yankees hits two
inside-the-park home runs at Yankee Stadium in an 11–6 victory over
the White Sox.

1926

FEBRUARY 1   Wally Pipp is sold to the Cincinnati Reds for $7,500.

1927

AUGUST 16   Babe Ruth is the first player to hit a ball over Comiskey
Park's roof.
SEPTEMBER 13   Babe Ruth hits two home runs, and the Yankees win a
pair from Cleveland to clinch the AL pennant with a 98–41 record.

SEPTEMBER 30   Hitting home run number 60 on the final day of the season, Babe Ruth breaks his own major-league single-season record.

1928

APRIL 20   The left-field stands are expanded to three decks as the Yankees begin their sixth Yankee Stadium season.

1929

Babe Ruth and family

APRIL 16   The Yankees make numbers a permanent part of their uniform. They are the first major-league team to do so.

MAY 19   Seeking cover from a cloudburst, fans at Yankee Stadium stampede in the standing-room-only right-field bleachers. Two die and sixty-two are injured. Jake Ruppert says he will never again sell more tickets than seats.

SEPTEMBER 25   Miller Huggins dies of blood poisoning from a boil.

OCTOBER 17   Former pitcher Bob Shawkey is signed as manager.

1930

MARCH 8   Babe Ruth signs a two-year contract for $160,000, making him the highest-paid player in baseball, a salary higher than President Hoover's. The Babe quips: "I had a better year than he did." Ed Barrow, Yankee GM, says, "No one will ever be paid more than Ruth."

JULY 5   The New York Lincoln Giants and the Baltimore Black Sox split a doubleheader before twenty thousand at Yankee Stadium as Negro League teams play there for the first time.

AUGUST 23   Shortstop Frank Crosetti's contract for the following season is purchased from the San Francisco Seals of the Pacific Coast League.

OCTOBER 10   Joe McCarthy signs a four-year contract to manage the Yankees.

1931

FEBRUARY 15   The Yankee training site in St. Petersburg, Florida, is renamed Miller Huggins Field, to honor the team's late manager.

APRIL 12   Joe McCarthy debuts as Yankee manager.

SEPTEMBER 13   Tony Lazzeri steals second base and home in the twelfth inning, giving Lefty Gomez a 2–1 victory over Detroit.

NOVEMBER 6   Jack Chesbro dies at age fifty-six in Conway, Massachusetts.

1932

MAY 30   A plaque honoring Miller Huggins is dedicated at Yankee Stadium.

JUNE 3   Lou Gehrig becomes the first modern-day player to hit four home runs in a game. The Yankees romp 20–13 over Philadelphia.

JULY 3   The first Sunday game at Fenway Park is played and Boston loses to the Yankees, 13–2.

SEPTEMBER 13   The Yankees clinch the American League pennant; Joe McCarthy becomes the first manager to win pennants in both leagues.

OCTOBER 1   Babe Ruth homers into the center-field bleachers in game three of the World Series off Chicago's Charlie Root. The home run will be known as the called shot. On this day Joe DiMaggio, a seventeen-year-old shortstop, appears in his first game for the San Francisco Seals in the Pacific Coast League.

DECEMBER 31   Colonel Jacob Ruppert hires George Weiss as general manager to create and supervise the Yankee farm system.

1933

JULY 6   The first major-league All-Star Game is played at Comiskey Park, and Babe Ruth's two-run home run gives the American League a 4–2 win. Yankee pitcher Lefty Gomez gets the win.

AUGUST 17   Lou Gehrig plays in his 1,308th consecutive game, breaking Everett Scott's major-league record, set in 1923.

1934

JUNE 3   Babe Ruth and Lou Gehrig homer in the same game for the final time.

JUNE 6   Yankee outfielder Myril Hoag ties an American League record with six singles in six at bats. Hoag has only sixty-seven hits that season.

JULY 14   Babe Ruth slams his seven hundredth career home run. It comes off Tommy Bridges in the second inning as the Yankees defeat Detroit 4–2 at Navin Field.

AUGUST 12   Making his final appearance in Boston in a Yankee uniform, Ruth draws a record crowd of 47,766 at Fenway Park. More than 20,000 are turned away.

SEPTEMBER 29 Babe Ruth hits his last home run as a Yankee in a doubleheader at Washington.

NOVEMBER 21 The New York Yankees obtain Joe DiMaggio from the San Francisco Seals for $50,000.

1935

FEBRUARY 26 Babe Ruth is released by the Yankees and signs with the Boston Braves.

DECEMBER 11 The Yankees trade pitcher Johnny Allen to Cleveland for Monte Pearson and Steve Sundra.

1936

MARCH 17 Joe DiMaggio makes his debut as a Yankee in a spring-training game and records four hits.

MAY 3 Joe DiMaggio's Yankee Stadium debut attracts an estimated twenty-five thousand Italian Americans, who wave the Italian flag. The rookie collects three hits in a 14–5 romp over St. Louis.

MAY 24 Tony Lazzeri hits two grand-slam home runs, setting an American League record for single-game RBIs—eleven.

SEPTEMBER 9 The Yankees clinch the pennant on the earliest date in history.

OCTOBER 4 Lou Gehrig paces a 5–2 win as another attendance record is set at Yankee Stadium with 66,669 on hand.

1937

APRIL 20 Yankee Stadium's fifteenth season begins with the right-field stands expanded to three decks. A concrete facility replaces the wooden bleachers. The distance to the center-field fence is reduced from 490 to 461 feet.

1938

MAY 30 A franchise-record crowd of 81,841 watches a Yankee doubleheader sweep of the Boston Red Sox. More than 6,000 fans are turned away; 511 are given refunds.

AUGUST 27   The first no-hitter is pitched at Yankee Stadium as Monte
  Pearson coasts 13–0 over Cleveland.
AUGUST 28   Joe DiMaggio ties a major-league record with three triples
  in a game against St. Louis.

1939

JANUARY 13   Colonel Jacob Ruppert dies at the age of seventy-one.
JANUARY 17   Ed Barrow is elected team president, succeeding Colonel
  Ruppert.
MAY 2   Lou Gehrig's playing streak of 2,130 straight games comes to an
  end. Babe Dahlgren takes over at first base. The Yankees crush Detroit,
  22–2.
JULY 4   Lou Gehrig Appreciation Day is held before 61,808 at Yankee
  Stadium. Gehrig's uniform number (4) is retired.
JULY 11   The All-Star Game is played at Yankee Stadium, and Joe
  DiMaggio's home run paces a 3–1 American League victory.
OCTOBER 24   Joe DiMaggio is the American League's Most Valuable
  Player.
DECEMBER 7   Lou Gehrig is elected to the Baseball Hall of Fame.

1940

Babe Dahlgren

SEPTEMBER 8   Second baseman Joe Gordon hits
  for the cycle.

1941

MAY 15   Joe DiMaggio's fifty-six-game hitting
  streak begins as he singles off Chicago's Edgar
  Smith.
JUNE 2   Lou Gehrig dies at the age of thirty-seven
  of amyotrophic lateral sclerosis exactly sixteen
  years to the day that he replaced Wally Pipp at
  first base in the Yankee lineup.
JUNE 28   Joe DiMaggio reaches across the plate to
  hit a pitch thrown by the Athletics' Johnny
  Babich and singles through the box, extending
  his hitting streak to forty games. Babich had
  tried to walk DiMaggio in each at bat to end his
  hitting streak.

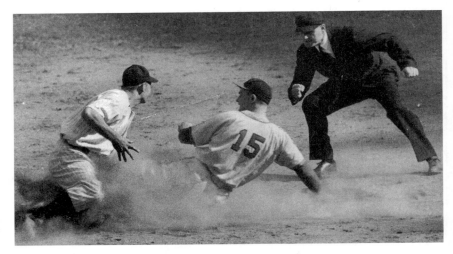

Joe Gordon tags out Walker Cooper of St. Louis in the 1943 World Series.

JUNE 29 In a doubleheader against the Washington Senators, Joe DiMaggio ties and then breaks the American League record of hitting safely in forty-one consecutive games. DiMaggio doubles in the opener and singles in the second game, breaking the record set by George Sisler of the St. Louis Browns in 1922.

JULY 2 Joe DiMaggio extends his hitting streak to forty-five consecutive games, breaking Willie Keeler's major-league record of forty-four.

JULY 17 Joe DiMaggio's consecutive-game hitting streak is ended at fifty-six. He is 0 for 3 in a 4–3 Yankee victory over Cleveland.

SEPTEMBER 4 With eighteen games remaining in the season, the Yankees record the earliest pennant-clinching date in history.

NOVEMBER 27 Joe DiMaggio edges Ted Williams 291–254 votes for the American League Most Valuable Player award.

1942

AUGUST 14 The Yankees turn seven double plays against the Philadelphia Athletics.

1943

OCTOBER 11 Spud Chandler pitches a ten-hit 2–0 shutout against the St. Louis Cardinals. The Yankees win the World Series in five games.

NOVEMBER 11 Pitcher Spud Chandler wins the American League MVP award.

1944

JUNE 26   To raise funds for war bonds, the New York Giants, Brooklyn Dodgers, and New York Yankees each play six innings against each other at the Polo Grounds.

1945

JANUARY 25   Dan Topping, Del Webb, and Larry MacPhail obtain the Yankees for $2.8 million from Colonel Jacob Ruppert's estate. The deal includes 400 players, 266 of them in military service, Yankee Stadium, parks in Newark and Kansas City, and leases on other minor-league ballparks. Jake Ruppert had paid more than that just for the ground on which Yankee Stadium was built in 1923.

1946

MAY 24   Joe McCarthy resigns and Bill Dickey replaces him as Yankee manager.

MAY 28   Before 49,917 fans, the first night game is played at Yankee Stadium. Washington defeats the Yankees 2–1.

1947

APRIL 27   Babe Ruth Day is celebrated in every baseball park in the United States and Japan. The Babe attends the celebration at Yankee Stadium but is too frail and ill to wear his old uniform.

OCTOBER 2   Yogi Berra homers off Brooklyn's Ralph Branca, becoming the first player to hit a pinch-hit home run in World Series history.

OCTOBER 5   Al Gionfriddo makes "the Catch," robbing Joe DiMaggio of a home run that would have tied the sixth game of the 1947 World Series.

OCTOBER 7   Just moments after the final game of the 1947 World Series, Larry MacPhail resigns as Yankee general manager. Dan Topping and Del Webb then buy out MacPhail's one-third interest in the club for $2 million.

NOVEMBER 27   Joe DiMaggio wins his third American League MVP. He edges out Ted Williams by a single point, setting off controversy as Williams, the Triple Crown winner, is left off one ballot.

1948

MARCH 29   The Yankees and Red Sox play through four hours and two minutes to a 2–2 tie in a spring-training game in which thirty-three players are used.

JUNE 13   Babe Ruth's uniform number (3) is retired at Babe Ruth Day at Yankee Stadium before 49,641 fans.

AUGUST 16   Babe Ruth passes away of throat cancer in New York City at age fifty-three.

OCTOBER 12   Casey Stengel takes over as manager, replacing Bucky Harris.

Mourners for Babe Ruth at Yankee Stadium on August 18, 1948

1949

FEBRUARY 7   Joe DiMaggio signs for $100,000, the first six-figure contract in baseball history.

APRIL 19   At the season opener, a granite monument to Babe Ruth is unveiled in center field. Plaques honoring Lou Gehrig and Miller Huggins are also presented.

SEPTEMBER 25   Despite seventy-one injuries, the Yankees remain alone in first place all season, until a 4–1 victory by the Red Sox moves Boston into a tie for first.

OCTOBER 2   A 5–3 victory over the Red Sox gives the Yankees the pennant.

1950

APRIL 18   Billy Martin becomes the first player to get two hits in one inning in his first major-league game. Martin's two hits are part of a nine-run Yankee eighth inning at Fenway Park.

MAY 13   Ed Barrow Day is staged at Yankee Stadium.

JULY 19   The Yankees purchase the contracts of their first black players: outfielder Elston Howard and pitcher Frank Barnes from the Kansas City Monarchs. Both are assigned to Muskegon in the Central League.

SEPTEMBER 10   Joe DiMaggio becomes the first player to hit three home runs in one game at Washington, D.C.'s, Griffith Stadium.

DECEMBER 18   Outfielder Tommy Henrich retires and becomes a Yankee coach.

1951

MARCH 26   Mickey Mantle blasts two monster home runs in an exhibition game played at Bovard Field at the University of Southern California.

APRIL 17   Mickey Mantle plays his first major-league game at Yankee Stadium. He gets one hit in four at bats against Boston.

MAY 1   Mickey Mantle hits his first major-league home run. It comes off Randy Gumpert of the White Sox in Chicago at Comiskey Park. The ball travels nearly five hundred feet.

MAY 16   Mickey Mantle hits his first major-league home run at Yankee Stadium.

JUNE 19   Mickey homers for the first time in both games of a doubleheader.

Joe DiMaggio and Mickey Mantle

JULY 12   Allie Reynolds no-hits the Indians at Municipal Stadium in Cleveland.

JULY 15   Mickey Mantle, not playing well, is optioned down to Kansas City of the American Association.

AUGUST 20   Mickey Mantle, back in a groove, is recalled from Kansas City.

SEPTEMBER 28   In game one of a doubleheader against Boston at Yankee Stadium, Allie Reynolds tosses his second no-hitter of the season, defeating the Red Sox 8–0.

OCTOBER 4   Mickey Mantle plays in his first World Series game.

OCTOBER 5   Mickey Mantle gets his first World Series hit but is injured when his spikes get caught in a sprinkler head while he is chasing down a fly ball hit by Willie Mays.

OCTOBER 10   Mickey Mantle wins his first world championship as the Yankees beat the Giants in six games.

NOVEMBER 8   Yogi Berra wins the first of three MVP awards.

DECEMBER 12   Joe DiMaggio announces his retirement.

1952

JULY 26   In Detroit, Mickey Mantle slams his first career grand slam. It lands in the upper deck in left center field.

SEPTEMBER 2   The Yankees shut out the Red Sox in both games of a doubleheader, 5–0 and 4–0.

SEPTEMBER 17   A mammoth home-run shot by Mickey Mantle off the upper-deck football press box in Detroit powers a Yankee win over the Tigers.

1953

APRIL 17   Mickey Mantle blasts a monster 565-foot homer off Chuck Stobbs at Griffith Stadium in Washington, D.C. Yankees PR director Red Patterson coins the term "tape-measure home run" by measuring the homer during the game. It may be the most famous home run ever hit. *The Guinness Book of World Records* lists it as the longest home run to be measured at the time it was hit.

JULY 6   Mickey Mantle slams his first pinch-hit home run. It travels over five hundred feet out of Shibe Park in Philadelphia.

World Series vs. Dodgers. The Yankees celebrate their 1952 World Series victory over the Dodgers.

AUGUST 7   Mickey Mantle hits his first inside-the-park home run as the Yankees beat Chicago 6–1 at Yankee Stadium.

OCTOBER 4   Mickey Mantle pounds a first-pitch grand slam into the upper deck in left center field as the Yankees beat the Dodgers 11–7 at Ebbets Field.

OCTOBER 5   The Yankees win their record fifth consecutive World Series championship, eliminating the Brooklyn Dodgers in six games.

OCTOBER 28   Red Barber resigns as Brooklyn Dodgers announcer. He signs on as an announcer with the Yankees.

1954

FEBRUARY 23   Vic Raschi's contract is purchased from the Yankees by the Cardinals for $85,000.

SEPTEMBER 6   Ten Yankee pinch hitters are used against the Red Sox.

SEPTEMBER 26   Casey Stengel's "power lineup" nips the Athletics 8–6 in that franchise's final game in Philadelphia. Yogi Berra plays third base for the first and only time in his professional career. Mickey Mantle plays shortstop.

NOVEMBER 3   Members of the Yankees tour Japan, drawing a record crowd of sixty-four thousand when they play the first game against the All-Japan Stars in Osaka. Andy Carey hits thirteen home runs and Elston Howard bats .468 on the twenty-five-game tour.

NOVEMBER 18   Don Larsen, Bob Turley, and Billy Hunter are traded to the Yankees from the Orioles for Harry Byrd, Jim McDonald, Hal Smith, Gus Triandos, Gene Woodling, and Willie Miranda.

DECEMBER 1   The deal is concluded with Mike Blyzka, Darrell Johnson, Jim Fridley, and Dick Kryhoski coming to New York for Bill Miller, Kal Segrist, Don Leppert, and minor-leaguer Ted DelGuercio. In all, seventeen players are involved in the largest trade in history.

1955

JANUARY 26   Joe DiMaggio is elected to the Baseball Hall of Fame.

APRIL 13   Mickey Mantle homers on Opening Day for the first time.

APRIL 14   Elston Howard singles in his major-league debut in a game against the Red Sox.

MAY 13   Mickey Mantle slugs three home runs, two batting left-handed and one from the right side. The only three-home-run game of his career, it is the first of ten times he homers from both sides of the plate. He goes 4 for 4 and drives in all five runs to pace a Yankee win over the Tigers in New York.

JUNE 6   Mickey Mantle hits the first home run ever to go over the center-field screen at Briggs Stadium in Detroit.

JUNE 7   Mickey Mantle smashes the first home run ever to go into the center-field "black seats" at Yankee Stadium. It travels 486 feet.

SEPTEMBER 23   The Yankees clinch the pennant, beating the Red Sox 3–2.

Mickey Mantle, May 1959

1956

APRIL 17   Mickey Mantle slashes two long Opening Day homers against the Senators at Griffith Stadium. President Eisenhower cheers Mantle on from his seat behind the Washington dugout.

MAY 30   Homering off Pedro Ramos, Mickey Mantle's shot nearly goes out of Yankee Stadium, hitting the right-field façade.

SEPTEMBER 30   Mickey Mantle nips Ted Williams in the batting title race on the last day of the season to win baseball's Triple Crown.

OCTOBER 8   Don Larsen pitches the only perfect game in World Series history. The Yankees defeat the Brooklyn Dodgers 2–0 in game five at Yankee Stadium. It is the sixth perfect game in major-league baseball history.

DECEMBER 18   Phil Rizzuto signs on as a Yankee radio-TV announcer.

1957

APRIL 20   Slugger Moose Skowron homers out of Fenway Park, just one of only six balls ever hit out of the park, to the right of the center-field flagpole.

JULY 14   Moose Skowron hits a then-major-league-record second pinch-hit grand slam of the season off Jim Wilson of the White Sox in the second game of a doubleheader.

JULY 23   Mickey Mantle hits for the cycle for his first and only time. He goes 4 for 5, scoring two runs and driving in four.

NOVEMBER 22   Mickey Mantle wins the MVP award.

1958

SEPTEMBER 17   Mickey Mantle slams a home run over the roof and out of Tiger Stadium in Detroit.

SEPTEMBER 20   Baltimore Orioles right-hander Hoyt Wilhelm, sporting a 2–10 record, no-hits the New York Yankees.

1959

DECEMBER 5   Yogi Berra visits Italy on behalf of major-league baseball to present baseball equipment and aid in the sport's development there.

DECEMBER 11   Roger Maris is acquired in a seven-player trade that sends Don Larsen, Hank Bauer, Marv Throneberry, and Norm Siebern to the Athletics.

1960

JULY 13   Yankee Stadium is the site of the All-Star Game. The National League wins 6–0.

AUGUST 13   Three days after his eighty-sixth birthday, former president Herbert Hoover throws out the first ball at the Old Timers' Day game at Yankee Stadium.

SEPTEMBER 10   Mickey Mantle hits a tremendous home run over the right-field roof at Tiger Stadium in Detroit. The ball crosses Trumbull Avenue and lands in a lumberyard. *The Guinness Book of World Records* lists it as the longest home run ever measured (after the fact) in baseball history.

OCTOBER 13   A bottom-of-the-ninth-inning home run by Bill Mazeroski of the Pirates breaks a 9–9 tie, defeats the Yankees, and gives Pittsburgh the world championship, winning four games to three.

OCTOBER 18   Casey Stengel is forced out as manager. Yankee co-owners Dan Topping and Del Webb institute a mandatory retirement age of sixty-five.

OCTOBER 20   Ralph Houk succeeds Stengel as manager.

NOVEMBER 2   Roger Maris edges out Mickey Mantle for the Most Valuable Player award, 225–222.

Yankees vs. Phillies at spring training on March 15, 1961. Elston Howard is #32.

1961

APRIL 26   Roger Maris homers for the first time in 1961 in Detroit off Paul Foytack.

OCTOBER 1   Roger Maris hits his sixty-first home run in the last game of the season off Boston's Tracy Stallard, breaking Babe Ruth's record of sixty.

OCTOBER 12   Manager Ralph Houk is given a two-year contract extension.

1962

APRIL 10   Mickey Mantle hits his last Opening Day home run. It goes some 425 feet into the right-center-field bleachers at Yankee Stadium, and the Yankees nip Baltimore 7–6.

JUNE 24   Yankee outfielder Jack Reed hits a twenty-second-inning home run that finally ends the longest game in franchise history. The Yankees win 9–7 at Detroit.

OCTOBER 16   The Yankees win the World Series against the San Francisco Giants. Second baseman Bobby Richardson snags Willie McCovey's two-on, two-out shot in the ninth inning of game seven.

Roger Maris, May 1962

1963

FEBRUARY 27   Mickey Mantle signs his first $100,000 contract.

NOVEMBER 7   Elston Howard is the American League's first black Most Valuable Player.

1964

AUGUST 12   Mickey Mantle sets a switch-hitting record, homering from both sides of the plate in one game for the tenth time.

OCTOBER 3   An 8–3 defeat of Cleveland gives the Yankees their fifth straight pennant.

OCTOBER 15   In his final World Series game, Mickey Mantle hits his eighteenth World Series home run to set the all-time Fall Classic home-run record.

OCTOBER 17   The Yankees lose the World Series to the St. Louis Cardinals and fire manager Yogi Berra.

NOVEMBER 2   CBS obtains 80 percent of the Yankees for $11.2 million, and later purchases the remaining 20 percent.

1965

JULY 20   Pitcher Mel Stottlemyre hits an inside-the-park grand-slam home run against Boston, giving New York a 6–3 win.

1966

JULY 25   Casey Stengel is inducted into the Baseball Hall of Fame.

SEPTEMBER 25   Only 413 show up at Yankee Stadium, the smallest crowd in the history of the franchise, as the White Sox beat the Yankees 4–1.

OCTOBER 13   Lee MacPhail is named general manager.

DECEMBER 8   Roger Maris is traded to the Cardinals for Charlie Smith.

1967

MAY 14   Mickey Mantle homers for the five hundredth time.

MAY 30   After playing in just seven games in 1967, Whitey Ford retires.

JUNE 7   Outfielder Ron Blomberg is selected by the last-place Yankees as their first pick in the free-agent draft.

Mickey Mantle at bat

1968

SEPTEMBER 20   Mickey Mantle hits his final home run, number 563. It comes off Jim Lonborg of Boston.

SEPTEMBER 28   At Fenway Park, Mickey Mantle plays in his final game—number 2,401, the most ever for a Yankee.

NOVEMBER 19   Pitcher Stan Bahnsen is named American League Rookie of the Year.

1969

JUNE 8   Mickey Mantle Day is celebrated before a record crowd at Yankee Stadium. His uniform number (7) is retired. A plaque is dedicated in honor of Joe DiMaggio in Monument Park.

JULY 21   At the All-Star banquet in Washington, D.C., Joe DiMaggio is named the Greatest Living Player, and Babe Ruth is selected as the Greatest All-Time Player.

1970

AUGUST 29   Mickey Mantle becomes the Yankee first-base coach.

NOVEMBER 25   Catcher Thurman Munson is selected as American League Rookie of the Year.

1972

MARCH 22   Southpaw Sparky Lyle is acquired from the Red Sox for Danny Cater.

AUGUST 7   Lefty Gomez and Yogi Berra are inducted into the Hall of
Fame.

AUGUST 8   The Yankees sign a thirty-year lease to play in a remodeled
Yankee Stadium beginning in 1976.

1973

JANUARY 3   George M. Steinbrenner III heads a limited partnership
that purchases the Yankees from CBS.

MARCH 5   Teammates Fritz Peterson and Mike Kekich announce at
spring training that their wives, families, and family dogs have been
swapped.

APRIL 6   Ron Blomberg bats as baseball's first designated hitter and
draws a first-inning walk from Boston's Luis Tiant.

AUGUST 1   Red Sox catcher Carlton Fisk and Thurman Munson brawl
at Fenway Park after the Yankee catcher attempts to score from third
base on a missed bunt attempt.

SEPTEMBER 30   Completing their fiftieth anniversary season at the old
Yankee Stadium, the Yankees play their final game there. Ralph Houk
resigns as manager.

1974

JANUARY 3   Bill Virdon becomes Yankee manager.

APRIL 6   Playing their first home game outside of Yankee Stadium since
1922, the Yankees begin the first of two seasons at Shea Stadium. They
defeat Cleveland 6–1.

AUGUST 12   Whitey Ford and Mickey Mantle are inducted into the
Baseball Hall of Fame.

NOVEMBER 27   George Steinbrenner is fined $15,000 by the courts and
then suspended for two years by baseball commissioner Bowie Kuhn
for illegal contributions to Richard Nixon's reelection campaign.

DECEMBER 31   Free agent pitcher Jim Catfish Hunter signs a five-year
contract worth $3.75 million.

1975

AUGUST 1   Billy Martin replaces Bill Virdon as manager. It is the first of
five turns for Martin as Yankee pilot.

Jim "Catfish" Hunter

1976

APRIL 15   A remodeled Yankee Stadium opens; the Yankees defeat the Minnesota Twins 11–4.

JUNE 15   A's owner Charlie Finley sells Vida Blue to the Yankees for $1.5 million.

JUNE 18   Commissioner Bowie Kuhn orders the Yankees to return Vida Blue to the A's, claiming the pitcher becoming a Yankee would change unfairly the balance of power in the league.

SEPTEMBER 24   The Yankees win the American League East playoffs, defeating the Tigers 8–0.

OCTOBER 14   Chris Chambliss's ninth-inning home run in game five of the ALCS against Kansas City seals the thirtieth pennant for the Yankees.

OCTOBER 21   The Yankees, in the World Series for the first time since 1964, are swept by the Reds.

NOVEMBER 18   Pitcher Don Gullett becomes the first free agent signed by the Yankees in the 1976 re-entry draft.

NOVEMBER 29   The Yankees sign free agent outfielder Reggie Jackson to a five-year contract.

1977

APRIL 5   Shortstop Bucky Dent is acquired from the White Sox for outfielder Oscar Gamble, pitchers LaMarr Hoyt and Bob Polinsky, plus an estimated $200,000.

JUNE 18   Reggie Jackson is removed by Billy Martin from a game against the Red Sox in Fenway Park for "loafing" on a fly ball.

JULY 19   The All-Star Game is played at Yankee Stadium. The National League wins 7–5.

SEPTEMBER 10   Expansion team Toronto rolls over the Yankees 19–3 in one of the worst defeats in franchise history.

OCTOBER 1   The Yankees win the AL East despite losing to the Tigers 10–7.

OCTOBER 9   The Yankees defeat the Royals 5–3 to win the pennant.

OCTOBER 18   Reggie Jackson hits three home runs in game six of the World Series against the Los Angeles Dodgers at Yankee Stadium. The Yankees win their twenty-first world championship.

OCTOBER 26   Sparky Lyle wins the American League Cy Young Award, becoming the first reliever to record that honor.

1978

JANUARY 13   Joe McCarthy dies at age ninety.

APRIL 13   At the Yankee home opener, "Reggie Candy Bar Day," Reggie Jackson smashes a first-inning three-run homer. Fans throw candy bars out all over the field.

APRIL 15   Joe "Flash" Gordon dies.

JUNE 17   Ron Guidry establishes a Yankee record by striking out eighteen batters in a four-hit 4–0 shutout over the Angels. The win boosts his record to 11–0, a record for American League left-handers.

JULY 24   Billy Martin resigns as Yankee manager. Ron Guidry records his third straight two-hitter, pitching his ninth shutout of the season.

JULY 25   Bob Lemon replaces Billy Martin as manager.

JULY 29   At Old Timers' Day, the announcement is made that Billy Martin will come back as manager in 1980, Bob Lemon will be general manager.

SEPTEMBER 7   The "Boston Massacre," a four-game sweep of the Red Sox, begins.

OCTOBER 2   Overcoming a fourteen-game deficit, the Yankees win the American League East by nipping the Red Sox 5–4 in the second play-off game in American League history.

OCTOBER 3   Reggie Jackson hits a three-run home run, singles, and doubles, leading the Yankees to a 7–1 victory over the Royals in the opening game of the AL Championship Series.

OCTOBER 7   The Yankees win the pennant by defeating the Royals 2–1.

OCTOBER 17   The Yankees win their twenty-second world championship, defeating the Dodgers 7–2, taking the series four games to two.

1979

JUNE 18   Billy Martin returns again as Yankee manager, replacing Bob Lemon.

AUGUST 2   Thurman Munson, age thirty-two, dies in a plane crash in Canton, Ohio.

OCTOBER 28   Dick Howser replaces Billy Martin as manager.

1980

SEPTEMBER 20   A bronze plaque is dedicated at Yankee Stadium to the memory of Thurman Munson.

OCTOBER 4   The Yankees win their fourth division title in five years by beating the Tigers 5–2.

OCTOBER 5   The Yankees set a new American League season attendance record of 2,627,417, breaking the record set by the 1948 Cleveland Indians.

NOVEMBER 21   Gene Michael is named manager after Dick Howser resigns.

DECEMBER 15   The Yankees sign free-agent outfielder Dave Winfield to a ten-year, $15 million contract. He becomes the highest-paid player in baseball.

Dave Winfield, July 4, 1982

1981

SEPTEMBER 6   The Yankees fire Gene Michael. Bob Lemon is named manager for the second time.

OCTOBER 11   Home runs by Reggie Jackson, Oscar Gamble, and Rick Cerone help the Yankees defeat the Brewers 7–3 and win their fifth division title in six years.

OCTOBER 15   The Yankees win their thirty-third American League pennant, beating the A's 4–0 as they complete a three-game sweep.

OCTOBER 28   The Dodgers win their fifth World Series title by beating the Yankees 9–2, taking the series in six games.

NOVEMBER 4   Outfielder Ken Griffey is traded to the Yankees for pitcher Fred Toliver and minor-leaguer Brian Ryder.

NOVEMBER 30   Dave Righetti is named Rookie of the Year in the American League.

DECEMBER 23   Outfielder Dave Collins signs as a free agent.

1982

JANUARY 22   Reggie Jackson leaves the Yankees and signs a free-agent contract with the California Angels.

APRIL 26   The Yankees fire Bob Lemon. Gene Michael is named manager for the second time.

AUGUST 3   Clyde King is named manager of the Yankess after Gene Michael is fired.

AUGUST 6   Bucky Dent is traded to the Texas Rangers for Lee Mazzilli.

DECEMBER 1   Don Baylor signs a five-year free-agent contract.

1983

JANUARY 11   Billy Martin becomes manager for the third time in eight years.

MAY 31   AL president Lee MacPhail suspends Yankee owner George Steinbrenner for one week, citing "repeated problems" with public criticism of umpires. The Yankee owner is banned from attending games or being in his Yankee Stadium office.

JULY 4   Dave Righetti no-hits the Red Sox 4–0 before 41,077 at Yankee Stadium.

JULY 24   The Yankees and Kansas City play the notorious "pine tar" game at Yankee Stadium. The game is suspended, and the teams agree to reschedule and conclude the game August 18.

AUGUST 7   Bobby Murcer day is celebrated.

AUGUST 18   The "pine tar" game concludes with the Royals winning 5–4.

DECEMBER 16   Yogi Berra is named manager after the Yankees fire Billy Martin.

1984

JANUARY 5   Free agent Phil Niekro is signed to a two-year contract. The signing will allow Dave Righetti to move to the bullpen to replace Rich Gossage.

AUGUST 5   Lou Piniella Day is celebrated at Yankee Stadium.

SEPTEMBER 23   The Detroit Tigers beat the New York Yankees 4–1, making Sparky Anderson the first manager to win more than one hundred games in each league.

SEPTEMBER 30   Don Mattingly edges out teammate Dave Winfield and wins the American League batting title with a .343 batting average on the final day of the season.

DECEMBER 5   Rickey Henderson is acquired in a trade with the A's.

1985

APRIL 28   Billy Martin is named Yankee manager for the fourth time. He replaces Yogi Berra.

JULY 13   The uniform numbers of Roger Maris (9) and Elston Howard (32) are retired.

AUGUST 4   On Phil Rizzuto Day, his uniform number (10) is retired.

SEPTEMBER 13   Bernie Williams signs with the Yankees on his seventeenth birthday.

SEPTEMBER 15   George Steinbrenner calls Dave Winfield "Mr. May" after the Yankees lose three key games to the Blue Jays. The Niekro brothers are reunited as the Yankees trade for forty-year-old Joe Niekro.

OCTOBER 6   Phil Niekro wins his three hundredth game.

OCTOBER 17   Billy Martin is fired for the fourth time. Lou Piniella takes over as manager.

NOVEMBER 20   Don Mattingly becomes the first player on a non-championship team to win the American League Most Valuable Player award.

DECEMBER 14   Roger Maris passes away at age fifty-one of cancer in Houston, Texas.

1986

JUNE 30   Ken Griffey is traded to the Braves for outfielder Claudell Washington and shortstop Paul Zuvella.

AUGUST 10   On Billy Martin Day, Martin's uniform number (1) is retired.

AUGUST 30   Tommy John, forty-three, and Joe Niekro, forty-one, pitch a doubleheader for the New York Yankees against Seattle. They are the first forty-plus teammates to start a doubleheader since 1922.

OCTOBER 2   Eclipsing the mark set by Earle Combs in 1927, Don Mattingly sets a Yankees record with his 232nd hit of the season in a 6–1 win over the Red Sox.

OCTOBER 4   Dave Righetti saves both ends of a doubleheader sweep of Boston, giving him a major-league record of forty-six saves.

Don Mattingly

1987

JANUARY 14   Pitcher Catfish Hunter is elected to the Baseball Hall of Fame.

JULY 18   Don Mattingly homers off Texas's Jose Guzman to tie Dale Long's major-league record of hitting a home run in eight consecutive games.

AUGUST 26   Southpaw Dennis Rasmussen is traded to Cincinnati for right-hander Bill Gullickson.

SEPTEMBER 29   Don Mattingly's sixth grand slam of the season, a major-league record, comes off Boston's Bruce Hurst.

OCTOBER 19   Billy Martin is hired for an unprecedented fifth time as manager.

1988

JANUARY 6   Jack Clark is signed as a free agent.

JUNE 23   Billy Martin is replaced as manager. Lou Piniella is named manager.

OCTOBER 24   Jack Clark is traded to San Diego.

DECEMBER 9   A twelve-year contract with the Madison Square Garden television network is signed.

1989

APRIL 28   Rickey Henderson sets a major-league record when he leads off a game with a home run for the thirty-sixth time in his career.

AUGUST 18   In the seventeenth managing change since George Steinbrenner took over the Yankees in 1973, Bucky Dent replaces Dallas Green as manager.

DECEMBER 25   An automobile accident claims Billy Martin's life. He was sixty-one years old.

1990

MAY 11   Dave Winfield, citing a no-trade clause in his contract, refuses to report to the Angels after being traded for Mike Witt. Five days later he relents.

JUNE 6   Stump Merrill takes over for Bucky Dent as Yankee manager.

JULY 1   Andy Hawkins throws a no-hitter against the White Sox, but loses the game 4–0.

JULY 6   Starting his first game since losing a no-hitter, Andy Hawkins pitches 11⅔ innings of shutout ball but loses in the 12th 2–0 to the Twins.

Derek Jeter

JULY 30   Commissioner Fay Vincent permanently bans George Steinbrenner from the day-to-day operations of the Yankees because of the Yankee owner's dealings with a known gambler.

AUGUST 2   With ten home runs in seventy-seven at bats, rookie Kevin Maas reaches that mark faster than any other player.

AUGUST 20   George Steinbrenner resigns as managing general partner of the Yankees.

OCTOBER 3   For the first time during the Steinbrenner era, the Yankees finish the season in last place.

1991

JULY 21   Bernie Williams strikes out five straight times to tie the major-league strikeout record mark for a nine-inning game. The Yanks lose 7–4 to the Royals.

OCTOBER 29   Buck Showalter is named manager of the Yankees, replacing Stump Merrill.

1992

JUNE 1   The Yankees use their sixth pick in the amateur draft to select Derek Jeter.

DECEMBER 6   The Yankees trade first baseman J. T. Snow and pitchers Jerry Nielsen and Russ Springer to the Angels for pitcher Jim Abbott.

1993

MARCH 1   George Steinbrenner is reinstated.

AUGUST 14   On Reggie Jackson Day, Jackson's uniform number (44) is retired.

SEPTEMBER 4   Jim Abbott hurls a 4–0 no-hitter over Cleveland at Yankee Stadium.

1994

FEBRUARY 25   Phil Rizzuto is elected to the Baseball Hall of Fame by the Veterans Committee.

APRIL 4   An Opening Day crowd of 56,706 is the largest in Yankee history.

AUGUST 9   Phil Rizzuto Hall of Fame Night is celebrated.

1995

AUGUST 13   Mickey Mantle dies of cancer in Dallas, Texas. He was sixty-three years old.

SEPTEMBER 6   Lou Gehrig's major-league record of 2,130 consecutive games played is broken. Cal Ripken, Jr., of the Orioles plays in his 2,131st straight game.

NOVEMBER 2   Joe Torre is named manager of the Yankees after Buck Showalter resigns.

1996

MAY 14   Dwight Gooden records the eighth regular-season no-hitter in franchise history. He blanks Seattle 2–0 at Yankee Stadium.

JUNE 16   Legendary broadcaster Mel Allen dies at age eighty-three.

AUGUST 25   A Mickey Mantle monument is unveiled in Monument Park.

SEPTEMBER 26   The Yankees win the AL East by defeating the Brewers 19–2.

David Wells

OCTOBER 5   The Yankees defeat Texas 6–4 and win the division series. Bernie Williams homers from both sides of the plate.

OCTOBER 9   Aided by Jeffrey Maier's glove in the outfield stands, the Yankees beat the Orioles in game one of the ALCS.

OCTOBER 13   The Yankees win the AL pennant by beating the Orioles 6–4. Bernie Williams is named the MVP of the ALCS.

OCTOBER 26   The Yankees win their twenty-third World Series title by beating the Braves 3–2 in game six. John Wetteland is named the series MVP.

1997

JANUARY 22   Don Mattingly retires.

AUGUST 31   Don Mattingly's number (23) is retired and he is given a plaque in Monument Park.

1998

MARCH 3   Lee MacPhail is elected to the Baseball Hall of Fame.

APRIL 13   A five-hundred-pound steel girder falls on a seat in an empty Yankee Stadium just hours before a game, forcing the postponement of two games against the Angels.

MAY 17   David Wells pitches a perfect game—only the fifteenth in baseball history—trimming Minnesota 4–0. Wells fans eleven batters.

JUNE 16   The Yankees host the Mets in their first-ever regular-season interleague game.

JULY 5   The Yankees beat the Orioles 1–0, setting a major-league record with sixty-one wins in the first half of a season.

JULY 25   Jim Bouton returns to Yankee Stadium as part of Old Timers' Day. The former pitcher had been declared persona non grata by the Yankees since the 1971 release of his behind-the-scenes book, *Ball Four.*

SEPTEMBER 4   The Yankees reach one hundred wins on the earliest date in major-league history with an 11–6 win over the Chicago White Sox.

SEPTEMBER 25   The Yankees set an American League record, winning their 112th game, 6–1, over Tampa Bay at the Stadium.

SEPTEMBER 27   Beating the Devil Rays 8–3, the Yanks set the AL record (later broken by Seattle) for wins in a season with 114.

The Yankee Clipper makes his final appearance at Yankee Stadium on Joe DiMaggio Day.

OCTOBER 21   The Yankees complete a four-game sweep of the San Diego Padres, winning their twenty-fourth world championship. The fourth-game 3–0 win gives the club a record of 125–50 (114–48 in the regular season, 11–2 in postseason).

1999

FEBRUARY 19   Pitchers David Wells and Grahame Lloyd, along with second baseman Homer Bush, are traded to the Blue Jays for five-time Cy Young Award–winner Roger Clemens.

MARCH 8   Joe DiMaggio passes away at age eighty-four in Hollywood, Florida.

APRIL 25   A monument honoring Joe DiMaggio is shown off at Monument Park.

JULY 18   On Yogi Berra Day, David Cone tosses the sixteenth perfect game in baseball history only one season after David Wells accomplishes the feat.

SEPTEMBER 9   Jim "Catfish" Hunter dies of ALS–otherwise known as Lou Gehrig's disease–in Hertford, North Carolina. He was fifty-three years old.

OCTOBER 27   The Yankees complete a four-game sweep of the Atlanta Braves, capturing their twenty-fifth world championship. The win is their twelfth straight in World Series play, tying the record of the 1927, 1928, and 1932 Yankees.

DECEMBER 10   Babe Ruth is voted Player of the Century by an Associated Press panel.

2000

Mariano Rivera

JUNE 19   The Yankees beat the Red Sox 22–1, handing Boston its most lopsided home loss ever. New York scores sixteen runs in the game's last two innings.

OCTOBER 26   The Yankees win their third straight world championship, their fourth title in five years, their twenty-sixth overall, defeating the Mets 4–2 in game five.

OCTOBER 30   A World Series Championship Victory Parade down the Canyon of Heroes is staged in Manhattan.

NOVEMBER 30   Pitcher Mike Mussina signs as a free agent for six years at $88.5 million.

2001

FEBRUARY 15   Mariano Rivera signs a four-year contract for $39.99 million, making him the highest-paid relief pitcher in history.

Paul O'Neill

MARCH 22   University of Michigan quarterback and third baseman
    Drew Henson agrees to a six-year, $17 million contract with the
    Yankees.

MAY 4   The Yankees meet with President George W. Bush in a White
    House Rose Garden ceremony celebrating their third straight World
    Series championship.

MAY 26   Roger Clemens strikes out eight Cleveland Indians, moving
    into fifth place on the career strikeout list as the Yankees romp 12–5
    over Cleveland.

JUNE 2   Gene Woodling, a member of five straight championship teams from 1949 to 1953, dies at age seventy-eight.

JULY 4   American League manager Joe Torre selects seven of his players—nearly one-third of the Yankee roster—for the All-Star Game in Seattle. Roger Clemens, Andy Pettitte, Mariano Rivera, Mike Stanton, Derek Jeter, Bernie Williams, and Jorge Posada are picked.

JULY 23   Roger Clemens moves past Tom Seaver into fourth place on the career strikeout list, notching his 3,641st strikeout, winning his tenth straight decision as the Yankees beat Toronto.

AUGUST 15   For the first time in thirty-two years, a major-league pitcher posts a record of 16–1. Roger Clemens pitches the Yankees past Tampa Bay 10–3.

AUGUST 18   New Hall of Famer Dave Winfield is honored by the Yankees.

AUGUST 25   Paul O'Neill becomes the oldest player to record twenty home runs and twenty steals in a season.

SEPTEMBER 2   Mike Mussina comes within one pitch of the seventeenth perfect game in major-league history, but Red Sox pinch hitter Carl Everett lines a 1-and-2 pitch for a base hit.

SEPTEMBER 5   Roger Clemens sets a Yankees record with his fifteenth straight victory, becoming baseball's first 19–1 pitcher in eighty-nine years as the Yankees defeat Toronto 4–3. At 19–1, Clemens becomes just the second player in major-league history to win nineteen of his first twenty decisions, passing Jack Chesbro and Whitey Ford for the longest winning streak in Yankee history.

SEPTEMBER 11   Within ninety minutes of the horrific attacks on the World Trade Center, Yankee Stadium is evacuated.

SEPTEMBER 25   The Yankees clinch their seventh straight postseason berth while losing to Tampa Bay 4–0 in the first game at Yankee Stadium in more than two weeks, as Baltimore trims Boston 12–7.

OCTOBER 15   The Yankees are the first team to win a best-of-five series after losing the first two games at home, beating the Athletics 5–3.

NOVEMBER 4   In game seven of one of the most thrilling World Series in history, set against the backdrop of the September 11 disaster at the World Trade Center and a recovering New York City and nation, and following two incredible come-from-behind wins, the Yankees are defeated by Arizona, who score two runs in the bottom of the ninth inning to win 3–2.

NOVEMBER 15   Roger Clemens wins his record sixth Cy Young Award.

NOVEMBER 27   Scott Brosius retires, becoming the third Yankee to do so in the off-season, joining Paul O'Neill and Luis Sojo.

DECEMBER 7   The Yankees trade outfielder David Justice to the Mets for third baseman Robin Ventura. Reliever Steve Karsay signs a four-year contract worth about $21 million.

DECEMBER 11   Joe Torre signs a new three-year contract with the Yankees.

DECEMBER 13   Jason Giambi signs a seven-year deal with the Yankees reported to be worth $120 million.

DECEMBER 18   Yankee star first baseman Tino Martinez signs a $21 million, three-year contract with St. Louis.

2002

JANUARY 10   David Wells becomes a Yankee again, signing a $7 million, two-year contract.

FEBRUARY 11   Frank Crosetti dies at age ninety-one in Stockton, California. He was the shortstop on eight New York Yankees world championship teams from 1932 to 1948.

MAY 9   Mariano Rivera saves his 225th game, tenth of the season, to set a new career saves record, breaking the mark set by Dave Righetti of 224.

JUNE 30   The Yankees become the first AL team since the 1954 White Sox to have All-Stars at all four infield positions and catcher. First baseman Jason Giambi, catcher Jorge Posada, and second baseman Alfonso Soriano were voted on by the fans. Joe Torre picked closer Mariano Rivera, shortstop Derek Jeter, and third baseman Robin Ventura.

JULY 6   A plaque honoring Reggie Jackson in Monument Park is dedicated at Old Timers' Day.

CHAPTER TWO

Stadium

"*Very few buildings managed to meld their history literally with the present. Yankee Stadium does. There is something glorious about knowing that the physical form of the structure (never mind how badly it has been altered) ties Derek Jeter to Joe DiMaggio.*"
      —PAUL GOLDBERGER, *New York Times* architecture critic

◆

"*Playing there as a Yankee, you had the feeling you were in a special ballpark, special town, special uniform, special history.*"
      —PHIL LINZ

ONLY WRIGLEY FIELD and Fenway Park are older. It's where Notre Dame coach Knute Rockne made his "Win One for the Gipper" speech, where Johnny Unitas won the 1958 NFL championship in the so-called Greatest Game Ever Played, where Muhammad Ali fought. It's where Casey Stengel hit the first World Series home run for the old New York Giants—an inside-the-park shot in game one of the 1923 World Series—where Mickey Mantle blasted a fly ball off the third-deck façade, 109 feet above the playing field and 374 feet from home plate. It's where Thurman Munson's locker remains the way it was the day he died in a 1979 airplane crash, with his number-15 jersey and catching gear still intact.

From 1903 until April 11, 1913, the New York Highlanders—on their way to becoming the New York Yankees—played all home games at Hilltop Park. Then they became tenants of the New York Giants at the Polo Grounds. In 1920, Yankee attendance, boosted by the drawing power of the sensational new slugger Babe Ruth, doubled to 1,289,422, over a hundred thousand more than the Giants.

The relationship between the two franchises, never especially cordial, turned even more testy following that 1920 season. The next year, the Giants told the Yankees they were no longer welcome as tenants at the Polo Grounds and should vacate the premises as soon as possible.

Ironically, Yankee co-owner Jake Ruppert had thought of demolishing the Polo Grounds and constructing a 100,000-seat stadium to be shared by the Giants and Yankees. Now, however, he and his partner, Colonel Tillinghast L'Hommedieu Huston, announced plans to build a new ballpark for the Yankees alone. It would be, Ruppert said, along the lines of the Roman Colosseum.

On February 6, 1921, the Yankees issued a press release announcing the purchase of ten acres of property on the site of a lumberyard in the west Bronx from the estate of William Waldorf Astor for $675,000. Directly across the Harlem River from the Polo Grounds, it was at the mouth of a little body of water called Crowell's Creek. Identified as City Plot 2106, Lot 100, the land had been a farm owned by John Lion Gardiner prior to the Revolutionary War. "It was all farmland," recalled former Giant ticket taker Joe Flynn. "It was beautiful. You could get fresh milk and vegetables there."

Two weeks after construction on the stadium began, Ruppert bought out Huston's ownership share of the Yankees for $1.5 million. The White Construction Company had begun work May 5, 1922, agreeing to complete the project "at a definite price" ($2.5 million), and by Opening Day 1923. The architectural firm, Osborne Engineering Company of Cleveland, Ohio, was under mandate to create the greatest and grandest ballpark of its day. Original plans called for the stadium to be triple-decked and roofed all the way around. It was to be shaped like the Yale Bowl and contain towering battlements enclosing the entire park that would render events inside "impenetrable to all human eyes, save those of aviators." Those without tickets would have no view of the action.

Alas, this initial, soaring grand plan was quickly abandoned in favor of less ambitious designs. Yankee Stadium was indeed a gigantic horseshoe-shaped edifice circled by huge wooden bleachers, but the triple-decked grandstand did not reach either foul pole. And whether Ruppert liked it or not, action on the playing field was to be highly visible from the elevated trains that passed by the outfield, as well as from the buildings that were to sprout up across River Avenue.

The new ballpark was to have unique touches, however, such as "eight toilet rooms for men and as many for women scattered throughout the stands and bleachers," and a decorative element that would become the signature feature of Yankee Stadium: a fifteen-foot-deep copper façade adorning the front of the roof, covering much of the stadium's third deck, giving it an elegant and dignified air. Another singular element of "The Yankee Stadium," as it was originally named, was a fifteen-foot-deep brick-lined vault underneath second base. The vault had electrical, telephone, and telegraph connections that made for the setting up of a boxing ring and press area on the infield feasible. Yankee executive offices were moved from midtown Manhattan and located between the main and mezzanine decks; an elevator connected them with the main entrance.

The first ballpark to be called a stadium, and the last privately financed park in the major leagues, the new park boasted 10,712 upper-grandstand seats and 14,543 lower-grandstand seats, all locked in place by 135,000 individual steel castings on which 400,000 pieces of maple lumber were held down by more than a million screws.

The right-field foul pole was but 295 feet from home plate; it was 429 feet to right center. The left-field pole was but a short 281-foot poke from home, but right-handed batters had to contend with a 395-foot left field and left center. The park's deepest points were a distant 490 feet away. The outfield warning track at first was composed of red cinders, later red brick dust.

Yankee Stadium's first game took place April 18, 1923. The Yankees triumphed 4–1 over the Red Sox, with a Babe Ruth home run thrilling the throng. The Yankee slugger had said: "I'd give a year of my life if I can hit a home run in this first game in this new park." He got his wish, and so did all those in attendance. A *New York Times* account read: "Governors, general colonels, politicians, and baseball officials gathered solemnly yesterday to dedicate the biggest stadium, in baseball . . . in the third inning with two team mates on the base lines, Babe Ruth smashed a savage home run into the right field bleachers, and that was the real baptism of Yankee Stadium."

In their first season at the stadium, the Yankees drew 1,007,066, posted a 98–54 record, and won their third straight pennant, finishing sixteen games in front. World Series competition for the third year in a row was the rival Giants of John J. McGraw, who banned his team from using the Yankee Stadium visitor's clubhouse. Instead the Giant players dressed in their Polo Grounds clubhouse and then in full uniform took cabs across the Harlem River over the

Central Bridge to Yankee Stadium, only to be defeated. "The House that Ruth Built" flew its first world-championship banner that first year.

With the opening of Yankee Stadium, property values all around the area skyrocketed. New parking lots, a small theater, restaurants, and bars opened. Drugstores installed lunch counters. The nearby Concourse Plaza Hotel did a brisk business catering to visiting players and others.

Almost from the start, the cathedral of a ballpark was a place where pigeons, bulging from peanuts and popcorn, lodged in the rafters and beams and flew up and about when the huge crowds cheered a Yankee's heroics.

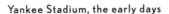
Yankee Stadium, the early days

Wooden bleachers surrounded the outfield during those early years. A grass slope came up to the outfield walls from foul pole to foul pole. Babe Ruth and other outfielders, as a matter of course, backed up the small hill in pursuit of fly balls. There were advertising signs on top of the bleachers, and a single manually operated wooden scoreboard in right center field. It provided the scores up to twelve innings for games played by every major-league team.

With flair and fanaticism, always tinkering and changing to keep ahead of his rivals, Jacob Ruppert presided over his Yankees and Yankee Stadium. He was fond of saying: "Yankee Stadium was a mistake—not mine, but the Giants."

Ruppert loved nothing more than seeing the twenty-two thousand bleacher seats at the stadium filled. In 1927, he cut the price of those seats from seventy-five to fifty cents. Third decks were added to left field and center field in 1927 and 1928. Right field had its third deck added a decade later.

In 1932, the Yankees began the tradition of honoring their legends with a monument for Miller Huggins. This was followed by monuments for Lou Gehrig and Babe Ruth. The monuments were located in straightaway center field as part of the playing field, ten feet in front of the wall forming part of the background for hitters in front of the flagpole. Outfielders always had to be wary as they ran back for long fly balls. There were times when long drives managed to roll behind the monuments. Retrieving the ball was sometimes an odd and "ghoulish" task for an outfielder as he jockeyed around the "gravestones."

On one occasion Casey Stengel watched in dismay as one of those long drives skipped past his center fielder and banged around the monuments. Exasperated, Casey bellowed: "Ruth, Gehrig, Huggins, someone throw that darned ball in here *now*!" At one time ticket holders exited through the center-field gates and viewed the monuments on their way out of the stadium.

A ball hitting the foul pole in the 1930s was in play, not a home run. "Death Valley," in deep left center field, was a place of heartbreak, as many a right-handed basher would watch in frustration as towering fly balls that seemed fated to be homers died there. A curse to straightaway hitters, center field in 1923 was 490 feet from home plate. By 1937, the distance was still a considerable 461 feet. A green curtain was installed in left center that was raised and lowered like a window shade; opposition hitters had a background of white-shirts of bleacher fans, Yankee hitters had a dark green background as their backdrop.

In 1937, the right-field stands were enlarged. Triple decks were extended beyond the foul pole in right field. Homers could now be hit into the upper decks in right and left field. In 1937–1938, an enlarged grandstand replaced "Ruthville," the original old wooden bleachers that Babe Ruth bashed so many homers into.

The Seating capacity of the Stadium was reduced to about 67,000 when outfield bench seats were replaced by chair seats in the 1930s and 1940s.

YANKEE STORIES
Monte Irvin

The Yankees have always been a part of my life in one way or other. When I was growing up in Orange, New Jersey, we would go down to see the Newark Bears, the great farm club of the Yankees in the International League. We saw so many of the players who went on to play for the Yankees so it was a natural thing for us to be Yankee fans. We grew up rooting for the Yankees. Very rarely were we disappointed.

The first time I went to Yankee Stadium was to see a Decoration Day doubleheader in 1936. It was the Yankees against the Red Sox, Lefty Gomez pitching against Lefty Grove. My brother and I took the Hudson tubes over to Penn Station and took the train up to the stadium. All we had was two dollars each but that was enough for a sandwich, soda, and seats for this wonderful doubleheader. We even came back home with a little money left over.

My favorite Yankee player was Joe DiMaggio, and his performance that day was just outstanding. Grove threw him a fast breaking curveball on the inside corner. He lined it just foul into the left-field stands. Then Grove came back with a fastball on the outside corner, and DiMaggio doubled down the right-hand side of first base. That was good hitting. To me, Joe was "the Man," very smooth and charismatic. I can remember the way he stood up there looking so elegant.

Five years later, I was on the field of Yankee Stadium when my Newark Eagles team played the Kansas City Monarchs in a Negro League game while the Yankees were on the road. I couldn't believe I was there. It was like playing on hallowed ground. My first hit in Yankee Stadium was a double off Satchel Paige. If I could hit Satchel, I thought, I could hit anybody.

A decade after that, I played in the World Series with the Giants against the Yankees in the last season of Joe DiMaggio. This was just after the Giants won the pennant on the Bobby Thomson home run, and we were still on a high from that game and the victory over Brooklyn. Without a chance to rest, we reported to Yankee Stadium the next day. I got four straight hits and also stole home.

My last time up, Yogi Berra said: "Monte, I don't know what to throw you. You have been hitting high balls and low balls and fastballs and curve balls. I'm gonna have you get a fastball right down the middle."

I didn't believe Yogi, but sure enough Reynolds threw me a fastball right down the middle. I hit a line drive that Joe Collins jumped up for and caught. I really wanted that hit. No one had ever gone five for five in the World Series.

Back in 1936 when I saw my first game in Yankee Stadium, I was still in high school and playing for my school team. I hit almost .700. My coach told both the Yankees and the Giants if they ever wanted to break the color barrier, they should take a look at me. Scouts were sent. They came back with terrific reports about me, but the Yankees and the Giants said they couldn't take a chance at that time. They thought the rest of the owners wouldn't go along with it. Later on, of course, the Giants did take a chance. But I always think of how I could have been a Yankee.

Through the 1930s and 1940s the Black Yankees of the Negro National League, one of the worst teams in that circuit, rented out Yankee Stadium when the Yankees were on the road. Monte Irvin was one of those who had the opportunity to play at the stadium as a member of the Newark Eagles. "It was being on hallowed ground," Irvin recalled. "We didn't get into the Yankee dressing rooms. We dressed together with the Black Yankees in the visitors' dressing room."

"Prior to the second world war," sportswriting veteran Red Foley made the point, "box seats were regular wooden chairs that went back about two or three rows from third to first base. They cost about $2.50. You had the low fences in left and right field, only about three feet high. Players could lean in and make a catch. There were a lot of pillars and people sat behind them and couldn't see very well. It was called 'an obstructed view.'"

Auxiliary scoreboards were built in the late 1940s, which covered up the 367 right-center sign and the 415 left-center sign. In 1946, $600,000 worth of renovations were made, including the installation of arc lights, which equaled the illumination of five-thousand full moons, as the Yankee press release bragged. Irish turf was brought in by Larry MacPhail so the grass was greener. And the stadium—now with a new paint job—was greener and bluer. The dugout locations were switched: visiting teams were located on the third-base side and the Yankees were on the first-base side of the infield. Another new feature was the creation of the Stadium Club for box holders, a place where the high and mighty and their guests congregated, ate and drank at what was for some time the largest bar in the state of New York.

Those were the only major changes made to Yankee Stadium until the winter of 1966–1967, when the team's new owner, CBS, spent $1.5 million to modernize the park with a very expensive paint job that made use of ninety tons of paint. The brown concrete exterior and the greenish copper façade were painted white, while the green grandstand seats were painted blue. "It was a light blue," veteran sportswriter Red Foley recalled, "much lighter than the blue used today." A new 463 sign and a 433 sign were placed in the power alleys.

Fans at Yankee Stadium, having a ball

YANKEE STORIES
Howard Elson

Duke Ellington may have taken the A train up to Harlem in the '40s, but for me, a kid living in Queens in the late '50s, early '60s, it was the F up to Lexington Avenue and then the number 4 to Yankee Stadium.

Back then it was impossible to come near a Yankee, let alone commemorate the event by having any of them sign something. If you had a bleacher ticket you were chain-link-fenced in. If you sat in the right-field stands hoping to catch a Mantle blast, the stadium guards wouldn't let you get close to the rich people in the box seats, much less hang over the box-seat railing.

Even after the game, when the now-civilian-clad Bronx Bombers came out of the players' entrance, a double line of police would form an impregnable blue-uniform-lined pathway that the players would walk through to their waiting cars. They would drive off without any inter-action, without so much as an acknowledgment of the hundreds waiting for a glimpse, a nod, a scribble.

Not so with the visiting ballplayers. They would walk out of a door on the other side of the stadium unencumbered by security and usually happy to oblige fans. Not too many kids hung around that side, but it sure was easy to get a Ted Lepcio autograph, or a Bobby Klaus, or a Frank Bolling. Once I asked Mike Garcia to show me the finger he lost; instead he showed me the middle finger he still has. But the next time the Indians were in town, he signed my Alvin Dark–model glove.

Still I had enough Sherm Lollars and Harvey Kuenns and Pete Runnels. I wanted a Yankee. Knowing it was useless to try and break through the police barricade, I snuck over to where the cars were parked and ducked down behind a car that was parked next to a car where a lady was sitting behind the wheel—obviously waiting for a Yankee.

With the little dull nub of an almost-used-up number-two Eberhard Faber pencil (only the Eb was left) in one hand, and a rolled-up, scrunched-up, folded, stained, and sweaty score-card in the other, I waited for the cop-lined cordon to wend its way to the car with the lady-in-waiting.

Finally the double line of blue uniforms slowly serpentined my way and stopped on the passenger side of the waiting car, and out comes . . . Ryne Duren! You couldn't miss him. He really did wear coke-bottle eyeglasses. I snuck over to the driver's-side window. I couldn't go around to the passenger side where Duren was sitting, the cops would have gotten me.

"Mr. Duren, Mr. Duren, can I have an autograph, please?" I shoved the nubby, dull, almost-used-up number-two pencil and the rolled-up, scrunched-up, folded-up, stained and sweaty scorecard through the half-open driver's side window. Whereupon the startled and angry Mrs. Duren proceeded to stare me down while she rolled the window up on my hands.

Just before she severed my fingers, I dropped my pencil and scorecard inside the car, then watched as the Yankees' premier reliever, the meanest lady in the world, and my pencil and scorecard drove away.

Although I continue to love my boyhood Yankees, I never attempted to get a Yankee auto-graph again.

But if you need a Turk Lown, or a Johnny Klippstein, or a Reno Bertoia, I'm the guy to see.

1974 FIRE SALE
OF THE OLD YANKEE STADIUM

Cuyahoga Wrecking Company of Cleveland, the firm hired to dismantle the original Yankee Stadium, began selling off artifacts and mementos.

- ◆ *$30,000: lights purchased by Osaka baseball team of Japan*
- ◆ *$10,000: foul poles purchased by Osaka baseball team of Japan*
- ◆ *$500: box seats, enlarged photos of Babe Ruth on Babe Ruth Day, and clubhouse stool purchased by Jim Bouton*
- ◆ *$300: Gate A sign*
- ◆ *$200: a huge picture of a young Joe DiMaggio*
- ◆ *$150: a photo of Dan Larsen making the last pitch of his perfect game*
- ◆ *$100: turnstiles*
- ◆ *$75: a locker-room scale*
- ◆ *$50: an old duffel bag that belonged to Joe Pepitone*
- ◆ *$20: box seats*
- ◆ *$10: groundskeeper's uniform*
- ◆ *$5: hot-dog vendor trays*
- ◆ *$3: men's lavatory In sign*
- ◆ *$3: a sheet of World Series tickets, unused from the 1972 Yankees' near miss*
- ◆ *50 cents: Scout Admission—50 Cents sign*

The total proceeds from the sale were $300,000—an eighth of the original Yankee Stadium construction cost. Twenty thousand letters that Mickey Mantle never answered were not bid on.

The final game at the old Yankee Stadium was played on September 30, 1973. There were 32,238 on hand, including the widows of Babe Ruth and Lou Gehrig. When Yankee Stadium celebrated its fiftieth anniversary in 1973, the team moved out to Shea Stadium. It would play in Queens for two seasons while its home was almost completely demolished and then rebuilt. Mementos from the stadium were sold off. The Smithsonian Institution received the bat racks and bullpen steps. Home plate was given to the widow of Babe Ruth, and first base to the widow of Lou Gehrig. Some seats were sold off to former players and fans. George Steinbrenner loaned another batch of seats to the producers of a new live television show, who used them as seats for the audience. The show was *Saturday Night Live*; the seats are still in use.

"When they started to tear down Yankee Stadium after the 1973 season," the restaurateur Tracy Nieporent said, "my brother Drew and I went uptown on the subway, bought a blue wooden chair and dragged it back on the subway. It had iron stanchions and was very heavy to carry. We found petrified gum stuck underneath it, and at first we were going to remove it. But then I said, 'You know maybe that gum was there when Joe DiMaggio had his hitting streak.' I still have the chair, and the gum is still there."

Yankee Stadium in 1960 during World Series game vs. Pirates. Ralph Terry is pitching with Yogi Berra as his catcher.

"Seeing the Yankees playing in Shea Stadium when Yankee Stadium was being redone was very strange and bizarre," recalled literary agent David Vigliano. "They were completely out of place. You could count on Bobby Murcer to hit thirty home runs at Yankee Stadium every year because of the short porch in right field. But at Shea Stadium he didn't hit many."

By the time the House that Ruth Built reopened on April 15, 1976, the stadium had undergone a $100 million facelift. Many obstructive steel columns that had supported the second and third decks and the roof had been removed. By "cantilevering" the upper decks and by lowering the playing field five feet while increasing the slope of the lower stands, sight lines were drastically improved. Old eighteen-inch wooden seats were replaced by twenty-two-inch plastic seats. There were now approximately 11,600 fewer seats, bringing the seating capacity down from 67,000 to about 54,200.

The original roof had been removed and the stadium's most-recognizable feature, the iron third-deck façade, was almost lost. But a portion was placed in the bleachers and an exact copy of it was constructed atop the new 560-foot-long scoreboard that stretched across the rear of the bleachers. That board included the first "telescreen" in baseball, providing instant replays and using a then-state-of-the-art "nine shades of gray." The new scoreboard cost thirty times Colonel Jacob Ruppert's purchase price for Babe Ruth from the Red Sox. And the scoreboard's girth and size eliminated the views many once had enjoyed from the 161st Street station of the IRT subway and the rooftops of adjacent apartment houses.

Three escalator towers, one at each of the three entrances, had been added, greatly improving access to the upper decks. The majestic look of the stadium was enhanced with ten additional upper deck rows of seats.

Fences in left and center field had been drawn in considerably but were still pokes of 430 feet and 417 feet, respectively. Death Valley in deep left center field was reduced from 457 feet to 417 feet. By 1988, it would be 399 feet.

In 1976, Monument Park was relocated between the Yankee and visitor bullpens. It would be moved to the left-field corner in 1985 and made available for public touring up to forty-five minutes before game time.

Miller Huggins, Jake Ruppert, Lou Gehrig, Babe Ruth, Casey Stengel, Edward Barrow, Joe DiMaggio, Mickey Mantle, Joe McCarthy, Lefty Gomez, Whitey Ford, Elston Howard, Phil Rizzuto, Don Mattingly, Billy Martin, Bill Dickey, Yogi Berra, Allie Reynolds, Pope Paul VI (who said mass at Yankee Stadium in 1965), and Pope Paul II (who said mass at Yankee Stadium in 1979) are among those honored in Monument Park. A section of plaques also exists for Yankees who had their numbers retired.

When the new Yankee Stadium opened on April 15, 1976, it was before the largest Opening Day crowd since 1946. Among the 52,613 present were legends Yogi Berra, Mickey Mantle, and Joe DiMaggio, as well as the widows of Babe Ruth and Lou Gehrig. Bobby Richardson delivered the pre-game prayer. Ceremonies honored the 1923 team. Bob Shawkey, eighty-five, who had won

the 1923 stadium opener, threw out the first ball of a game that saw the Yanks defeat the Twins 11–4. That 1976 season, echoing the first season of the old Yankee Stadium in 1923, saw the team from the Bronx host a World Series.

Yankee Stadium, 1997

"When I first came to Yankee Stadium I used to feel like the ghosts of Babe Ruth and Lou Gehrig were walking around in there," Mickey Mantle said. "After they remodeled Yankee Stadium I didn't feel that the ghosts were there anymore. It just wasn't the same."

"It had a sort of plastic look," veteran New York City sportswriter Red Foley noted. "When they took the frieze down they found out that it was made of galvanized steel. The dugouts before were different, a little bigger, more intimidating."

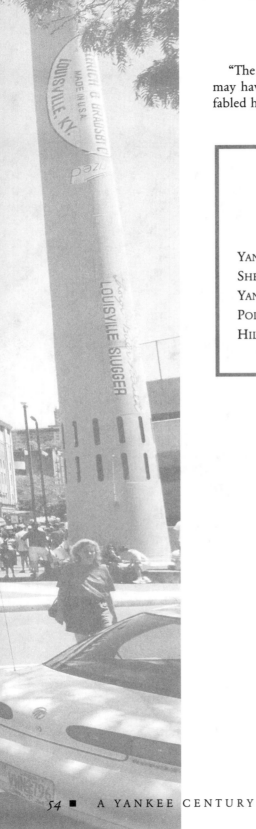

"The American League Baseball Grounds," "the House that Ruth Built," may have lost some character and gained some comfort. Still, it remains the fabled home of baseball's most fabled franchise.

CHRONOLOGY
YANKEE BALLPARKS

PLACE	TIME	SEATING CAPACITY
YANKEE STADIUM II	1976–present	57,746
SHEA STADIUM	1974–1975	55,101
YANKEE STADIUM	1923–1973	67,224
POLO GROUNDS II	1913–1922	38,000
HILLTOP PARK	1903–1912	15,000

CHAPTER THREE

Memorable
MOMENTS

F ROM THE PERFECT games of Don Larsen, David Wells, and David Cone
to an almost-perfect game by Mike Mussina to back-to-back no-hitters by
Allie Reynolds; from Ruth calling (or not) the shot to the Lou Gehrig homers,
the Dent homer, the Chambliss homer, the Reggie Jackson homers, the Leyritz
homer, and the Jeffrey Maier catch; from the eighteen Ks by Guidry to the 2001
World Series and its thrills an inning—here are some of the most memorable
moments in New York Yankees history.

◆

THE FIRST HOME GAME: *April 30, 1903*

HILLTOP PARK WAS a slum of a ballpark from the beginning, and it became worse as time went by. It was built in six weeks, a hastily constructed wooden ballpark. Lacking a clubhouse, players at first dressed in hotels. Parking space was minimal too, until 1906, when lots were set up inside the grounds behind the grandstand for carriages and cars.

The formal name for the park was New York American League Ball Park, but its location at the highest point in Manhattan earned it the name Hilltop Park. The official name for the team was the New York Americans, but again, because of the park's lofty location, fans and sportswriters used the team nickname Hilltoppers. Others preferred Highlanders because of the elevated playing site and because club president Gordon's name evoked the fabled British army unit the Gordon Highlanders. Other names to describe the new American League entry included Hill Dwellers, Porch Climbers, Burglars, and Cliffmen.

The franchise had been bought for $18,000 by well-known gambler Frank Farrell and former New York City Chief of Police William S. "Big Bill" Devery. The duo owned hundreds of poolrooms and nearly as many politicians. The team had a decidedly local flavor, with most players coming from the New York–New Jersey–Pennsylvania area. It had a patchwork look, though, with a roster including seven rookies and others whose roots were with eleven different teams.

There were two former National League stars—Wee Willie Keeler, thirty-one, of "hit 'em where they ain't" fame, and ace pitcher "Happy Jack" Chesbro. The five-feet-four-inch Keeler brought to the Highlanders his 30½-inch bat—the shortest in major-league history—a .371 lifetime batting average, and all kinds of superstitions. Chesbro brought along his spitball.

Each of the 16,294 who attended the balmy Opening Day game of the brand-new American League franchise received a small American flag, a gift from the new league president, Ban Johnson. Many of the fans arrived at Hilltop Park that day via the new subway station at 168th Street. A seat in the single wooden grandstand that extended from first base around to third base cost fifty cents. Bleacher seats were seventy-five cents, box seats a dollar.

Those who sat in the upper-level seats behind home plate enjoyed a unique view of the Hudson River, two blocks to the west of the ballpark, and the Palisades in New Jersey beyond that. Located on the west side of Broadway and Ft. Washington Avenue, between 165th and 168th Streets in Washington Heights, the new park was ten blocks north of the Polo Grounds, with its main entrance facing Broadway. The roof of the grandstand was not yet in place.

It was estimated that more than $200,000 had been spent excavating twelve thousand cubic yards of rock. At a cost of $15,000, the hastily constructed wooden ballpark was created in six weeks on the roughly cleared site.

1903 HIGHLANDERS
ROSTER

Doc Adkins, Monte Beville, Elmer Bliss, Jack Chesbro, Wid Conroy, Ernie Courtney, Lefty Davis, John Deering, Kid Elberfeld, Dave Fultz, John Ganzel, Paddy Greene, Clark Griffith, Fred Holmes, Harry Howell, Tim Jordan, Willie Keeler, Herman Long, Pat McCauley, Herm McFarland, Jack O'Connor, Ambrose Puttmann, Eddie Quick, Jesse Tannehill, Jimmy Williams, Snake Wiltse, Barney Wolfe, Jack Zalusky

The surface of the playing field was dirt on rock, dirt on dirt. An unsightly hollow in right field was roped off. Players hitting a ball past the ropes were awarded a double. That June, when a fence was put up in front of the hollow, players hitting a ball over the fence would be awarded a home run. Left field was 365 feet from home plate, center field was a monstrous 542, and right field was 400 feet.

At 3 P.M., the Highlanders and Washington Senators marched from the outfield to home plate. The two squads stood at attention as the Sixty-ninth Regiment band played the "Washington Post March" and then the "Star-Spangled Banner." The first ball was thrown out by Ban Johnson, and the game began.

Behind the pitching of Jack Chesbro, the Highlanders won 6–2. The franchise's first home game was in the history books. That first season the Highlanders won seventy-two games, finishing in fourth place, seventeen games out of first.

THE CHESBRO WILD PITCH: *October 10, 1904*

THE PLACE WAS Hilltop Park. The event was a last-day-of-the-season doubleheader between the New York Highlanders and the Boston Pilgrims. To win the pennant, the Highlanders needed a doubleheader sweep.

New York had been atop the American League standings throughout most of the 1904 season, but Boston surged at the end to move in front by a game and a half. Spectators in the estimated crowd of 25,584 overflowed the playing field and stood ten and twenty deep in the outfield.

Spitballer Happy Jack Chesbro, a forty-one-game winner, was on the mound for the Highlanders. Boston's Bill Dineen, a twenty-two-game winner, opposed him. The game was scoreless until the fifth, when New York scored twice. In the seventh inning, Boston tied the score with two unearned runs on a pair of errors by New York second baseman Jimmy Williams.

The tension kept increasing. The game moved to the ninth, a 2–2 tie. Boston catcher Lou Criger singled and was sacrificed to second base. A ground ball moved him to third. Freddy Parent was next for Boston. Chesbro worked the count to one ball and two strikes. Then the spitter fluttered to the plate. Perhaps there was too much on it. Perhaps all the innings Chesbro had pitched that season caught up with him. The ball sailed over the head of catcher Jack "Red" Kleinow. Wild pitch—Criger scored.

The Highlanders failed to score in the bottom of the ninth. Boston had its second straight pennant. New York would go on to win the second game of the doubleheader 1–0, in ten innings, but the win meant nothing.

There were those who took some solace in the fact that the Highlanders doubled their first season's attendance, that they won twenty more games than they had the season before. But that 1904 season would be the closest the American League New York team would come to winning a pennant in its first eighteen years of existence.

FIRST YANKEE NO-HITTER: *George Mogridge, April 24, 1917*

GEORGE ANTHONY MOGRIDGE out of Rochester, New York, pitched for the Yankees from 1915 to 1920 six seasons and posted a 48–55 record. His ERA was 2.71, a sign that he had a lot on the ball—including resin.

But the lean and long lefty is best remembered for what he achieved on April 24, 1917. He hurled the first no-hitter in Yankee history, the only Yankee regular-season no-hitter until Dave Righetti's in 1983. Mogridge's no-hitter was one of his nine wins that 1917 season.

When the American League banned the use of resin in 1920, Mogridge worked the powder into the underside of the bill of his cap. It worked for him as a convenient, efficient, and never-detected technique.

Traded off to the Washington Senators in 1921 as the Yankees were entering their first great years, Mogridge served with pitcher Walter Johnson to anchor the Senators' staff. When the career of the well-traveled southpaw finally ended in 1927 after 440 games, the one game he talked about the most was the no-hitter he pitched that April day in 1917 as a member of the Yankees.

YANKEE STADIUM OPENS: *April 18, 1923*

A MASSIVE CROWD showed up for the proudest moment in the history of the Bronx. Many in the huge assemblage wore heavy sweaters, coats, and hats. Some sported dinner jackets. Game-time temperature was forty-nine degrees. Wind whipped Yankee pennants. Dust blew up from the dirt road that led to the stadium. The announced attendance was 74,217, later changed to 60,000.

The fire department, concerned about the conditions created by the huge throng, ordered the gates closed. More than 25,000 were turned away and many of them lingered outside in the cold listening to the sounds of music and the roar of the crowd inside the stadium.

The day's dominant sound was the march beat played by the Seventh Regiment Band, directed by John Philip Sousa. Both the Yankees and Red Sox were escorted out to the deep-center-field flagpole by the band. The American flag and the 1922 pennant were hoisted.

Seated in the celebrity box were baseball commissioner Kenesaw Mountain Landis, New York City mayor John Hylan, Yankee owner Colonel Jacob Ruppert, and New York governor Al Smith. At 3:25, Babe Ruth was presented with an oversized bat handsomely laid out in a glass case. At 3:30, Governor Smith threw out the first ball to Yankee catcher Wally Schang. And at 3:35, home-plate umpire Tommy Connolly shouted: "Play ball!"

A third-inning RBI single by Joe Dugan scored Yankee pitcher Bob Shawkey with the first run of the game. Ruth stepped to the plate. There were two Yankees on base, Whitey Witt and Dugan.

The Bambino said before the game: "I'd give a year of my life if I can hit a home run in the first game in this new park." Boston's Howard Ehmke tried to get a slow pitch past the Sultan of Swat, who turned it into a fast pitch, hammering it on a line into the right-field bleachers—the first home run in Yankee Stadium history.

Roaring, the crowd was on its feet. Ruth crossed the plate, removed his cap, extended it at arm's length in front of him, and waved. The game played out into the lengthening afternoon shadows. Sailor Bob Shawkey, wearing a red sweatshirt under his Yankee jersey, pitched the home team to a 4–1 victory, making the first Opening Day at Yankee Stadium a matter of record.

SAM JONES'S NO-HITTER: *September 4, 1923*

SAM JONES'S MAJOR-LEAGUE career began with the Cleveland Indians on June 13, 1914, continued with the Boston Red Sox from 1916 to 1921, with the Yankees from 1922 to 1926, the St. Louis Browns in 1927, the Washington Senators from 1928 to 1931, and the Chicago White Sox from 1932 to 1935. Twice a twenty-game winner, Samuel Pond Jones out of Woodsfield, Ohio, won 229 games and lost 217 in twenty-two American League seasons.

A stylish right-hander, one of the first major-leaguers to wear eyeglasses on the field, Jones had his ups and downs. Like most pitchers of his time, he was both a starter and a reliever. His eight saves in 1922 led the league. In 1923, he won twenty-one games, but lost a league-high twenty-one in 1925 as the Yanks dropped to seventh place.

Jones won sixty-seven games as a Yankee in five seasons. But no game was more memorable for him than his September 4, 1923, no-hitter, a 2–0 gem

Tony Lazzeri

against the Athletics. It capped his career year, a time he was *the* Yankee ace, hurling New York to its first world championship.

TONY LAZZERI STRIKEOUT: *October 10, 1926*

THERE WERE 38,093 in attendance on a gloomy and overcast day at Yankee Stadium for game seven of the 1926 World Series, Yankees versus Cardinals. The game played on into the seventh inning with St. Louis clinging to a 3–2 lead.

Yankee stopper Waite Hoyt had pitched well enough to win, giving up just the three runs on five hits. Jess Haines, the St. Louis hurler, had been touched for a homer by Babe Ruth but was still on the long end of the score.

Then he came apart in the seventh inning—a single, a sacrifice, an intentional pass to the Babe, and a walk to Gehrig. Bases loaded for the Yankees. Two out. Whether it was because of a blister Haines had developed on his finger or whether it was because Cardinal manager Rogers Hornsby itched to go to the same well one more time, Grover Cleveland Alexander was brought in to pitch to the Yankee rookie Tony Lazzeri, who had gone 0 for 4 against the thirty-nine-year-old right-hander the day before. Alexander, however, had already pitched complete-game victories in games two and six. It was also said that he was recuperating from too much imbibing while celebrating his victory the previous day.

Cardinal catcher Bob O'Farrell told Alexander to take his time and relax. The first pitch was a curve. The twenty-two-year-old Lazzeri swung with gusto. Strike one. The next pitch was a curve. Line drive into the left-field seats. Foul ball.

"Lazzeri swung where that curve started but not where it finished," Alexander said later. "The ball got a hunk of the corner and then finished outside. If that line drive Lazzeri hit had been fair, Tony would be the hero, and I'd just be an old bum."

Then an overanxious Lazzeri swung and missed—strike three. Alexander breezed through the eighth, and then, with two outs in the ninth, Babe Ruth walked. Incredibly, he was thrown out trying to steal second base, the only player to end a World Series by being thrown out on a stolen-base attempt.

But despite the unique ending that gave the Cardinals the victory, it was the Lazzeri-Alexander battle that provided high drama for the game and World Series.

MURDERERS' ROW WINS WORLD SERIES: *1927*

THE 1927 PITTSBURGH Pirates were a very talented team. Their fans bragged about players like Pie Traynor, National League MVP, batting champ Paul Waner, and his brother, Lloyd, who set a rookie record for hits.

The only problems for the Pirates in the 1927 series was that they were unfortunately matched up against "Murderers' Row," probably the greatest team ever, winner of 110 games.

The Yanks had Lou Gehrig, who batted .373 and drove in 175 runs—tops in the American League that year. His forty-seven home runs were second to Babe Ruth, who rapped out sixty. In comparison, the Philadelphia Athletics, second as a team to the Yanks in homers, hit only fifty-six.

It was reported that Gehrig, while preparing for game one of the series, hit ten home runs in batting practice. Then Ruth stepped in for batting practice. Pirate players gaped at the man who had hit six more home runs during the season than their entire team. Then the Babe hit ten more homers.

"Okay, sonnies," Ruth snarled. "If any of you want my autograph, go out there and get those balls and I'll sign them for you."

The strength of the 1927 Yankees, however, was not solely in their hitting. Anchored by twenty-two-game winner Waite Hoyt, the Yankee pitching staff was deep and often almost unhittable. Hoyt matched up against Pittsburgh nineteen-game winner Ray Kremer in the first game of the series. The Yankees won 5–4, helped by a couple of Pirate flubs. In game two, pitcher George Pipgras used a live fastball to go the distance in the 6–2 New York triumph. Herb Pennock had a perfect game to the eighth inning in game three. He finished with a three-hitter as the Yankees won 8–1.

Game four was a 3–3 tie as the bottom of the ninth got under way. Pirate relief pitcher John Miljas walked Earle Combs. Mark Koenig bunted his way on. With Ruth at bat, a flustered Miljas delivered. Wild pitch. Koenig was on second. Combs was on third. Ruth was intentionally walked, loading the bases. Gehrig fanned. Bob Meusel fanned. Tony Lazzeri stepped in. Miljas delivered—another wild pitch. Combs scored from third. The Yanks won 4–3 and had their series sweep.

"If the two teams had played a hundred games," recalled a member of that Pittsburgh team, "I honestly think the Yankees would have won them all. That's how intimidated we were."

Babe Ruth

BABE RUTH, SIXTY HOME RUNS: *1927*

THEY WERE CALLED the home run twins, Babe Ruth and Lou Gehrig, and throughout much of the 1927 season, they changed places holding the American League home-run lead.

On August 15, Gehrig was ahead 38–36. But the Iron Horse managed just nine more home runs the rest of the season. Anguish over his mother's health had him fretting during games and sent him to the hospital to see her after each home game.

Ruth, however, was having no such problems. The Sultan of Swat swatted his fortieth home run on August 22; he would smash twenty-four homers in his last forty-two games, including a September surge of seventeen dingers in his last twenty-nine games. One of those homers was on September 2—number forty-four, the four hundredth of his career. On September 6, he hit three home runs in a doubleheader at Fenway Park. Numbers forty-eight and forty-nine came the next day.

Numbers fifty-one and fifty-two came in a doubleheader sweep over Cleveland on September 13, the Yankee pennant clincher. At Yankee Stadium on September 29, Ruth smashed home runs off two different Washington pitchers—the second home run tied his single-season record of fifty-nine.

On September 30, southpaw Tom Zachary was on the mound. "I had made up my mind," the Senator pitcher said, "that I wasn't going to give him a good pitch to hit."

The game moved to the bottom of the eighth inning, score tied 2–2. The Babe had singled and scored in his first two at bats. No home run, not yet. Number fifty-nine had been hit just the day before with the bat Ruth called Black Betsy. His other bats were the ash-blond Big Bertha and the reddish Beautiful Bella.

Ruth carried Bella with him as he stepped into the batter's box lusting for number sixty.

There was one out, and Mark Koenig, who had tripled, was on third base. The count was one and one. "I don't say it was the best curve I ever threw, but it was as good as any I ever threw," Zachary said.

Lou Gehrig and Babe Ruth

Ruth reached out for the ball and pulled it into the first row of the bleachers near the right-field foul pole, fair by about ten feet. Number sixty.

Ruth doffed his cap a few times to the eight thousand in attendance, who cheered him as he slowly trotted out the historic home run and carefully touched each base.

As he crossed home plate, a double line of Yankees greeted Ruth. His fans in "Ruthville" in right field waved handkerchiefs and cheered the Babe as he took his fielding position in right field in the top of the ninth.

Later Zachary explained: "I gave Ruth a curve, low and outside. It was my best pitch. The ball just hooked into the right-field seats and I instinctively cried 'foul.' But I guess I was the only guy who saw it that way. If I'd a known it was gone be a famous record, I'd a stuck it in his ear."

LOU GEHRIG, FOUR HOME RUNS: *June 3, 1932*

THE DAY COULD have gone down in history as the one when Lou Gehrig pounded five home runs. But he had to settle for four.

In his first-inning at bat at Shibe Park in Philadelphia before a crowd of seventy-three hundred, Gehrig mashed the ball into the left-center stands for a two-run shot. His second home run of the day went over the right-field wall in the fourth inning. Home run number three went into the stands in the fifth inning.

The Athletics' George Earnshaw gave up the first three homers. Philly manage Connie Mack replaced Earnshaw with Leroy Mahaffey, who gave up Gehrig's fourth homer in the seventh inning. That shot screamed over the right-field wall.

Gehrig had two more chances to become the first player to hit five homers in a game (Bobby Lowe and Ed Delahanty each had four in the nineteenth century). When the Yankee hero came to bat in the eighth inning, Philadelphia fans cheered, urging him on, beseeching him to hit another home run. He grounded out.

The Yankee first baseman came up for the final time in the game in the ninth inning against pitcher Ed Rommel. Gehrig missed a fifth home run by just inches as Al Simmons made a one-handed snatch in the farthest part of the park in deep center field.

Although he fell short of breaking the record, Lou Gehrig did have the distinction of becoming the first player in the twentieth century to hit four homers in one game.

BABE RUTH'S
SIXTY HOME RUNS
1927

HOME RUN	GM	DATE	PITCHER (right- or left-hander), CLUB	HOME OR AWAY	INNING	PLAYERS ON BASE
1	4	Apr 15	Howard Ehmke (R), Philadelphia	H	1	0
2	11	Apr 23	Rube Walberg (L), Philadelphia	A	1	0
3	12	Apr 24	Sloppy Thurston (R), Washington	A	6	0
4	14	Apr 29	Slim Harriss (R), Boston	A	5	0
5	16	May 1	Jack Quinn (R), Philadelphia	H	1	1
6	16	May 1	Rube Walberg (L), Philadelphia	H	8	0
7	24	May 10	Milt Gaston (R), St. Louis	A	1	2
8	25	May 11	Ernie Nevers (R), St. Louis	A	1	1
9	29	May 17	Rip H. Collins (R), Detroit	A	8	0
10	33	May 22	Benn Karr (R), Cleveland	A	6	1
11	34	May 23	Sloppy Thurston (R), Washington	A	1	0
12	37	May 28	Sloppy Thurston (R), Washington	H	7	2
13	39	May 29	Danny MacFayden (R), Boston	H	8	0
14	41	May 30	Rube Walberg, (L), Philadelphia	A	11	0
15	42	May 31	Jack Quinn (R), Philadelphia	A	1	1
16	43	May 31	Howard Ehmke (R), Philadelphia	A	5	1
17	47	June 5	Earl Whitehill (L), Detroit	H	6	0
18	48	June 7	Tommy Thomas (R), Chicago	H	4	0
19	52	June 11	Garland Buckeye (L), Cleveland	H	3	1
20	52	June 11	Garland Buckeye (L), Cleveland	H	5	0
21	53	June 12	George Uhle (R), Cleveland	H	7	0
22	55	June 16	Tom Zachary (L), St. Louis	H	1	1
23	60	June 22	Hal Wiltse (L), Boston	A	5	0
24	60	June 22	Hal Wiltse (L), Boston	A	7	1
25	70	June 30	Slim Harriss (R), Boston	H	4	1
26	73	July 3	Hod Lisenbee (R), Washington	A	1	0
27	78	July 8	Don Hankins (R), Detroit	A	2	2
28	79	July 9	Ken Holloway (R), Detroit	A	1	1
29	79	July 9	Ken Holloway (R), Detroit	A	4	2
30	83	July 12	Joe Shaute (L), Cleveland	A	9	1
31	92	July 24	Tommy Thomas (R), Chicago	A	3	0
32	95	July 26	Milt Gaston (R), St. Louis	H	1	1
33	95	July 26	Milt Gaston (R), St. Louis	H	6	0
34	98	July 28	Lefty Stewart (L), St. Louis	H	8	1
35	106	Aug 5	George S. Smith (R), Detroit	H	8	0

HOME RUN	GM	DATE	PITCHER (right- or left-hander), CLUB	HOME OR AWAY	INNING	PLAYERS ON BASE
36	110	Aug 10	Tom Zachary (L), Washington	A	3	2
37	114	Aug 16	Tommy Thomas (R), Chicago	A	5	0
38	115	Aug 17	Sarge Connally (R), Chicago	A	11	0
39	118	Aug 20	Jake Miller (L), Cleveland	A	1	1
40	120	Aug 22	Joe Shaute (L), Cleveland	A	6	0
41	124	Aug 27	Ernie Nevers (R), St. Louis	A	8	1
42	125	Aug 28	Ernie Wingard (L), St. Louis	A	1	1
43	127	Aug 31	Tony Welzer (R), Boston	H	8	0
44	128	Sep 2	Rube Walberg (L), Philadelphia	A	1	0
45	132	Sep 6	Tony Welzer (R), Boston	A	6	2
46	132	Sep 6	Tony Welzer (R), Boston	A	7	1
47	133	Sep 6	Jack Russell (R), Boston	A	9	0
48	134	Sep 7	Danny MacFayden (R), Boston	A	1	0
49	134	Sep 7	Slim Harriss (R), Boston	A	8	1
50	138	Sep 11	Milt Gaston (R), St. Louis	H	4	0
51	139	Sep 13	Willis Hudlin (R), Cleveland	H	7	1
52	140	Sep 13	Joe Shaute (L), Cleveland	H	4	0
53	143	Sep 16	Ted Blankenship (R), Chicago	H	3	0
54	147	Sep 18	Ted Lyons (R), Chicago	H	5	1
55	148	Sep 21	Sam Gibson (R), Detroit	H	9	0
56	149	Sep 22	Ken Holloway (R), Detroit	H	9	1
57	152	Sep 27	Lefty Grove (L), Philadelphia	H	6	3
58	153	Sep 29	Hod Lisenbee (R), Washington	H	1	0
59	153	Sep 29	Paul Hopkins (R), Washington	H	5	3
60	154	Sep 30	Tom Zachary (L), Washington	H	8	1

THE CALLED SHOT: *October 1, 1932*

A HEAVIER, SLOWER, and older Babe Ruth had much more to prove in 1932. And prove he did! Batting .341, driving in 137 runs, slugging 41 homers, the Sultan of Swat pushed the New York Yankees to another pennant. The Chicago Cubs would be their opposition in the World Series.

There had been a good deal of bad blood between the two teams over the past several years. Yankee manager Joe McCarthy had been let go as Chicago manager in 1930. He wanted payback. Ruth's old buddy Mark Koenig, now a Cub, had helped his new team win the pennant. His Chicago teammates voted Ruth's old buddy only a half World Series share. The Babe was not happy about that.

On October 1 in Chicago during batting practice, Ruth shouted: "Hey, you damn bum Cubs, you won't be seeing Yankee Stadium again. This is going to be all over Sunday." The Babe was referring to the fact that the Yanks had won the first two games in New York. Game three got under way before 49,986. Lemons from the stands and curses from the Cubs were heaped upon the Yankees. Chicago fans showered Ruth with fruits and vegetables and other projectiles when he was on defense in the outfield. The Babe smiled, doffed his cap, felt the fire.

When he came to bat in the fifth inning, Ruth had already slugged a three-run homer into the right-center-field bleachers—but the best was yet to come. Right-hander Charlie Root got a strike on Ruth, who as accounts go, raised up one big finger and yelled, "Strike one!"

Another fastball strike. Ruth, as the story continues, raised two fingers and bellowed, "Strike two!"

Then, as the story has been handed down, the thirty-eight-year-old Yankee legend stepped out of the batter's box and pointed. Some said he pointed at Root; others said he pointed at the Chicago bench; others said at the center-field bleachers.

"To tell the truth," Joe McCarthy said, "I didn't see him point anywhere at all. But maybe I turned my head for a moment."

"The Babe pointed out to right field," said George Pipgras, who pitched and won that game, "and that's where he hit the ball."

The count was 2–2 when Babe swung from his heels. Johnny Moore, the Chicago center fielder, started back, then stopped. The ball disappeared into the right-field bleachers, 436 feet from home plate, the fifteenth and last World Series home run for Babe Ruth, and the longest home run ever hit at that point in time in Wrigley Field.

"As I hit the ball," Ruth would say later, "every muscle in my system, every sense I had, told me that I had never hit a better one, that as long as I lived nothing would ever feel as good as this one."

Chicago fans cheered and applauded the Babe as he rounded the bases, yelling out a different curse for each Cub infielder as he passed them by. When the Sultan of Swat reached third base, he paused—and bowed toward the Chicago dugout. Then he came across home plate.

Through the years the debate has continued. Did he or did he not call the home run?

Babe Ruth later explained:

"I didn't exactly point to any spot, like the flagpole. I just sorta waved at the whole fence, but that was foolish enough. All I wanted to do was give the thing a ride . . . outta the park . . . anywhere. Every time I went to the bat the Cubs on the bench would yell 'Oogly googly.' It's all part of the game, but this particular inning when I went to bat there was a whole chorus of oogly googlies. The first pitch was a pretty good strike, and I didn't kick. But the second was outside and I turned around to beef about it. As I said, Gabby Hartnett said, 'Oogly googly.' That kinda burned me and I said, 'All right, you bums, I'm gonna knock this one a mile.' I guess I pointed, too."

LOU GEHRIG, 2,130 CONSECUTIVE GAMES STREAK

IT BEGAN INNOCENTLY enough when Yankee manager Miller Huggins sent Lou Gehrig up to bat for Pee-Wee Wanninger on June 1, 1925. The husky twenty-two-year old singled. The next day regular first baseman Wally Pipp was hit on the side of the head during batting practice. "Has anyone an aspirin tablet?" asked Pipp.

"Take a couple of days off," manager Miller Huggins said. "I'm going to start young Gehrig in your place." In the previous two seasons, Gehrig had accumulated just thirty-eight at bats. He was told by Huggins that if he did well as a replacement, he might become a regular.

He did well in the game against Washington, rapping out a double and two singles in his first major-league start. When the season ended, Gehrig had twenty-nine home runs and a .295 average. Half of his hits were for extra bases. Pipp never got his job back; he was traded to the Reds after the season ended.

There is the misconception that the day Gehrig replaced Pipp was the day the 2,130-game streak began. It actually began the day before when he pinch-hit for Pee-Wee Wanninger.

On June 23, 1932, Gehrig played in his 1,103rd straight game. On June 14, 1933, he was at 1,249 straight games. However, on that day Gehrig and manager Joe McCarthy were tossed out of the game. Marse Joe was given a three-game suspension. Gehrig played on.

On August 17, 1933, Gehrig broke the record of 1,308 set by Everett Scott. On July 13, 1934, Gehrig's pain was so intense from what was diagnosed as lumbago that in the first inning of a game against Detroit he had to be helped off the field.

Lou Gehrig

There were those who said "the streak" was over. But the next day, listed first in the Yankee batting order and penciled in to play shortstop, the Yankee legend singled in his first at bat. Then he was replaced by a pinch runner.

On June 5, 1936, Lou Gehrig appeared in his 1,700th consecutive game. On May 31, 1938, his wife asked: "Why not stop at 1,999?" The streak reached 2,000 on August 3, 1937.

Then in the final third of the 1938 season, Gehrig faltered; his great strength seemed to be waning. But he played on.

On September 9, rapping out four hits, the Iron Horse pushed his batting average to .300 and the streak to 2,100.

The season of 1938 ended, and it was clear that Lou Gehrig's great vitality was no longer there. His hand trembled when he held a cup of coffee.

In spring training of 1939, his physical condition worsened. He was advised to take some time off. On Opening Day, in the fifth inning, star pitcher Lefty Grove of the Red Sox, who had once called the Iron Horse the toughest man he'd ever faced, intentionally walked Joe DiMaggio to face Gehrig, who grounded weakly into a double play.

The three-time MVP would pop up, hit little fly balls. Shaken, he still played on. Tommy Henrich remembered, "It looked like he was trying to run uphill."

Off the field, sudden falls were becoming common. He had difficulty tying his shoelaces.

A week into the season, Gehrig had driven in just one run and his batting average was well below .200. The eighth game of the season was the end. Three Senator pitchers held Gehrig hitless in four at bats. He dropped an easy throw to first in an early inning.

"Take some time off," Gehrig's wife, Eleanor, said. "Get yourself checked out and find out what is wrong with you."

Lou responded, "I will be able to work this out. This is the only way for me to go."

On the last day of April 1939, more than 600,000 passed through the turnstiles at the opening of the World's Fair in New York. In the Bronx, only 23,712 were at Yankee Stadium. The Senators nipped New York 3–2. In his 2,130th straight game, Lou Gehrig went 0 for 4. His batting average dropped to .143. A somber Gehrig told Joe McCarthy: "You'd better take me out. I guess that's all."

An announcement was made to the fans in Detroit on May 2 that the great Gehrig had taken himself out of the starting lineup. As he walked back off the field he was given a standing ovation. Removing his cap and tipping it to the fans, the handsome Yankee settled in a corner of the dugout.

Babe Dahlgren, Gehrig's replacement, had waited three years. He homered in the third inning. The first player out of the Yankee dugout to congratulate him was Lou Gehrig.

With the game ended—the first Yankee game he had missed in fifteen years—and with the streak stopped, the gentlemanly Gehrig answered all questions.

"Maybe a rest will do me some good. Maybe it won't. Who knows? Who can tell? I'm just hoping."

It would be sixty-two years before Gehrig's streak of 2,130 consecutive games played would be broken. Yet although Cal Ripken, Jr., now holds the record, the magic and the drama of Gehrig's fabled streak will always remain with the Yankee first baseman.

MONTE PEARSON'S NO-HITTER: *August 27, 1938*

HIS FULL NAME was Montgomery Marcellus Pearson, but everyone called him Monte. Out of Oakland, California, a Yankee from 1936 to 1940, a two time All Star, Pearson went 63–27 with four World Series wins for the Bronx Bombers, including a two-hit shutout of the Reds in 1939.

Pearson had a lot of talent—he was a two-time All Star—but battled control problems and various illnesses, real and imagined, throughout his career. He walked 135 batters one year, 113 another. There were days when he just did not want to pitch, blaming his lack of enthusiasm on one ailment or another.

But that was not the case on August 27, 1938. On that day he spun the first no-hitter in Yankee Stadium history as the Yankees beat up on a hard-hitting Cleveland team 13–0. The win was just one of Pearson's 16 victories that 1938 season.

LOU GEHRIG APPRECIATION DAY,
FAREWELL SPEECH: *July 4, 1939*

IT WAS YANKEES versus Senators on July 4, 1939, a doubleheader at Yankee Stadium. Most of the 61,808 on hand were there to honor Lou Gehrig in a ceremony between games. Two weeks earlier, Gehrig had made public that he had ALS.

Players, officials, writers, and employees at the park outdid themselves with gifts for the Iron Horse. A parade launched the forty-minute ceremony as the Seventh Regiment Band escorted Babe Ruth, Waite Hoyt, Bob Meusel, Herb Pennock, Joe Dugan, Tony Lazzeri, Mark Koenig, Benny Bengough, Wally Schang, Everett Scott, Wally Pipp, George Pipgras, and Bob Shawkey to the center-field flagpole. A banner was hoisted saluting the 1927 Yankees.

Then the group of former stars, all wearing street clothes, assembled shoulder to shoulder near the pitcher's mound. Yankees and Senators formed a semi-circle around a microphone at home plate.

"We want Lou, we want Lou," the chant began. Led out of the dugout by Yankees president Ed Barrow, Gehrig doffed his cap. The crowd roared. Gehrig fought back tears.

Sid Mercer, the master of ceremonies, announced, "Ladies and gentlemen, Lou Gehrig has asked me to thank you all for him. He is too moved to speak."

"We want Lou! We want Lou," The chant was a plea for Gehrig to speak.

Coaxed by manager Joe McCarthy, Gehrig wiped his eyes, blew his nose. On unsteady feet, the seven-time All Star moved toward the microphone to give the speech he had written the night before.

"Fans, for the past two weeks you have been reading about a bad break I got. Yet today, I consider myself the luckiest man on the face of the earth. I have been in ballparks for seventeen years and I have never received anything but

kindness and encouragement from you fans. Look at these grand men. Which of you wouldn't consider it the highlight of his career just to associate with them for even one day? Sure I'm lucky. Who wouldn't have considered it an honor to have known Jacob Ruppert? Also, the builder of baseball's greatest empire, Ed Barrow? To have spent six years with that wonderful little fellow, Miller Huggins? Then to have spent the next nine years with that outstanding leader, that smart student of psychology, the best manager in baseball today, Joe McCarthy? Sure, I'm lucky. When the New York Giants, a team you would give your right arm to beat and vice versa, sends you a gift, that's something. When everybody down to the groundskeeper and those boys in white coats remember you with trophies, that's something. When you have a father and mother work all their lives so that you can have an education and build your body, it's a blessing. When you have a wife who has been a tower of strength and shown more courage than you dreamed existed, that's the finest I know. So I close in saying that I might have had a bad break, but I have an awful lot to live for."

Until season's end, "the Pride of the Yankees" was there with and for his team. He spent every day on the bench and traveled with the Yankees on road trips. He sat through all four of the 1939 World Series games.

Lou Gehrig gave his farewell speech on Lou Gehrig Appreciation Day, July 4, 1939. He would continue to travel with the team and attend games until the end of the season.

On June 3, 1941, Lou Gehrig died at his home, 5204 Delafield Avenue, in the Fieldston section of the Bronx. He would have been thirty-eight years old on June 19.

JOE DIMAGGIO'S FIFTY-SIX-GAME HITTING STREAK

IT WAS TRULY remarkable—a hit every game for two months, from May 15 through July 17, 1941, in Yankee wins and defeats, in games played in the daytime and those played at night. Single games, doubleheaders, meaningless games and ones that really counted—Joe DiMaggio was locked in for fifty-six straight. And what made the epic feat even more dramatic was that it took place in the summer of 1941, a time America was locked into news of the triumphs and tragedies of World War II.

The Yankee Clipper started the 1941 season slumping. He managed a single in four at bats on May 15 against Edgar Smith in a game the Yankees lost to the White Sox 3–1.

On May 24 in his final at bat of a game against the Red Sox, DiMaggio singled in two runs. He had a modest ten-game hitting streak, but hardly anyone paid it any attention. On May 30 the Yankee center fielder made three errors in the second game of a doubleheader. He was pressing. In the fifth inning, his fly ball to right was lost in the sun by Boston outfielder Pete Fox. DiMag, credited with a hit, had pushed the streak to sixteen.

Hits in both games of a doubleheader on June 1 against the Indians moved the streak to eighteen. It was at nineteen the next day, the day Lou Gehrig died. The American League record set by George Sisler of forty-one straight seemed out of reach. But there was lots of speculation in the newspapers and on the radio about the possibility of him reaching it.

"That's when I became conscious of the streak," DiMaggio said. "But at that stage I didn't think too much about it."

Newspaper and radio began to dramatize what Joe DiMaggio was doing. Most games then were played in the afternoon. Radio announcers would routinely interrupt their programs with the news of the Yankee Clipper's progress, and the Les Brown Orchestra's "Joltin' Joe DiMaggio" recording was played by radio disc jockeys day and night:

On June 17, DiMaggio's grounder to short bounced up and hit Chicago's Luke Appling on the shoulder. Official scorer Dan Daniel credited him with a hit. The streak stood at thirty. The George Sisler American League consecutive-game hit record of forty-one was in reach.

Over the next week and a half, DiMaggio continued to hit. Then on June 29, DiMaggio singled off Washington knuckleballer Dutch Leonard in the first game of a doubleheader. A seventh-inning single off Walt Masterson in the second game set a new record—forty-two. The taciturn DiMaggio became

America's most famous athlete, pestered by the media, ogled by fans, adored by his Yankee teammates.

Before 52,832 at Yankee Stadium on July 1, DiMag paced a doubleheader sweep of Boston. The Yankee Clipper rapped out two hits in the first game. The nightcap was called after five innings, but DiMaggio got a hit and tied the forty-three-year-old major-league record of forty-four set by Willie Keeler.

The next day DiMag moved the streak to forty-five, homering off Dick Newsome of the Sox. Even the All-Star Game did not stop Joe DiMaggio's streak. "I doubled"–the Clipper smiled remembering the time–"and [brother] Dom drove me in with a single."

The sixteenth of July saw the Yankees in Cleveland for the start of a series with the Indians. Joe Di stroked a first-inning single. Fifty-six!! The crowd at vast Municipal Stadium cheered.

On July 17, 1941, DiMag and Lefty Gomez were headed in a cab to the ballpark in Cleveland. "I've got a feeling that if you don't get a hit your first time up tonight," the cabby told him, "they're going to stop you."

"Who the hell are you?" Gomez snapped at the cabby. "What are you trying to do, jinx him?"

Before 67,468–40,000 of whom had purchased their tickets some time in advance–veteran left-hander Al Smith took the mound for Cleveland. It was not the Indians the throng came out to see. It was Joltin' Joe DiMaggio.

In inning one, DiMaggio slashed a 1–0 pitch past third base but Ken Keltner, playing deep, backhanded the ball and fired to first. Out! In the fourth inning, DiMag was walked.

The intense Yankee came to bat in the seventh inning lusting to extend the streak. The noise level in the huge ballpark was almost deafening. A shot to third, a pickup by Keltner. DiMaggio out at first base.

In the eighth inning the bases were loaded with one out when the Yankee Clipper came up, displaying no emotion. But there was plenty in the rocking, rowdy stands. The count was 1–1. Ground ball to Lou Boudreau at short. The flip to Ray Mack at second, who pivoted and threw to first. Double play. The streak was over.

"I can't say I'm glad it's over," DiMaggio said after the game. "Of course, I wanted it to go on as long as it could."

During the streak Joe DiMaggio had ninety-one hits, twenty-two multi-hit games, five three-hit games, four four-hit games, a 408 batting average that included fifteen home runs and fifty-five runs batted in. Incredibly, with the streak over, DiMaggio began a new one. He hit in sixteen consecutive games—giving him the distinction of having hit safely in seventy-two of seventy-three games in the 1941 season.

A P.S. to the remarkable streak took place more than thirty-years later. Joe DiMaggio recalled: "The guy said he was that cab driver. He apologized and he was serious. I felt awful. He might have been spending his whole life thinking he had jinxed me, but I told him he hadn't. My number was up."

JOE DIMAGGIO'S
FIFTY-SIX-GAME HITTING STREAK
1941

DATE	GAME	PITCHER(S)	OPPONENT	AB	R	H	2B	3B	HR	RBI
May 15	1	Eddie Smith	Chicago	4	0	1	0	0	0	1
May 16	2	Thornton Lee	Chicago	4	2	2	0	1	1	1
May 17	3	Johnny Rigney	Chicago	3	1	1	0	0	0	0
May 18	4	Bob Harris/Johnny Niggeling	St. Louis	3	3	2/1	1	0	0	1
May 19	5	Denny Galehouse	St. Louis	3	0	1	1	0	0	0
May 20	6	Elden Auker	St. Louis	5	1	1	0	0	0	1
May 21	7	Schoolboy Rowe/Al Benton	Detroit	5	0	1/1	0	0	0	1
May 22	8	Archie McKain	Detroit	4	0	1	0	0	0	1
May 23	9	Dick Newsome	Boston	5	0	1	0	0	0	2
May 24	10	Earl Johnson	Boston	4	2	1	0	0	0	2
May 25	11	Lefty Grove	Boston	4	0	1	0	0	0	0
May 27	12	Ken Chase				1				
		Red Anderson	Washington	5	3	2	0	0	1	3
		Alex Carrasquel				1				
May 28	13	Sid Hudson	Washington	4	1	1	0	1	0	0
May 29	14	Steve Sundra	Washington	3	1	1	0	0	0	0
May 30	15	Earl Johnson	Boston	2	1	1	0	0	0	0
May 30	16	Mickey Harris	Boston	3	0	1	1	0	0	0
June 1	17	Al Milnar	Cleveland	4	1	1	0	0	0	0
June 1	18	Mel Harder	Cleveland	4	0	1	0	0	0	0
June 2	19	Bob Feller	Cleveland	4	2	2	1	0	0	0
June 3	20	Dizzy Trout	Detroit	4	1	1	0	0	1	1
June 5	21	Hal Newhouser	Detroit	5	1	1	0	1	0	1
June 7	22	Bob Muncrief				1				
		Johnny Allen	St. Louis	5	2	1	0	0	0	1
		George Caster				1				
June 8	23	Elden Auker	St. Louis	4	3	2	0	0	2	4
June 8	24	George Caster/Jack Kramer	St. Louis	4	1	1/1	1	0	1	3
June 10	25	Johnny Rigney	Chicago	5	1	1	0	0	0	0
June 12	26	Thornton Lee	Chicago	4	1	2	0	0	1	1
June 14	27	Bob Feller	Cleveland	2	0	1	1	0	0	1
June 15	28	Jim Bagby	Cleveland	3	1	1	0	0	1	1
June 16	29	Al Milnar	Cleveland	5	0	1	1	0	0	0
June 17	30	Johnny Rigney	Chicago	4	1	1	0	0	0	0
June 18	31	Thornton Lee	Chicago	3	0	1	0	0	0	0
June 19	32	Eddie Smith/Buck Ross	Chicago	3	2	1/2	0	0	1	2

DATE	GAME	PITCHER(S)	OPPONENT	AB	R	H	2B	3B	HR	RBI
June 20	33	Bobo Newsom/Archie McKain	Detroit	5	3	2/2	1	0	0	1
June 21	34	Dizzy Trout	Detroit	4	0	1	0	0	0	1
June 22	35	Hal Newhouser/Bobo Newsom	Detroit	5	1	1/1	1	0	1	2
June 24	36	Bob Muncrief	St. Louis	4	1	1	0	0	0	0
June 25	37	Denny Galehouse	St. Louis	4	1	1	0	0	1	3
June 26	38	Elden Auker	St. Louis	4	0	1	1	0	0	1
June 27	39	Chubby Dean	Philadelphia	3	1	2	0	0	1	2
June 28	40	Johnny Babich/Lum Harris	Philadelphia	5	1	1/1	1	0	0	0
June 29	41	Dutch Leonard	Washington	4	1	1	1	0	0	0
June 29	42	Red Anderson	Washington	5	1	1	0	0	0	1
July 01	43	Mickey Harris/Mike Ryba	Boston	4	0	1/1	0	0	0	1
July 01	44	Jack Wilson	Boston	3	1	1	0	0	0	1
July 02	45	Dick Newsome	Boston	5	1	1	0	0	1	3
July 05	46	Phil Marchildon	Philadelphia	4	2	1	0	0	1	2
July 06	47	Johnny Babich/Bump Hadley	Philadelphia	5	2	2/2	1	0	0	2
July 06	48	Jack Knott	Philadelphia	4	0	2	0	1	0	2
July 10	49	Johnny Niggeling	St. Louis	2	0	1	0	0	0	0
July 11	50	Bob Harris/Jack Kramer	St. Louis	5	1	3/1	0	0	1	2
July 12	51	Elden Auker/Bob Muncrief	St. Louis	5	1	1/1	1	0	0	1
July 13	52	Ted Lyons/Jack Hallett	Chicago	4	2	2/1	0	0	0	0
July 13	53	Thornton Lee	Chicago	4	0	1	0	0	0	0
July 14	54	Johnny Rigney	Chicago	3	0	1	0	0	0	0
July 15	55	Eddie Smith	Chicago	4	1	2	1	0	0	2
July 16	56	Al Milnar/Joe Krakauskas	Cleveland	4	3	2/1	1	0	0	0
		TOTALS		**223**	**56**	**91**	**16**	**4**	**15**	**55**

MICKEY OWEN, CALLED THIRD STRIKE:
October 5, 1941

IT WAS SUNDAY baseball at Ebbets Field in Brooklyn before a standing-room-only crowd of 33,813. Yankees against Dodgers, game four of the World Series, the first for Brooklyn in twenty-one years.

The ceremonial first pitch was thrown out by New York City mayor, Fiorello La Guardia. Everyone settled in on that summerlike day to watch the matchup of Brooklyn's Kirby Higbe and New York's Atley McDonald in the first Subway Series between the two teams.

As the game moved to the ninth inning with the Brooks clinging to a 4–3 lead, Higbe and McDonald were long gone and in their places were Brooklyn's Hugh Casey and Yankee reliever Johnny Murphy.

The burly Casey got Johnny Sturm and Red Rolfe on ground balls. That made it seven in a row for him. Outfielder Tommy Henrich was next. The count ran full.

"Casey goes into the windup," Mel Allen described it. "Around comes the right arm, in comes the pitch. A swing by Henrich . . . he swings and misses, strike three! But the ball gets away from Mickey Owen. It's rolling back to the screen. Tommy Henrich races down toward first base. He makes it safely. And the Yankees are still alive with Joe DiMaggio coming up to bat." That fabled call by Allen succinctly and dramatically described what happened.

Stunned, shaken by the dramatic turn of events, Casey lost his command and was roughed up for four runs. The Yankees wound up beating the Dodgers 7–4. Later, Tommy Henrich recalled: "That ball broke like no curve I'd ever seen Casey throw. As I start to swing, I think, 'No good. Hold up.' That thing broke so sharp, though, that as I tried to hold up, my mind said, 'He might have trouble with it.' "

Owen was the goat ironically, that season he had set the National League record of 476 consecutive errorless chances accepted by a catcher while setting a Dodger season record by fielding .995.

There were those who thought the game was over when Henrich swung and apparently struck out on the Casey 3–2 pitch. A few Yankee players were headed down the runway to their locker room. Police, positioned in the Dodger dugout, were out on the field getting ready to handle crowd control. An issue for Owen trying to come up with the passed ball were the police on the field.

The next day a four-hitter by Ernie (Tiny) Bonham gave the Yankees a 3–1 victory and the world championship, again. For the Dodgers, it was "Wait 'til Next Year" again.

THE BEVENS NO-HITTER LOST: *October 3, 1947*

THE 1947 WORLD Series game-four starter for the Yankees before 33,443 frenzied fans at Ebbets Field was an unlikely choice—Bill Bevens. The thirty-one-year-old right-hander had lost thirteen of twenty decisions during the regular season.

His record would have been a lot better had he not walked seventy-seven in 165 innings. His luck was a lot better in the World Series start—or so it seemed.

Going into the ninth inning, Bevens had a 2–1 lead. Much more important—he was pitching a no-hitter. But by the ninth, he was getting tired, he had thrown a lot of pitches, going deep in the count with quite a few batters—everyone was waiting to see what would happen.

Brooklyn catcher Bruce Edwards hit a high fly ball for the first out in the ninth. The Bevens, laboring, walked Carl Furillo. It was his ninth walk of the game. Spider Jorgensen fouled out, weakly. Just one more out and the first World Series no-hitter would be sealed.

Then, in Dodger broadcaster Red Barber's phrase, "the wheels were turning." Speedy pinch runner Al Gionfriddo came in for Furillo. "Pistol Pete" Reiser came in to hit for relief pitcher Hugh Casey. With the count 3–1 on Reiser, Gionfriddo stole second base. Bevens intentionally walked Reiser, his tenth walk of the game. Eddie Miksis came in to run for Reiser. The Dodgers now had two very fast runners on base.

Bill Bevens, Red Embree, Allie Reynolds, Frank Shea, and Ed Lopat

Eddie Stanky headed for the plate, bud Dodger manager Burt Shotton pulled him and sent in veteran Harry Arthur "Cookie" Lavagetto as a pinch hitter.

Pitch number 136 from Bevens drew a swing and a miss by Lavagetto. The next pitch, one pitch too many, was slightly off the plate.

"The pitch was right out there and I got hold of it good," said Lavagetto. Line drive toward the right-field wall. Tommy Henrich, in front of the scoreboard in right center field, watched as the ball struck high, near the center of the Gem Razorblade sign. It bounced around and Henrich finally picked it up, turned, and threw.

"I ran down to first base," Lavagetto said, "and turned and saw the two runs scoring and that's all there was to it."

"Friends," Red Barber said, "they're killin' Lavagetto . . . his own teammates . . . they're beatin' him to pieces and it's taking a police escort to get Lavagetto away from the Dodgers!"

The two-out double not only broke up the Bill Bevens no-hitter, it also pinned the loss on the Yankee hurler and tied the series at two games each. Goat Bevens and hero Lavagetto would never again wear major-league uniforms after the 1947 World Series.

THE CATCH BY AL GIONFRIDDO:
October 5, 1947

JUST TWO DAYS before, he had been one of those cast in history's spotlight. He scored as Bill Bevens lost game four and his no-hitter. But the five-feet-six, 165-pound Albert Francis Gionfriddo, who played in only thirty-seven games that 1947 season for the Brooklyn Dodgers, would end up having an even larger role in game six of the hard-fought World Series.

There were 74,065 on hand at Yankee Stadium, a World Series record, on a beautiful day for baseball. Most of them had come to see the home team, now leading three games to two, wrap up another world championship.

Allie Reynolds started for the Yankees against little left-hander Vic Lombardi for the Dodgers. Neither would be around when the game ended.

"Dem Bums" had made up a 5–4 deficit against reliever Joe Page, taking an 8–5 lead as the game moved to the bottom of the sixth inning. As the Dodgers took the field, Gionfriddo was put in for defensive purposes.

A George Stirnweiss walk and a two-out single by Berra set the stage for Joe DiMaggio—the potential tying run. The Yankee Clipper mashed the first pitch he saw from Dodger reliever Joe Hatten. Dodger broadcaster Red Barber shouted "Back, back, back" as Gionfriddo raced toward the bullpen railing. He lost his cap, turned, leaped, and stuck out his glove. The catch was made just to the left of the 415-foot marker in front of a low metal gate.

It was said that the catch was one of the greatest in baseball history. It was said the only time Joe DiMaggio ever showed real emotion on the ball field was that moment. In disbelief as he neared second base, DiMag shook his head and kicked at the dirt.

The game lasted three hours and nineteen minutes. There were a total of thirty-eight players used. Brooklyn hung on to eke out an 8–6 win and force a seventh game, which the Yankees would go on to win 5–2.

And Gionfriddo? After the series ended, he joined Bill Bevens and Cookie Lavagetto in the distinction of never playing in another major-league game.

BABE RUTH'S FINAL APPEARANCE:
June 13, 1948

BABE RUTH DEVELOPED throat cancer in 1946. Surgery and radiation treatments did very little to help. He was released from the hospital on February 15, 1947. His wife and doctors kept the horrific diagnosis from him, but Ruth knew the end was near.

"The termites have got me," he told Connie Mack and others. The surgery had damaged his larynx, transforming the sound of his once-exuberant voice into a smoky rasp.

On June 13, 1948, Babe made his final appearance in Yankee Stadium, an occasion for commemorating the twenty-fifth anniversary of the House that Ruth Built and for the Babe's uniform number (3) to be retired.

Friends had to help him into his old uniform, which now fit him like a loose sack. The Yankee clubhouse was lined with his teammates from the 1923 team, who were there to play a two-inning exhibition game against veterans from other years. The Babe would only watch.

It was raining that day and someone put a camel's-hair coat over his shoulders. The Babe's old teammates were introduced one by one to booming cheers. Finally, announcer Mel Allen called him to home plate. Using a bat as a cane, Ruth walked out slowly. The thunderous ovation shook Yankee Stadium.

"Thank you very much, ladies and gentlemen." The Babe struggled to talk into the microphones. "You know how bad my voice sounds. Well, it feels just as bad. You know this baseball game of ours comes up from the youth. That means the boys. And after you've been a boy, and grow up to know how to play ball, then you come to the boys you see representing themselves today in our national pastime.

"The only real game in the world, I think, is baseball. As a rule, people think that if you give boys a football or a baseball or something like that, they naturally become athletes right away. But you can't do that in baseball. You got to start from way down, at the bottom, when the boys are six or seven years of age. You can't wait until they're fourteen or fifteen. You got to let it grow up with you, if you're the boy. And if you try hard enough, you're bound to come

Babe Ruth's last public appearance, June 13, 1948

out on top, just as these boys here have come to the top now. There have been so many lovely things said about me today that I'm glad to have had the opportunity to thank everybody."

When the ceremonies finally ended and the media and old-timers gathered in the locker room, Joe Dugan poured a beer for his old friend. "So" Joe asked, "how are you, Babe?"

"Joe, I'm gone," Ruth said and then began to cry.

Back in the hospital after that poignant day, the man who was the national pastime signed autographs, watched baseball on television, listened to his wife read him some of the hundreds of letters sent to him every day. Visitors came and went. The Babe tried to look upbeat.

At 8:01 P.M., on August 16, 1948, Babe Ruth died. He was fifty-three years old. He lay in state in the House that Ruth Built for two days as more than two hundred thousand paid last respects. Grieving fathers held up their sons and daughters for one final look at arguably the greatest baseball player of all time.

Three days later the funeral was held at St. Patrick's Cathedral. There were tens of thousands in the streets outside and tens of thousands more lined the funeral cortege route. At the funeral's somber scene, Ruth's old teammates were pallbearers. Claire Ruth, Babe's widow, would live on at their apartment at 100 Riverside Drive for another twenty-eight years until her death.

THE JOE DIMAGGIO SHOW AT FENWAY PARK:
June 28–30, 1949

IT WAS BITTER rivalry time again, Yanks versus Red Sox. New York had a hold on first place but Boston had won four straight, ten of their last eleven.

Joe DiMaggio was returning to the baseball wars after missing sixty-five games because of a bone spur in his foot. Fenway was jammed with 36,228 for the Friday-night three-game-series opener on June 28.

In his first American League at bat in eight months, DiMag faced Mickey McDermott. "He could throw hard," DiMaggio said. "My timing was off. I kept fouling pitch after pitch to right field. Then I lined a hit over shortstop. It felt good."

It felt even better for the Yankee center fielder his second time up—a two-run home run. The rabidly partisan Red Sox fans gave DiMag a standing ovation. "I don't think I was ever booed at Fenway," he said. "The fans there always respected clean competition and good baseball."

With the Red Sox trailing 5–4 in the bottom of the ninth inning, Joe DiMaggio hauled in an extra-base bid by Ted Williams. That catch ended the Red Sox winning streak and broke the hearts of the Fenway faithful. The Yankee Clipper was back.

Game two on Saturday saw the Yanks down 7–1 after four innings. A DiMaggio three-run dinger sliced the Sox lead. Then in the eighth inning, it was that man DiMaggio again—a two-run home run over the Green Monster. The Bronx Bombers had a 9–7 come-from-behind triumph. "You can hate the Yankees," one sign read, "but you've got to love Joe DiMaggio!"

The third game on Sunday saw an SRO crowd in attendance. After seven innings in a tight battle, it was Yankees 3, Red Sox 2. A three-run smash by the Yankee center fielder off the light tower gave the New Yorkers a 6–3 win and a sweep of the Sox.

It was truly the Joe DiMaggio show. He batted .455 in the three games, hit four home runs and a single, droving in nine runs.

"I think," Joe DiMaggio said later, "I was the most surprised guy in all of Boston."

THE ELEVEN-WALK INNING: *September 11, 1949*

IT WAS SUNDAY at Yankee Stadium. The New York Yankees were matched up against the Washington Senators, the two wildest pitching staffs in the major leagues. The New Yorkers had surrendered 5.27 free passes per nine innings; Washington, 4.99.

Game one of the doubleheader played that eleventh day of September saw the Senator pitchers outdo themselves in bestowing walks. The Yankees were given seventeen free passes, including eleven in the third inning, a major-league record surpassing the previous high of eight.

The frenetic fifty-minute bottom of the third inning saw eighteen Yankees bat. Four Yankees were walked twice in the inning—another major-league record.

Phil Rizzuto walked (1). (The parenthetical number indicates walks yielded by Senator pitchers). Cliff Mapes walked (2). A Bobby Brown double scored Rizzuto and Mapes. Eddie Yost threw a Joe DiMaggio ground ball off the Yankee Clipper's shoulder into right field. Brown scored. Yogi Berra doubled to center. DiMaggio scored. Washington pitcher Paul Calvert was removed from the game. Charlie Keller was walked by relief pitcher Dick Welteroth (3).

The bases were loaded when Joe Collins walked (4). Yogi Berra scored when Jerry Coleman walked (5). An Allie Reynolds single drove in two more runs; Washington left fielder Bud Stewart and shortstop Sam Dente ran into each other. Both had to leave the game. Stewart was carried off on a stretcher. Jerry Coleman was trapped off second and tagged out in a rundown. Reynolds moved to second. A Rizzuto single to left sent Reynolds to third. For the second time in the inning, Mapes walked (6). The bases were loaded. Welteroth was removed from the game. Julio Gonzalez replaced him.

Reynolds scored when Brown walked (7). DiMaggio made the second out by flying out to Clyde Vollmer in left, scoring Rizzuto. Mapes to third. Berra walked (8), reloading the bases. Keller also walked (9), forcing home Mapes. Collins walked (10), scoring Brown. Buzz Dozier replaced Gonzalez. Coleman walked (11), forcing home Berra. Reynolds popped out to first.

It was wild, all right—and many more records for wildness (read bases on balls) could have been broken if not for the presence of Washington's Buzz Dozier, a hurler who plied his trade wearing sunglasses. He pitched the final five innings and walked only four Yankees.

The final score of the game was Yanks 20, Senators 5.

FINAL WEEKEND OF THE 1949 SEASON

"THE RED SOX–YANKEE rivalry was one of the most unique things in baseball history," said former Boston pitching great Mel Parnell. "We were criticized as being a country club ball club being pampered by Mr. Yawkey. The differences in our ball clubs were that we were probably a step slower than the Yankees. They also had more depth.

"In 1949, I won twenty-five games and Ellis Kinder won twenty-three. As the season came to its end we were either in the game or in the bullpen for nineteen consecutive days. We were pretty well worn out."

It was Joe DiMaggio Day at Yankee Stadium on Saturday, October 1, 1949, as the Yankees and Red Sox prepared to battle in the final two games of the season. A winner in fifty-nine of its last seventy-eight games, Boston needed

Phil "Scooter" Rizzuto
(sliding)

just one more victory to clinch the pennant. More than 140,000 would be on hand for the two games. Many, without tickets, would mill around outside of the stadium, listening to the games on bulky portable radios.

Mel Parnell of the Sox was pitted against Allie Reynolds in the October 1 game. "We were behind four to nothing," Phil Rizzuto recalled. "We were behind but not beaten. Casey had told Joe Page, who came in for Allie, 'Just hold them, Joe, just hold them.' I went up to hit and Boston catcher Birdie Tebbets, who always talked to me, this time got me angry.

" 'Oh, Phil,' he said, 'we're gonna be drinking a lot of champagne tonight and we're gonna have a party because we're gonna clinch the pennant today and a kid from the minors will be pitching for us tomorrow.' Holy cow, I was annoyed. I told Casey and some of the other guys when I got back to the bench and they were not too happy with what Birdie had said. I don't think that was the only factor in getting us back in the game, but it sure helped."

It sure helped. An eighth-inning home run by Johnny Lindell gave the Yanks the margin of their 5–4 victory. That set the stage for the next day, Sunday, October 2—the final day of the 1949 season.

The line for bleacher seats was more than a block long. Ellis Kinder, a twenty-game winner, was the Boston starter. Vic Raschi took the ball for the New Yorkers. As the shadows of autumn started to fill Yankee Stadium, the chances for Boston grew less and less. Kinder had surrendered only two hits but trailed 1–0.

Joe McCarthy, who had managed those many years for the Yankees, made a move now as Boston pilot that would be questioned for years. He pinch hit for Kinder. It was to no avail. And then he brought in Mel Parnell, who had given his all the day before, to hurl the bottom of the eighth inning. "I don't make excuses," Parnell recalled. "I was tired, but I was a professional and professionals are paid to pitch." The Yanks scored four times. The Sox fought back, scoring three times in their half of the eighth. Ultimately, it was the same old story—a Yankee victory over the Red Sox. Casey Stengel, savoring the moment and the 5–3 pennant-clinching triumph, screamed out in the locker room: "Fellas, I want to thank you all for going to all the trouble to do this for me."

ALLIE REYNOLDS—THE TWO NO-HITTERS: *1951*

CLEVELAND, 1–0, JULY 12, 1951

BOSTON, 8–0, SEPTEMBER 28, 1951

CLEVELAND ACE BOB Feller took the mound to face Allie Reynolds on July 12. The two had been roommates on the Indians and knew each other very well.

The game moved through five innings, a taut, tight pitching duel. Neither team had a hit. Then Gene Woodling homered for the Yanks in the seventh. That was the only run the man they called "Chief" needed.

Retiring the last seventeen batters to face him, Reynolds struck out Bobby Avila for the final out. In the game, the big right-hander faced just twenty-nine batters. He won his tenth game, his fifth shutout of the year. More importantly—he gave up no hits.

The second no-hitter was before forty thousand at Yankee Stadium against the Red Sox, the hottest-hitting team in the American League.

"I was very much aware of the no-hitter and the ninth inning," Reynolds said. "All I had to get out was Ted Williams. Most times I tried to walk the damn guy. In my opinion it was just stupid to let an outstanding hitter like him beat you."

With two out in the ninth, Ted Williams was all that stood in the way of the Reynolds no-hitter and the Yankees clinching the American League pennant.

Reynolds got a fastball strike on Williams. The next pitch—a fastball again. Williams popped it up behind home plate. Yogi Berra was under it, waiting. The ball bounced off his glove, then Yogi bounced off Reynolds, who was backing up the play.

Helping Berra to his feet, a tired and anxious Reynolds was kind: "Don't worry, Yogi, we'll get him next time."

An exasperated and annoyed Williams told Berra: "You sons of bitches put me in a hell of a spot. You blew it, and now I've got to bear down even harder even though the game is decided and your man has a no-hitter going."

On the next Reynolds offering, Williams again popped up. This time Berra squeezed the ball good. Reynolds had his second no-hitter and the Yankees had an 8–0 triumph and their third straight American League flag.

Gene Woodling, striking a pose

MICKEY MANTLE'S TAPE-MEASURE SHOT:
April 17, 1953

MEL ALLEN ALWAYS had a way with words. Here is his call of the epic Mickey Mantle home run:

"Yogi Berra on first. Mickey at bat with the count of no strikes. Left-handed pitcher Chuck Stobbs on the mound. Mantle, a switch-hitter batting right-handed, digs in at the plate. Here's the pitch . . . Mantle swings . . . there's a tremendous drive going into deep left field! It's going, going, it's over the bleachers and over the sign atop of the bleachers into the yards of houses across the street! It's got to be one of the longest home runs I've ever seen hit. How about that! . . . We have just learned that Yankee publicity director Red Patterson has gotten hold of a tape measure and he's going to go out there to see how far that ball actually did go."

Washington outfielders at Griffith Stadium never moved. Only twice before had a ball ever been hit over the Griffith left-field wall—once by Joe DiMaggio and once by Jimmie Foxx. Their shots, however, bounced in the seats before clearing the final barrier.

Mantle's shot was blasted toward left center, where the base of the bleachers wall was 391 feet from the plate. The distance to the back of the wall was sixty-nine feet more. A football scoreboard was atop the wall. The ball struck about five feet above the wall, caromed off to the right and flew out of sight.

"Look out!" Yankee third-base coach Frank Crosetti screamed at Mantle. Billy Martin stayed at third base and pretended to tag up. Mickey ran the bases with his head down and didn't notice Billy standing there and almost ran him over.

"That was the hardest ball I ever saw hit," Martin complimented his buddy.

Scrambling, Donald Dunaway, ten years old, was the first to get to the ball in the backyard of a house across a major thoroughfare and four houses up a bisecting street. Scuffed in two spots, the ball finally stopped in the backyard of a house about 565 feet from home plate.

In one of the best trades in all of baseball history, Yankee publicity director Arthur E. Patterson obtained the Mantle home-run ball for one dollar and three new baseballs to be autographed to Dunaway by the Yankee players.

That wasn't all Patterson had going for him that day. It was the wily publicist who measured the monster shot's distance with a tape measure and coined the term "tape-measure home run."

Mickey Mantle's gargantuan shot may be the most famous home run ever hit. The *Guinness Book of World Records* lists it as the longest home run to be measured at the time it was hit.

DODGERS FINALLY BEAT YANKS
IN WORLD SERIES: *October 4, 1955*

"DEM BUMS" OF Brooklyn won the National League pennant in 1916, 1920, 1941, 1947, 1949, 1952, and 1953. But the team had never won the World Series. Going into the 1955 Fall Classic, their last five defeats were at the hands of the Yankees. The Brooks and their fans were understandably frustrated.

Whitey Ford bested Don Newcombe as the Yankees won game one of the series. That was the game with the controversial "steal" of home by Jackie Robinson. Brilliant pitching by thirty-five-year-old Tommy Byrne gave the Yanks a victory in game two. Brooklyn fans took heart in the fact their team dropped the first two contests by a combined total of just three runs. But no team in the history of major-league baseball had ever won a seven-game World Series after losing the first two games.

In game three, Dodgers pitcher Johnny Podres came up big, limiting the powerful Yankees to seven hits. The Brooks won 8–3. They won again in game four, 8–5. The series was tied.

The largest crowd to ever see a World Series game at Ebbets Field showed up on October 2. Sophomore manager Walt Alston started slim rookie Roger Craig in game five. Stengel tabbed 1954 Rookie of the Year Bob Grim. Incredibly, the Dodgers managed to win once again, 5–3. One more win and the team from Flatbush would do the unthinkable—defeat the mighty Yankees in the World Series.

Game six. It was southpaw Karl Spooner against southpaw Whitey Ford at Yankee Stadium. It was no contest. Spooner lasted only through the first inning, giving up five runs. Spooner would never pitch in the major leagues again.

Ford, at the top of his game, in the fourth year of what would be a brilliant sixteen-year Hall of Fame career, was having fun, toying with the Dodgers.

After Ford gave up a hit, Yogi Berra told him: "Your slider ain't workin' good, Whitey. Don't throw no more."

"Aw, Yog," Ford said, "don't be a spoil sport. I need the practice. Let me throw it to this guy."

"No more," Berra insisted. "The World Series ain't the right time to horse around."

So Ford stopped horsing around. He gave up just four hits as the Yankees stayed alive with a 5–1 win.

On October 4, 1955, twenty-three-year-old Johnny Podres took the mound for the most important game of his life. Tommy Byrne, a dozen years his senior, took the ball for the Yankees. Each pitcher had won a game in the series. There were 62,465 in attendance at Yankee Stadium.

Hits by Gil Hodges in the fourth and sixth innings gave the Dodgers a 2–0 lead. In the bottom of the sixth, Junior Gilliam came in from left field to play second base. Sandy Amoros took his place in the outfield. The moves were little noticed at the time.

The Yankee sixth began with a walk to Mantle. McDougald bunted for a single. Berra was next. Mel Allen's call brings back the moment:

"Johnny Podres on the mound. Dodgers leading 2–0. . . . The outfield swung away toward right. Sandy Amoros is playing way into left center. Berra is basically a pull hitter. Here's the pitch. Berra swings and he does hit one to the opposite field, down the left-field line . . . Sandy Amoros races over toward the foul line . . . and he makes a sensational, running, one-handed catch! He turns, whirls, fires to Pee Wee Reese. Reese fires to Gil Hodges at first base in time to double up McDougald. And the Yankees' rally is stymied!"

"I run and run and run" was how Amoros characterized what took place. After all these years Yankee pitcher Jerry Coleman is not as impressed with what happened as others: "It wasn't so much that Amoros made a great catch. It was the way he went after it in the sun. A better fielder would have made it easier . . . the circumstance was that we may have had a tie ball game . . . as it turned out, that was our last chance."

With two outs in the bottom of the ninth inning, Mel Allen, loyal to a fault, turned the microphone over to Vin Scully: "Howard hits a ground ball to Reese. He throws to Hodges . . . the Brooklyn Dodgers are world champions."

The precise moment was 3:43 P.M. on October 4, 1955. Brooklyn streets were clogged with celebrating fans. Honking car horns, clanging pots and pans, and shredded newspaper all punctuated that one singular moment.

In the borough-wide party that night, there were fifty complaints of noise and ten false fire alarms. Some one billion flakes of tickertape, shredded newspapers, and torn telephone books were swept off Court Street in downtown Brooklyn the following morning.

In their eighth attempt, the Dodgers finally won. "It was the first and only world championship the Brooklyn Dodgers ever had," their storied center fielder, Duke Snider, said. "You had to pinch yourself. We finally had done it."

DON LARSEN, THE PERFECT GAME:
October 8, 1956

"I HAVE BEEN asked a million times about the perfect game," Don Larsen said. "I never dreamed about something like that happening and everybody is entitled to a good day and mine came at the right time. I still find it hard to believe I really pitched the perfect game. It's almost like a dream, like something that happened to somebody else."

The image of the Yankee right-hander almost nonchalantly tossing the ball from a no-stretch windup to Yogi Berra remains as part of baseball lore.

Just two seasons earlier Don Larsen, while pitching for Baltimore, had one of the worst records, winning just three of twenty-one decisions. He became a Yankee in the fall of 1954 in a seventeen-player trade. "Nobody lost more games than me in the American League that year," Larsen said. "But two of my wins came against the Yankees. That's probably why I came to them."

In 1956, "Gooneybird," as his teammates called him for his late-night behavior, posted an 11–5 record. In his next-to-last start of that season, Larsen showed off his no-windup delivery. "The ghouls sent me a message," he joked, explaining why he had suddenly switched to the highly unorthodox pitching motion.

Casey Stengel tabbed Larsen to start game two of the World Series against Brooklyn. It was not a good outing, as the tall right-hander lasted just 1⅔ innings, walking four and giving up four runs.

When Larsen arrived at Yankee Stadium for game five, he was shocked when Stengel told him that he would be the starter.

Larsen struck out Junior Gilliam on a breaking ball to begin the game. Then the 3–2 count on Pee Wee Reese—and the strikeout. Then it all seemed to blend—the autumn shadows and the smoke and the haze at the stadium, the World Series buntings on railings along the first- and third-base lines, the scoreboard and the zeroes for the Dodgers of Brooklyn inning after inning.

The six-feet-four, 240-pound hurler threw no more than fifteen pitches in any one inning against the mighty Dodgers of Campanella, Reese, Hodges, Gilliam, Robinson, Snider, and Furillo.

"A second-inning Jackie Robinson line-drive shot to my left," Andy Carey said, "was what I lunged for. It went off the tip of my glove fingers to McDougald and he barely threw Robinson out. That was probably one of the closest things to a hit." Mantle's great jump on a fifth-inning line drive by Gil Hodges positioned him for a backhand grab of the ball. "It was a fantastic catch," Carey said. "It would have been a home run in Brooklyn. Only Mickey could have caught the ball."

"Everybody suddenly got scared we weren't playing the outfield right," Stengel said. "I never seen so many managers." The Yankee infield of first baseman Joe Collins, second baseman Billy Martin, shortstop Gil McDougald, and third baseman Andy Carey were ready for any kind of play. "It wasn't until the seventh inning," Carey recalled, "that we started to think about it."

Gil Hodges's eighth-inning shot down the third-base line was converted into an out by Andy Carey. Sandy Amoros and Duke Snider of the Dodgers hit balls into the right-field seats—foul, but just barely so.

The Yankees clung to a 2–0 lead scratched out against veteran pitcher Sal Maglie, age thirty-nine. Jim Gilliam hit a hard one-hopper to short to open the seventh inning. He was thrown out by Gil McDougald. Pee Wee Reese flied out. Duke Snider flied out.

In the eighth, Jackie Robinson grounded back to Larsen. "Hodges hit a little line drive that I caught three inches off the ground," Carey said. "I threw it to first base just to make sure that the umpires didn't say I trapped the ball. Amoros struck out."

The 64,519 in attendance cheered each out. The game moved to the bottom of the ninth inning.

"If it was nine to nothing, Larsen would've been paying little attention," Berra remembered. "It was close, and he had to be extremely disciplined. He was. At the start of the ninth I didn't say a thing about how well he was throwing. I went to the mound and reminded him that if he walked one guy and the next guy hit one out, the game was tied."

"The last three outs were the toughest," Larsen recalled. "I was so weak in the knees that I thought I was going to faint. I was so nervous I almost fell down. My legs were rubbery. My fingers didn't feel like they belonged to me. I said to myself, 'Please help me, somebody.'"

The jam-packed stadium was almost silent. Four pitches were fouled off by Furillo. Then he hit a fly ball to Bauer in right field. Campanella was up next but grounded out weakly to Billy Martin at second base. Left-handed batter Dale Mitchell was sent up to pinch-hit for Sal Maglie. It would be the final major-league at bat for the thirty-five-year-old, a lifetime .312 hitter.

NBC-TV announcer Bob Wolff called it this way:

"Count is one and one. And this crowd just straining forward on every pitch. Here it comes . . . a swing and a miss! Two strikes, ball one to Dale Mitchell. Listen to this crowd! I'll guarantee that nobody—but nobody—has left this ballpark. And if somebody did manage to leave early, man he's missing the greatest! Two strikes and a ball . . . Mitchell waiting, stands deep, feet close together. Larsen is ready, gets the sign. Two strikes, ball one, here comes the pitch. Strike three! A no-hitter! A perfect game for Don Larsen!"

That final pitch—Larsen's ninety-seventh of the game that took just two hours and six minutes—was the only one that elicited controversy.

"The third strike on Mitchell was absolutely positively a strike on the outside corner," Berra maintains to this day. "No question about it. People say it was a ball and that I rushed the mound to hug Larsen to make the umpire think it was a strike. Nonsense. It was a perfect strike."

After the same, Berra says, "Casey Stengel was asked: Was that the best game he had ever seen Larsen pitch.

"So far," was his response.

"He was great," Yogi Berra said. "I've never caught a greater pitcher than Don was today."

On the day Larsen reached perfection, his estranged wife—whom he married only because they had a daughter together but with whom he never lived—filed for back payment of court-ordered support. It was hours after the game when Larsen wrote out a check to cover the seven weeks he was behind—for $420.

Named the MVP of the series by Sport magazine for his epic feat Larsen received a Corvette. He also earned about $35,000 in endorsements and appearances, including $6,000 for being on Bob Hope's TV show. Larsen spent

$1,000 for plaques commemorating the game and gave them to his teammates, Yankee executives, the six umpires, his parents, and close friends.

The man who reached perfection also received many letters and notes, including this one:

> Dear Mr. Larsen: It is a noteworthy event when anybody achieves perfection in anything. It has been so long since anyone pitched a perfect big league game that I have to go back to my generation of ballplayers to recall such a thing—and that is truly a long time ago.
>
> This note brings you my very sincere congratulations on a memorable feat, one that will inspire pitchers for a long time to come. With best wishes,
>
> Sincerely,
>
> Dwight D. Eisenhower
> President of the United States

The rest of Larsen's fourteen-year career—with eight teams—was marked by consistent mediocrity interrupted from time to time with flashes of brilliance. He finished his time in the majors with an 81–91 record and 3.78 ERA. But he did rise to the occasion at World Series time, compiling a 4–2 record and a 2.75 ERA in five different Autumn Classics.

"I pitched for fourteen years with eight different clubs and won only eighty-one games," Larsen said. "Hey, I gave it my best shot and I tried and I wish my record had been better but I was very pleased to get into the World Series and pitch the perfect game. And I guess that is what I will always be remembered for."

THE COPA INCIDENT: *May 16, 1957*

DESPITE YOGI BERRA'S emphatic denial—"Nobody did nothin' to nobody"—a lot did happen at the Copacabana nightclub in Manhattan when Mickey Mantle, Yogi Berra, Hank Bauer, Whitey Ford, and Johnny Kucks gathered to celebrate Billy Martin's twenty-ninth birthday.

Mickey Mantle recalled what happened: "Two bowling teams came in to celebrate their victories. Sammy Davis, Jr., was the entertainer. They kept calling him Little Black Sambo and stuff like that. Billy and Hank kept telling them a couple of times to sit down. They kept standing up. The next thing I knew was that the cloak room was filled with people swinging. I was so drunk I didn't know who threw the first punch. A body came flying out and landed at my feet. At first I thought it was Billy (Martin) so I picked him up. But when I saw it wasn't I dropped him back down. It looked like Roy Rogers rode through on Trigger, and Trigger kicked the guy in the face."

The fracas resulted in Ford, Bauer, Berra, Mantle, and Martin being fined $1,000 each. It also resulted in a Bronx delicatessen owner suffering a concussion and a fractured jaw. It also resulted in Casey Stengel dropping Hank Bauer to eighth in the lineup the day after the incident but leaving Mantle batting third in the order.

"I'm mad at him, too, for being out late," the Yankee skipper said. "But I'm not mad enough to take a chance on losing a ball game and possibly the pennant."

The main result of the episode was the trading away of Billy Martin to Kansas City.

"I'm gone," Martin told Mantle and Ford the day after the incident. "George Weiss is just looking for an excuse to get rid of me."

"I needed him this one time in my life and Casey let me down," was how Martin felt about Stengel, who he thought let him down by not sticking up for him.

"Billy thought that Casey got rid of him," Mantle said. "I never thought that. It was the farthest thing from the truth. Casey loved Billy."

BILL MAZEROSKI'S WORLD SERIES HOMER:
October 13, 1960

AFTER SLIPPING TO third place in 1959, the Yankees were back in the World Series again in 1960. The competition was Pittsburgh.

The Pirates won the first game of the series. Then Yankee bats took over. The New Yorkers won game two 16–3 and game three 10–0. Behind the pitching of Vern Law and Harvey Haddix, Pittsburgh won the next two to take a three-games-to-two lead. The seesaw series saw New York tie things up with a 12–0 shutout from Whitey Ford.

All of that set the stage for game seven in Pittsburgh, a contest that stands as one of the most memorable games in World Series history.

The Yankees rallied from a 4–0 deficit to take a 7–4 lead going into the bottom of the eighth. The Pirates scored five runs in the eighth inning, the final three on Hal Smith's homer, to take a 9–7 lead. A Yankee two-run rally in the top of the ninth tied the score 9–9. Forbes Field was a madhouse.

Pittsburgh second baseman Bill Mazeroski led off the ninth against Yankee right-hander Ralph Terry. The count on Maz was 1–0. At 3:36 P.M., it seemed there was no other sound in the ballpark except for the crack of Mazeroski's bat against the ball pitched by Terry. Maz thought the ball would reach the wall, so he ran all-out from the batter's box.

Yogi Berra backed up in the left field, then he circled away from the wall, watching the ball go over his head and over the wall. Then Yogi dropped to his knees in despair and anger.

Forbes Field was just the opposite—it rocked. The Pittsburgh Pirates had their first world championship since 1925. Bill Mazeroski became the first player to end a World Series with a home run.

"It's hard to believe it hadn't been done before," Mazeroski, the greatest fielding second baseman in Pirate history, said. "Every day of my life I think of that home run. Wouldn't you if you had hit it? People always are reminding me of it. I suppose it must be the most important thing I've ever done."

"I was an eight-year-old Yankee fan in 1960," Bob Costas mused. "I literally wept when Bill Mazeroski's home run cleared the ivy-covered wall of Forbes Field. I believe I have come to terms with it, and can see Mazeroski for what he really was: one of baseball's all-time great players."

Mickey Mantle batted .400 with three homers, eleven RBIs, eight runs scored and eight walks in the series. It was not enough. "We outscored them 55–27," Mantle complained, "and that was not enough. The best team lost."

Five days after the series ended, Casey Stengel was fired as manager of the Yankees.

JOHNNY BLANCHARD, FOUR STRAIGHT HOMERS: *July 21–26, 1961*

MOST PEOPLE ASSOCIATE home-run hitting and the Yankees with 1961 and Roger Maris. But it was also the time of Johnny Blanchard. The third-string catcher nearly quit in 1960 when Casey Stengel toyed with activating forty-year-old Jim Hegan as a backup to Yogi Berra when Elston Howard was hurt. In the end, Casey was glad he stuck with Blanchard instead of Hegan; Blanchard had a career year and was competent behind the plate. And he also did some special home-run hitting.

On July 21, Johnny B. hammered a ninth-inning, two-out, pinch-hit grand-slam home run at Fenway Park to push the Yanks to an 11–8 victory over the Red Sox. The next day Blanchard hit another ninth-inning pinch-hit homer to spark a second come-from-behind victory over Boston.

On July 26, the man they called Super-Sub slashed his third and fourth home runs at Yankee Stadium against the Chicago White Sox. The homers drove in four runs as the Yanks beat the White Sox 5–2.

Four straight homers over three games tied a major-league record. Not bad for a guy who was ready to pack in his career the year before.

ROGER MARIS, THE SIXTY-FIRST HOME RUN: *October 1, 1961*

"WHEN ROGER MARIS was going for the home-run record he would eat only bologna and eggs for breakfast," his friend Julie Isaacson recalled. "Every morning we would have breakfast together at the Stage Deli. We had the same waitress, and I'd leave her the same five-dollar tip every time. After, I would drive Roger up to the stadium."

In 1956, Mickey Mantle had smashed fifty-two home runs for the Bronx Bombers and there were many who saw him as the man to break Babe Ruth's season record of sixty. Mantle was the favorite. Maris had come to the Yankees in a trade with Kansas City; he was the outsider, the loner.

In 1961, Maris did not hit a home run in his first ten games, but by the end of May he had a dozen. There were twenty-seven by the end of June. By the end of July Maris had forty home runs—and was six ahead of Ruth's record total that had stood since 1927.

"My going off after the record started off such a dream," the Yankee outfielder said. "I was living a fairy tale for a while. I never thought I'd get a chance to break such a record."

Reporters lined up by the Maris locker in ballparks all over the American League. "How does it feel to be hitting so many home runs? Do you ever think of what it means?"

"How the hell should I know?" Maris, short-tempered, surly, shot back.

There were all kinds of commercial capitalizations. An enterprising stripper went by the name of Mickey Maris. The sales of M&M candy skyrocketed—a tip of the cash register to the "M&M Boys," who had not endorsed the confection.

Newspapers printed endless stories and charts comparing Mantle and Maris, Maris and Ruth, Ruth and Mantle, et cetera, ad nauseam. There were stories that claimed animosity existed between Mantle, who earned $75,000 that season, and Maris, paid $42,000. The stories were completely untrue.

"Roger," Mantle insisted, "was one of my best friends." The two shared a Queens apartment with Bob Cerv. The three young Yankee outfielders rode in Maris's open convertible back and forth from Yankee Stadium.

Media scrutiny was in Maris's face. Photographers insisted on pairing Mantle and Maris together in all kinds of posed shots. Maris was irked; Mantle was bemused. "We've taken so many pictures together," Mantle joked, "that I'm beginning to feel like a Siamese twin."

All through the summer, Maris continued to hit. Then, against his former Kansas City teammates on August 26 in his 128th game of the 1961 season, Maris smashed Number 50. He was now eight ahead of the Ruth pace. It was about that time that Commissioner Ford Frick ruled that an asterisk would be placed next to Maris's name in the record books if he broke the Babe's record. Frick pointed out that Ruth set the record in a 154-game season. Maris was playing in a season with a 162-game schedule.

The Mick managed only one home run from September 10 on—number fifty four. With Mantle a shell of himself and no longer a factor in the home-run race, the pressure was now totally on Roger Maris.

Maris had fifty-eight home runs by September 18 when the Yankees came to Baltimore for a four-game series. In a twi-night doubleheader, games 152 and 153, Maris did not homer.

Roger Maris and
Mickey Mantle

On September 20, in a night game, Maris faced Milt Pappas of the Orioles.
It was a media circus, with reporters from all over the country converged on
the scene. But there were only twenty one thousand or so in the stands.

The man they called Rajah lined solidly to right field his first time up. In the
third inning, Maris stroked a Pappas pitch and blasted it almost four hundred
feet into the bleachers in right field—home run number fifty-nine! He had passed
Jimmie Foxx and Hank Greenberg. Maris had three more chances that night to
tie the Babe Ruth record. But he struck out, flied out, and grounded out.

Five days later at Yankee Stadium, on September 26, in game number 158
for the Yankees, Jack Fisher of Baltimore threw a high curveball in the third
inning. "The minute I threw the ball," Fisher moaned, "I said to myself, that
does it. That's number sixty."

The record-tying home run pounded onto the concrete steps of the sixth row
in the third deck in Yankee Stadium. The ball bounced back onto the field and
was picked up by Earl Robinson, the Oriole right fielder, who tossed the ball to

ROGER MARIS'S
SIXTY-ONE HOME RUNS IN 1961

DATE	PITCHER, TEAM	HOME OR AWAY	INNING	PLAYER ON BASE
April 26	Paul Foytack (R), Detroit	A	5	0
May 3	Pedro Ramos (R), Minnesota	A	7	2
May 6	Eli Grba (R), L.A.	A	5	0
May 17	Pete Burnside (L), Washington	H	8	1
May 19	Jim Perry (R), Cleveland	A	1	1
May 20	Gary Bell (R), Cleveland	A	3	0
May 21	Chuck Estrade (R), Baltimore	H	1	0
May 24	Gene Conley (R), Boston	H	4	1
May 28	Cal McLish (R), Chicago	H	2	1
May 30	Gene Conley (R), Boston	A	3	0
May 30	Mike Fornieles (R), Boston	A	8	2
May 31	Billy Muffett (R), Boston	A	3	0
June 2	Cal Mclish (R), Chicago	A	3	2
June 3	Bob Shaw (R), Chicago	A	8	2
June 4	Russ Kemmerer (R), Chicago	A	3	0
June 6	Ed Palmquist (R), Minnesota	H	6	2
June 7	Pedro Ramos (R), Minnesota	H	3	2
June 9	Ray Herbert (R), K.C.	H	7	1
June 11	Eli Grba (R), L.A.	H	3	0
June 11	Johnny James (R), L.A.	H	7	0
June 13	Jim Perry (R), Cleveland	A	6	0
June 14	Gary Bell (R), Cleveland	A	4	1
June 17	Don Mossi (L), Detroit	A	4	0
June 18	Jerry Casale (R), Detroit	A	8	1
June 19	Jim Archer (L), K.C.	A	9	0
June 20	Joe Nuxhall (L), K.C.	A	1	0
June 22	Norm Bass (R), K.C.	A	2	1
July 1	Dave Sisler (R), Washington	H	9	1
July 2	Pete Burnside (L), Washington	H	3	2
July 2	Johnny Klippstein (R), Washington	H	7	1
July 4	Frank Lary (R), Detroit	H	8	1
July 5	Frank Funk (R), Cleveland	H	7	0
July 9	Bill Monbouquette (R), Boston	H	7	0
July 13	Early Wynn (R), Chicago	A	1	1
July 15	Ray Herbert (R), Chicago	A	3	0
July 21	Bill Monbouquette (R), Boston	A	1	0
July 25	Frank Baumann (L), Chicago	H	4	1

DATE	PITCHER, TEAM	HOME OR AWAY	INNING	PLAYER ON BASE
July 25	Don Larsen (R), Chicago	H	8	0
July 25	Russ Kemmerer (R), Chicago	H	4	0
July 25	Warren Hacker (R), Chicago	H	6	2
Aug 4	Camilo Pascual (R), Minnesota	H	1	2
Aug 11	Pete Burnside (L), Washington	A	5	0
Aug 12	Dick Donovan (R), Washington	A	4	0
Aug 13	Bennie Daniels (R), Washington	A	4	0
Aug 13	Marty Kutyna (R), Washington	A	1	1
Aug 15	Juan Pizarro (L), Chicago	H	4	0
Aug 16	Billy Pierce (L), Chicago	H	1	1
Aug 16	Billy Pierce (L), Chicago	H	3	1
Aug 20	Jim Perry (R), Cleveland	A	3	1
Aug 22	Ken McBride (R), L.A.	A	6	1
Aug 26	Jerry Walker (R), K.C.	A	6	0
Sep 2	Frank Lary (R), Detroit	H	6	0
Sep 2	Hank Aguirre (L), Detroit	H	8	1
Sep 6	Tom Cheney (R), Washington	H	4	0
Sep 7	Dick Stigman (L), Cleveland	H	3	0
Sep 9	Mudcat Grant (R), Cleveland	A	7	0
Sep 16	Frank Lary (R), Detroit	A	3	1
Sep 17	Terry Fox (R), Detroit	A	12	1
Sep 20	Milt Pappas (R), Baltimore	A	3	0
Sep 26	Jack Fisher (R), Baltimore	H	3	0
Oct 1	Tracy Stallard (R), Boston	H	4	0

umpire Ed Hurley, who gave it to Yankee first-base coach Wally Moses, who rolled it into the Yankee dugout. The ball and Maris, running out the sixtieth home run, arrived in the dugout of the Bronx Bombers at about the same time.

Maris picked up the ball and barely looked at it; cheering fans kept calling for him to come out and take a bow. Finally, Maris emerged. Standing sheepishly on the top step of the dugout, he waved his cap. An especially interested onlooker was Mrs. Claire Ruth, widow of the Babe.

It came down to the final three games of the 1961 season. It was Yankees versus Red Sox. It was Maris versus Ruth. The Yankee slugger was shut out in the first two games by Boston pitchers, each of whom was determined not to be the one to be linked with him in the record books.

It was October 1. A tired, bedraggled Maris faced twenty-four-year-old Red Sox right-hander Tracy Stallard. In the Yankee bullpen in right field the pitchers and the catchers watched as the action played out. A $5,000 reward had been promised by Roger Maris to the one who caught the ball.

"I told them," Maris said, "that if they got the ball not to give it to me. Take the $5,000 reward."

Stallard retired Maris in his first at bat. The 23,154 roaring fans at Yankee Stadium were quieted. In the fourth inning, Maris came to bat again.

The voice of Phil Rizzuto broadcast the moment: "They're standing, waiting to see if Maris is gonna hit number sixty-one. We've only got a handful of people sitting out in left field, but in right field, man, it's hogged out there. And they're standing up. Here's the windup, the pitch to Roger. Way outside, ball one . . . And the fans are starting to boo. Low, ball two. That one was in the dirt. And the boos get louder . . . Two balls, no strikes on Roger Maris. Here's the windup. Fastball, hit deep to right! This could be it! Way back there! Holy cow, he did it! Sixty-one for Maris!"

The ball traveled 360 feet, went over outfielder Lu Clinton's head and slammed into box 163D of section thirty-three into the sixth row of the lower deck in right field. And a melee broke out as fans scuffled and scrambled, fighting for the ball and the $5,000 reward.

Roger Maris trotted out the historic home run. A kid grabbed his hand as he turned and ran past first. The proud Yankee shook hands and then did the same thing with third-base coach Frank Crosetti as he turned past third and headed for home.

His Yankee teammates formed a human wall in front of the dugout, refusing to let him enter. Four times he tried, to no avail. Finally, Maris waved his cap to the cheering crowd, and his teammates finally let him into the dugout.

"He threw me a pitch outside and I just went with it," Maris would say later. "If I never hit another home run—this is the one they can never take away from me."

"I hated to see the record broken," Phil Rizzuto said. "But it was another Yankee that did it. When he hit the sixty-first home run I screamed so loud I had a headache for about a week."

MCCOVEY LINES OUT TO BOBBY RICHARDSON:
October 16, 1962

YOGI BERRA, WHO has seen it all, said: "When McCovey hit the ball, it lifted me right out of my shoes. I never saw a last game of a World Series more exciting."

Restaurateur Tracy Nieperont recalled: "I can still remember being in the playground the fall of 1962. We were playing stickball. The radio was on. Willie McCovey hit the line drive to Bobby Richardson, if Richardson didn't catch it, the Giants would win the Series. But Richardson did catch it and the Yankees did."

Three days of rain had finally ended. Candlestick Park was finally dry. But the outfielders were still at the mercy of the whipping, gusting wind.

Game seven matched New York's Ralph Terry, winless in four World Series decisions, against San Francisco's twenty-four-game-winner Jack Sanford, who Terry had lost to in game two.

With two outs in the sixth inning, Terry had a perfect game going and the Yankees were clinging to a 1–0 lead. Relaxing out in the Giants bullpen was "Mr. Perfect Game," Don Larsen. He watched a Sanford single break up Terry's bid for perfection. Entering the bottom of the ninth, Terry had allowed only two hits to the Giants.

With two outs, the Giants had runners at second and third. It could have been worse. Willie Mays, coming off a forty-nine-homer, 141-RBI season, doubled to right, but Roger Maris ran and grabbed the bounding ball. His quick throw to cutoff man Bobby Richardson forced Matty Alou to hold at third base.

The twenty-six-year-old Terry, two years earlier, had been the goat in the World Series when he gave up the game-winning home run to Bill Mazeroski in game seven. Now, he had a chance to make up for it. With first base open, Giants cleanup hitter Willie McCovey moved toward the plate. Orlando Cepeda was in the on-deck circle.

Yankees manager Ralph Houk decided to let right-hander Terry pitch to the left-handed-hitting McCovey, who had tripled in his previous at bat. The count was one and one on the big Giant they called Stretch.

The next pitch was inside and McCovey hit a line drive. It was about five feet off the ground when it blurred by the pitcher's mound. But Yankees second baseman Bobby Richardson was perfectly positioned. Moving slightly to his left, he threw up his glove—and caught it. A second straight world championship—New York Yankees.

Terry, who wound up with a four-hitter and gave up no walks, was jubilant and also modest. "I was thankful to have the opportunity to pitch a seventh game and have a real shot at redemption."

THE HARMONICA INCIDENT: *August 20, 1964*

DESPITE A STRING of four straight pennants and counting, the Yankees were a bust throughout much of the 1964 season. Yogi Berra had succeeded Ralph Houk as skipper and there were reports that he got more laughs than lauds from his players. It was getting to be late August; the Yankees were in third place behind Baltimore and Chicago. On the team bus heading to O'Hare Airport, losers of four straight to the White Sox, winless in ten of their last fifteen games, the Yankees were disgusted and demoralized. They had just been shut out 5–0 by Chicago's John Buzhardt.

In his third New York season, Phil Linz, number 34, reserve infielder and a career .235 hitter, was a tough, aggressive player who loved being a Yankee. But he was regarded by some as un-Yankee-like, along with teammates Joe Pepitone and Jim Bouton.

"I sat in the back of the bus," Linz recalled. The bus was stuck in heavy traffic. It was a sticky, humid Chicago summer day. "I was bored. I pulled out my harmonica. I had the Learner's Sheet for 'Mary Had a Little Lamb.' So I started fiddling. You blow in. You blow out."

An angry Berra snapped from the front of the bus: "Knock it off!" But Linz barely heard him. When asked what their manager had said, Mickey Mantle said, "Play it louder." Linz played louder.

Berra stormed to the back of the bus and told Linz to "shove that thing."

"I told Yogi that I didn't lose that game," Linz related. Berra smacked the harmonica out of Linz's hands. The harmonica flew into Joe Pepitone's knee and Pepitone jokingly winced in pain. Soon the entire bus—except for Berra—was in stitches.

Another version has it that Linz flipped the harmonica at the angered Berra and screamed: "What are you getting on me for? I give a hundred percent. Why don't you get on some of the guys who don't hustle?"

Linz was fined $200—but as the story goes, he received $20,000 for an endorsement from a harmonica company. "The next day"—Linz gives his version—"the Hohner Company called and I got a contract for $5,000 to endorse their harmonica. The whole thing became a big joke."

Actually, the whole thing changed things around for the Yankees. The summer of 1964 was Linz's most productive season. Injuries to Tony Kubek made the "super-sub" a regular: Linz started the majority of the games down the stretch, and every World Series game, at short.

New respect for Yogi propelled the Yanks to a 22–6 record in September and a win in a close pennant race over the White Sox. A loss in the World Series to the St. Louis Cardinals in seven games cost Berra his job. But there were those who said he was on his way out the day of the "Harmonica Incident."

There are a few postscripts. In 1967, Linz and Berra were together again as player and coach on the New York Mets. What better thing to do than to relive the old times. There for all to see, they reenacted the famous harmonica incident at the Mayor's Trophy Game at Yankee Stadium.

The final P.S.: It is rumored that Phillip Francis Linz today carries a harmonica with him at all times, signing his autograph accompanied by a musical note.

MICKEY MANTLE DAY: *June 8, 1969*

THE LINE MOST of those who were there that day will remember is this one by Mel Allen in his introduction: "Ladies and gentlemen, a magnificent Yankee, the great number seven, Mickey Mantle."

June 8, 1969, was all Mickey Mantle—the Yankee legend had his number, 7, retired before 61,157 at the stadium. At that time the only other retired numbers were 3, 4, and 5—for Babe Ruth, Lou Gehrig, and Joe DiMaggio.

"When I walked into this stadium eighteen years ago," Mantle said in his speech, "I felt much the same way I do right now. I don't have words to describe how I felt then or how I feel now, but I'll tell you one thing, baseball was real good to me and playing eighteen years in Yankee Stadium is the best thing that could ever happen to a ballplayer."

The Mick received a ten-minute standing ovation. Kids paraded around the field with posters in tribute to the onetime kid from Oklahoma. And Mantle and Joe DiMaggio exchanged plaques, which later were placed on the center-field wall.

Mantle was driven around the stadium on a golf cart to the rising roar and cheers of the huge crowd.

"And the guy that was driving me," Mantle recalled, "was Danny, one of the ground-crew guys who came up at about the same time I did in fifty-one.

"The last time around the park. That gave me goose pimples. But I didn't cry. I felt like it. Maybe tonight when I go to bed, I'll think about it. I wish that could happen to every man in America. I think the fans know how much I think about them—all over the country. It was the most nervous I've ever been but the biggest thrill."

FIRST DESIGNATED HITTER, RON BLOMBERG: *April 6, 1973*

THE 1966 YANKEES finished in last place, so they had the first pick in the 1967 free-agent draft. That selection was Ron Blomberg. He made his major-league debut September 10, 1969, with three hits in six at bats late in the season.

Then on Opening Day, April 6, 1973, he was on the scene ready to make baseball history at Fenway Park. Blomberg, who had played first base and the outfield from 1970 to 1972 but was now limited in mobility due to injuries, was baseball's first "designated pinch hitter."

"With Bobby Bonds in right field," Blomberg joked, "and three first basemen, I might as well have donated my glove to charity. I asked Ellie [Howard], 'What do I do?' He said, 'The only thing you do is go take batting practice and just hit.' They announced the lineup. Bob Sheppard, he was great, a great voice up there, said, 'Ron Blomberg, DH.'

"When it was my time to hit, the bases were loaded. I was batting sixth in the Yankee order against Luis Tiant. I walked and forced in a run.

"I was left at first base, and I was going to stay there because normally that was my position. Elston said, 'Come on back to the bench, you aren't supposed to stay out here.' I went back and said, 'What do I do?' He said, 'You just sit here with me.' "

The brand-new DH went 1 for 3 in the game, drove in a run and scored a run. After the game ended, Blomberg's bat was shipped off to the Baseball Hall of Fame. The DH was now a part of baseball history.

Rob Blomberg is remembered most of all as the first DH (to bat), but he was a very talented athlete, slowed and hampered by injuries. His lifetime batting average is just below .300. When the Yankees made him the first overall pick in 1967, Blomberg had hundreds of scholarship offers to play football and basketball.

"I went into the Hall of Fame through the back door," he said. "Everywhere I go, people always talk about me being the first DH in baseball."

For the record, the complete and original "designated hitter" list:

BALTIMORE, Terry Crowley

BOSTON, Orlando Cepeda

CALIFORNIA, Tom McCraw

CHICAGO, Mike Andrews

CLEVELAND, John Ellis

DETROIT, Gates Brown

KANSAS CITY, Ed Kirkpatrick

MILWAUKEE, Ollie Brown

MINNESOTA, Tony Oliva

NEW YORK, Ron Blomberg

OAKLAND, Bill North

TEXAS, Rico Carty

THE YANKEE BOX FOR THE DAY OF THE FIRST DESIGNATED HITTER

NAME	POS	AB	R	H	RBI
HORACE CLARKE	2B	5	0	1	0
ROY WHITE	LF	5	0	0	0
MATTY ALOU	RF	5	2	2	0
BOBBY MURCER	CF	3	1	0	0
GRAIG NETTLES	3B	2	2	1	2
MEL STOTTLEMYRE	P	0	0	0	0
LINDY MCDANIEL	P	0	0	0	0
CASEY COX	P	0	0	0	0
RON BLOMBERG	DH	3	0	1	1
FELIPE ALOU	1B	4	0	3	2
THURMAN MUNSON	C	3	0	0	0
GENE MICHAEL	SS	4	0	0	0

CHRIS CHAMBLISS'S HOME RUN: *October 14, 1976*

THE NIGHT WAS cold and misty as October nights in New York City often are. The opposition for the Yankees that night was the Kansas City Royals. The teams had split four hard-fought games. Now they were in a winner-take-all fifth game of the ALCS.

The game, like the series, had seesawed back and forth. As the eighth inning began, the Yankees had a 6–3 lead. Some of their fans were already celebrating. Wiser ones in the throng were just there watching the outs tick off. A three-run homer by George Brett stopped the buzz.

Bottom of the ninth, score tied 6–6. "You can't get any tenser than that," Chris Chambliss recalled. Mainly well behaved throughout the game, some fans now turned restless and ugly. Debris cascaded onto the playing field; firecrackers, too.

There was a delay as groundskeepers cleaned up the mess. The Yankee first baseman, Chambliss, set to lead off the ninth, poked around at the bat rack in the dugout. "It was cold," he recalled. "I was a little anxious. That was a trying time. I just wanted to be aggressive. I didn't want to be taking."

Reliever Mark Littell, a saver of sixteen games, a winner of eight, who had given up only one home run that year, was on the mound for KC. The left-handed-hitting Chambliss swung in that classic way of his. Littell had given up another—home run to right field—just over the glove of Hal McRae. The time was 11:13 P.M.

A highly excited Chambliss watched the ball disappear over the right-center-field fence. Throwing his arms into the air, he did a little victory dance heading down the line to first base. After a dozen years of waiting, the Yankees had their thirtieth pennant.

Howard Cosell, for ABC-TV, called it this way: "Chris Chambliss has won the American League pennant for the New York Yankees. . . . A thrilling, dramatic game. . . . What a way for the American League season to end!"

"I was in the middle of a mass of people," Chambliss said. "It was scary. The fans ran on the field, and I had a little trouble touching all the bases."

"Fans came on the field," Littell remembered. "Nobody touched me. That was amazing. I went down to the dugout and looked out. I didn't know what to think. I went to the clubhouse and sat in the showers."

"By the time Chris got to third base," Thurman Munson recalled, "all hope of reaching the plate was gone. He never did make it."

Earlier in the game, public-address announcer Bob Sheppard had cautioned fans not to throw objects on the field after a call that went against the Yankees. "In the Chambliss incident, I did absolutely nothing," Sheppard recalled. "The game was over, the Yankees had won, ten thousand people, as if they were shot out of a cannon, ran out on the field and I just folded my arms and let them do it."

Hours later, in an empty ballpark under the protective and watchful eyes of two security guards, Chambliss touched home plate. "It was the greatest moment of my career," said Chambliss, who hit an ALCS record .524 with eight RBIs. He was named ALCS MVP.

"The Chambliss home run," Willie Randolph recalled, "was the highlight of our season. We celebrated that night and flew all the way to Cincinnati for a World Series game the next day."

Carroll Christopher Chambliss hit .279 over his career with 185 home runs and 972 RBIs. He was the AL Rookie of the Year with the Indians in 1971 and went on to win the World Series with the Yankees in 1977 and 1978. He played for the Yankees for six seasons and appeared in 911 games. He also later coached for the Yanks.

But what he is best remembered for is the home run he hit that misty October night.

TWELFTH-INNING SINGLE BY PAUL BLAIR:
October 11, 1977

THE DODGERS AND Yankees met for the ninth time in the World Series of 1977. The pitching matchup in game one was Don Gullet for the New Yorkers and Don Sutton for Los Angeles. Both clubs had staggered through tumultuous seasons to get to this point before 56,668 fans at Yankee Stadium.

L.A. scored two in the top of the first; the Yankees came back with one in their half of the inning, then tied the game in the bottom of the sixth on a Willie Randolph lead-off homer.

In the bottom of the eighth, a Thurman Munson double drove Randolph, who had walked, home. The Yanks led 3–2. But the Dodgers tied the game in the ninth when pinch hitter Lee Lacy singled off reliever Sparky Lyle, scoring Dusty Baker from second base.

The 3–3 deadlock held through the tenth and eleventh innings. In the bottom of the twelfth, Willie Randolph was at it again, doubling off the fifth Dodger hurler, Rick Rhoden. Thurman Munson was intentionally walked, setting the stage for Paul Blair, who had replaced Reggie Jackson in the ninth for defense.

It was only the first of four Yankee seasons for Blair after thirteen years with Baltimore.

Attempting unsuccessfully to bunt, the fleet Blair saw the count go to 2–2. Coaching at third base, Dick Howser called for time, then went through a few motions to remove the bunt restrictions. Blair was happy he did. He slapped the next pitch to right field. Randolph flew home as the Yankees winning run, ending the three-hour-and-twenty-four-minute contest.

REGGIE JACKSON'S THREE HOME RUNS, GAME SIX, 1977 WORLD SERIES: *October 18, 1977*

AT FENWAY PARK on June 18, 1977, manager Billy Martin pulled Reggie Jackson from the game "for not hustling" on a Jim Rice double. Jackson and Martin nearly came to blows with the eyes of the nation watching.

That moment was just another roller-coaster ride for Reggie Jackson that 1977 season, a season when he batted .286, smacked thirty-two homers and drove in 110 runs.

Mr. October, Reggie Jackson

But going into game three of the 1977 World Series against the Dodgers, Reggie was hitting a puny .100 in postseason. The next four games, however, would be a complete turn-around for him.

His game of games took place October 18, 1977, game six of the series. A sign of what was going to happen showed up in batting practice. Reggie smacked a few homers.

Second baseman Willie Randolph urged: "Save some of those for the game."

"No problem," Jackson said. "There are more where those came from."

In his first at bat, Reggie Jackson was walked on four pitches by Dodger veteran Burt Hooton. When Jackson came to bat in the fourth inning, he wasn't about to be walked again—he rocked Hooton's first pitch for a two-run homer into the lower bleacher seats in right field. As Jackson went around the bases trotting out the "hook shot," the attention-seeking Yankee mouthed, "Hi, Mom," two times to TV cameras.

In the fifth inning, Jackson was up against Elias Sosa. First pitch—slugged into right center field. His second two-run home run of the game. The Yankees led 7–3.

"All I had to do was show up at the plate," Jackson remembered. "They were going to cheer me even if I struck out." Many in the crowd of 56,407 stomped their feet and chanted "REGGIE! REGGIE! REGGIE!"

It was Reggie versus knuckleballer Charlie Hough, eighth inning. First pitch—home run deep into the blackness of the tarp in center field. The matter-of-fact call by Ross Porter. "Jackson, with four runs batted in, sends a fly ball to center field and deep! That's going to be way back! And that's going to be gone! Reggie Jackson has hit his third home run of the game!"

Those who saw it at the stadium or on television will never forget the image—"Mr. October" dropping the bat and watching the ball fly into the inky blackness of that night.

Dodger Steve Garvey said afterward: "I must admit when Reggie hit his third home run and I was sure nobody was looking, I applauded in my glove."

"I felt like Superman," Jackson said after the game. "If they had tied it up and we played eight more extra innings, I'd have hit three more home runs on the first pitch that night." Then warming up to the topic, Jackson added: "Nothing can top this. Who in hell's ever going to hit three home runs in a deciding World Series game? I won't. Babe Ruth, Hank Aaron, Joe DiMaggio . . . at least I was with them for one night."

The memorable moment—three home runs on the first pitch off three different pitchers—helped the Yankees become world champions for the first time in fifteen years. Jackson became the only player other than Babe Ruth to hit three homers in a World Series game, and the first to blast five homers in one World Series.

Reggie set Fall Classic records for home runs (five), total bases (twenty-five) and runs (ten). He batted .450, and his unbelievable 1.250 slugging percentage set a new standard.

"It was the happiest moment of my career," Jackson said. "I had heard so many negatives about Reggie Jackson. I had been the villain. Couldn't do this. Couldn't do that. And now suddenly I didn't care what the manager or my teammates had said or what the media had written."

RON GUIDRY'S EIGHTEEN STRIKEOUTS:
June 17, 1978

THEY WERE TALKING on the California bench about Ron Guidry, and the word was out that he could be hit that night of June 17, 1978. It was remarkable to hear that kind of talk about a pitcher whose record was 10–0. But the slender Guidry had bad-mouthed himself to teammate Sparky Lyle before the game began. "I've got nothing tonight," he said.

Ron Guidry

If ever a pitcher was wrong about his stuff!

The game began with a Bobby Grich double. But "Louisiana Lightnin'" reached back and fanned two to get past the first inning. He was just getting started. After four innings Guidry had fanned nine. After five innings, he had eleven strikeouts. "I wasn't trying to strike out guys," Guidry explained later. "I was throwing fastballs right down the middle, and they couldn't hit it and then the crowd started to get into it."

Oh, did the crowd get into it. Guidry had fourteen Ks after six innings, and another strikeout in the seventh inning made it fifteen. One more in the eight made it sixteen.

Going into the ninth inning, all that was left was for Guidry to fan the side and tie the strikeout record for a single game. He got numbers seventeen and eighteen. Each Angel had struck out at least once in the game.

Designated hitter Don Baylor, who had fanned in his last two at bats, came up. "I wasn't going to be number nineteen," Don Baylor said. He singled. Then he was forced out at second base by a Ron Jackson ground to end the game. The "Gator" had the record for the most strikeouts in a single game by a left-handed hurler.

"It was one of those games," the soft-spoken Guidry mused, "where they were swinging and missing."

Willie Randolph played second base behind Guidry that 1978 season. "He was so dominating that it wasn't even funny," the Yankee veteran said. It was like he was cheating. He grunted on every pitch. He had that slider. I can still see Thurman putting down slider, slider, slider."

For Ron Guidry, what he accomplished against California on June 17, 1978, was in his phrase "perhaps my greatest single thrill."

THE BOSTON MASSACRE: *September 7–9, 1978*

THAT SEASON OF 1978 was a study in contrasts for the Yankees and Red Sox. Early on it seemed to all who were watching that Boston was by far the superior team. But as the season moved down through the dog days of August, the first-place Sox seemed to be chasing the second-place Yankees.

On the seventh day of September, Boston's lead was just four games over a charging Yankee team. The Red Sox had played 25–14 ball since their fourteen-game lead of July 24. The Yankees in that same time had won 35 of 49.

The pitching matchup in the first game of the four-game series was Mike Torrez of Boston versus Catfish Hunter of New York.

After two innings, the Yanks led 5–0. They led 7–0 after three. After four innings it was 12–0 Yankees. The final score that broke Red Sox hearts was 15–3.

The next day two rookies started against each other—Jim Wright for the humbled Sox and Jim Beattie for the high-flying Yankees. Boston was thrashed again—13–2. In two games, the Bronx Bombers had pounded out twenty-eight runs to Boston's five, and had outhit the Sox 38–14. Worst of all were the nine errors committed by Boston.

"Boston's got the best record in baseball," Yankee super-scout Clyde King said. "I could understand if an expansion team fell apart like his. It can't go on like this."

Beleaguered Red Sox manager Don Zimmer put his best pitcher out on the mound for the third game of the series. Dennis Eckersly had a 16–6 record and had won his last nine decisions at Fenway. The Yankees did Boston more than one better. Ron Guidry took the mound against him with his 20–2 record, his popping fastball, and dancing slider. Final score, 7–0 Yanks.

Boston catcher Carlton Fisk underscored his team's frustration: "How can a team get thirty-something games over .500 in July and then in September see its pitching, hitting and fielding all fall apart at the same time?"

Reggie Jackson explained the Yankee turnaround: "This team is loaded with tough guys. This team is loaded with professionals."

Game four of the series pitted rookie Bobby Sprowl of Boston against Ed Figueroa. The Yanks had a 6–0 lead at the end of four and held on to win 7–4.

It was called "the Boston Massacre," and it was.

The Yankees pounded out forty-two runs and sixty-seven hits. Boston managed just nine runs and twenty-one hits. The Sox also committed a dozen errors. The Yankees won all four games by an average margin of over eight runs. For the long suffering fans of the Boston Red Sox, it was like an old time horror movie–replayed with the volume turned up. But there was still October 2, 1978 on the horizon.

BUCKY DENT'S HOME RUN: *October 2, 1978*

"When I hit the ball," Bucky Dent recalled, "I knew that I had hit it high enough to hit the wall. But there were shadows on the net behind the wall and I didn't see the ball land there. I didn't know I had hit a homer until I saw the umpire at first signaling home run with his hand. I couldn't believe it."

Neither could the Red Sox.

Don Zimmer, then Boston's skipper, changed the Yankee shortstop's name to "Bucky F——g Dent." Red Sox fans had even more salty phrases.

Dent's home run was the headline-grabber in that one-game playoff game between the historic rivals at Fenway Park before 32,925. The Yankees were down to the Sox in the AL East by fourteen games on July 19. After Billy Martin was fired as manager, Bob Lemon led the team to a 52–21 record. After losing fourteen of seventeen in September, the Sox made a late-season run, winning their last eight games, catching the Yankees on the last day of the season.

New York's twenty-four-game winner Ron Guidry gave up two runs to Boston through six–a home run to Carl Yastrzemski and a Jim Rice RBI single. Mike Torrez, a former Yankee, was the Boston pitcher.

Chris Chambliss singled. Roy White singled. That's how the top of the seventh began for the Yankees, setting the stage for Russell Earl Dent, born Russell Earl O'Dey, out of Savannah, Georgia. A fine defensive shortstop but not much of an offensive threat, he had hit but .243 for the season. For the last twenty games he had batted a puny .140. But the Yankees were out of infield replacements. Regular second baseman Willie Randolph was injured. Fred Stanley, the only other available mid-infielder, was slotted to come in and replace Brian Doyle, who he had hit for earlier in the inning.

Dent stepped in. Just hoping to make contact, the five-feet-nine-inch Yankee peered out at Torrez, the six-feet-five-inch Red Sox pitcher. The two were locked in, locked up.

Dent fouled the second pitch off his foot. The count was one and one. There was a brief delay as the Yankee trainer tended to Dent. Mickey Rivers, the on-deck batter, pointed out that there was a crack in the infielder's bat. Dent borrowed a bat from Rivers.

All set, Dent swung at the next pitch; the ball cleared the infield, heading out to the left-field wall. The wind and destiny moved the ball higher to its date with the Green Monster.

"Deep to left!" Bill White, the Yankee broadcaster, shouted. "Yastrzemski will not get it!"

Yaz backed up. He had been in this position before. But he knew it was hopeless. The ball sailed into the twenty-three-foot net above the Green Monster, the thirty-seven-foot wall in left field. Three-run home run!

White, Chambliss, and the entire Yankee bench were there waiting at home plate. It was all Bucky Dent that October day.

"I was so damned shocked," Torrez said. "I thought maybe it was going to be off the wall. Damn, I did not think it was going to go out."

Not many remember that the Red Sox still had a chance in the bottom of the ninth. But Goose Gossage got Carl Yastrzemski to pop out with two on and two out. Not many remember that the victory in that game was earned by Ron Guidry, moving his record to 25–3.

"I had a dream as a kid," Dent said. "I dreamed someday I would hit a home run to win something."

GOSSAGE VERSUS BRETT: *October 10, 1980*

TALK ABOUT LIFE imitating art and art imitating life.

It was a moment right out of *The Natural*. Better.

The situation was a matchup of powerful closer Goose Gossage against bat wizard George Brett. Both men were not the most likable of personalities, but they could do things on a baseball field very few could match.

The noisy crowd at Yankee Stadium was more than fifty-six thousand strong. It was the top of the seventh inning. The Yankees were barely holding on to a 2–1 lead, down two games to none in the best-of-five playoff series. There were two outs. A Willie Wilson double off Yankee pitcher Tommy John brought in Goose Gossage and his ninety-eight-mile-per-hour fastball. Shortstop U. L. Washington, using all his speed, scratched out an infield single. Enter slugger George Brett.

The Yankees had closed out the Royals three times in the 1970s. "Beating the Yankees," Brett said, "had become the biggest obstacle in our lives. Walking up to home plate, I could hear the roar of the crowd, the anticipation. But once I got in that batter's box . . . I never heard a thing. I hit the ball, didn't feel any reverberation in my hands. I knew I'd hit it good."

The home run was a three-run shot into the upper deck. George Brett ran the bases. The huge Yankee stadium crowd was silenced.

"I was devastated," said Gossage, who sought sanctuary after the game in the bowels of Yankee Stadium, in a players' lounge with a no-media area. He sat there, alone. George Brett and the Kansas City Royals celebrated. They had finally gotten the Yankee money off their back, at least for a while.

DAVE RIGHETTI'S NO-HITTER: *July 4, 1983*

HE CAME TO the Yankees in a multiple-player deal that sent Sparky Lyle to Texas. His major-league debut was as an end-of-the-season call-up on September 16, 1979. It wasn't until 1981 that Dave Righetti came back to the Yankees to stay.

American League Rookie of the Year that 1981 season (8–4, 2.06 ERA), the player they called Rags won twice against Milwaukee in divisional play and once over Oakland in the LCS.

But his moment of moments in a Yankee uniform took place on July 4, 1983, a very hot day. Many in the holiday crowd of 41,077 took their seats wearing Yankee caps. Thousands had been given out as a promotional ploy.

Then they settled down and watched as Dave Righetti pitched a 4–0 no-hitter against the Boston Red Sox. Righetti fanned nine and walked four. Wade Boggs, batting .357, was the last out. A hard slider put him away.

It was the first no-hitter by a left-hander in Yankee Stadium history, the first no-hitter by a Yankee pitcher since 1956, when Don Larsen tossed a perfect game in the World Series. It was only the sixth regular-season no-hitter in Yankee history and the first since 1951.

PINE TAR INCIDENT: *July 24, August 18, 1983*

THE 1983 SEASON was an up-and-down one for the Yankees. But on July 24, things were on the upside. They were positioned to take over first place as they prepared to play the Kansas City Royals at Yankee Stadium.

Dave Righetti

The game that was played that day was fairly ordinary. As it moved to the top of the ninth inning, the Yankees had a 4–3 lead. As the Royals came to bat, no one could have forecast what would come next.

There were two outs. Goose Gossage was one out away from wrapping up the Yankee victory. George Brett had other ideas. Home run, into the stands in right field!

The Royal superstar ran out the homer that had apparently given his team a 5–4 lead. But just seconds after crossing the plate and going into his dugout, Brett saw Yankee manager Billy Martin approach home-plate rookie umpire Tim McClelland.

"I was feeling pretty good about myself after hitting the homer," Brett said. "I was sitting in the dugout. Somebody said they were checking the pine tar, and I said, 'If they call me out for using too much pine tar, I'm going to kill one of those SOBs.' "

McClelland called to the Royal dugout and asked to see Brett's bat. Then he conferred with his umpiring crew. Martin watched from a few feet away. Brett looked out from the bench. Then McClelland thrust his arm in the air. It was the signal that indicated George Brett was out—for excessive use of pine tar on his bat.

McClelland had brought forth rule 1.10(b): "a bat may not be covered by such a substance more than 18 inches from the tip of the handle." The umpire ruled that Brett's bat had "heavy pine tar" 19 to 20 inches from the tip of the handle and lighter pine tar for another three or four inches.

The home run was disallowed. The game was over. The Yankees were declared 4–3 winners. Brett, raced out of the dugout. Then mayhem and fury took center stage. Brett, not your calmest player, lost it completely.

At one point, umpire Joe Brinkman had Brett in a choke hold. That was the easy part for the Royal superstar. When the other players stormed the field things got really out of control.

Royals pitcher Gaylord Perry grabbed the bat from McClelland, tossed it to Hal McRae, who passed it on to Royals pitcher Steve Renko, who was halfway up the tunnel to the team clubhouse. Then Yankee Stadium security guards grabbed him and grabbed the bat, which was then impounded.

The Royals lodged a protest of the Yankee victory. The Yankees went off to Texas, where they won three games and took over first place for the first time that season.

The almost-comical mess was debated by baseball fans all over the nation. The media couldn't get enough of it. "Why a .356 hitter like George Brett," *Time* magazine commented, "would lumber along with a Marv Throneberry Model (lifetime .237) is the sort of paradox that, scientists say, has trees talking to themselves."

Eventually American League president Lee MacPhail overturned McClelland's decision. Acknowledging that Brett had pine tar too high on the bat, MacPhail explained that it was the league's belief that "games should be won and lost on the playing field—not through technicalities of the rules."

Yankee owner George Steinbrenner was miffed. "I wouldn't want to be Lee MacPhail living in New York!" he snapped.

The Brett home run was reinstated. The Royals' protest was upheld. The contest was declared "suspended." Both teams were told to find a mutually agreeable time, continue playing the game, and conclude it.

The date was August 18. Play was resumed for the last four outs of a game that had begun on July 24. The Yankees, strangely anxious to make a few more bucks, announced they would charge regular admission for the game's continuation. There were fan mumblings of protest. The Yankees quietly changed the admission idea. It was too late and to no avail. Only twelve hundred fans showed up.

The atmosphere was bizarre. To show their rage and annoyance at the whole turn of events, the Yankees played pitcher Ron Guidry in center field and outfielder Don Mattingly (a left-hander) at second base for the final out of the top of the ninth. Guidry played center field because the Yankees had traded away Jerry Mumphrey, who had been in the original game for defensive purposes. New York's George Frazier struck out McRae for the third out. In the bottom of the ninth, Royals reliever Dan Quisenberry was able to retire the Yankees in order. The final score of the game was Royals 5; Yankees 4.

KANSAS CITY ROYALS

NAME	POS	AB	R	H	RBI
WILLIE WILSON	CF	3	0	0	0
PAT SHERIDAN	PH-CF	2	0	0	0
U.L. WASHINGTON	SS	5	1	1	0
GEORGE BRETT	3B	5	1	3	2
HAL MCRAE	DH	3	0	0	0
AMOS OTIS	RF	4	0	1	0
JOHN WATHAN	1B-LF	3	2	1	0
LEON ROBERTS	LF	3	0	2	0
WILLIE AIKENS	PH-1B	1	0	0	0
FRANK WHITE	2B	4	1	2	2
DON SLAUGHT	C	4	0	3	1
TOTALS		37	5	13	5

NEW YORK YANKEES

NAME	POS	AB	R	H	RBI
BERT CAMPANERIS	2B	4	1	2	0
GRAIG NETTLES	3B	3	0	0	0
LOU PINIELLA	RF	4	1	1	0
JERRY MUMPHREY	CF	0	0	0	0
DON BAYLOR	DH	4	1	1	2
DAVE WINFIELD	CF-LF	4	1	3	2
STEVE KEMP	LF-RF	4	0	0	0
STEVE BALBONI	1B	2	0	0	0
DON MATTINGLY	1B	1	0	0	0
ROY SMALLEY	SS	3	0	1	0
RICK CERONE	C	2	0	0	0
TOTALS		31	4	8	4

MATTINGLY VERSUS WINFIELD, BATTLE FOR THE BATTING TITLE: *1984*

ON AUGUST 18, 2001, Don Mattingly and Dave Winfield were reunited, after a fashion. "Donnie Baseball" gave the player George Steinbrenner labeled "Mr. May" the keys to a new car at Yankee Stadium. The occasion was an honoring (but not a retiring of the number) of Winfield, a twelve-time All Star who in 2001 was admitted to the Baseball Hall of Fame.

"Donnie and I got along," Winfield said after the ceremonies. "We played well together. There were some differences. I was really glad to see him today."

Whenever the names Don Mattingly and Dave Winfield come up, the spirited batting race of 1984 comes up, too. That season Mattingly became the regular Yankee first baseman and took big strides toward establishing himself as one of the top stars of the 1980s. The veteran Winfield, goaded by a Steinbrenner comment that he was unable to "hit for average," cut down on his big swing. That set up a run for the batting title against Mattingly.

"Donnie and I were at different points in our careers," Winfield said. "He was a young kid who had a lot of support from the public. I know what I experienced was much different from him. I had a lot of things going on with the [Winfield] Foundation, stuff in the newspapers."

Don Mattingly

The battle for the American League batting crown came down to the final game. All through the season the bias was clear, the favoritism among Yankee officials—if not the entire Yankee family—toward Mattingly. Winfield was booed by fans at Yankee Stadium.

Mattingly collected four hits in five at bats; Winfield managed one hit in four at bats in the Yankee season-ending 4–2 win over the Tigers. Mattingly edged Winfield .343 to .340 to win the title and become the first Yankee left-handed hitter to bat over .340 since Lou Gehrig hit .351 in 1937.

The batting championship secured, Don Mattingly's popularity with Yankee fans soared even more. Dave Winfield's relationship with the fans and media, however, turned even more sour.

ANDY HAWKINS'S NO-HITTER: *July 1, 1990*

JUST ABOUT A month before the Yankees were poised to release journeyman hurler Andy Hawkins, an injury to another pitcher kept him on the roster. Hawkins, who had been a star prospect at the beginning of his career, had lost four of five decisions for the Yankees in 1990.

But this first day of July, 1990, against the Chicago White Sox at Comiskey Park was very different for the tall Texan. Hawkins had pitched into the eighth inning four outs away from a no-hitter.

The first two outs in the eighth came on pop-ups by Ron Karkovice and Scott Fletcher to second baseman Steve Sax. Then Sammy Sosa hit a bouncer to third baseman Mike Blowers, who back-handed the ball but then dropped it and picked it up and threw hurriedly to first.

A head-first slide, Sosa safe. Then a steal of second. A walk to Ozzie Guillen. A walk to Lance Johnson on four straight balls. Bases loaded.

Robin Ventura shot a can-of-corn to left-fielder Jim Leyritz. Spinning the wrong way, Leyritz wobbled, then lunged. The ball dropped off the tip of his glove. Two-base error. The three base runners scored. Ventura to second.

"It was hit right at me," said Leyritz. "It got caught up in the wind, and I couldn't reach it."

The next batter, Ivan Calderon, hit a high similar fly ball to center fielder Jesse Barfield, who said later: "I lost it in the sun coming down." Ventura scored. Calderon ended up on second.

The Texas native finally got out of the inning with the no-hitter intact but he was down 4–0. The Yankees failed to score in their half of the ninth. Melton Andrew Hawkins had spun a no-hitter, but he lost the game, suffering the most lopsided no-hit defeat in history.

Still, for a guy who finished the season with a 5–12 record and a 5.37 ERA, that July 1 no-hit outing against the Sox was something special.

JIM ABBOT'S NO-HITTER: *September 4, 1993*

JIM ABBOTT WAS born without a right hand, but he persevered—more than persevered. A graduate of the University of Michigan, he carried the United States flag during the opening ceremonies at the 1987 Pan American Games in Indianapolis and pitched for the 1988 U.S. Olympic team.

In 1989, at the age of twenty-two, he went directly from the University of Michigan to the Angels' starting rotation. A solidly built southpaw, the intense Abbott won a dozen games and posted a 3.92 ERA in his rookie season. On the mound, he wore a right-hander's fielder's glove over the stump at the end

JIM ABBOT NO-HITTER

CLEVELAND

NAME	POS	AB	R	H	RBI
KENNY LOFTON	CF	3	0	0	0
FELIX FERMIN	SS	4	0	0	0
CARLOS BAERGA	2B	4	0	0	0
ALBERT BELLE	LF	3	0	0	0
RANDY MILLIGAN	1B	1	0	0	0
MANNY RAMIREZ	DH	3	0	0	0
CANDY MALDONADO	RF	3	0	0	0
JIM THOME	3B	2	0	0	0
JUNIOR ORTIZ	C	1	0	0	0
SANDY ALOMAR, JR.	PH-C	1	0	0	0
TOTALS		**25**	**0**	**0**	**0**

YANKEES

NAME	POS	AB	R	H	RBI
WADE BOGGS	3B	4	1	1	0
DION JAMES	LF	4	1	2	1
GERALD WILLIAMS	LF	0	0	0	0
DON MATTINGLY	1B	3	0	1	0
DANNY TARTABULL	DH	4	0	1	0
PAUL O'NEILL	RF	4	0	0	0
BERNIE WILLIAMS	CF	3	0	1	0
MATT NOKES	C	4	0	1	0
MIKE GALLEGO	2B	3	1	0	0
RANDY VELARDE	SS	3	1	1	1
TOTALS		**32**	**4**	**8**	**2**

of his right arm. After delivering a pitch and completing his follow-through, he adroitly switched the glove to his left hand to be in a position to handle any balls batted back to him.

In 1991 he looked like one of the best young left-handers in the game after winning eighteen games for the Angels while posting a 2.89 ERA. The Yankees traded their best prospect, first baseman J. T. Snow, and pitchers Russ Springer and Jerry Nielsen to California for Abbott on December 6, 1992. The media spotlight in New York City seemed to be on him daily.

Abbott said he wanted to be like Nolan Ryan and not like Pete Gray, the one-handed outfielder.

Abbott had his ups and downs during his two seasons in the Bronx. His record was 20–22. But he did have one especially shining moment. It came just six days after he had been racked for ten hits and seven runs in only three and a third innings against Cleveland.

Facing Cleveland again, in the heat of the pennant race, Abbott tossed a 4–0 no-hitter against the Indians. "I remember it was a cloudy day. A day game, the kind of game I like to throw."

DWIGHT GOODEN'S NO-HITTER: *May 14, 1996*

ON OCTOBER 16, 1995, Dwight Gooden was signed by the New York Yankees. His days of glory in New York City baseball pitching with the Mets were behind him. Drugs and alcohol had ravaged the body and the mind of the once-overpowering hurler.

The 1996 season was more of the same for the Tampa native: failure. At the beginning of the season, George Steinbrenner had claimed that the thirty-one-year-old hurler could win fifteen games. But he was struggling to win one. Gooden was sent to the Yankee bullpen with an 0–3 record and an 11.48 ERA.

"I've just got to keep working on my mechanics," the Doc said. "It's complete frustration more than anything else."

Overwork and injury depleted the Yankee pitching staff, bringing Gooden back onto center stage. He was rushed into the rotation on April 27. There were six strong innings hurled against the Twins, a half dozen shutout innings over the White Sox. Then in his next outing, Gooden notched his first victory since June 19, 1994. It was a gem against the Tigers, the final twenty batters retired in a row.

On Tuesday night, May 14, 1996, Dwight Gooden, his father in a Tampa hospital slated for double bypass surgery the next day, took the mound against Seattle.

As the Mariners came to bat in the ninth inning, most of the 20,786 fans, hoarse from screaming inning after inning, were edgy, standing up. Gooden had thrown more than a hundred pitches and was going on grit now.

The Mariners managed to get runners on first and second base. "It was Dwight's game all the way," said Joe Torre. A wild pitch to the dangerous Jay

Buhner moved the runners to second and third with one out. Gooden reached back. He fanned Buhner. Two out.

Gooden's 135th pitch of the game was a swerving curve to Paul Sorrento. High pop to Jeter—no-hitter! Yanks win 2–0! Yankee Stadium rocked! Gooden was carried off the field on the shoulders of his Yankee teammates. The final score of the game was Yankees 2, Mariners, 0.

"This is the greatest feeling of my life," he said. "I never thought I could do this, not in my wildest dreams. A year and a half ago I thought I had pitched my last game, so being able not only to make it back but to throw a no-hitter, that's been an incredible blessing for me."

It was the eighth regular-season no-hitter by a Yankee hurler. For Dwight Gooden that performance ended a streak of twenty-three months without a major-league victory and saw him rebound from an 0–3 start to win eleven of his next thirteen decisions.

JIM LEYRITZ AND THE GREAT WORLD SERIES COMEBACK: *October 23, 1996*

THE GAME WAS played before 51,881 on a Wednesday night at Fulton County Stadium in Atlanta, Yanks versus Braves, the Braves with a 2–1 lead in the World Series.

Through five innings it looked as if the home team was headed for another victory. Their fans, tomahawk chopping in earnest, were pumped up over Atlanta's six-run lead. Pitcher Denny Neagle was shutting down New York.

But in the sixth, the Yanks scored three times. Enter Jim Leyritz, number 13, as a defensive replacement for Joe Girardi. The muscular Leyritz had spent much of the game in the weight room.

To preserve the lead, Braves skipper Bobby Cox started the eighth inning with closer Mark Wohlers, who could hit one hundred miles per hour on the radar gun. With two on, Leyritz stepped into the box. He worked the count to 2–2, fouling off two blistering fastballs.

Then Wohlers hung a slider. Leyritz sent the ball deep to left and over the wall. Leyritz hung three runs on the scoreboard. The Yankees hadn't won the game and tied the series with one swing, but it sure seemed that way.

"I'm not thinking home run right there," Leyritz said. "I'm thinking I've got an opportunity to drive in one run if I get a base hit."

"I lost it," Wohlers said. "I blew it."

The game moved to the tenth, tied at 6. Southpaw Steve Avery, the replacement for Mark Wohlers, got the first two batters. Then Tim Raines walked. Jeter got an infield single. Bernie Williams was intentionally walked to get at Yankee rookie Andy Fox. Joe Torre inserted his last pinch hitter, Wade Boggs, who walked. A run was forced in. The Yanks had their first lead. Then another run was tacked on.

It took seven pitchers, five pinch hitters, a reserve catcher, and a pinch runner—the whole Yankee bench, not including pitchers, for the victory to be achieved, but the Yankees won the game, finally, 8–6.

For journeyman Jim Leyritz, who triggered the comeback, that home run was his greatest moment in baseball. "Because it was in the World Series," he said. "It helped us get the momentum back and go on to win the World Series. And it really made my mark as far as being a Yankee."

DEREK JETER'S HOME RUN (COURTESY OF JEFFREY MAIER): *October 9, 1996*

IT WAS THE first game of the 1996 ALCS, Yankees against Baltimore. October baseball at Yankee Stadium. The home team was losing 4–3 in the eighth inning.

Up came Derek Jeter, finishing off a splendid rookie season. He drove a pitch off Oriole reliever Armando Benitez, the ball heading out into the night toward the right-field stands. Outfielder Tony Tarasco started tracking the ball from the crack of the bat. Heading back to the wall, he waited.

So did twelve-year-old Jeffrey Maier, a rabid Yankees fan who had played hooky that day. The truant reached out over the railing in the stands with his black baseball glove and made the catch. Incredibly, right-field umpire Rich Garcia ruled that the youngster did not interfere with the play. A TV replay indicated otherwise. A heated dispute ensued but it did the O's no good. Jeter's shot was ruled a home run. The game was tied.

The Yankees went on to win 5–4 in an eleven-inning decision over the Orioles on a Bernie Williams home run (non-controversial) to left field. They went on to triumph over Baltimore in the series in five games.

Jeffrey Maier of Old Tappan, New Jersey, became an instant celebrity. "I don't think there's any reason to be mad at me," Maier said later. "I'm just a twelve-and-a-half-year-old kid going for the ball."

It seemed every talk show had him on, and the video of his catch was repeated over and over. He even managed to be interviewed by the likes of Regis and Kathie Lee. Not bad for a truant.

DAVID WELLS'S PERFECT GAME: *May 17, 1998*

GOING INTO THE game on May 17, 1998, the season had been a checkered one for the burly flake David Lee Wells of Torrance, California. He took the mound with a 5.23 ERA. Consistency was his problem, some said inconsistency.

Wells marched to his own drummer, one game wearing an actual Babe Ruth hat on the mound before he was told by manager Joe Torre to take it off. In a

David Wells

start on May 6 in Texas, he had been lifted by Torre. Wells not too tactfully flipped the ball to his miffed manager as he left the mound.

On this seventeenth day of May, three days shy of his thirty-fifth birthday, Wells took the mound on a Sunday against the Minnesota Twins. He was locked in right from the start, fanning the first three batters with ease. Between innings, he sat next to David Cone, who was a calming influence.

In the seventh inning, Cone told him: "It is time to break out the knuckle-ball." Wells let out a big if nervous laugh. "I started getting really nervous,"

BOX SCORE

MINNESOTA

NAME	POS	AB	R	H	RBI
MATT LAWTON	CF	3	0	0	0
BRENT GATES	2B	3	0	0	0
PAUL MOLITOR	DH	3	0	0	0
MARTY CORDOVA	LF	3	0	0	0
RON COOMER	1B	3	0	0	0
ALEX OCHOA	RF	3	0	0	0
JON SHAVE	3B	3	0	0	0
JAVIER VALENTIN	C	3	0	0	0
PAT MEARES	SS	3	0	0	0
TOTALS		**27**	**0**	**0**	**0**

NEW YORK

NAME	POS	AB	R	H	RBI
CHUCK KNOBLAUCH	2B	4	0	0	0
DEREK JETER	SS	3	0	1	0
PAUL O'NEILL	RF	4	0	0	0
TINO MARTINEZ	1B	4	0	0	0
BERNIE WILLIAMS	CF	3	3	3	1
DARRYL STRAWBERRY	DH	3	1	1	1
CHAD CURTIS	LF	3	0	1	1
JORGE POSADA	C	3	0	0	0
SCOTT BROSIUS	3B	3	0	0	0
TOTALS		**30**	**4**	**6**	**3**

Wells recalled. "I knew what was going on, I was hoping the fans would kind of shush a little bit. They were making me nervous."

In the bottom of the eighth inning, Wells went through neck and arm stretches in the dugout. The crowd of 49,820 gave him a standing ovation as he came out to pitch the ninth, with the Yankees leading 4–0.

The Twins went quickly. Rookie Jon Shave flew out to right. Javier Valentin fanned, the eleventh K for Wells. Then Pat Meares lofted a fly to right and the entire stadium seemed to hold its breath, waiting to see what would happen. Paul O'Neill gloved it—perfect game! Wells pumped his left fist twice after the final out that sealed his perfect day on the mound after two hours and forty minutes. It was just the fifteenth perfect game in major league history. Swarmed over by his teammates, Wells was carried off the field.

Billy Crystal walked into the clubhouse after the game, walked over to the ecstatic Wells, and asked: "I got here late, what happened?"

DAVID CONE'S PERFECT GAME: *July 19, 1999*

IT WAS YOGI Berra Day at the stadium. The Squat Yankee legend had made up with George Steinbrenner and was at the park for the first time in years. Don Larsen was among the 41,930 in attendance. He was there to throw out the first pitch to Berra, who caught his perfect game in the 1956 World Series.

The plan was for Larsen to tarry a while in a seat behind home plate, watch a few innings, and then go back to his hotel and relax. But Larsen, like all the others in the park that day, was riveted to what Yankee starter David Cone was doing to the Montreal Expos.

Cone threw all manner of pitches from an assortment of arm angles. Even

David Cone

a thirty-three-minute rain delay in the third inning had little effect on his peerless pitching performance. In the eighth inning, Montreal's Jose Vidro grounded sharply up the middle. Second baseman Chuck Knoblauch, moving right, backhanded the ball and threw him out.

"When Knoblauch made the great play," Cone said, "I decided there was some kind of Yankee aura. Maybe this was my day."

As the ninth got under way, Cone was given a standing ovation as he walked to the mound. The large crowd remained standing. Cone got the final out on Orlando Cabrera, a pop-up. Cone grabbed the sides of his head, dropped to his knees, and was quickly lifted by his teammates onto their shoulders.

The Yankees had a 6–0 win. Cone had the sixteenth perfect game in modern history. He hadn't gone to a three-ball count all day. He threw eighty-eight pitches, sixty-eight of them strikes, getting thirteen fly outs, ten strikeouts, and four groundouts.

"You probably have a better chance of winning the lottery than this happening," he said. "The last three innings, that's when you really think about it. You can't help feel the emotion of the crowd. I felt my heart thumping through my uniform."

BOX SCORE

MONTREAL

NAME	POS	AB	R	H	RBI
WILTON GUERRERO	DH	3	0	0	0
TERRY JONES	CF	2	0	0	0
JAMES MOUTON	CF	1	0	0	0
RONDELL WHITE	LF	3	0	0	0
VLADIMIR GUERRERO	RF	3	0	0	0
JOSE VIDRO	2B	3	0	0	0
BRAD FULLMER	1B	3	0	0	0
CHRIS WIDGER	C	3	0	0	0
SHANE ANDREWS	3B	2	0	0	0
*RYAN MCGUIRE	PH	1	0	0	0
ORLANDO CABRERA	SS	3	0	0	0
TOTALS		**27**	**0**	**0**	**0**

*Flied out for Andrews in the 9th inning.

NEW YORK

NAME	POS	AB	R	H	RBI
CHUCK KNOBLAUCH	2B	2	1	1	0
DEREK JETER	SS	4	1	1	2
PAUL O'NEILL	RF	4	1	1	0
BERNIE WILLIAMS	CF	4	0	1	1
TINO MARTINEZ	1B	4	0	1	0
CHILI DAVIS	DH	3	1	1	0
RICKY LEDEE	LF	4	1	1	2
SCOTT BROSIUS	3B	2	1	0	0
JOE GIRARDI	C	3	0	1	1
TOTALS		**30**	**6**	**8**	**6**

THE FLYING BAT: *October 22, 2000*

IT WAS SUBWAY World Series game two on October 22, 2000, Yankees versus Mets. Winners of game one in dramatic fashion, the Yankees were counting on Roger Clemens to give them a 2–0 lead.

The main story, the moment that was eagerly anticipated and built up in the media for weeks before, was the matchup of Piazza and Clemens—the first "meeting" of the two since the Rocket had beaned the Mets catcher earlier in the season with a pitch. Clemens retired the first Mets batters with ease. The air that night at Yankee Stadium was electric as Piazza stepped into the batter's box. Two quick inside fastballs gave Clemens two quick strikes. His third pitch was inside and backed Piazza off the plate. The buzz picked up.

The next pitch was inside again and Piazza fouled it off, shattering his bat. The ball wound up in the Yankee dugout. Piazza, not knowing where it was, started running to first. A chunk of the splintered bat was fielded by Clemens, who fired it right into the path of the running Piazza.

The wood barely missed hitting Piazza, who started a slow walk toward Clemens, snarling. "It was bizarre," the Mets catcher said later. "I never had a bat come back at me."

Both benches cleared. There was mumbling, milling about, grumbling, a few curses. Piazza approached Clemens, and in his phrase, "I just kept asking him, 'What's your problem; what is your problem?' I didn't get a response. I didn't know what to think."

The umpires ruled that Clemens had not intended to hit Piazza with the bat, so the game resumed. Clemens then retired Piazza on a ground ball and went on to dominate the Mets for eight innings. The Yankees went on to win the game and the series in five games.

It was just another in the long line of incidents in the sometimes rocky history of New York City baseball. It was just another incident that underscored the sour side image of Roger Clemens.

MIKE MUSSINA'S NEAR-PERFECT GAME:
September 2, 2001

IT WAS YANKEES versus Red Sox, September baseball between the two age-old rivals. Mike Mussina against David Cone. Through eight innings, no score. Mussina, no walks, no hits given up. As the man they called Moose took a perfect game into the eighth for the third time in his career, the Yankees dugout was quiet.

The ninth inning began with a Tino Martinez single. A sharp grounder by Paul O'Neill that second baseman Lou Merloni erred on put runners on first and third. Clay Bellinger pinch-ran for Martinez. He came home on an Enrique Wilson hit. Score 1–0 Yankees.

Boston's Troy O'Leary, pinch hitting for Shea Hillenbrand, hit a liner that Bellinger, playing first base, dove for and caught. He tossed the ball to Mussina. One out.

"I thought maybe this time it was going to happen," said Mussina, "considering that I thought that ball was through for sure."

Lou Merloni struck out. Carl Everett was in the clubhouse hitting off a tee; he got the call to pinch-hit for Joe Oliver. The moody Everett, in a 3-for-32 slump, was 1 for 9 with seven strikeouts in his career against Mussina.

The switch-hitter fouled off the first pitch. He swung at strike two. Pitch number three to Everett was a ball. The next pitch was a high fastball. Everett fought it off, lofting a soft liner to left center between Chuck Knoblauch and Bernie Williams. It dropped—a single.

Mussina knew immediately. "I thought it was a hit," he said. "I'm going to think about that pitch until I retire, but that was the pitch I threw." All Mussina could do was hang his head and give a little smile. "It was just a phenomenal game," Mussina said. "I was disappointed, I'm still disappointed. It just wasn't meant to be."

"I've never been part of a no-hitter before as an opponent," Everett said. "It was very satisfying to get the hit. It was very satisfying to hit the high fastball."

The game ended when Mussina got Trot Nixon on a groundout to second baseman Alfonso Soriano. The Yankee pitcher then weakly pumped his fist as his teammates ran out onto the field.

Mussina finished with his fourth career one-hitter, and struck out a season-high thirteen. Nine came on called third strikes, as his breaking ball fooled the Red Sox all night. The Yankees completed a three-game sweep of Boston, handing them their eighth straight loss and putting the Sox nine games back in the AL East.

CAL RIPKEN'S LAST YANKEE STADIUM GAME:
September 30, 2001

THE DAY WAS drizzly and cold. The Yankees played against the Orioles for fifteen innings, until the game was finally called because of the rain. There were 55,351 fans around at the start and far fewer at the finish.

Many in the crowd had come out to see Cal Ripken, Jr., playing in his 126th game at Yankee Stadium, the most by an opposing player. His first game there had been on June 18, 1982.

There was an orange number 8 painted on third base, as well as on the Orioles' on-deck circle. Ripken threw out the game's first pitch to Derek Jeter. Gifts presented to the Oriole legend included a sterling silver press pin from Don Mattingly, a watch, an enlarged and framed copy of the commemorative ticket each fan was given, which read "Farewell Cal Ripken." Black-and-white pictures of Ripken and Gehrig were on the tickets.

Ripken's pregame speech near home plate was staged close to where a dying Lou Gehrig had said good-bye. "I know there will be many things that I'll miss about baseball, but coming to New York and playing in Yankee Stadium will always be at the top," Ripken said. "I remember Graig Nettles making diving catches," Ripken continued. "I remember Louisiana Lightning. I didn't like facing him that much. . . . Willie Randolph and Dave Winfield. It's really been a great run. Let's get to the game."

The game was in Ripken's words: "Eerie. The weather, the gray sky, the wind, the rain. I was punched out four times and went 0 for 7, but I still had a lot of fun competing."

TWO NIGHTS, TWO COMEBACKS, 2001 WORLD SERIES: *October 31–November 2, 2001*

"THIS IS THE most incredible couple of games I've ever managed," Joe Torre said of games four and five of the 2001 World Series.

"This is some of the most exciting baseball I've ever been a part of," Arizona manager Bob Brenly said.

On back-to-back nights in the big ballpark in the Bronx, the New York Yankees did the unthinkable, the unimaginable, becoming the first team in postseason history to win two straight games when trailing after eight innings.

Big Apple newspapers over-reached with headlines:

"LAST LICKS TASTING SWEETER"
"DEREK DINGER REAL STINGER"
"MAGIC!"
"MIDNIGHT MADNESS"
"ENCORE"

In game four, Tino Martinez saved the Yankees with a first-pitch, two-out, two-run homer to right center in the ninth, off closer Byung-Hyun Kim. The shot, clubbed off a fastball at 11:35 P.M., tied the game and moved it into extra innings.

Curt Schilling, who had started the game that Wednesday night on three days' rest and pitched seven brilliant innings, holding the Yankees to one run and three hits, slouched in the Arizona dugout. He was in deep denial. He would feel worse soon.

Along came Derek Jeter with two outs in the bottom of the tenth inning as October turned into November. The 55,863 on the scene screamed themselves hoarse as the stadium scoreboard flashed "Welcome to November Baseball."

Jeter, who had gone 1 for 15 in the World Series, lined Kim's sixty-first pitch in his third inning of work for a full-count homer, an opposite-field drive into the seats in right. It was the first game-ending homer of the Yankee shortstop's brilliant career.

"In the postseason," Jeter said, "you can throw everything you've done out the window. In every at bat you have a chance to do something huge. I've never hit a walk-off home run before so it was a special experience."

The time was 12:04 A.M. EST Thursday and the Yanks had a 4–3 win. The World Series was tied at two games each.

The next night it seemed the Yankees had the edge with ace Mike Mussina matched against journeyman Miguel Batista. But the thirty-year-old outpitched Mussina going in to the eighth inning, leading 2–0 with two on and two outs.

By the bottom of the ninth, the stadium shook with the sound of the fans, and there were many in the sellout crowd who covered their ears against the deafening din. Kim, despite having thrown sixty-two pitches the night before—and having been the goat—came in to pitch once again.

"He is our closer," Diamondback pilot Brenly would explain. "He wanted the ball in that situation."

Young Byung-Hyun Kim, intense on the mound, knew the opportunity was there for him to erase the stigma and memory of blowing game four.

Jorge Posada doubled to the corner in left to start the Yankee ninth. Kim retired Shane Spencer on a grounder, then struck out Knoblauch. Scott Brosius, the 1998 World Series MVP, stepped in.

The time was 11:46 P.M. The count was 1–0. The pitch came in. Brosius swung—a long drive to left field. Raising his arm in the air, he knew it. Kim knew it. The ballpark erupted.

In his final career at bat in Yankee Stadium, Brosius had slashed a tying, two-run homer. He fist-pumped his way around the bases. Kim sank to his knees, covering his head with his glove.

For the second straight night, there was a game-tying homer with two outs in the bottom of the ninth inning of the 2001 World Series.

"You know they have to be thinking. 'I can't believe this is happening.' Not one night, but two nights in a row," Mussina said.

"It seemed like the whole situation was set again, and it happened again," Brosius said.

The Yankees went on to win the four-hour, fifteen-minute marathon in the twelfth inning—an Alfonso Soriano single did the trick.

Arizona, however, came back to win the world championship in the seventh game. "Somebody told me that we beat the Yankees in the bottom of the ninth!" veteran first baseman Mark Grace said and smiled. "I still don't believe it!"

There are still many fans of the mighty Yankees who don't believe it. But they and the people of New York City, still picking up the pieces and trying to get on with the normalcy of their lives after the tragic events of September 11, had a baseball team they could brag about and be proud of.

PART

2

CHAPTER FOUR

A *Yankee* WHO'S WHO

WITH TWENTY-FOUR HALL of Famers who spent the majority of their careers with the team, and another dozen who were onetime Yankees, second and third teams could easily be created by the Bronx Bombers that would be far more talented than the first teams of many other franchises.

Not everyone on this list of the "greatest Yankees" is a player, but for one good reason or another, each one is deserving of being on the roster.

◆

MEL ALLEN

"How 'bout that, sports fans?"

IN HIS HEYDAY as a broadcaster, Mel Allen received more than a thousand letters a week. His was the most recognizable voice in all of baseball broadcasting.

The son of Russian Jewish immigrants, Melvin Allen Israel was born in 1913 near Birmingham, Alabama. At 'Bama, he earned degrees in political science and law but stayed on as a speech instructor, covering football for a Birmingham radio station. In 1936, he was hired as an announcer by CBS.

Three years later, Allen became the announcer for Giants and Yankees home games. He was lead announcer on radio and then television for the Yankees from 1940 to 1964. Yankee fans loved him; Yankee haters could not tolerate him. "He was accused of being prejudiced for the Yankees," Eddie Lopat recalled. "One year we won thirty-nine games in the seventh, eighth and ninth. He had to get riled up."

The articulate Allen brought the game to millions in a cultivated, resonant voice, coining such nicknames as "Joltin' Joe" DiMaggio, "Scooter" for Phil Rizzuto, "Old Reliable" for Tommy Henrich; expressing emotion with his signature phrase, "How about that!"; and calling home runs with "Going, going, gone!" or—to keep beer and tobacco sponsors happy— "Ballantine Blasts" and "White Owl Wallops."

Mel Allen

At the end of the 1964 season, after having announced twenty World Series and twenty-four All-Star Games, Allen was let go without notice. "The Yankees never even held a press conference to announce my leaving," the announcer said. "They left people to believe whatever they wanted—and people believed the worst."

But the affable Allen continued his career through the 1970s, doing assorted voice-overs and commercials. In 1977, he became the host of ESPN's *This Week in Baseball.*

The following year, Mel Allen was inducted into the Baseball Hall of Fame, along with Red Barber, with whom he had been paired in the Yankee broadcasting booth for over a decade, the first broadcasters to receive that honor. When Allen returned in 1985 to the Yankees to do their cablecasts, many said "the Voice of the Yankees" is back where it belongs.

The Voice of the Yankees was stilled on June 16, 1996, when eighty-three-year-old Mel Allen suffered a

YANKEE STORIES
Barry Deutsch

When I was a kid growing up in the Bensonhurst section of Brooklyn, there was no television. You saw occasional glimpses of baseball games in newsreels. You traded baseball cards. But mainly, you listened to the radio and envisioned what was going on.

My becoming a Yankee fan had a lot to do with hearing Mel Allen on the radio. I liked his mellifluous voice, the way he described the game and talked about the players. Listening to Mel Allen was my first exposure to baseball, so to me, the Yankees were baseball.

The first game I ever saw was between the Yankees and the Philadelphia Athletics at Yankee Stadium. It was a spring day in 1948. My father and I schlepped all the way from Brooklyn to the Bronx by the IRT subway, leaving in the morning to be there in time for the game. It was Passover then, and we couldn't eat baseball food. My mother packed a lunch of gefilte fish cakes and matzoth for us.

My father had chosen that particular game because he had grown up in Philadelphia and was an Athletics fan—which was rare for someone living in Brooklyn. Allie Reynolds was pitching for the Yankees and Lou Brissie was pitching for the Athletics. Brissie had come back from the war with a wooden leg, and the buzz around baseball was that other teams were bunting on him. "The Yankees would never do that," my father told me. "They are so good, they don't have to cheat." I don't remember anybody bunting that game.

They had big hitters—Johnny Lindell, Charlie Keller, Tommy Henrich, Joe DiMaggio. Everybody loved DiMaggio. It was almost a cliché. But my particular affinity was for Tommy Henrich—it might have been the nickname Old Reliable or the fact that he was a marine.

The next year, the Yankees were in the World Series. We still didn't have a television set, but we were invited to watch the games in the one apartment in our building that did. I brought along my two cousins from the Bronx who were visiting that weekend. We all started rooting for the Yankees and got thrown out.

Since those days, I have traveled quite a lot and lived in a number of places outside the United States, and it strikes me as significant that wherever I am, if I mention the Yankees, almost everyone seems to know who they are.

To me, the team always seemed corporate; the players always seem to know what they are doing. One time I was sitting behind third base and watching Gil McDougald during batting practice. He didn't joke with anybody or talk to anybody. Every ball that came to him, he picked up and dealt with. And he did not miss a ball. It was such a professional approach to the game. I never got that sense with any other team.

heart attack in his Greenwich, Connecticut, home, having just watched a tele-vised broadcast of a Yankee game.

Jerry Coleman, who had worked with him in the broadcasting booth, said, "Mel Allen was the persona of the great broadcast voice. He was magnificent in what he did and how he did it. And he could talk forever."

ED BARROW

"The Yankee Empire Builder"

BASEBALL'S FIRST REAL general manager, Ed Barrow was the power behind the New York Yankee dynasties of the 1920s, 1930s, and 1940s—a time in which the Yankees won fourteen pennants and ten World Series.

Barrow's baseball roots stretched back to 1894, when he partnered with Harry Stevens operating concessions for the Pittsburgh Pirates. He moved quickly up the rungs: minor-league manager, owner, and president of the Eastern League, by 1918 the man known as Cousin Ed and Cousin Egbert was managing the Boston Red Sox, leading them to a world championship. He got some help from a young southpaw pitcher he converted to an outfielder, Babe Ruth.

At the end of the 1920 season, Barrow became the Yankee GM and began to strip the Sox roster of its stars, acquiring players like Wally Schang, Waite Hoyt, Joe Bush, Everett Scott, Joe Dugan, and Herb Pennock in 1923.

From 1921 to 1923, Barrow presided over the franchise's first three pennants. In his first eight years on the job, the Yankees won six pennants. George Weiss was brought to the Yankees by Barrow, and together the two developed the far-flung, productive farm system. Instrumental in establishing a scouting network, innovative and daring, Barrow took risks. Other teams were fearful of giving Tony Lazzeri a chance because he was an epileptic. Barrow was not. Other teams shied away from Joe DiMaggio because of his knee injury, dubbing him damaged goods. Barrow took the chance.

Opposed to ballpark promotions, averse to night baseball, Barrow allowed neither to be part of the Yankee scene in his time. Old school, quick to anger, quick to use his fists, Barrow ran the affairs of the Yankees from the stadium and his office on 42nd Street. A two-time Major League Executive of the Year, Barrow was respected but also feared by his peers.

His relationship with Jacob Ruppert was especially close. When the Yankee owner died in 1939, Barrow continued on the job as team president. When Ruppert's heirs sold the Yankees to Larry MacPhail, Dan Topping, and Del Webb in 1945, Barrow was appointed chairman of the board; however, he had many differences with the new owners.

He retired in 1947, ending his twenty-four-year reign as the Yankees' top executive. Three years later, the Yankees honored him with Ed Barrow Day.

Three years after that, Edward Grant Barrow was elected to the Baseball Hall of Fame, and the following year a plaque in his honor was dedicated at Yankee Stadium. He was called many things, but the phrase that fit him best is "the Yankee Empire Builder."

HANK BAUER

"Don't mess with my money!"

TOUGH, GRITTY, AND dependable were just a few of the adjectives used to describe outfielder Hank Bauer. A Yankee for 1,406 games spread over a dozen

Hanke Bauer

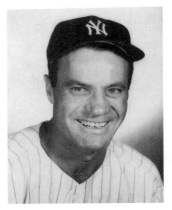

Hank Bauer

seasons, a three-time All Star, and one of Casey Stengel's favorites, Bauer didn't make mental mistakes and was very unhappy when his teammates did.

He was born in East St. Louis, Illinois, on July 31, 1922, and only managed to get through the eighth grade. But he was educated by life. Serving with the marines during World War II, Bauer was at the battle of Okinawa. "We went in with sixty-four," he recalled, "and six of us came out."

After the war, Bauer signed with the Yankees and moved up the minor-league rungs. Promoted from Kansas City late in the 1948 season, he was hustling away in the outfield in his usual style when he noticed center fielder Joe DiMaggio glaring at him.

"Did I do something wrong?" Bauer asked.

"No, you didn't do anything wrong," DiMaggio countered. "But you're the first son of a bitch who ever invaded my territory."

Bauer, it was noted, never did that again. Casey Stengel often platooned him in the outfield. "I didn't like it," Bauer said. "But there wasn't much I could do about it. He was the boss. Later on in my career I finally realized he probably prolonged my career a couple of years."

"He had that rough, grumbled talk, but was a real nice guy," Bauer's old teammate Irv Noren said. "He was a tough guy who got a lot of respect—no one wanted to fight him, not even Billy Martin."

Henry Albert Bauer, a solid hitter with the power and speed to take the extra base, had eighteen first-inning leadoff career home runs. In 1956, he had career highs in homers and RBIs. Bauer set a World Series record by hitting in seventeen straight games from 1956 to 1958.

Playing on nine pennant winners for the Yankees from 1949 through 1959, Bauer had a favorite expression: "Don't mess with my money!" He yelled it loud and often at teammates when he thought they weren't putting out as much as required. He just loved the way those World Series checks kept coming in. However, they ended for Bauer in 1960 when he was traded to Kansas City in a deal that brought Roger Maris to the Yankees.

Though Bauer played for other teams, he is best remembered as a New York Yankee.

YOGI BERRA

"I want to thank all the people for making this night necessary."

IN HIS PRIME, Lawrence Peter Berra was the heart and soul of the great Yankee teams of 1949–1955. He led the Yanks in RBIs each season during that stretch and won three MVP awards.

The kid who grew up on the Hill in St. Louis eating banana sandwiches with mustard went on to become one of the legends of Yankee baseball. As an inexperienced catcher in 1947, Yogi Berra once fielded a bunt in a game against the St. Louis Browns. He tagged the hitter and a runner coming home from third on a squeeze play. "I just tagged everything in sight," said Yogi, "including the umpire."

From 1946 to 1965, Yogi averaged about five hundred at bats a year and never struck out more than thirty-eight times in a season. He played in fifteen straight All-Star Games, and won fourteen pennants and ten world championships, more than any other player in history. He is "Mr. World Series," holding records for games (75), at bats (259), hits (71), and doubles (10).

Casey Stengel referred to him as "Mr. Berra" and "my assistant manager." One of the great clutch hitters of all time, Berra golfed low pitches for deep home runs and stroked high pitches for line drives. Eight times he led the league in games caught and chances accepted, six times he paced all catchers in double plays, five times he posted more than one hundred RBIs.

Yogi Berra sliding into third in the 1949 World Series

Yogi was one of only four catchers to ever have a perfect fielding record in a season (1958). Between July 28, 1957, and May 10, 1959, he set major-league records by catching in 148 consecutive games and accepting 950 chances without making an error. His lifetime fielding percentage was a glittery .988.

When he broke a finger in 1949, Berra was forced to play part of that season with one finger pushed outside of his catcher's mitt. That became standard practice for catchers.

Incredibly, Berra never led the league in a single offensive category, although he did just about everything else. In 1972 he was very deservingly elected to the Baseball Hall of Fame.

YOGI BERRA, MOSTS

Most postseason games: Yogi Berra holds the record for appearing in the most postseason games—seventy-five. In his nineteen-year career, Berra and the New York Yankees went to the postseason fourteen times. Since Berra played during the years before divisional play, all of the games he appeared in were World Series games, meaning he also holds the record for most World Series games appeared in. Berra also has the record for most World Series at bats with 259, and is third behind Mickey Mantle and Babe Ruth in World Series home runs, with twelve.

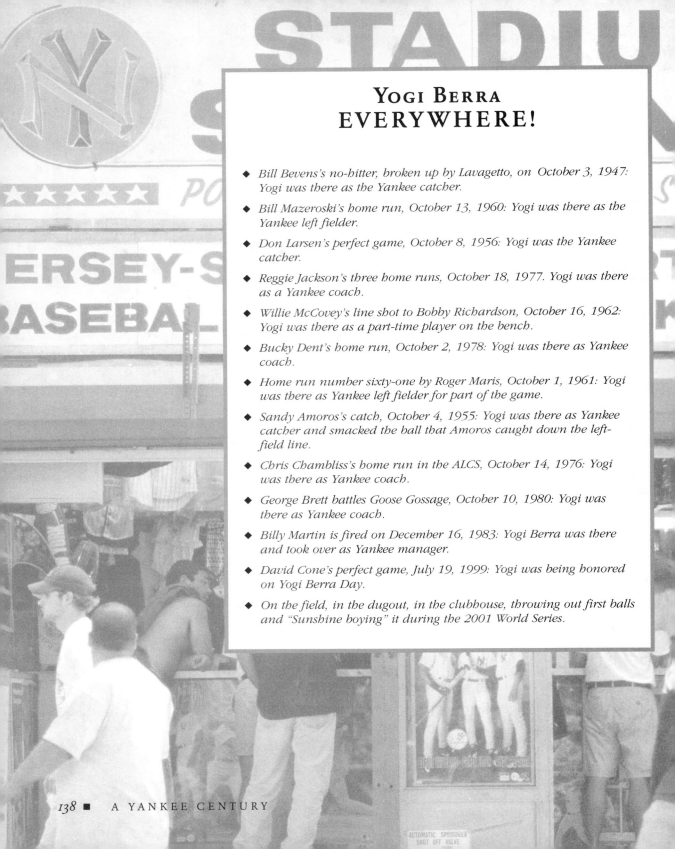

Yogi Berra
EVERYWHERE!

◆ *Bill Bevens's no-hitter, broken up by Lavagetto, on October 3, 1947: Yogi was there as the Yankee catcher.*

◆ *Bill Mazeroski's home run, October 13, 1960: Yogi was there as the Yankee left fielder.*

◆ *Don Larsen's perfect game, October 8, 1956: Yogi was the Yankee catcher.*

◆ *Reggie Jackson's three home runs, October 18, 1977. Yogi was there as a Yankee coach.*

◆ *Willie McCovey's line shot to Bobby Richardson, October 16, 1962: Yogi was there as a part-time player on the bench.*

◆ *Bucky Dent's home run, October 2, 1978: Yogi was there as Yankee coach.*

◆ *Home run number sixty-one by Roger Maris, October 1, 1961: Yogi was there as Yankee left fielder for part of the game.*

◆ *Sandy Amoros's catch, October 4, 1955: Yogi was there as Yankee catcher and smacked the ball that Amoros caught down the left-field line.*

◆ *Chris Chambliss's home run in the ALCS, October 14, 1976: Yogi was there as Yankee coach.*

◆ *George Brett battles Goose Gossage, October 10, 1980: Yogi was there as Yankee coach.*

◆ *Billy Martin is fired on December 16, 1983: Yogi Berra was there and took over as Yankee manager.*

◆ *David Cone's perfect game, July 19, 1999: Yogi was being honored on Yogi Berra Day.*

◆ *On the field, in the dugout, in the clubhouse, throwing out first balls and "Sunshine boying" it during the 2001 World Series.*

CHRIS CHAMBLISS

*"If you're not having fun in baseball,
you miss the point of everything."*

ON APRIL 27, 1974, Chris Chambliss came to the Yankees in a seven-player trade with Cleveland. And although he played in only half a dozen Yankee seasons, 1974–1979, he left his mark on franchise history.

Chambliss struggled somewhat in his first Yankee season but hit his stride in 1975, batting .304. Consistency and reliability were hallmarks of the Chambliss game. He played in 150 or more games for four straight seasons, 1975–1978. A very important part of the Yankee pennant winners in 1976 through 1978, the stocky Chambliss drove in at least ninety runs in each of those seasons.

In the time of the "Bronx Zoo," characterized by big mouths and even bigger egos, Chambliss was steady, an almost refreshingly calm presence among the hyperactive Yankees of that time. An All Star in 1976, he averaged ninety-two RBIs in those years. His classic left-handed swing enabled him to hit the ball where it was pitched.

When Chambliss first began his major-league career, he was below par as a defensive first baseman. But he made himself into the best defensive first baseman in the American League, leading that position in fielding (.997) in 1978, winning the Gold Glove. He was especially adroit at handling bad throws.

His career moment came in the final game of the 1976 championship series when Chambliss, who already had ten hits and seven RBIs in the series, homered off Kansas City pitcher Mark Littell to put the Yankees into the World Series against Cincinnati. Although he had 954 hits and seventy-nine home runs as a Yankee, none was bigger than the one hit off Littell.

In the 1990s, his playing days over, the classy Chambliss returned to the Yankees as batting coach and helped the team win four World Series championships in five seasons.

SPUD CHANDLER

"Carnesville Plowboy"

BILL DICKEY CALLED Spud Chandler the best pitcher he ever caught. "He's got five pitches," Dickey said. "He's got that fastball. He's got the curve. He's got the slider. He's got the forkball. He's got the screwball. You can call for any one of them at any time."

Born September 12, 1907, in Commerce, Georgia, Spurgeon Ferdinand

Spud Chandler

Chandler was raised on a farm. He went on to play baseball and football for the University of Georgia, but spurned offers to play professional football, signing with the Yankees instead.

He was twenty-nine years old when he made his major-league debut with the Yanks on May 6, 1937, beginning a career filled with eye-catching headlines. Spud Chandler, the winning pitcher in the 1942 All-Star Game, won two games for the Yankees in the 1943 World Series. That was his best season, the one in which he notched the most wins, the best winning percentage, most complete games, and most shutouts of any American League pitcher. His 1.64 ERA was the lowest in the American League in twenty-four seasons. In 1943, he was named the American League Most Valuable Player.

A four-time All Star, Chandler was 20–8 in 1946. During his illustrious career he recorded twenty-six shutouts and wound up 109–43 for a .717 winning percentage—still best ever in major-league history for pitchers with ten or more years of service. Chandler's career was a relatively brief one due to military service and injuries, but he never had a losing season.

Catcher Bill Dickey called the "Carnesville Plowboy" the best pitcher he ever handled. Yankee manager Joe McCarthy named Chandler to his "All-time Yankee Team."

HAL CHASE

"I am an outcast and I haven't a good name."

VIEWED AS ONE of the most unsavory characters in the history of the game, Yankee first baseman Hal Chase is one of baseball's more enigmatic figures. It was said that he threw games when he bet against his own team and was involved in the Black Sox scandal, which resulted in his being banned from baseball for life.

But the record also shows that Chase was one of the most popular players of his time, that he revolutionized the way first base was played, that he still ranks third all-time on the Yankee stolen-base list, that he set team fielding records.

Born in 1883, Hal Chase grew up in the Santa Cruz Mountains, where his father operated a sawmill. The Yankees signed him after he attracted attention in the minor leagues.

From the time of his major-league debut April 14, 1905, Chase stood out. Most first basemen of the time stood on the bag awaiting a throw. Chase, however, played off the bag and was the first to charge bunts, tag the runner, or throw out a runner trying to advance a base. His fielding skills, solid hitting, and sparkling personality made him one of the game's most popular stars.

Dubbed Prince Hal because of his elegant bearing, Chase led AL first basemen in errors seven times, and holds the AL career first baseman's mark for errors (285). But he also did remarkable things around first base. On September 21, 1906, he tied the major-league record for putouts by a first baseman in a nine-inning game with twenty-two; two other times he had twenty-one putouts.

His reputation for consorting with gamblers always followed him around, no matter how he played. Fans would often chant "What's the odds?" when Chase was up at bat or playing first base.

The Sporting News said of him: "That he can play first base as it never was and perhaps never will be played is a well-known truth. That he will is a different matter."

In 1910, Yankee manager George Stallings accused Chase of throwing games. But Chase, using charm and guile and a powerful personality, beat the charge and Stallings. He then used his popularity to become Yankee manager for the last few games of the season. Chase's real talent, however, lay in his playing first base—not being a manager. In 1911, with Chase in charge, New York dropped from a second-place finish (88–63) in 1910 to sixth place (76–76).

Chase batted .284 in 1,059 games for the Yankees. His range in the field, soft hands, and keen eye at the plate were all assets that popular opinion claimed were diminished by his gambler's spirit.

Playing baseball until he was in his fifties, drifting in and out of the news, the then-alcoholic Harold Homer Chase died in 1947 at the age of sixty-four. "I'm the loser just like all gamblers are," he said. "I was a wise guy, a know-it-all, I guess."

JACK CHESBRO

"Happy Jack"

BORN JUNE 5, 1874, in North Adams, Massachusetts, Jack Chesbro grew up to be a stocky five-feet-nine-inch right-handed hurler whose specialty was the spitball. He said he could make the ball drop from two or three inches to more than a foot and a half.

Chesbro was one of many National League players who jumped to the new American League, signing with New York and winning twenty games for the third straight season in 1903. A member of the Highlanders from 1903 to 1909, the man they called Happy Jack because of his sunny disposition pitched the first game the Highlanders played. He lost it 3–1 to Al "the Curveless Wonder" Orth and Washington.

Chesbro's season of seasons, however, was 1904. Completing forty-eight games in fifty-one starts—both twentieth-century major-league records—winning forty-one and losing just twelve, Chesbro completed his first thirty starts and pitched 454 innings in fifty-five games. In the 454⅔ innings he pitched, his earned-run average was a stingy 1.82.

From May 14 to July 4, the workhorse hurler won fourteen straight games. From his last eight innings on June 26 through his first six innings on July 16, Chesbro spun a string of forty consecutive scoreless innings. He led the American League in wins, innings pitched, winning percentage, games pitched, and complete games. Along with Ed Walsh, Chesbro remains the only pitcher to win more than forty games in a season in the twentieth century.

The only negative for Chesbro in that sterling year took place on the season's final day. His New York team needed a sweep of a doubleheader with Boston to take over first place. Chesbro pitched the first game of the doubleheader and was going for his forty-second victory but it was not to be. With two outs in the ninth inning he threw a wild pitch that allowed the winning run to score and the Red Sox to clinch the pennant.

The wild pitch was said to haunt him all his life. Old friends seemed to always bring up the subject; new acquaintances always asked him about it. Any time a wild pitch caused a game to be lost, the Chesbro wild one that got away was brought back into the news. Never quite able to come close to what he accomplished that forty-one-victory season in 1904, Jack Chesbro was released by New York during the 1909 season.

ROGER CLEMENS

"I enjoy representing New York City from the point of view of the history, the tradition, the pride that goes with it."

HE CAME TO the Yankees from Toronto in a trade that involved David Wells on February 18, 1999. And although Roger Clemens made his major-league debut with the Red Sox way back on May 15, 1984, it seemed, given his personality and skills, he was always destined to be a New York Yankee.

Before every start he made at the stadium, Roger Clemens would wipe the sweat from his brow when exiting the bullpen and gently touch the head of Babe Ruth while passing his monument. The ritual, he explained, helped him connect with the glory of Yankee times past.

At six feet four inches and 220 pounds, an imposing figure on the mound, Clemens has a pitching repertoire that includes a nearly unhittable forkball, a four-seam fastball, and a slider. He also has never been shy about throwing his ninety-five-mile-per-hour fastball inside.

Throwing inside has not made him Mr. Popularity with many opposing players, fans, and the press. But like Frank Sinatra, Clemens has done it his way.

Before coming to New York, Clemens had won five Cy Young Awards but never a World Series. Earning his first World Series ring in 1999, Clemens in the 2000 American League Championship Series hurled one of his most memorable games—a one-hit, fifteen-strikeout complete-game shutout at Seattle, the first complete-game one-hitter in LCS history.

A week later, in game two of the World Series, Clemens whiffed nine Mets in eight innings and won the game. Yet for all that, what most remember about Clemens in that series was his first-inning confrontation with Mike Piazza. Clemens shattered the Met catcher's bat with an inside pitch and then threw a piece of the shattered bat at Piazza. Both benches cleared, but calmer personalities prevailed. Vilified in the press, Clemens was fined $50,000 for "throwing" that piece of bat. Most agreed with the vilification and the fine.

But for those who admire him and even those who can't abide him, there is no denying that Roger Clemens is a baseball legend, a walking record book, a player who personifies the glory of the Yankee present.

On April 2, 2001, the Rocket became the American League strikeout king, passing Walter Johnson's mark in the Yankee season opener. In 2001, he set a Yankee record with his fifteenth consecutive win, breaking the previous record of fourteen set in 1904 by Jack Chesbro, matched in 1961 by Whitey Ford. Clemens also became only the second pitcher in major-league baseball history to begin the season with nineteen wins in his first twenty decisions.

"Rocket is remarkable," Joe Torre said. "Nineteen and one is one thing, thirty-nine years old is another thing. To still be the power pitcher, the dominant pitcher that he is, is remarkable."

In 2001, he led New York to their fourth consecutive AL pennant, posting a 20–3 record, fanning 213, winding up the season with 280 career wins. On November 15, 2001, Roger Clemens won his record sixth Cy Young Award, a major league record. At the age of thirty-nine, he became the third-oldest recipient of that honor.

As a youngster, the Rocket idolized all-time strikeout king Nolan Ryan. But William Roger Clemens could never have dreamed that long ago May 15, 1984, when he made his debut with the Boston Red Sox, what the fates had in store for him—a to-be Hall of Famer and Yankee immortal.

JERRY COLEMAN

*"The Yankees were not our team,
they were our religion."*

HALL OF FAMER Frankie Frisch thought so much of second baseman Jerry Coleman he claimed the handsome Californian would one day join him in

Jerry Coleman

Cooperstown. Injuries and two different tours of military duty denied Coleman that honor, but he still ranks in the top echelon of infielders ever to wear pinstripes.

Gerald Francis Coleman was born on September 14, 1924, in San Jose, California. Baseball was his life all through his childhood. In 1942, Coleman was signed by the Yankees and sent to Class D Pony League with the Wellsville Yankees. World War II, however, interrupted his budding career. He flew fifty-seven bombing missions in the Solomon Islands, not returning to his baseball career until 1948.

"Spring training of 1948," Coleman said, "I was in Florida trying to make the Yankees. I was the last man cut. I played for the Newark Bears in the International League and came up to the Yankees at the end of the season. I didn't even think I would be brought up. I'd had a poor season at Newark.

"My first major-league game was April 20, 1949. We were playing the Senators. The first batter hit a ground ball to me and it went right through my legs. The next guy up was Sherry Robertson. He hit a one-hop shot at me. I caught it, turned it into a double play and the day was saved.

"The way we were indoctrinated, the Yankees were not our team, they were our religion. That was what we lived for. It wasn't money then, it was winning or losing. If you came in second place, you lost. It was the glory of winning and the ring."

An All Star in 1950 and that year's World Series MVP, Coleman experienced the glory of being on six Yankee pennant-winning teams and batting .275 in half a dozen World Series.

The biggest hit of his career came on October 2, 1949, the last day of the season, Yankees versus Red Sox. The winner would be the American League pennant winner. Going into the eighth inning, the Yankees clung to a 1–0 lead. A four-run eighth inning put the game away for the Yankees—the key hit was Coleman's bases-loaded single.

The sure-handed Coleman was the regular second baseman from his rookie season in 1949, and he led AL second basemen in fielding through 1951. His 137 double plays in 1950 set a Yankee record for second basemen.

When the Korean War broke out, the gentlemanly Coleman went back into military service and missed the 1952 and 1953 baseball seasons. He flew 120 missions and won two distinguished flying crosses.

Jerry Coleman played nine seasons for the Yankees, was in 723 games and had a .263 career batting average. This true American hero, who gave some of the best years of his life in service of his country, could have had much grander career stats had it not been for military service in two wars. He was a class act all the way.

EARLE COMBS

*"I thought the Hall of Fame was for superstars,
not just average players like me."*

OUT OF PEBWORTH, Kentucky, gifted with a great eye and exceptional speed, Earle B. Combs was the table setter, the leadoff batter for the terrific Yankee teams of the 1920s and early 1930s. Averaging almost two hundred hits and seventy walks a season during his prime, the quiet center fielder compiled a .325 career batting average in a dozen Yankee seasons.

Earle Combs

The triple was his specialty. He hit three in a 1927 game, led the American League in triples three times, and collected 154 in his career. A deft bunter as well, Combs batted in the lineup ahead of Babe Ruth and Lou Gehrig. His on-base career percentage was .397.

The Yankees purchased his contract for $50,000 from Louisville in the minors, where he was a great base stealer. His nickname then was Mail Carrier. Yankee manager Miller Huggins told him: "Up here, we'll call you 'the waiter' "–a reference to his waiting for Ruth or Gehrig or Meusel to hit one out.

Combs made his debut with the Yankees on April 16, 1924, hitting .400 in his first twenty-four games before fracturing his ankle and missing the rest of the season. He came back to hit .342 with 203 hits and 117 runs scored for the 1925 Yankees, a seventh-place team.

After slipping to .299 in 1926, the former one-room-schoolhouse teacher batted over .300 for the next eight seasons. In 1927, Combs led the American League in hits with 231 and batted .356. His adoring fans bought him a gold watch.

Combs was a churchgoer, a nonsmoker and nondrinker who never cursed. He was a graceful and fleet performer. A left-handed hitter, Combs batted .325 lifetime; nine times he batted well over .300. He especially excelled during World Series games, hitting .357 in 1926, .313 in 1927, and .375 in 1932. He had a twenty-nine-game hitting streak in 1931.

Midway through the 1934 season, "the Kentucky Colonel" smashed into the wall while chasing a fly ball at Sportsman's Park in St. Louis, fracturing his skull. After that, he was never the same player again. His final Yankee season was 1935, when he batted .282 in eighty-nine games.

In a ritual that has been repeated many times by many different players in Yankee history, Combs instructed his replacement, rookie Joe DiMaggio, in all the nuances of Yankee Stadium outfield play.

Inducted into the Hall of Fame in 1970, Combs said: "I thought the Hall of Fame was for superstars, not just average players like me." Always self-effacing, the Kentucky Colonel was anything but average.

FRANK CROSETTI

"The Crow"

A FINE FIELDING shortstop who anchored the Yankee infield for almost seventeen seasons, Frank Crosetti was on nine pennant-winning and eight world-championship-winning teams. He came to the Yankees on April 12, 1932, replacing Lyn Lary as the regular shortstop. He stayed until 1968 as player and coach–thirty-seven straight seasons in a Yankee uniform, a team record.

Listed at five feet ten and 165 pounds, exaggerated stats, Crosetti was much stronger than he looked. He even managed to surprise many an opposing

(L to R): Johnny Neun, Frank Crosetti, Casey Stengel, Jim Turner, and Bill Dickey

pitcher with his power. Four times he had seasons with double-digit home-run totals.

The San Francisco native was an All Star in 1936 and 1939. In 1938 and 1939 he led AL shortstops in putouts and double plays. He topped the league with twenty-seven stolen bases in 1938, and his 757 plate appearances that year set a major-league record for a 154-game season. Eight times he led the American League in being hit by pitches. The man they called the Crow was one of the game's great sign stealers and a master of the "hidden-ball trick" (when the infielder hides the ball in his glove, instead of returning it to the pitcher he tags out unsuspecting runners strolling off base).

After retiring as a player in 1948, Crosetti remained on the scene as the Yankee third-base coach for twenty years, and participated in fifteen more World Series. "He was very basic and down to earth, consistency was everything," Jerry Coleman said.

On the scene for 122 series games, Crosetti received so many World Series rings that he tired of getting them. "So he would take cameras and shotguns in their place," former Yankee third baseman Andy Carey recalled. "If he had kept all the rings he would have had a small fortune."

BILL DICKEY

"A catcher must want to catch."

ONE OF THE top catchers in baseball history, an eleven-time All Star, Bill Dickey has records that grab your attention. Eleven times he batted over .300. In 1936, he hit a lofty .362, the highest mark for a catcher in the twentieth century. His lifetime batting average was .313. He had 202 career home runs. In sixty-three hundred at bats, he struck out only 289 times.

In 1928, Dickey joined the Yankees and was straining to impress manager Miller Huggins with his home-run swing. Huggins snapped at him: "Stop unbuttoning your shirt on every pitch. We pay one player here for hitting home runs, and that's Babe Ruth. So choke the bat and drill the ball."

Being a Yankee, drilling the ball, and being as great a catcher as he could be–these things defined Dickey. "A catcher must want to catch," Dickey once said. And Dickey did want to catch. He never played a single game at another position. The right-handed-throwing and left-handed-batting backstop played his entire seventeen-season career as a Yankee. He set a major-league record by catching one hundred or more games for thirteen straight years.

An expert handler of pitchers with a highly accurate throwing arm, Dickey three times led American League catchers in assists and fielding, five times in putouts. He did not allow a passed ball in 125 games behind the plate, an American League record.

The Hall of Famer played in eight World Series, in thirty-eight World Series games. As player, and as coach from 1947 to 1957, Dickey was part of eighteen pennant-winning Yankee teams.

JOE DIMAGGIO

"I'd like to thank the good Lord
for making me a Yankee."

"THERE WAS AN aura about him," Phil Rizzuto said.

"Joe didn't sweat," veteran sportswriter Red Foley said, "he perspired."

He was born Giuseppe Paolo DiMaggio on November 25, 1914, in Martinez, California, one of nine children of Rosalie and Giuseppe DiMaggio, a crab fisherman and émigré from Sicily. It was all planned for Joe to become a fisherman like his father.

But his real passion was playing baseball, a game his father called "a bum's game." On the sandlots of San Francisco, the young DiMaggio developed baseball skills by hitting balls with a broken oar from a fishing boat. The kids he played with called him Long Legs, in Italian. He was always tall for his age, and skilled in baseball through high school.

With the San Francisco Seals of the Pacific Coast League in 1933, DiMag hit safely in sixty-one straight games. The next year, playing shortstop, he batted .341, but injured his knee. Yankee scouts Joe Devine and Bill Essick downplayed the injury in their reports to general manager Ed Barrow. "Don't back off because of the kid's knee," Essick recommended. "He'll be all right."

"Getting him," George Weiss said on many occasions, "was the greatest thing I ever did for the Yankees." The deal contained the clause that DiMaggio be allowed to play one more season for the Seals. And did he ever play! That last season with the Seals, DiMaggio batted .398, recorded 270 hits, and drove in 154 runs.

Joe DiMaggio being greeted by his teammates at the dugout after homering

In 1936, permission was granted for DiMag to drive cross-country with fellow San Franciscans Tony Lazzeri and Frank Crosetti to the Yankee spring-training camp in Florida. Lazzeri turned to DiMaggio after driving most of their first day of travel and asked: "Would you like to take over and drive?"

"I don't drive." It was reported that those were the only words uttered by DiMag in that three-day cross-country trek.

"Joe DiMaggio was a guy who didn't graduate from high school," noted second baseman Jerry Coleman. "He went to about the tenth grade. He was totally insecure, and consequently his quietness came from his saying nothing rather than saying something that would make him look bad."

On March 2, 1936, DiMaggio reported to spring training. Red Ruffing greeted him with, "So you're the great DiMaggio?"

He played in his first major-league game on May 3, 1936, at Yankee Stadium against the St. Louis Browns. In his first time at bat, he hit the second pitch into left field for a single. His next time up he had another single, and then a triple to left field. Joe DiMaggio played 138 games in his rookie season, hit .323, with twenty-nine home runs and 125 runs batted in.

He would step into the batter's box and stub his right toe into the dirt in back of his left heel. It was almost a dance step. His feet were spaced approximately four feet apart, with the weight of his frame on his left leg. Erect, almost in a military position, Joe Dee would hold his bat at the end and poise it on his right shoulder—a rifle at the ready. He would peer at the pitcher from deep in the batter's box with a stance that almost crowded the plate. He was ready.

"DiMag held the bat back, and didn't stride very much, maybe four or five inches," noted former Dodger outfielder Monte Irvin. "I watched that. I became a pretty good hitter because I watched Joe. In later years I told him that I copied him."

In DiMaggio's first four seasons (1936–1939), the Yankees not only won four straight World Series but lost only three series games.

"Joe was the complete player in everything he did," said his former manager, Joe McCarthy. "They'd hit the ball to center field and Joe would stretch out those long legs of his and run the ball down. He never made a mistake on the bases and in Yankee Stadium, a tough park for a right-hander, he was a great hitter, one of the best."

As determined as he was about not making mistakes on the ballfield, Joe DiMaggio was also fiercely concerned about his public image. Being silly in public was not for him. His shoes were always shined, all his buttons were always buttoned, his impeccably tailored clothes fit seamlessly. DiMaggio led the major leagues in room service. On road trips, no one ate alone in his hotel room as often as he did. It all fit DiMaggio's personality, which seemed placid, disciplined, calm.

Only those in the Yankee clubhouse saw the legs scraped and raw from hard slides or diving catches. Only those in the clubhouse saw him sit for a half hour or more in front of his locker after the Yankees had lost or when he thought he had played beneath his own exceptionally high standards.

In 1941, the Yankee Clipper put together his season of seasons. He batted .351, paced the American League with 125 RBIs, hit thirty home runs and struck out just thirteen times. But the centerpiece of that marvelous season was DiMaggio's fifty-six-game hitting streak, a feat that led to his winning the MVP award, narrowly edging out Ted Williams, who batted .406.

Military service and injuries limited DiMaggio to just thirteen years in pinstripes, but in that time the Yankees won ten pennants and nine world championships.

On Joe DiMaggio Day in 1949, the Yankee Clipper said: "When I was in San Francisco, Lefty O'Doul told me, 'Joe, don't let the big city scare you. New York is the friendliest town in the world.' This day proves it. I want to thank my fans, my friends, my manager, Casey Stengel; my teammates, the gamest, fightingest bunch of guys that ever lived. And I want to thank the good Lord for making me a Yankee."

During the course of his thirteen-year Yankee career, DiMaggio won three MVP awards, two batting titles, was named to the All-Star team every season he played, slammed 361 homers, was struck out just 369 times, averaged 118 RBIs a season and had a .325 lifetime batting average. The Yankee Clipper homered once every 18.9 at bats, his homer-to-hit ratio was 1 to 6.13. He won home-run titles eleven years apart, 1937 and 1948, and slugging-percentage titles thirteen years apart, 1937 and 1950.

"Those statistics," teammate Eddie Lopat said, "don't even tell half the story. What he meant to the Yankees, you'll never find in the statistics. He was the real leader of our team. He was the best."

In 1951, the man they called the Yankee Clipper retired at age thirty-six. Management attempted to get him to perform in pinstripes for one more season, but he had too much pride, and too much pain.

"I no longer have it," DiMaggio said. "I can no longer produce for my club, my manager, my teammates and my fans. It has become a chore for me to play. . . . When baseball is no longer fun, it's no longer a game."

Joseph Paul DiMaggio will always be remembered as a player who moved about in the vast center field of Yankee Stadium with a poetical grace. He was one who played when he was fatigued, when he was hurt, when it mattered a great deal, and when it didn't matter at all. "I was out there to play and give it all I had all the time," he said.

"Joe could do more things just a little better than others," former Yankee pitcher Jim Turner recalled. "He was a superb athlete. So graceful, both at bat and in the field. It would be hard to match him for genuine dignity. He probably was the greatest team player in the history of the game."

Elected to the Hall of Fame in 1955, Joe DiMaggio passed away on March 8, 1999, at age eighty-four.

GIFTS
Presented to Joe DiMaggio
on His Day at Yankee Stadium
October 1, 1949

Cadillac automobile, Dodge auto for his mother, Cris-Craft boat, Longine Baro Thermo calendar watch, Waltham watch chain knife, golf cuff links, gold belt buckle, 14-karat gold cufflinks and tie pin, 51" loving cup trophy, Admiral television set, Dumont television set, deer rifle, bronze plaque, $100 fedora hat, golf bag, 25 volumes of Joe DiMaggio Capitol records for Yankee Juniors, set of Lionel trains for Joe Jr., driving and sun glasses for Yankee Juniors, 500 Joe DiMaggio shirts in Joe's name to Yankee Juniors, oil painting of Joe DiMaggio, carpeting for his living room in Amsterdam, NY, a Westinghouse toaster, a 14-karat gold money clip, open house privileges at hotels Concourse Plaza and Martinique in the Bronx (these hotels also provided a four-year college scholarship for a boy of Joe's selection), 300 quarts of Cardini ice cream for any institution designated by Joe, a statuette neckerchief and clip from the Boy Scouts of America, a case of shoestring potatoes, a case of Ventura County oranges, a sack of walnuts, a case of lemonade and frozen lima beans, a hand-painted tie, sterling silver rosary beads for Joe Jr., a cocker spaniel from the American Spaniel Club, taxi service for 300 fans from Newark ("This ride is on Joe D.") from the Brown and White Cab Company of Newark, NJ.

JOE DUGAN

"For five hundred dollars you can take the whole family."

ANTHONY DUGAN WAS born on May 12, 1897, in Mahanoy City, Pennsylvania. He went to Holy Cross College and was playing ball there when he came to the attention of Connie Mack, owner of the Philadelphia Athletics.

A $500 bonus was offered to Dugan's father for his son to sign on with Philadelphia. "My father looked at the money," Dugan recalled. "Then he glanced at my seven brothers and sisters. He couldn't contain himself. 'For five hundred dollars you can take the whole family.' "

The tall, rangy infielder went directly from the campus of Holy Cross to the Athletics in 1917. Playing shortstop his first three seasons, he went on to become one of the finest all-around third basemen of his era.

In January of 1922, Dugan was part of a three-team trade that sent him to the Red Sox. Then in late July of the same year Joe Dugan unexpectedly became a New York Yankee. It was another in a series of deals that year that did in Boston and helped create the Yankee dynasty. The controversial trade, picking up a top player made in the heat of a pennant race caused an uproar. It helped bring about the creation of the June 15 trading deadline the following year.

Third base had been the only weak position on the 1922 Yankees. With Dugan now on board, the position—and the team—was solidified. The Yanks would go on to win the American League pennant that year, although they would ultimately lose the World Series to the Giants. In seven Yankee seasons, Dugan batted .286, and performed admirably in five World Series, including posting a .333 average in the 1926 Fall Classic.

Dugan twice led the league in fielding as a Yankee. He had a powerful throwing arm, and agility and ability with a snap throw made him an expert handler of bunts. In 1924, Dugan set a major-league record for third basemen with four unassisted double plays.

One of Babe Ruth's best friends on the Yankees, the lively infielder was famous for the line "Born? Hell, Babe Ruth wasn't born, he fell from a tree." Dugan didn't fall from any tree, but he was able to swing with the best of them, Ruth included.

WHITEY FORD

*"I came here in 1950 and was wearing
fifty-dollar suits. And I'm leaving wearing
two-hundred-dollar suits, and I'm gettin'
'em for eighty dollars. So I guess I'm doing
all right."*

EDWARD "WHITEY" FORD was born in New York City ten days before Halloween, 1928. Yankee scout Paul Krichell spotted the teenager playing first base at a tryout in 1946 and signed him to a minor league contract, switching his position to pitcher. Krichell said, "I never saw a kid with a curveball like his. It just came natural to him."

As the story goes, Casey Stengel received a phone call telling him that his best chance of winning the pennant was to bring up Whitey Ford from the minors. Casey always insisted that it was Ford who made the call.

Brought up to the Yankees in June 1950, Ford won his first nine decisions on his way to becoming the "Chairman of the Board," the backbone of the Yankee powerhouse teams of the 1950s and 1960s. With him on the scene, the Yankees won eleven pennants and seven World Series.

"I don't care what the situation was," his buddy Mickey Mantle said, "how high the stakes were—the bases could be loaded and the pennant riding on every pitch. It never bothered Whitey. He pitched his game. Cool. Crafty. Nerves of steel."

Whitey Ford with $2 bill

A stylish southpaw and a gifted all-around athlete, Ford rapped out 177 major-league hits. But it was what he did on the mound that the Yankees paid him for. On the mound he was into every game, every pitch that he threw at different speeds to different locations through 3,170 career innings.

He posted a 236–106 lifetime record, winning 69 percent of his games, with a career ERA of 2.75. He paced the American League in victories three times, in ERA and shutouts twice. He holds many World Series records, including ten wins, thirty-three consecutive scoreless innings, and ninety-four strikeouts. There were forty-five career shutouts, eight of them 1–0 victories. Pressure was what Ford thrived on.

"Whitey didn't begin cheating until late in his career," former American League umpire Bill

Valentine recalled. It was said Ford used his wedding ring and belt buckle to gouge the baseball. "Elston Howard would make believe he had lost his balance and would go down in the dirt," Valentine said. "He would scratch up or muddy up the ball for Ford."

"I didn't cheat when I won the twenty-five games in 1961," Ford said. "I don't want anybody to get any ideas and take my Cy Young Award away. And I didn't cheat in 1963 when I won twenty-four games. Well, maybe a little."

On May 30, 1967, Edward Charles "Whitey" Ford called it a career after sixteen seasons in pinstripes and a franchise record of 236 wins. His resume shines: all-time Yankees leader in wins, innings pitched, strikeouts and shutouts. Ford won the Cy Young Award in 1961 and had a .690 career winning percentage, best ever for pitchers with at least two hundred wins. In 1974, Ford was admitted to the Baseball Hall of Fame.

LOU GEHRIG

*"I consider myself the luckiest man
on the face of the earth."*

THEY CALLED HIM Larrupin' Lou, Iron Horse, Biscuit Pants, Columbia Lou, and Buster. But whatever they called him, he *was*, above all, "the Pride of the Yankees."

Born Heinrich Ludwig Gehrig II on June 19, 1903, in New York City to poor German immigrants, he was the only one of four children to survive infancy.

Labeled "the Babe Ruth of the schoolyards" after hitting a tremendous ninth-inning grand-slam home run over the right-field fence for his Commerce High School team in a special "national championship" game at Wrigley Field in Chicago, Gehrig then became a star at Columbia University.

"I did not go there to look at Gehrig," Yankee scout Paul Krichell said. "I did not even know what position he played, but he played in the outfield against Rutgers and socked a couple of balls a mile. I sat up and took notice. I saw a tremendous youth, with powerful arms and terrific legs. I said, here is a kid who can't miss."

Lou Gehrig

Despite his mother's protestations, Gehrig signed with the Yankees for a $1,500 bonus. After brief minor-league stints in 1923 and 1924, Gehrig came to stay with the Yankees in 1925, batting .295 in 126 games his first full season.

When Lou Gehrig stepped into the batter's box as a pinch hitter on June 1, 1925, for shortstop Pee-Wee Wanninger, it began a string of fifteen seasons of Yankee box scores with the name Gehrig always in the lineup.

In 1927, his second full season with the Yankees, he was voted the Most Valuable Player in the American League. His .363 average in 1934 gave Gehrig the batting championship. There were thirteen straight seasons of 100 RBIs, seven seasons of more than 150 RBIs. Gehrig's power came from his big shoulders, broad back, and powerful thighs.

A two-time MVP, a three-time home-run king, a five-time RBI champ, Gehrig led the American League in batting average just once—with a .363 average in 1934, when he became the first Yankee to win the Triple Crown. Three times, however, he batted higher than .363, contributing to his .340 career batting average.

Among his records are: 184 RBIs in 1931, an American League record, and twenty-three career grand slams, a major-league record. On June 3, 1932, he became the first modern-day player to hit four home runs in a game. In his thirteen full seasons, Gehrig averaged 147 runs batted in. He hammered 493 career home runs—73 were three-run homers, 166 were two-run homers. Gehrig homered once every 16.2 at bats. His home-run-to-hit ratio was 1 to 5.51.

There are estimates that he earned $361,500 in salary from the Yankees. Playing in seven World Series pushed the total income above $400,000. Gehrig received $3,750 in his first season, $6,500 in his second year. This advanced $1,000 in 1927. For the next five years he received $25,000 and then he dropped to $23,000 for 1933 and 1934, after which he received $31,000 in 1935 and 1936, $36,750 in 1937, $39,000 in 1938 and $35,000 for 1939, a season when he played only eight games.

He was worth every penny as he was a major part of seven pennant winners and six world champions.

In one of the bittersweet moments of baseball, on May 2, 1939, Wally Pipp, whose place Gehrig had taken those long years ago, came to Tiger Stadium to watch a Tigers-Yankees game. On that day, an ailing Gehrig ended his 2,130-consecutive-games streak by taking himself out of the lineup. Positioned near home plate, the Iron Horse was a mere presenter of the lineup card.

The great Gehrig would languish a while like a bent oak, still the captain, still the Pride of the Yankees, still the bringer of the lineup card out to umpires before each game.

MOVIE:
PRIDE OF THE YANKEES

Nominated for eleven Academy Awards, Pride of the Yankees *is still regarded as one of the finest baseball movies ever made. Gary Cooper portrayed Lou Gehrig. The film features several of Gehrig's real-life teammates playing themselves, including Bill Dickey, Bob Meusel, Mark Koenig and, of course, Babe Ruth.*

On June 19, 1939, the day of his thirty-sixth birthday, Lou Gehrig left the Mayo Clinic with a sealed envelope. Inside was a letter: "Mr. Gehrig is suffering from amyotrophic lateral sclerosis. This type of illness involves the motor pathways and cells of the central nervous system and in lay terms is known as a form of infantile paralysis. The nature of this trouble makes it such that Mr. Gehrig will be unable to continue his active participation as a baseball player."

In December 1939, the Baseball Hall of Fame waived the mandatory five-year waiting period for Lou Gehrig and inducted him. On June 2, 1941, exactly sixteen years to the day that he replaced Wally Pipp at first base, Gehrig passed away. On the Fourth of July 1941, a monument was erected in center field at Yankee Stadium:

HENRY LOUIS GEHRIG

June 19, 1903–June 2, 1941

A MAN, A GENTLEMAN, AND A GREAT BALLPLAYER WHOSE AMAZING RECORD OF 2,130 CONSECUTIVE GAMES SHOULD STAND FOR ALL TIME. THIS MEMORIAL IS A TRIBUTE FROM THE YANKEE PLAYERS TO THEIR BELOVED CAPTAIN AND TEAMMATE

LEFTY GOMEZ

"I'd rather be lucky than good."

THE LICENSE PLATE on his car read "GOOF." He was known as El Goofo, Goofy, Singular Señor, the Happy Hidalgo, Yankee Doodle Zany, Gay Castillian, and the Gay Caballero. He was a parade of one-liners, quick quips, self-deprecating humor, and wild antics. But all kidding aside, Vernon Louis Gomez of Mexican descent out of Rodeo, California, was one hell of a pitcher.

The Yankees purchased his contract from the Pacific Coast League San Francisco Seals in 1929 for $35,000. Manager Joe McCarthy switched Gomez from his sidearm style to a straight overhand delivery, and the effort resulted in Gomez becoming one of the most dominant hurlers of the 1930s.

A four-time twenty-game winner, Gomez helped the Yankees win five American League pennants and world championships. Twice, the slight six-feet-two-inch hurler with the high leg kick and blazing fastball led the league in winning percentage and in ERA, three times in strikeouts. His records include a 6–0 World Series won-lost mark—the most wins without a loss in major-league history—and five starts with three wins (1933, 1935, and 1937) in All-Star Game competition.

Gomez ranks third in wins, second in complete games, fourth in shutouts and strikeouts among all Yankee hurlers. In 1972, he was admitted into the Baseball Hall of Fame, the second Hispanic player to be inducted.

JOE GORDON

"Hitting, what is there to it? You swing and if you hit the ball, there it goes."

AT THE UNIVERSITY of Oregon, Joseph Lowell "Flash" Gordon played baseball, football, soccer, and was a star long jumper. He also played in the school orchestra. As a sophomore, he batted .418. Yankee scout Bill Essick, who signed him, wrote in his report: "At his best when it meant the most and the going was toughest."

Joe Gordon leaping for the ball

On April 18, 1938, Gordon joined the Yankees as their starting second baseman, another example of an up-and-coming star replacing an aging Yankee star. Joe Gordon for Tony Lazzeri.

Through his first four All-Star Yankee seasons Gordon averaged twenty-five home runs and 101 RBIs. In 1942, Gordon was the AL MVP, hitting .322 with 103 RBIs. The acrobatic Gordon was one of the top second basemen of his era with great range in the field and pop in his bat. He holds the American League second baseman's records for career home runs (246) and season home runs (32 in 1948).

He prided himself on his fielding. "Hitting," Gordon said, "what is there to it? You swing and if you hit the ball, there it goes. Ah, but fielding. There's rhythm, finesse, teamwork and balance."

A major player on five pennant-winning Yankee teams, Gordon was an eight-time All Star. Gordon's career was interrupted when he was called into military service, causing him to miss two seasons. When he came out in 1946, he batted a meager .210. After a thousand games and a thousand hits for the Yankees, Gordon was traded to Cleveland for Allie Reynolds.

GOOSE GOSSAGE

"Goooooose!"

OUT OF COLORADO Springs, Colorado, Richard Michael Gossage was one of the most consistent relief pitchers ever. A glowerer on the mound, always staring a batter down, Gossage's big cowboy-style mustache, wild mane of hair,

Rich "Goose" Gossage

thick stubble, and wide body made him an intimidator. The Goose also threw wicked heat that usually made him unhittable.

Signing as a free agent with the Yankees in 1978, he took over the Sparky Lyle stopper role and saved twenty-seven games, leading the late-season Yankee charge to catch Boston. It was Gossage who got the save in the one-game American League East playoff game against the Red Sox.

"Gossage was this big hulking guy who would get out of this little Toyota with pinstripes on it," recalled Irv Kaze, who was on the scene then as publicity director for the Yankees. "It seemed he unfolded as he came out of the car. He had that Fu Manchu mustache—and there he was sixty feet away with seemingly the ability to throw a ball through a wall. But he was a gentle man."

One of the best relievers in baseball in the years of the "Bronx Zoo," Gossage twice saved more than thirty games a season and was always good for a wisecrack at someone else's expense, always good for one kind of headline or another.

In 1980, Gossage led the American League in saves, but is probably remembered most for the homer he gave up to George Brett that torqued KC's surprising sweep of the Yanks in the ALCS. Brett versus Gossage was an item again in 1983 in the "pine tar" game.

"I want out," was how Gossage began one of his famous tirades. He seemed to always be starting one or ending one. "I'm sick of everything that goes on around here. I'm sick of all the negative stuff and you can take that upstairs to the fat man and tell him I said it."

The "fat man" (George Steinbrenner) heard those words and others. In 1983, Gossage's half-dozen-plus Yankee seasons ended. He left behind some splendid numbers—a 2.14 ERA, an average of almost a strikeout an inning, and a franchise record fifty-one saves in one season that would eventually be broken by Dave Righetti.

RON GUIDRY

"Winning twenty-five games in the big leagues is easy, it's losing only three games that's hard."

RONALD AMES GUIDRY pitched for the New York Yankees for thirteen seasons. But the real season to remember was 1978.

In that magical season, the man they called Louisiana Lightning won twenty-five of twenty-eight decisions for a winning percentage of .893, third best major-league record ever, posted a 1.74 ERA and set franchise records for strikeouts (248) and consecutive wins to start the season (thirteen). In that 1978 season, Guidry fanned eighteen against California on June 17. He tied Babe

Ruth's American League record for a lefty with nine shutouts. The southpaw won the Cy Young Award and finished second in MVP balloting.

Surprisingly, Guidry did not find a regular place in the Yankee rotation until 1977, when he was twenty-six years old. In 1977 and 1978, Guidry was 41–10 and led the league in ERA, pacing the Yanks to two World Series titles.

Using a wicked slider and a live fastball, Guidry went on to lead the majors in victories from 1977 through 1987 with 168, posting records of 18–8 (1979), 21–9 (1983), and 22–6 (1985). The "Gator" won five straight Gold Gloves (1982–1986).

A four-time All Star and three-time twenty-game winner, Guidry is second in franchise history in career strikeouts, fourth in wins, sixth in innings pitched, and seventh in games pitched and shutouts. His career won-lost record is a splendid 170–91.

TOMMY HENRICH

"I was always a Yankee fan."

THOMAS DAVID HENRICH was born in Massillon, Ohio, February 20, 1913. At an early age he took to playing baseball often and well.

Tommy Henrich

In April 1937, Commissioner Landis ruled Henrich a free agent after he had been illegally hidden in the Cleveland farm system. He signed with the Yankees for a reported $25,000 and debuted with New York on May 11, 1937.

Along with Joe DiMaggio and Charlie Keller, Henrich formed one of baseball's most storied outfields for the Yankees before and after WWII. Henrich played from 1937 through 1950 and was Joe DiMaggio's teammate longer than any other player.

Henrich's career batting average was .282. In 1948, he led the league in triples and runs scored, batted .308 with twenty-five homers and one hundred RBIs. In 1949, his consistent clutch hitting helped keep the injury-racked Yankees in the pennant race.

Although Henrich played in only four World Series because of injuries and three years of military service, he was a key figure in two of the most memorable series games.

He struck out with two outs in the ninth in game

four of the 1941 series, but Dodger catcher Mickey Owen couldn't hold on to the ball, allowing Henrich to safely reach first; in 1949, his ninth-inning homer off Don Newcombe in game one gave the Yankees the win and set the tone for that World Series.

Moments like those inspired Mel Allen to nickname the four-time All Star Old Reliable, after a train that ran from Cincinnati through the Yankee announcer's home state of Alabama and was always on time.

RALPH HOUK

"I'm on the players' side."

RALPH HOUK GREW up on a farm in Stull, Kansas. There was a brief stint as a Yankee farmhand at Binghamton. Then in 1942, he enlisted in the army, where he advanced from private to major in the Rangers, was at Omaha Beach on D-day, and was awarded the Silver Star, Purple Heart, and Bronze Star.

From 1947 on, Houk shuttled back and forth from the Yankees to the minors for eight seasons, getting into just eighty-one games. He was a catcher, but so was Yogi Berra. In 1955, Houk became manager of Denver in the American Association, and two years later he piloted the Bears to the Little World Series championship.

Grooming was in vogue at Denver. Houk groomed players like Tony Kubek, Ryne Duren, Ralph Terry, Johnny Blanchard, and Bobby Richardson. Yankee owner Dan Topping groomed Houk for a managerial role with the Yankees.

By 1961, Casey Stengel was out and Ralph Houk was in as Yankee manager. Houk told Mickey Mantle that it was the Mick's time to take over as leader of the Yankees. Houk switched Bobby Richardson and Clete Boyer from platoon roles into everyday players. Whitey Ford was "saved" by Casey. Houk gave the classy southpaw the ball every fourth day.

The man they called the Major was his own man, letting the Yankees play ball, always trying to say something positive about each player. He was opposed to curfews and elaborate rules.

The 1961 Yankees rolled to the pennant under Houk and racked the Reds in five games in the World Series. For the rookie manager who had been a part of the Yankee organization from the time he was nineteen years old, it was the best of times. In 1962, Houk notched his second straight pennant and world championship.

In 1963, Mantle and Maris missed a combined 186 games because of injuries. But the Yankees were pitching rich with Whitey Ford, Jim Bouton, Al Downing, and Ralph Terry. Nonetheless, the Dodgers swept the Yanks in the 1963 World Series, holding Houk's team to a puny .171 batting average. On October 22, 1963, Ralph Houk was appointed vice president and general manager of the Yankees. Yogi Berra became manager.

Johnny Keane then replaced Berra in 1965. Then in 1966 with the Yankees at 4–16, Houk fired Keane and took over for his second tour of duty as manager.

Maris, Mantle, Ford, and Howard were all past their primes. The team's top pitchers were Fritz Peterson and Mel Stottlemyre. Each won a dozen games in 1966, but Peterson also lost eleven games and Stottlemyre lost twenty. Managing just seventy wins, the Yanks finished 28½ games out in tenth place for the only time in their history. Over the next seven seasons, there was the one remarkable "throwback" season of 1970, when Houk piloted the Yankees to ninety-three wins and a second-place finish behind the powerful Baltimore Orioles. For that accomplishment he was voted the Manager of the Year.

On September 30, 1973, the final day of the Yankees fiftieth anniversary season, Ralph Houk, unhappy with the CBS ownership, resigned. In eight years as manager, he had won 944 games and lost 805.

And even though Mickey Mantle had his greatest years playing under Casey Stengel, he said that Ralph Houk was "the best manager I ever played for."

ELSTON HOWARD

*"No one in the Yankee organization
made me conscious of my color."*

"ELSTON WAS QUIET, efficient, with a quick and accurate arm," Monte Irvin said. "He paved the way for the first blacks on the Yankees."

Elston Howard was the International League's Most Valuable Player in 1954 and could have been the regular catcher for most major-league teams in 1955, but not the Yankees. Lawrence Peter Berra was in his prime.

"So Howard bided his time," Irvin said. He also had to suffer through the indignity in spring training of not being able to stay with the rest of the team at their hotel in segregated St. Petersburg; he had to be put up by a family in the black section of town. He bore up under this, too.

Casey Stengel utilized Howard from 1955 to 1957 at first base, in the outfield, and as catcher. An American League All Star nine straight seasons (1957–1965) and a two-time Gold Glove catcher, Howard batted over .300 three times.

Howard especially showed off his talents in the 1958 World Series against the Braves. In the fifth game, with the Yankees trailing three games to one, Howard, playing in left field, robbed the Braves of a hit, doubling a runner off first base. In game six he collected two hits, and in the final game drove in the run that gave the Yankees the series. He was named the World Series MVP, the first black to receive that award.

Elston Howard

In 1961, new manager Ralph Houk moved the aging Yogi Berra to left field. It created the opportunity for Howard to finally be the everyday Yankee catcher. He batted a career-high .348 with twenty-one homers. In 1962, he again hit twenty-one homers, upping his RBI total to ninety-one.

Mickey Mantle and Roger Maris missed playing time in 1963 with injuries; Howard often batted cleanup, taking up the slack as team leader, hitting .287 with a career-high twenty-eight home runs. He won the 1963 American League MVP award.

In 1964, he won his second Gold Glove, and led American League catchers with a .998 fielding mark as the Yankees won their fifth straight pennant.

An exceptional defensive catcher and a deft handler of pitchers, Howard pioneered the hinged catcher's mitt that led to the modern one-handed catching techniques.

Traded to Boston in 1967, Howard returned to the Yankees a couple of years later, where he was a coach for eleven years. When Howard passed away in 1980, Red Barber said: "The Yankees lost more class than George Steinbrenner could buy in ten years."

WAITE HOYT

"It's great to be young and a Yankee."

THE SON OF a professional minstrel, Waite Charles Hoyt threw three no-hitters at Brooklyn's Erasmus Hall High School, and at age fifteen was pitching batting practice at the Polo Grounds. When he asked for financial compensation for his labors, Giant manager John McGraw obliged him. After Hoyt's father signed the contract, he was handed a five-dollar bill and the kid hurler known as Schoolboy became one of the youngest players ever to turn professional.

After pitching in just one game for the Giants in 1918, Hoyt moved on to the Red Sox, where he developed a friendship with Babe Ruth; the two were reunited in 1921 when Hoyt was traded to the Yankees.

One of the most sophisticated players of his era, the broad-shouldered right-hander was a fixture on the Yankee pitching staff from 1921 to early 1930, winning 157 games and helping the Bronx Bombers win six pennants and three World Series.

In the 1921 World Series, he went twenty-seven innings without allowing an earned run, winning two of three decisions. In 1927, he led the American League in wins (twenty-two) and winning percentage (.759). In 1928, he was 23–7 and led the league in saves with eight.

Hoyt, who had just one losing season with the Yankees, augmented his income in unusual ways. An artist, writer, and singer, in the late 1920s he appeared in vaudeville, dancing and singing, even performing a few times at the Palace Theater in New York City. He also went into business as a mortician, and once said of his two off-season careers, "I'm knocking 'em dead on Seventh Avenue while my partner is laying 'em out up in Westchester."

In a twenty-year Hall of Fame career, Waite Hoyt won 237 games. He ranks among the Yankee all-time leaders in shutouts, complete games, winning percentage, wins, and innings pitched.

MILLER HUGGINS

*"A manager has his cards dealt to him
and he must play them."*

AT FIRST JAKE Ruppert did not want Miller Huggins to manage the Yankees. For Miller Huggins, the feeling was mutual. He viewed the American League as a step down from his days with St. Louis in the National League.

When the two first met, Ruppert looked at what he called "the worker's clothes, the cap perched oddly on Huggins's head, the smallness of the man." Truth be told, Miller Huggins was an unlikely Yankee. The Cincinnati native was five feet four and 140 pounds, a sufferer from real and imagined medical problems, aloof, and superstitious. He had a law degree but never practiced law.

The eighth manager in the franchise's sixteen-year history was in place as the 1918 season began. Miller Huggins, thirty-nine, was dwarfed by Babe Ruth and other Yankees in reputation and size. Huggins said: "New York is a hell of a town. Everywhere I go in St. Louis or Cincinnati, it's always 'Hiya, Hug.' But here in New York I can walk the length of Forty-second Street and not a soul knows me."

In his first season as Yankee manager, Huggins managed a fourth-place finish, then third-place finishes the next two seasons. In 1921, the Yankees won ninety-eight games and their first American League pennant, but lost to the Giants in the World Series.

There was another pennant in 1922, but again another loss to the Giants and no world championship. Another pennant followed in 1923, and this time, finally, a World Series victory over the Giants.

When the Yankees dropped to a seventh-place finish in 1925, Hug held sway over the retooling for 1926. The Yankees won sixteen straight games in May, wound up with ninety-one victories overall, and Huggins had another pennant winner. In 1927 they won another world championship as Huggins presided over Murderers' Row.

"Huggins was almost like a school master in the dugout," Waite Hoyt noted. "There was no goofing off. You watched the game and you kept track not only of the score and the number of outs, but of the count on the batter. At any moment Hug might ask you what the situation was."

In 1928, Miller Huggins piloted the Yankees to their third straight pennant, their sixth in eight seasons. A four-game sweep over St. Louis gave the Yanks a string of eight straight World Series game victories.

The two sweeps in the World Series and the half dozen pennants in just eight years had never before happened. The "Mite Manager" was the mighty manager. He was also self-effacing, claiming: "Great players make great managers."

The superstitious Huggins would change his seat on the bench to change the luck of the Yankees. Day in and day out throughout the 1929 season he moved about. Nothing worked. The powerful Philadelphia Athletics kept widening their lead. With each setback, the health of Huggins seemed to decline through an assortment of ailments including boils.

By the middle of August the Yankees were twenty-five games over the .500 mark, but the Athletics were forty-five games over. Huggins, wearing down from the strain of it all, was diagnosed as having severe blood poisoning caused by a carbuncle. Then on September 25, 1929, Miller James Huggins passed away at age fifty.

On May 30, 1932, the first monument ever at Yankee Stadium was dedicated to "the odd little man," in Waite Hoyt's phrase, "the greatest manager who ever lived," who moved the franchise from mediocrity to greatness. Baseball Hall of Fame admission came for Huggins in 1964.

CATFISH HUNTER

"I figured the people in there were like gods."

JAMES AUGUSTUS HUNTER was born on April 8, 1946, in Hertford, North Carolina, into a family of sharecroppers. Throwing baseballs at a hole in his father's barn door taught him the pinpoint control that enabled him to star in high school and American Legion competition. Tossing no-hitters became a part of his pitching profile and eased his path to the majors.

Given the name "Catfish" by Oakland owner Charles Finley, who thought it was colorful, Hunter had four consecutive years with at least twenty wins, four World Series wins with no losses, and a 1974 league-leading earned-run average of 2.49.

On December 13, 1974, Hunter was declared a free agent—the first shot in the free-agency revolution. He signed a $3.75 million five-year deal with the Yankees in December 1975, making him the highest-paid pitcher in baseball.

In his first season in New York, Catfish went 23–14, and managed to keep his down-home sense of humor and style. "The same crazy stuff," he said, "happens in Oakland and New York. But in Oakland there weren't as many reporters to write about it."

With Hunter on the scene, the Yankees recorded three straight pennants, 1976 through 1978. In March 1978, Hunter had been diagnosed with diabetes. He still won twelve games that year and was the winning pitcher in New York's 7–2 World Series–clinching victory over the Los Angeles Dodgers in game six.

However, the years of arm strain and the effects of diabetes finally caught up to the star hurler; in 1979, at the age of thirty-three, Hunter retired.

After retiring from baseball, Catfish went back to his roots, farming in North Carolina. In 1987, Hunter was elected to the Baseball Hall of Fame. His record included a Cy Young Award, a perfect game, and five consecutive twenty-win seasons. He played five seasons in the pressure cooker of the Bronx Zoo when he anchored most things Yankee.

But he was modest to a fault. "I didn't think I would make it," he admitted. "I figured I wasn't good enough. I figured the people in there were like gods." Hunter resisted pressure from the Yankees and Athletics and went into the Hall with neither team's insignia on his cap.

In 1998, Hunter was tragically diagnosed with ALS–also known as Lou Gehrig's Disease. On September 9, 1999, he passed away at age fifty-three.

CAPTAIN TILLINGHAST L'HOMMEDIEU HUSTON

"The Man in the Iron Hat"

CAPTAIN HUSTON WAS a big-bodied, self-made man out of Ohio who began his working career as a civil engineer in Cincinnati. A captain during the Spanish-American War, he made a fortune bringing the sewage system and harbor of Cuba into the modern age.

Together with Jacob Ruppert, Tillinghast L'Hommedieu Huston purchased the Yankees on January 11, 1915. Huston impressed everyone by peeling off 230 thousand-dollar bills–his share of the purchase price.

Players and sportswriters referred to Huston as Cap. There were others who called him the Man in the Iron Hat because of the derby hat, generally crumpled, that he always wore, which matched his crumpled suits.

But if his clothing left something to be desired, he was instrumental in having the Yankees dressed in freshly laundered uniforms day after day, having the team stay at good hotels and enjoy restful hours in railroad sleeping cars.

Owner of a thirty-thousand-acre hunting lodge in Georgia where he enjoyed entertaining friends, good food and liquor, Hutson also took pride in the estate he designed and built in the middle of the Altamaha River in Georgia. Designing things was one of his real passions. He supervised all aspects of the building of Yankee Stadium in 1922–1923, from the selection of materials to the quality and quantity of concrete used.

When World War I started, Huston served in France and rose to the rank of colonel, while Ruppert took over running the Yankees. The pair had never gotten along. Their order of importance in the New York Yankees scheme of things was underscored by job titles. Ruppert: club president; Huston: vice president.

One of the prime divisive issues between them was manager Miller Huggins, who Ruppert favored and Huston did not. A loss in the 1922 World Series made Huston determined to fire the little manager. But it was the man they called Cap who went away.

On May 21, 1923, Colonel Ruppert bought out Huston as Yankee owner for $1.5 million, giving Huston a 650 percent profit for his seven-year tenure. There was talk that Huston had plans in motion to purchase the Red Sox. It was only talk. Huston's time in baseball ended with the Ruppert buyout.

REGGIE JACKSON

"Some people call October a time of pressure.
I call it a time of character."

WHEN REGGIE JACKSON was elected to the Hall of Fame in 1993, he went in as a Yankee, even though he played just five of twenty-one seasons with the team, and even though there had once been all that bad history between him and George Steinbrenner and some of his teammates.

The Reginald Martinez Jackson story in New York began when Reggie flew in for his first meeting with Steinbrenner and was whisked from La Guardia Airport directly to the 21 restaurant. After lunch, Steinbrenner and Jackson strolled down the street on the warm November afternoon, and everywhere Jackson turned people greeted him with a smile, urging him to sign with the Yankees. There followed a Thanksgiving breakfast in Chicago, many phone calls back and forth.

Reggie Jackson and
George Steinbrenner

The deal got done—Reggie for five years and a then-record $2.96 million contract. "Steinbrenner took it upon himself to hunt me down," Jackson explained. "Several clubs offered several hundred thousand dollars more, but the reason I'm a Yankee is that George Steinbrenner outhustled everybody else." And then Jackson, never, ever shy, added that playing in New York he was sure a candy bar would be named after him.

Jackson had been a main cog pushing the A's to three consecutive titles. His Oakland teammate Darold Knowles had said of him: "There isn't enough mustard in the world to cover that hot dog." His time as a Yankee would be marked by hot-dogging and triumph.

His giant ego got him off on the wrong foot when he arrived in the Big Apple, and he never overcame that. Phrases like "the magnitude of me," his being "the straw that stirred the drink," along with the battles with manager Billy Martin and others were just part of the Reggie persona.

On the playing field, however, he did get results. Each season Jackson played for the Yankees, he was an All Star. In 1977, Jackson smashed thirty-two home runs and led the Yankees in RBIs, doubles, and slugging percentage. And it was his play that helped push New York to the World Series. In game six against the Dodgers, Jackson hit three consecutive home runs, each on the first pitch. The Yankees clinched their first World Series title since 1962.

In 1978, the Reggie Bar—in Catfish Hunter's phrase, "Open it and it tells you how good it is"—was introduced to much fanfare at Yankee Stadium on Opening Day. The sellout crowd received free samples. Reggie blasted a three-run homer to beat the Chicago White Sox, and thousands of the orange-wrapped candies were thrown out onto the field.

That 1978 season the feud between Jackson and Billy Martin worsened. Both men became a bit hoarser. But it didn't affect Jackson's offense. Hitting twenty-seven homers, Reggie led the Yankees in RBIs (ninety-seven) and slugging percentage (.477). The Yankees returned to the World Series.

In that World Series, Jackson picked up where he left off the year before. He homered in the first game to give him six round-trippers in four consecutive series games (another record), and in the sixth game to give him seven in back-to-back series (still another record). It was his two-run homer in game six that clinched a second consecutive world championship for the Yankees.

In 1980, Jackson belted forty-one homers, notched 111 RBIs, and hit .300, his best offensive year as a Yankee. But the following year, in the strike-shortened 1981 season, things came apart for Reggie. He hit just .237 with fifteen homers in ninety-four games. Postseason was still a time of accomplishment for him. In eleven games he hit .400 with five home runs and fifteen RBIs.

The Yankees lost the World Series to the Dodgers and George Steinbrenner went into an apologetic monologue for the benefit of Yankee fans.

But Reggie snapped: "I don't have to apologize to anyone. I played my best." That comment more or less ended it in New York for him. On January 22, 1983, Jackson signed a five-year deal with the Angels.

Audacious, outspoken, controversial, many times unlikable—it seemed that Reggie was always opening his mouth. Sometimes it was all or nothing with him—a strikeout or a home run. He homered once every 17.5 at bats in his career and his home-run-to-hit ratio was 1 to 4.58. He was a piece of work as a player and a person.

DEREK JETER

"All I ever wanted to be was a Yankee."

IT WAS A Derek Jeter moment that will live on in replays. On October 14, 2001, with two outs in the seventh in game three of the ALCS, Oakland's Jeremy Giambi chugged home ready to tie the score. Yankee outfielder Shane

Spencer's throw bounced through the infield. Along came shortstop Derek Jeter, seemingly out of nowhere. He was about twenty feet up the first-base line. The Yankee shortstop cut off Spencer's throw and flipped the ball backhanded to Jorge Posada. Giambi was out. The play preserved Mike Mussina's 1–0 win. The crowd's roar was deafening, and FOX-TV replayed the moment again and again and again.

"The kid has great instincts," Joe Torre said. "That was obviously the play of the game."

"I guess that's the reason he's wearing so many rings," Oakland manager Art Howe said. "This kid is as good as they come. Whenever they need a big play, he's there to make it. Whenever they need a big hit, he gets it."

Derek Jeter was a kid from Kalamazoo who visited his grandmother in the summer in New Jersey. They spent many weekends in the bleachers at Yankee Stadium. Jeter told his parents that when he grew up he wanted to play shortstop for the Yankees. His junior high yearbook even dubbed him "most likely to play shortstop for the New York Yankees."

Derek Jeter

Selected sixth by the Yankees in the 1992 free-agent draft, and Minor League Player of the Year in 1994, Jeter made his Yankee debut on May 29, 1995, and his boyhood dream came true in 1996. He was the Yankees Opening Day shortstop.

Jeter's first Yankee season was also Joe Torre's first season as manager. Jeter still calls his manager Mr. Torre. Rookie of the Year in 1996, the handsome athlete showed off remarkable consistency, clutch hitting, solid and at times spectacular shortstop play, maturity and leadership skills.

He batted .324 and had nineteen home runs, eighty-four RBIs, and thirty stolen bases in 1998. In his first five seasons the Yankees won four World Series. His 996 hits (1996–2000) were the most of any major-leaguer. He became just the third Yankee with three straight two-hundred-hit seasons, joining Lou Gehrig (1927–1929) and Don Mattingly (1984–1986).

Only Joe DiMaggio and Mickey Mantle amassed more hits by age twenty-six than Jeter. Possessor of the second-largest contract in sports history, the first player to be the recipient in the same season of the MVP award in the All-Star Game and World Series, Jeter was hobbled by nagging injuries in 2001. Still, he batted .311 with 191 hits and twenty-seven stolen bases in thirty attempts.

"God," Jeter once said, "I hope I wear this jersey forever." On Opening Day in 2001, Jeter, just twenty-seven years old, signed a contract that extends through the 2010 season. The six-feet-three, 175-pound Derek Sanderson Jeter has many more milestones to reach as he adds to his luster as a Yankee legend.

WEE WILLIE KEELER

*"I keep my eyes clear and
I hit 'em where they ain't."*

AT FIVE FEET four and only 140 pounds, Willie Keeler was one of the smallest men to ever play in the major leagues. As befitting his slight size, he used the smallest bat in history, one that was thirty inches and weighed only twenty-nine ounces. During his nineteen years in the majors Keeler had a lifetime batting average of .343 and slapped out 2,947 hits.

William Henry Keeler began his career on September 30, 1892, with the New York Giants, then started for the old Baltimore Orioles and then Brooklyn. In 1903, the native Brooklynite jumped from the National League to the New York Highlanders of the American League when he was offered the highest salary in baseball at the time: $10,000.

A precise bunter and place hitter as well as a master of the "Baltimore chop" off the hardened dirt in front of home plate, Keeler choked his short bat almost halfway up, and with a quick wrist snap would punch the ball over infielders' heads.

The phrase "hit 'em where they ain't" was Keeler's simple and succinct explanation for the success of his hitting technique. His best of seven years with the Highlanders was 1904, when he batted .343, one of four .300-plus years for the team.

After he batted .304 in 1906, his production fell off. Although Keeler was offered the opportunity to manage the Highlanders in 1908, he declined. Keeler played for the Dodgers for just one season, appearing in only nineteen games before he finally retired at the end of the season in 1910. In 1939, Keeler was inducted into the Baseball Hall of Fame.

CHARLIE KELLER

"King Kong"

AT A MUSCULAR five feet ten and 190 pounds, Charlie Keller made his debut as a Yankee on April 22, 1939. With the Newark Bears, he had won the International League batting crown and Minor League Player of the Year honors in 1937. But the Yankees made him wait in line for his chance to play—there was just so much talent on the big club.

Keller played right field that 1939 season and batted .334, fifth best in the American League. The star of the 1939 World Series, the southpaw slugger paced the Yankee sweep of the Cincinnati Reds.

In game one in the bottom of the ninth with the score tied 1–1, his triple drove in the winning run. In game three, Keller banged out two two-run homers.

In game four, he homered leading off the seventh inning, getting things going for the Yankees. In the top of the tenth inning he was on first base and Frank Crosetti was on third. DiMaggio singled. Crosetti scored as the ball was fumbled in the outfield. Keller raced home and was beaten by the throw, but "King Kong" leveled catcher Ernie Lombardi, who lay stunned. DiMag also scored. That World Series was truly the "Charlie Keller Show." He batted .438, hammered three homers and drove in six runs in sixteen at bats.

Charlie Keller

In 1940, Keller's batting average dropped but his home-run production increased from eleven as a rookie to twenty-one. His 106 walks led the league and he was second in triples. Foreshadowing Reggie Jackson's antics, Keller took center stage in the World Series against the Brooklyn Dodgers by batting .389, leading his teammates in runs scored and hits.

The 1942 season may have been Keller's best. Posting career highs in runs and walks, finishing third in the AL in homers, RBIs, home-run ratio and total bases, he paced another Yankee pennant run.

Keller is ranked among the top long-ball threats in major-league history, averaging a home run every 20.5 at bats. He was a five-time All Star who helped the Yankees win six pennants and three world championships.

Unfortunately, back problems and the loss of nearly two seasons to World War II service derailed Keller's career. By age thirty, he was a part-timer. Five years later he retired and went on to become a highly successful thoroughbred horse breeder back home in Maryland.

TONY KUBEK

"Those were fun times."

ON JANUARY 25, 1966, Tony Kubek announced his retirement. A Mayo Clinic diagnosis in 1965 revealed that he had fused vertebrae in his back. He was warned that if he continued playing baseball, a collision could paralyze him.

If not for his premature retirement at the age of twenty-nine, there are many who believe Tony Kubek would be considered one of the top three shortstops in Yankee history.

The handsome athlete was signed by the Yankees in September of 1953, a month before his seventeenth birthday. In spring training of 1957, Casey Stengel took a shine to the youngster and decided to keep him with the big club that season.

The quiet, gentlemanly Kubek didn't smoke or drink. "Here's a boy who sits on the bench without opening his mouth," Casey Stengel said. "So you don't know which side he's on. But when he goes out on the field, you know."

The twenty-year-old Kubek made his Yankee debut on April 20, 1957. That year he played fifty games in the outfield, forty-one at shortstop, thirty-eight at third base, one game at second, and batted .297 in the first of nine Yankee seasons.

Named Rookie of the Year, Kubek helped the Yankees win the pennant. In the World Series against the Milwaukee Braves, playing before his hometown folks, the multitalented Kubek put on a show. His two game-three homers paced a 12–3 Yankee victory. His versatility was on display throughout the seven-game series as the strong-armed youngster started games in center field, left field, and third base.

The Yankees lost the 1957 series to the Braves but were winners against them in 1958. The all-purpose Kubek was the starting shortstop in that series.

A two-time All Star, Kubek played wherever he was needed. For eight seasons he and second baseman Bobby Richardson were one of baseball's best double-play combinations. Possessing tremendous range and sure hands, Kubek led all shortstops in total chances in 1961; in 1963, he posted the fifth best fielding percentage by a Yankee shortstop ever, .980.

Day to day, season to season, with the juggling done by Casey Stengel, Tony Kubek, number 10, sometimes didn't know where he was going to play. He played in 1,092 games for the Yankees, and wherever he played, he was always successful.

TONY LAZZERI

"Poosh 'em up."

ON AUGUST 6, 1946, the baseball world was saddened to learn of the death in San Francisco of Tony Lazzeri at age forty-two. He fell down a stairway in his home from an epileptic seizure.

The son of a blacksmith, Anthony Michael Lazzeri was born on December 6, 1903, in San Francisco. Lazzeri carried the memory of his growing-up years with him: "I was a pretty tough kid," he said. "The neighborhood wasn't one in which a boy was likely to grow up a sissy, for it was fight or get licked, and I never got licked."

Playing for the Salt Lake City Bees in the Pacific Coast League in 1925, assisted by the altitude and almost two-hundred-game schedule, Lazzeri pounded sixty home runs, drove in 222 more and scored an amazing 202 runs.

The Yankees knew he was an epileptic, but they also knew he could play ball. For $55,000 and five players, the quiet second baseman became a Yankee.

He debuted April 13, 1926. During that rookie season of 1926, he batted .275, hit eighteen home runs and drove in 114 runs.

Although Lazzeri often seemed aloof, in reality it was his epilepsy that made him almost painfully quiet. But Lazzeri's talent said it all. He was a clutch hitter with power, a deadly combo that fit the mix of six Yankee Murderers' Row pennant winners.

Lazzeri was baseball's first Italian-American superstar, a magnet for Italian fans at Yankee Stadium, who would scream out "Poosh 'em up, Tony," urging him to hit home runs.

The main right-handed power hitter on the 1927 Yankees, five times a .300 hitter, Lazzeri drove in over a hundred runs seven times. On June 3, 1932, Lazzeri hit for the cycle, capping the day with a grand-slam homer. Not that many took notice of his terrific accomplishment, for in that same game Lou Gehrig slammed four home runs. On May 24, 1936, he became the first major-leaguer to hit two grand slams in one game and set a still-standing AL record with eleven RBIs.

Tony Lazzeri appeared in six World Series in a dozen Yankee seasons and played in the very first All-Star Game. In 1991, he was admitted to the Baseball Hall of Fame.

EDDIE LOPAT

*"My main purpose was to make
a hitter off-stride."*

HE WAS BORN Edmund Walter Lopatynski. "As a kid growing up in New York City," said the man who would be known as Eddie Lopat, "I was always a Yankee fan. I wondered what made them tick."

After four seasons with the White Sox, Lopat was traded to New York before the 1948 season. It was the first trade George Weiss made.

Rookie manager Casey Stengel pitched the left-handed "Steady Eddie" between right-handed flamethrowers Allie Reynolds and Vic Raschi, making Lopat's slow stuff appear even slower.

It was said that Lopat could pitch three different ways: slow, slower and slowest. He gave fits to free-swinging batters and teams like the Indians, who he was 40–12 lifetime against.

"My main purpose," Lopat said, "was to make a hitter off-stride. I couldn't overpower hitters so I had to operate from a different angle." Frustrated hitters called him the Junk Man and other earthier phrases.

He averaged sixteen wins a year 1949 through 1953. World Series time, however, was when Lopat especially strutted his stuff. In the 1951 World Series against the Giants, Lopat pitched complete-game victories in games two and five, yielding just one earned run in eighteen innings. In five World Series, Lopat pitched fifty-two innings, won four games while losing only one, and posted a 2.60 ERA.

A spot starter in 1952 because of a sore arm, Lopat managed to open the season at 7–0, complete ten of his nineteen starts, and post a 10–5 record. In 1953, Lopat was not part of the regular rotation but still put up terrific numbers, leading the American League in ERA and going 16–4.

Consistency was Lopat's way. He won 113 games and lost 59 as a Yankee. Five straight seasons he paced Yankee pitchers in ERA while starting thirty or more games. Five years in a row his winning percentage was between .667 and .800. Not too shabby for a "Junkman."

SPARKY LYLE

"Why pitch nine innings when you can get just as famous pitching two?"

SPARKY LYLE WAS a three-time All Star, yet he never started a major-league game in a sixteen-year career. But he sure was able to do the job as a relief pitcher. In 1977, he became the first reliever to win the Cy Young Award. In a league-leading seventy-two appearances, Lyle was 13–5 with twenty-six saves and a 2.17 ERA. He added a win in the World Series as the Yankees beat the Dodgers in six games.

Albert Walter Lyle came to the Yankees from the Red Sox before the 1972 season in a one-for-one trade for first baseman Danny Cater, one of the worst trades in Boston history. Lyle led the league with thirty-five saves in 1972, recording a 1.91 ERA. There were twenty-seven saves in 1973. There was a career-low 1.66 ERA in 1974.

A wisecracking left-hander with a sizable paunch quite visible beneath his uniform, Lyle relied almost exclusively on a sensationally tough slider. His fastball and curve were above average.

"Some people say you have to be nuts to be a relief pitcher. But the truth is I was nuts before I ever became one," he said. The hyper Lyle would do anything to get a laugh—exiting from a coffin, sitting around nude, showing up at spring training with his limbs in casts.

The image of his coming into games at Yankee Stadium in that pinstriped Toyota to the accompaniment of "Pomp and Circumstance" enhanced the zany image of the man they called the Count.

On the mound, though, he was all business. In seven Yankee seasons the rubber-armed Lyle pitched in more games than any other Yankee, posting a 57–40 record with 141 saves and a 2.41 ERA. Those stats helped get the Yankees into three World Series.

George Steinbrenner's signing of relief aces Rich Gossage and Rawley Eastwick ticked Lyle off. He was traded to Texas in a ten-player deal that brought Dave Righetti to the Yankees.

JOE MCCARTHY

> *"So I eat, drink and sleep baseball*
> *twenty-four hours a day.*
> *What's wrong with that?"*

"A BALLPLAYER HAS only two hours of concentrated work every day with occasional days off," the square-jawed Joe McCarthy said. "If he cannot attend to business with the high pay and the working hours so pleasant, something is wrong with him and he ought to move on."

That statement underscored the no-playing-games-with-me approach of Hall of Famer Joseph Vincent McCarthy, who managed for two dozen winning seasons in the majors and posted a .614 winning percentage.

A minor-league player for fifteen seasons, McCarthy never played in the major leagues, but he is the winningest major-league manager of all time. Fired by the Cubs after the 1930 season, McCarthy took over as manager of the Yankees in 1931 and was on the scene until 1946.

"Marse Joe" had his own Ten Commandments of Baseball and a severe dress code. He even had the team's caps and uniforms cut larger so his Yankees would appear bigger and stronger. Players were told to shave before they came to the ballpark. "This is your job. Shave before you come to work."

Joe McCarthy, pondering

He held sway over all things from his seat in the dugout. "I never roamed the dugout," he said. "I was there seated in the middle, the command post." Arguing with umpires was not for him. "I wanted to be around to manage," he said. "I'm no good to the team if I'm not there."

"Never a day went by," Joe DiMaggio said, "when you didn't learn something from McCarthy." There were no hot dogs or peanuts

Joe McCarthy's
TEN COMMANDMENTS
for Success in the Major Leagues

1. *Nobody can become a ballplayer by walking after a ball.*

2. *You will never become a .300 hitter unless you take the bat off your shoulder.*

3. *An outfielder who throws after a runner is locking the barn door after the horse is stolen.*

4. *Keep your head up, and you may not have to keep it down.*

5. *When you start to slide, slide. He who changes his mind may have to change a good leg for a bad one.*

6. *Do not alibi on bad hops. Anybody can field the good ones.*

7. *Always run them out. You can never tell.*

8. *Do not quit.*

9. *Do not fight too much with the umpires. You cannot expect them to be as perfect as you.*

10. *A pitcher who hasn't control, hasn't anything.*

in the Yankee dugout. All players except for the starting pitcher had to show up for breakfast in jackets and ties before 8:30 A.M. For McCarthy, his only focus was the game. He permitted himself no diversions, no hobbies, no distractions.

It was McCarthy who was the first manager to separate a pitching staff into starters and relievers. In 1932, McCarthy became the first manager to win pennants in both leagues when his Yankees beat his former team, the Cubs, in the World Series.

Then came three consecutive second-place finishes—and the unkind tag of "Second-Place Joe" was put on him by writers. The phrase stuck in the craw of the manager obsessed with winning and with control.

Joe, however, had both the success and the control he craved during the 1936–1939 seasons. The Yankees, featuring power baseball, won four consecutive world championships in those years. There were pennants in 1941, 1942, and 1943. But then the Yanks dropped to third place in 1944 and fourth place in 1945. McCarthy was drinking more than ever. There was a fourth-place finish in 1945.

"He was drinking too much," Joe DiMaggio told reporters. "He wasn't eating right, and he was worried about the team because it was playing so lousy."

The team's play was lousy, and so was McCarthy's relationship with new Yankee owners Dan Topping, Del Webb, and Larry MacPhail. On May 24, 1946, thirty-five games into the season, Joseph Vincent McCarthy quit. In his sixteen years in pinstripes his teams recorded 1,460 wins, 867 losses, an astounding .627 winning percentage.

McCarthy returned to baseball in 1948 as manager of the Boston Red Sox, and over the course of his tenure there encountered some fierce battles with the Yankees.

He passed away in 1977 at age ninety.

LARRY MACPHAIL

"My heart can't take it anymore."

PART OF A group of WWI plotters that nearly succeeded in kidnapping Kaiser Wilhelm, Larry MacPhail was better known for what he did in baseball. Few executives have had a more profound effect on the game.

At Cincinnati, he introduced night baseball and commercial air travel to the major leagues. When he took over the Brooklyn Dodgers as general manager in 1938, the franchise made money for the first time since 1920. Branch Rickey succeeded him as general manager in 1942. MacPhail enlisted in the U.S. Army.

"He bought the Yankees for $3 million," his grandson Andy said, "even though he didn't have a penny, really. As he often did, he went to 21 for a drink to try to figure out what to do." He met Dan Topping, his tenant when he owned the Brooklyn Tigers football team. Topping was always interested in buying a baseball team with MacPhail. Later Bing Crosby recommended builder Del Webb, who joined in with MacPhail and Topping to become a partial owner of the Yankees.

In 1946, MacPhail quickly got to work with the Yankees, removing the flagpoles that stuck out from the stadium roof and replacing them with structures to hold hundreds of electric lights—night baseball.

He originated the Stadium Club and season box seats. Individualized dining and seating increased corporate patronage and was a harbinger of things to come throughout baseball. A brand-new clubhouse for the Yankees and a new press box for media coincided with MacPhail's transfer of the franchise office to Fifth Avenue.

MacPhail orchestrated Yankee travel by air on a regular basis. He arranged the first major-league TV contract in a time when there were but five hundred television sets in the New York area. He installed women ushers and a women's lounge at the stadium. His promotions included free nylon stockings for women, foot races and archery competitions. Under MacPhail, the Yankees became the first team to draw over two million at home in a season.

Leo Durocher said of MacPhail: "There is a thin line between genius and insanity, and in Larry's case it was sometimes so thin you could see him drifting back and forth."

In the festive Yankee clubhouse after the 1947 World Series triumph over the Dodgers, the mercurial MacPhail, cigarette in one hand, bottle of beer in the other, lashed out insults, punched a writer, and announced his resignation: "I'm through. I'm through. My heart just can't stand it anymore."

Apparently neither could his partners, Dan Topping and Del Webb. The next day they bought him out, leaving MacPhail with a $2 million profit on his investment. All season long he had feuded with his fellow owners and with players and had threatened to pack it all in. Now he had. Never again would the innovative, tempestuous MacPhail participate in the sport he loved.

But he did found a family dynasty. He and his son, Lee MacPhail, because of their remarkable executive skills, formed the first-ever father-son tandem to be elected to the Baseball Hall of Fame. His grandson Andy has served as general manager of the Minnesota Twins and Chicago Cubs.

LEE MACPHAIL

"I saw my first game in 1939.
DiMaggio hit a homer."

LELAND STANFORD MACPHAIL, Jr., was quiet, soft-spoken, and introverted, a personality that contrasted dramatically with that of his extroverted father. Beginning his baseball career as business manager at Reading in the Interstate League in 1941, Lee moved up the rungs, gaining much experience through employment in front offices of minor-league teams.

After World War II military service, MacPhail served as an executive in the far-flung Yankee farm system. Director of player personnel from 1948 through 1958, he constructed one of the strongest farm systems in baseball history. In his time the Yankees won seven World Championships in ten years.

MacPhail moved on to Baltimore as general manager from 1959 to 1965, laying the foundations for some top Orioles teams. In 1966, he returned to the Yankees as executive vice-president and GM, holding sway over a last-place team. MacPhail made some good moves, like trades for Sparky Lyle and Graig Nettles, but essentially he and the Yankees were in a holding pattern.

When George Steinbrenner took over as owner in 1973, MacPhail knew things would not be the same. He exited and went on to become American League president from 1974 to 1983. There were conflicts with Steinbrenner and Billy Martin; MacPhail suspended them for public criticism of umpires.

YANKEE STORIES
Bobby Brown

During World War II, I was in the navy and played a lot of baseball against service teams. They were comprised of professional players, so the competition was extremely good. That experience sharpened my skills.

Larry MacPhail, one of the owners of the Yankees at that time, was a colonel in the service and in San Francisco. He visited my dad and asked him what it would take for me to sign a contract with the New York Yankees. My dad was an executive with the Schenley Distilleries so he knew something about business. He told MacPhail what he thought was fair.

"Fine," MacPhail said. They shook hands and that was it.

When I got out of the navy in January 1946, I was eligible to sign a baseball contract. The Yankees not only offered me a substantial bonus, they allowed me to continue my education— I had been pre-med at Stamford when I went into the navy—while playing ball. That really swung the decision for me to sign with them.

I was assigned to the Newark Bears, the top Yankee farm team in the International League. We had a good team with Yogi Berra, Vic Raschi, Allie Clark. But it was Montreal, a Brooklyn Dodger farm team, that won the pennant. They had Jackie Robinson. He was not easy to play against and could aggravate another team. But he was a heck of a player. I think we ended up one and two in the batting race that year. Jackie hit .349. I hit .341. I was right there with history happening.

That 1946 season the Boston Red Sox had clinched the pennant and the Yankees were in second place. Yogi and I and another player named Frank Coleman drove from Newark to the stadium for a Sunday doubleheader against Philadelphia. Vic Raschi also was there. The four of us all joined the Yankees on that same day. Joe McCarthy, who had started the year as manager, resigned in mid-season. Then Bill Dickey was in charge for a while, but he didn't like it. Johnny Neun was the manager the last few weeks on an interim basis. Yogi and I played every one of the remaining ten games. Vic Raschi pitched in the regular turn.

My career was 548 games for the Yankees and also 17 World Series games. They claimed I was the hitting star in four World Series, which was a nice thing to say. In 1954, I retired from baseball to practice medicine.

He also overruled his umpires, ruling against the Yankees in the 1983 "pine tar" game.

In 1998, Lee MacPhail, Jr., a front-office executive for forty-five years, was elected to the Baseball Hall of Fame. It gave the Yankees the distinction of having the first executive father-son team in Cooperstown.

MICKEY MANTLE

*"I figure I got all the breaks. Otherwise I'd
have been in the mines."*

IN 1949, THERE were not a lot of scouts watching the semipro Baxter Springs, Kansas, Whiz Kids. But super scout Tom Greenwade of the Yankees was all over the Whiz Kids' shortstop from Commerce, Oklahoma, Mickey Mantle, named after the great catcher Mickey Cochrane.

"I now know how scout Krichell must have felt the first time he saw Lou Gehrig," Greenwade said. "Mickey possessed tremendous power from both sides of the plate, had blinding speed and a great arm."

Greenwade and Mantle's father, "Mutt," worked out a deal sitting in the scout's 1947 Oldsmobile in the parking lot during a rain delay one day. Mantle was signed for a bonus of $1,150 and a salary of $140 a month.

In two minor-league seasons, the kid they called the Commerce Comet made 102 errors. But he hit .317 in 1949 and .383 with twenty-six homers and 136 RBIs in 1950. He was clocked running from home to first base in 3.1 seconds. "You should time him going from first to second," Bill Dickey said. "That's when he's really moving."

"He was a real country boy," Whitey Ford recalled. "All shy and embarrassed. He arrived with a straw suitcase and two pairs of slacks and one blue sports jacket that probably cost about eight dollars."

"Mickey Mantle came into the 1951 Phoenix rookie camp as a young phenom," recalled Andy Carey, who at the time was also a young phenom on the scene. "He came up as a shortstop, but in this game he was playing center field and he lost the ball in the sun and fell down. There was a big scurry of scouts and trainers. They thought they lost the damn franchise."

During spring training in 1951, Casey Stengel switched Mantle to the outfield and said: "I never saw a player who had greater promise. That young fellow has me terribly confused. He should have a year in Triple A ball, but with his combination of speed and power he should win the triple batting crown every year. In fact, he should do anything he wants to do."

Only nineteen years old, Mickey Mantle made his major-league debut on April 17, 1951, playing right field with Joe DiMaggio next to him in center. It was an exciting time for Mantle, but he had difficulty adjusting to big-league

Mickey Mantle

YANKEE STORIES
Bill Valentine

I actually saw the Yankees for the first time in Detroit in 1963, my first year as an American League umpire. I called Mickey Mantle out the first time he came up on a very good pitch. He was very good about not turning around and arguing with umpires. But he could talk a lot without looking at you. He never took a strike in his life that he thought was a strike.

His next time up I called him out again. And Mantle said: "Every time one of you dagos get off the boat they hand you an umpire indicator."

I flipped my mask back. "Why, you sandlobber from Oklahoma," I said, "I'm from Little Rock, Arkansas, and if you don't think that was a strike you had better be swinging every time I am behind this plate."

After that I probably widened the plate a little bit whenever he was up. I called Mantle out four times in that game. It started an ongoing feud that lasted for about six years.

This was now late in Mantle's career and Joe Pepitone said to me: "Bill, the Mick is really going bad. Why don't you give him a break?"

I said, "This has been going on for so long, his constant remarks, let him just tell me 'Stop the feud.' "

It was late in the season, a meaningless game. Dean Chance was pitching for the Angels and Bob Rodgers was catching. Mantle came up the second game of a doubleheader. He stepped in the left side and said: "I give up, you son of a bitch."

The count went 2–2. The next pitch was a perfect pitch, just right on the knees on the outside corner. I just missed it. "Ball," I said.

Mantle straightens out, goes out of the batter's box, looks at me and says: "God, I should've given up five years ago."

pitching. Sent down on July 15 to the Yankees' Kansas City farm team, Mantle continued to struggle and toyed with the idea of quitting.

Mickey Mantle

"I thought I raised a ballplayer," his father told him. "You're nothing but a coward and a quitter." Then his father started packing his son's bags. Mantle changed his mind.

In the very next game, Mantle broke out of his slump. After forty games and fifty RBIs with Kansas City, Mantle was back with the Yankees. His 1951 rookie season numbers were respectable: .267, thirteen home runs, sixty-five RBIs.

In game two of the 1951 World Series, running down a fly ball hit by Willie Mays that ended up being caught by DiMaggio, Mantle's spikes caught in a sprinkler head covering and he tore up his right knee. The mishap foreshadowed the tough luck and injury bug that would haunt Mantle through the 2,401 games he played in his eighteen-year Yankee career.

In 1952, with DiMag retired, Mantle moved to center field. The Yankees became his team, and he became the most feared hitter on the most successful team in history. Able to run like the wind until the injuries finally had their way with his body, Mantle hit tape-measure home runs and also hit for average. He was the first power-hitting switch-hitter, the greatest switch-hitter of all time.

Mantle collected more than one hundred walks a season ten times; he scored one hundred or more runs in nine straight seasons; he won the American League home-run and slugging titles four times. He collected 2,415 hits, batted .300 or better ten times, won three MVP awards, and was on an astounding twenty All-Star teams. He scored more runs than he drove in (1,677 to 1,509), a rarity among power hitters. He pounded 536 homers.

"He was fairly amazin' in several respects," Casey Stengel noted.

"I used to limp around my neighborhood imitating him," said comic Billy Crystal. "I did my Bar Mitzvah with an Oklahoma drawl."

"He hit balls over buildings," said Stengel.

They still talk about the 565-foot blast he hit off southpaw Chuck Stobbs in Washington in 1953, the first of the tape-measure homers. A year later, he missed hitting the first ball out of Yankee Stadium by only eighteen inches—his drive off right-hander Pedro Ramos hit the top of the right-field upper-deck façade and stayed in the park.

"After I hit a home run," Mantle said, "I had a habit of running the bases with my head down. I figured the pitcher already felt bad enough without me showing him up rounding the bases."

"Even in his declining years when he would come up to bat, you would stick around to watch him because you never knew what was going to happen," said restaurateur Tracy Nieporent. "I was at the game when he hit his five hundredth home run. It was against the Orioles. I think it was Bat Day. We stood on the seats and waved the bats at him."

In his final four years (1965–1968), the Mick batted .255, .288, .245, and .237. Injuries and drinking contributed to the decline. "Falling under .300," Mantle said, "was the biggest disappointment of my career."

"Sometimes," Mantle said in retirement, "I sit in my den at home and read stories about myself. Kids used to save whole scrapbooks on me. They get tired of them and mail them to me. I'll go in there and read them, and you know what? They might as well be about Musial or DiMaggio. It's like reading about somebody else."

"When I retired," Mantle said, "I was probably an alcoholic but didn't know it. God gave me a body and the ability to play baseball and I just wasted it."

On August 13, 1995, in Dallas, Mickey Mantle died of liver cancer. He was sixty-three years old.

Mickey Mantle at bat, with Bill Fischer pitching for Kansas City

MICKEY MANTLE
HALL OF FAME SPEECH
AUGUST 12, 1974

"*Thank you very much, Commissioner. I would really like to thank you for leaving out those strikeouts. He gave all those records, but he didn't say anything about all those strikeouts. I was the world champion in striking out and everything, I'm sure. I don't know for sure, but I'm almost positive I must have had that record in the World Series, too. I broke Babe Ruth's record for all-time strikeouts. He only had, like, 1,500, I think. I ended up with 1,710. So that's one that no one will ever break probably, because, if you strike out that much, you don't get to play very long. I just lucked out.*

"*One of the reasons I'm in the Hall of Fame right now is not because of my speaking, so everybody be patient here. I know it's hot and I'll try to get through with what I gotta say real fast here. I was named after a Hall of Famer. I think this is the first time it's ever happened that a guy's ever come into the Hall of Fame that was named after one. Before I was born, my father lived and died for baseball and he named me after a Hall of Famer: Mickey Cochrane. I'm not sure if my dad knew it or not, but his real name was Gordon. I hope there's no Gordons here today, but I'm glad that he didn't name me Gordon. He had the foresight to realize that someday in baseball that left-handed hitters were going to hit against right-handed pitchers and right-handed hitters were going to hit against left-handed pitchers; and he taught me, he and his father, to switch-hit at a real young age, when I first started to learn how to play ball. And my dad always told me if I could hit both ways when I got ready to go to the major leagues, that I would have a better chance of playing. And believe it or not, the year that I came to the Yankees is when Casey started platooning everybody. So he did realize that that was going to happen someday, and it did. So I was lucky that they taught me how to switch-hit when I was young.*

"*We lived in a little town called Commerce, Oklahoma, and my mother, who is here today—I'd like to introduce her right now . . . Mom. We didn't have a lot of money or anything. She used to make my uniforms and we would buy the*

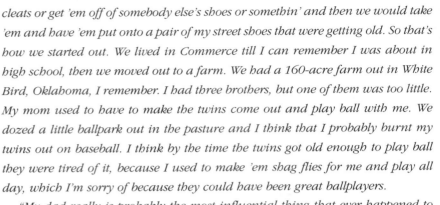

cleats or get 'em off of somebody else's shoes or somethin' and then we would take 'em and have 'em put onto a pair of my street shoes that were getting old. So that's how we started out. We lived in Commerce till I can remember I was about in high school, then we moved out to a farm. We had a 160-acre farm out in White Bird, Oklahoma, I remember. I had three brothers, but one of them was too little. My mom used to have to make the twins come out and play ball with me. We dozed a little ballpark out in the pasture and I think that I probably burnt my twins out on baseball. I think by the time the twins got old enough to play ball they were tired of it, because I used to make 'em shag flies for me and play all day, which I'm sorry of because they could have been great ballplayers.

"My dad really is probably the most influential thing that ever happened to me in my life. He loved baseball, I loved it and, like I say, he named me after a baseball player. He worked in the mines, and when he came home at night, why, he would come out and, after we milked the cows, we would go ahead and play ball till dark. I don't know how he kept doing it.

"I think the first real baseball uniform—and I'm sure it is—the most proud I ever was when I went to Baxter Springs in Kansas and I played on the Baxter Springs Whiz Kids. We had—that was the first time—I'll never forget the guy, his name was Barney Burnett, gave me a uniform and it had a BW on the cap there and it said Whiz Kids on the back. I really thought I was somethin' when I got that uniform. It was the first one my mom hadn't made for me. It was really somethin'.

"There is a man and a woman here that were really nice to me all through the years, Mr. and Mrs. Harold Youngman. I don't know if all of you have ever heard about any of my business endeavors or not, but some of 'em weren't too good. Probably the worst thing I ever did was movin' away from Mr. Youngman. We went and moved to Dallas, Texas, in 1957, but Mr. Youngman built a Holiday Inn in Joplin, Missouri, and called it Mickey Mantle's Holiday Inn. And we were doin' pretty good there, and Mr. Youngman said, 'You know, you're half of this thing, so why don't you do something for it.' So we had real good chicken there and I made up a slogan. Merlyn doesn't want me to tell this, but I'm going to tell it anyway. I made up the slogan for our chicken and I said, 'To get a better piece of chicken, you'd have to be a rooster.' And I don't know if that's what closed up our Holiday Inn or not, but we didn't do too good after that. No, actually, it was really a good deal.

"Also, in Baxter Springs, the ballpark is right by the highway, and Tom Greenwade, the Yankee scout, was coming by there one day. He saw this ball-game goin' on and I was playing in it and he stopped to watch the game. I'm making this kind of fast; it's gettin' a little hot. And I hit three home runs that

day and Greenwade, the Yankee scout, stopped and talked to me. He was actually on his way to Broken Arrow, Oklahoma, to sign another shortstop. I was playing shortstop at that time, and I hit three home runs that day. A couple of them went in the river—one right-handed and one left-handed—and he stopped and he said, 'You're not out of high school yet, so I really can't talk to you yet, but I'll be back when you get out of high school.'

"In 1949, Tom Greenwade came back to Commerce the night that I was supposed to go to my commencement exercises. He asked the principal of the school if I could go play ball. The Whiz Kids had a game that night. He took me. I hit another home run or two that night, so he signed me and I went to Independence, Kansas, Class D League, and started playing for the Yankees. I was very fortunate to play for Harry Craft. He had a great ball club there. We have one man here in the audience today who I played with in the minors, Carl Lombardi. He was on those teams, so he knows we had two of the greatest teams in minor-league baseball at that time, or any time probably, and I was very fortunate to have played with those two teams.

"I was lucky when I got out. I played at Joplin. The next year, I came to the Yankees. And I was lucky to play with Whitey Ford, Yogi Berra, Joe DiMaggio, Phil Rizzuto—who came up with me—and I appreciate it. He's been a great friend all the way through for me. Lots of times I've teased Whitey about how I could have played five more years if it hadn't been for him, but, believe me, when Ralph Houk used to say that I was the leader of the Yankees, he was just kiddin' everybody. Our real leader was Whitey Ford all the time. I'm sure that everybody will tell you that.

"Casey Stengel's here in the Hall of Fame already and, outside of my dad, I would say that probably Casey is the man who is most responsible for me standing right here today. The first thing he did was to take me off of shortstop and get me out in the outfield where I wouldn't have to handle so many balls.

"At this time I'd like to introduce my family. I introduced my mother. Merlyn, my wife, we've been married twenty-two years. That's a record where I come from. Mickey, my oldest boy, David, Billy and Danny. That's my family that I've been with for so long.

"I listened to Mr. Terry make a talk last night just for the Hall of Famers, and he said that he hoped we would come back, and I just hope that Whitey and I can live up to the expectation and what these here guys stand for. I'm sure we're going to try to. I just would—before I leave—would like to thank everybody for coming up here. It's been a great day for all of us and I appreciate it very much."

ROGER MARIS

"I never wanted all this hoopla."

THE STORY OF Roger Eugene Maras (his birth name) began on September 10, 1934, in Hibbing, Minnesota. The son of first-generation Croatian Americans, Rudy and Corrine Maras, Roger's grandfather Steve Maras had emigrated to the United States from Croatia around 1910.

In 1939, Roger's father moved his family to Grand Forks, North Dakota, and then to Fargo, where the young Maras would go on to excell in baseball, basketball, and football in high school.

Maras was recruited to play football at Oklahoma, but he instead signed with the Cleveland Indians and played with Fargo-Moorhead of the Northern League. In 1955, convinced that a spelling change would make it easier for baseball fans to pronounce his name, Roger Maras changed his surname to Maris. Another reason for the change was the memory of his boyhood, when mean-spirited kids called him "Mar-Ass."

After four seasons in the minors, Maris joined the Indians in 1957. In June 1958, he was traded to the Kansas City Athletics. A year later he hit thirty-nine home runs for KC, and was traded in December 1959 to New York along with two other players for four Yankees, including Hank Bauer and Don Larsen.

The six-feet, 197-pound outfielder thought of himself as the odd man out in Yankee pinstripes, but he fit right in as a powerful left-handed pull hitter with the invitingly close right-field stands at Yankee Stadium.

Maris made his Yankee debut on April 19, 1960, on Opening Day in Fenway Park against Boston, and smashed two home runs, went 4 for 5, and had four RBIs. That 1960 season he belted thirty-nine homers, one less than league-leader Mickey Mantle, and topped the AL with 112 RBIs, a .581 slugging percentage, and was awarded his only Gold Glove. He also won the first of two straight MVP awards.

Maris began the 1961 season hitting only one homer in April. But by the end of August, batting third in the powerful Yankee lineup, he had 50 round-trippers, the first player in history to reach that mark so quickly. Of the 275 homers Maris hit in his twelve-year career, the record 61 that broke Babe Ruth's single-season home-run record came in 1961.

But Maris paid a big price: "Every day I went to the ballpark in Yankee Stadium, as well as on the road, people were on my back," he said. "The last six years in the American League were mental hell for me. I was drained of all my desire to play baseball."

After being named to the All-Star team for the fourth straight year in 1962, injuries limited him to just ninety games and twenty-three homers in the 1963 season. But he helped the Yanks take a fourth straight pennant.

In his last two Yankee seasons, 1965 and 1966, Maris saw his playing time significantly reduced because of a hand injury. In December of 1966, the Yankees traded him to the Cardinals, who he helped win two pennants.

Embittered at being traded, Roger Maris stayed away from a number of Yankee Old Timers' games, but in 1978 finally returned to Yankee Stadium. The reception was warm. "It's like obituaries," Maris said. "When you die, they give you good reviews."

He had the glory, but he also had the hurt of being an unliked and unlikely hero. On December 14, 1985, Roger Maris, who had homered once every 18.5 at bats in his career and had a home-run-to-hit ratio of 4.81, died of lymphatic cancer. He was only fifty-one years old.

Roger Maris

"People just remember the sixty-one home runs," said Bill Skowron. "They forget that Roger was an excellent base stealer and a superb right fielder. He was the best defensive right fielder in the majors. He was an all-around ballplayer, a humble guy, a real team player. History never gave him his due."

BILLY MARTIN

*"When I get through managing,
I'm going to open a kindergarten."*

WHEN HE WAS old enough to listen, Alfred Manuel "Billy" Pesano's mother told him: "Don't take nothing from nobody. If you can't hit 'em, bite 'em." He never forgot what she said.

Martin spent two seasons as a player with Oakland in the Pacific Coast League, where he became "Casey's boy." When Stengel took over as Yankee manager in 1949, the two were reunited. Undersized and pugnacious, Martin did not fit the typical Yankee image.

But he was a contributing member of those great Yankee teams of the 1950s, batting .333 lifetime in the World Series and making the 1956 All-Star team. In 1957, "Billy the Kid" was part of a fight at the Copacabana nightclub, and George Weiss, never a fan of Martin, traded him away to Kansas City as a result.

"Guys on the street shook hands and said they'd miss me," Martin recalled.

Billy Martin forcing out Jackie Robinson at second base in first inning, fourth game of the 1953 World Series

"And the first time I came to bat for Kansas City in Yankee Stadium, they gave me a terrific hand. I just want to tell them all, 'thanks.'"

On Old Timers' Day 1975, after eighteen-plus years of being out of pinstripes, Billy Martin returned, put on the uniform with number 1 and took over as Yankee manager. The Yanks won the pennant in 1976, then another pennant and the World Series in 1977. Fans loved Billy Martin and his "Billy Ball," which was daring and unpredictable.

Then on July 25, 1978, George Steinbrenner fired Billy Martin. Four days later at Old Timers' Day, it was announced that Martin would return as manager in 1980. His return came a bit earlier than announced. On July 19, 1979, the hyper Martin replaced Bob Lemon, who had replaced him as manager.

In his second stint, Martin guided the Yankees to fourth place in the American League East. Key injuries, subpar hurling by Catfish Hunter, Thurman Munson's death—all contributed to the mediocre performance of the Yankees. Then in October of 1979, Martin had a fight with a marshmallow salesman in a Minnesota hotel and was fired for the second time.

The 1981 "split season," interrupted by a players' strike, was also a split season with managers for the Yankees. Gene Michael replaced Bob Lemon, who had returned to replace Martin a second time. The Yankees were matched up in the American League Championship Series against Oakland, now managed by Billy Martin, who had taken control of the moribund franchise in 1980 and driven it to a second-place finish, winning the Manager of the Year award in the process. "Bobby Ball" (Bob Lemon) versus "Billy Ball." The Yankees with just too much talent prevailed, sweeping Oakland in three games.

The 1982 Yankees finished in fifth, one game out of last place. On January 11, 1983, Billy Martin was signed on as manager for the third time in eight years. The Yanks were in sixth place on May 16. Attendance was down. Martin was out of control.

In midsummer Martin was suspended for three days for kicking dirt on one umpire, and then suspended for a couple of games for calling another umpire "a stone liar." Martin would close himself off in the manager's office. Drinking more and more, his nastiness increased. The 1983 Yankees finished in third place.

Coach Don Zimmer, along with players like Steve Kemp, Ken Griffey, and Goose Gossage, made it clear: if Billy returned in 1984, they would not. On December 16, 1983, it was "Hello, Yogi Berra. Good-bye, Billy Martin!"

Billy Martin with George Steinbrenner, who is holding his eight-year-old son, Hal, in victory celebration after the 1977 World Series triumph over the Dodgers. General Manager Gabe Paul is the other figure in photo.

The 1985 Yankees added speedy Rickey Henderson to a lineup that included Mattingly, Winfield, and Baylor. Off to a 6–10 start, the headlines on April 25, 1985, blared: "YOGI'S OUT, BILLY'S BACK."

Despite the MVP season of Don Mattingly, the twenty-win season of Ron Guidry, the performances of Winfield, Henderson, and Baylor, it was another frustrating season. The Yankees fell two games shy of Toronto in the American League East.

On October 27, 1985, Martin was fired for the fourth time, replaced for two seasons by Lou Piniella. On October 19, 1987, Billy Martin returned as manager for the fifth time, but by June 23, 1988, Billy Martin was out as manager yet again.

In sixteen years as a manager with five different franchises, Billy Martin managed 2,267 games, winning 1,253, losing 1,013. But the team he really belonged to was the New York Yankees, where he was Number One. His record as Yankee manager was 556 wins, 385 losses, with two American League titles and one world championship.

Five times he was manager of the Yankees. On Christmas Day 1989, Billy Martin, sixty-one, was tragically killed in an automobile accident.

"We used to tease each other about whose liver would go first," Mickey Mantle said. "I never thought it would end for him this way."

DON MATTINGLY

"I like being close to bats."

THE YANKEE FIRST baseman at the start of the 1984 season was Ken Griffey, Sr. Waiting in the wings was Don Mattingly, and manager Yogi Berra did not make him wait too long. Once he was installed as the full-time first sacker, Mattingly really showed his stuff.

In his first full season, Mattingly won the American League batting title with a .343 average, edging out teammate Dave Winfield on the last day of the season. The player they would call Donnie Baseball was the first Yankee left-handed hitter to bat over .340 since Lou Gehrig's .351 in 1937. He also was league leader in hits and doubles. Committing just five errors, Mattingly led all first basemen in fielding.

A throwback to the Yankees of years past, the Evansville, Illinois, native wore his cap settled low on his head, bill down, trademark lampblack always under the eyes. The 1980s were his time.

From 1984 until 1989, Mattingly hit better than .300 each season. In that six-year span, with the exception of 1988, he tallied at least twenty home runs and drove in one hundred runs each season, and his combined 684 runs gave him the highest total of any player in major-league baseball.

MVP in 1985, Mattingly set the major-league record for most home runs in seven consecutive games (nine), and eight consecutive games (ten). He also led the majors with 145 RBIs. In 1986, he batted .352 and topped the American League with 238 hits and fifty-three doubles. Setting a major-league record by hitting a home run in eight consecutive games in 1987, Mattingly also slammed a record six grand slams. On July 20, he made twenty-two putouts to tie the record for first basemen in one game.

By the late 1980s and into the 1990s, back problems affected Mattingly's skills. But he still ranked as the toughest player to strike out in the American League from 1990 to 1994.

Mattingly is only one of three players to have produced two thousand-plus hits, four hundred-plus doubles, two hundred-plus home runs, one thousand-plus RBIs, and a .300-plus career batting average while wearing Yankee pinstripes. The others were Lou Gehrig and Babe Ruth.

A nine-time Gold Glove winner and a six-time All Star, Mattingly was the tenth player in Yankee history to be named captain. His number, 23, was retired in 1997.

"He was a great hitter and a great ballplayer," Yogi Berra said. "It's just a shame his career had to end so soon. I guess in the end that back just got too bad."

It was also a shame that after playing for fourteen years, in 1,785 games, Mattingly's first postseason competition did not take place until 1995, against

Don Mattingly

Seattle. He batted .417. The quiet star was perhaps the greatest Yankee who never got to play in a World Series.

BOB MEUSEL

"Long Bob"

OUT OF SAN Jose, California, Robert William Meusel, younger brother of National League star Irish Meusel, played his Yankee career in the shadows of Babe Ruth and Lou Gehrig. But he was a star in his own right, batting .311 in his decade with the Yankees.

Casey Stengel said: "He had lightnin' on the ball."

The player with baseball's best arm, Meusel was the regular left fielder at Yankee Stadium. Babe Ruth once said of Meusel: "I never saw a better thrower." When the Yankees were on the road, he generally switched places with the Babe and played right field.

At six feet three, he was the tallest member of the 1927 Yankees. He had speed, power, and could hit for average. In seven of his first eight seasons, Meusel batted .313 or better. Babe Ruth was the only Yankee from 1920 to 1929 with more RBIs than Meusel. Five times, Meusel led the Yankees in stolen bases. He ranks among the all-time Yankee leaders in doubles, triples, RBIs, and batting average.

But while Meusel had a lot going for him, there was a lack of good character. Miller Huggins said he was "indifferent." Others had less kind words. With bat in hand in 1924, Meusel charged a Detroit pitcher, triggering one of the worst riots in modern baseball history.

Bob Meusel should have been a candidate for inclusion in the Baseball Hall of Fame, but the general negative feelings about him on the part of the media, fans, and even his teammates mitigated against that happening.

THURMAN MUNSON

"I'm a little too belligerent.
I cuss and swear at people."

THURMAN MUNSON DID have shortcomings as a person, but not very many as a baseball player. And he died much too soon.

On August 2, 1979, his Cessna Citation jet crash-landed just short of the runway at the Akron-Canton (Ohio) Regional Airport. Munson was killed. The driven athlete, who made his major-league debut on August 8, 1969, after playing in just ninety-nine games in the minors, was just thirty-two years old.

On September 20, 1980, his uniform number, 15, was retired and a bronze plaque was put into Yankee Stadium Memorial Park. His locker remains empty in perpetuity.

When Munson was appointed team captain—just the fifth in Yankee history—on April 17, 1976, he said: "Maybe they made me captain because I've been here so long. If I'm supposed to be captain by example, then I'll be a terrible captain."

Munson's eleven-year Yankee career began with his winning the Rookie of the Year honors in 1970. In 1976, he won the MVP award. A seven-time All Star, Thurman Lee Munson, incredibly, is not in the Hall of Fame. But a re-creation of his locker, including spikes, glove, and jersey, are all preserved in Cooperstown.

Munson remains, especially for those who saw him play, the undisputed leader of the exciting Yankee teams that won three American League pennants (1976–1978) and two world championships. A defensive presence and an expert handler of pitchers, the Ohio native won three straight Gold Glove awards (1973–1975). From 1975 to 1977, over a span of 423 games, Munson drove in more than one hundred runs and hit better than .300.

Thurman Munson

"I remember seeing Munson when he was a rookie September call-up, so I always had a soft spot for him," David Vigliano noted. "He was my favorite Yankee, the consummate professional, the heart and soul of those 1970s championship teams."

JOHNNY MURPHY

"Fireman"

A NEW YORKER through and through, John Joseph Murphy made his major-league debut with the Yankees on May 19, 1932. He appeared in just two games that first season, but once he got started he was always working.

In 1934, he posted a 14–10 record. Then in 1955, Joe McCarthy moved the big right-hander to the bullpen—the first real instance of a winning pitcher being placed there. McCarthy's decision to move Murphy definitely paid off: Ten times in a twelve-year career Murphy would lead the Yankees in saves.

A control pitcher with a big breaking curveball, Murphy's 104 saves and seventy-three wins in relief held up as major-league records until the 1960s. He had losing records in only two seasons, and led the majors in saves in four seasons. His best save year was 1939, when he had nineteen. Murphy's career season was 1941, when he saved fifteen games, had a 1.98 ERA, and an 8–3 record.

One pitcher who especially liked having him around was Lefty Gomez. Asked one season to predict how many games he would win, Gomez smiled and said: "Ask Murphy."

Fifth all-time still on the Yankee save list with 104, sixth in games pitched, thirteenth in winning percentage, seventeenth in wins, Murphy won ninety-three games and lost fifty-three in a dozen Bronx seasons.

As general manager of the Mets, he was the architect who brought the team from its hapless days to the 1969 world championship. He surely did contribute much to New York City baseball. He passed away from a heart attack at age sixty-one on January 14, 1970, in New York City.

GRAIG NETTLES

*"When I was a little boy, I wanted to be
a baseball player and join a circus.
With the Yankees I've accomplished both."*

GRAIG NETTLES'S MAJOR-league debut was on September 6, 1967, with Minnesota. He went on to have a twenty-two-year career, half of which was spent as a Yankee, from 1973 to 1983. The best all-around third baseman of the 1970s, probably the best defensive one ever, Graig Nettles had pop in his bat and also in his mouth. Slamming twenty or more home runs in eight of his seasons with the Yankees, in 1976 he led the American League in home runs, helping the Yanks win their first pennant in a dozen years.

The left-handed power hitter had a career year in 1977 when he hit thirty-seven homers, drove in 107 runs, scored 99 runs, and led the Yankees to the first of back-to-back World Series titles over the Dodgers.

Nettles was almost as well known for his mouth as he was for his baseball skills. Moody and sarcastic, Nettles was a master of one-liners like: "What the Yankees need is a second base coach"; when fined for missing a luncheon, he sniped: "If this club wants somebody to play third base, they've got me. If they want somebody to go to luncheons, they should hire George Jessel."

A two-time Gold Glover, a five-time All Star, Nettles was named Yankee captain in 1982. It was, however, a brief honor. During spring training 1984, the Yankees traded him away to San Diego.

PAUL O'NEILL

"I hit the jackpot."

"WHEN I FIRST came to the Yankees," Joe Torre said, "people told me Paul was selfish. That couldn't be further from the truth. He just wanted to win so badly."

A three-time All Star, the lanky and reserved Paul O'Neill was the backbone of Yankee baseball during the 1990s. Joe Torre called him the heart and soul of the Yankees.

Tempestuous, talented, driven, sometimes on the brink of rage, the rangy left-handed batter with the vicious swing was always a threat to opposing pitchers.

Paul Andrew O'Neill came to the Yankees from the Reds on November 3, 1992, in exchange for outfielder Roberto Kelly. Born and raised in Ohio and signed by Cincinnati out of high school, O'Neill was devastated by the trade. His father knew better. "This will turn out to be the best thing that happened to you."

At the start, there were doubts. Not only were the Yankees a subpar team at that time, but O'Neill had his car stolen—twice. Before he came to the Bronx, the Cincy native was a dead pull hitter. Playing in the stadium, however, transformed O'Neill into a professional batsman. In 1994, O'Neill batted over .400 for the first two months of the season. His .359 final average, a career high, gave him the American League batting title.

In his first six seasons, the intense O'Neill batted .300 or better. O'Neill's power hitting made some lose sight of his fielding prowess. But the Cincinnati native could flat-out play defense.

It was what he did in the clutch, however, that showed everyone what made O'Neill, O'Neill.

In 1996, he batted .320 and had fifty-two RBIs before a painful hamstring slowed him. But he did manage a career-high 102 walks. The hamstring woes continued in the Yankees' three postseason series; O'Neill managed just seven hits in thirty-eight at bats. Joe Torre nevertheless stayed with him. In game three, of the World Series against Atlanta tied at a game apiece, the Yanks clung to a 1–0 lead, desperate to win after losing the first two games. In the bottom of the ninth inning with two outs and two on, a John Wetteland pitch was ripped by Luis Polonia toward the right-center-field alley. O'Neill, clearly in pain, almost willed himself to the ball. His arm and glove fully extended, the intense Yankee grabbed the liner. Victory Yankees!

Paul O'Neill

In 1997, O'Neill batted .324 with a career-high 117 RBIs. In game one of the Division Series against the Indians, O'Neill homered following dingers by Tim Raines and Derek Jeter, helping his team to an 8–6 win. In game three he drove in five Yankee runs—four of them on a grand slam that broke the game open. In game five, O'Neill came up in the top of the ninth, the Yankees trailing 4–3 and an out away from elimination, and slammed a Jose Mesa fastball high off the center-field wall. Indians center fielder Marquis Grissom fired the ball to second base and Omar Vizquel. O'Neill appeared to be beaten by the throw, but he beat the tag, sliding, stretching out his hand, reaching the far side of the base. His face bloodied, O'Neill balked when Joe Torre took him out for a pinch runner. That sequence of events truly characterized Paul O'Neill's Yankee time.

A direct descendant of Mark Twain, O'Neill was frequently called a warrior by George Steinbrenner. In 1998, O'Neill was the backbone of the 114-win Yankee season, batting .317, slashing twenty-four home runs, and keeping his teammates on the stick.

Going into the 1999 season, O'Neill had a .317 career average—only Babe Ruth, Lou Gehrig, Joe DiMaggio, and Earle Combs had done better. That average was pulled down as he struggled to bat .285, the aches and pains of all the years and injuries catching up with him.

Hobbled by injuries in 2000, O'Neill still drove in one hundred runs for the fourth straight year, but he hit a disappointing .283. Yet the Subway World Series against the Mets somehow served as a wakeup call. Hitting almost two hundred points higher than his season average in the World Series, O'Neill's Fall Classic play was marked by a memorable ten-pitch at bat against Armando Benitez, setting off a Yankee rally in game one.

Starting in his ninth straight Opening Day for the Yankees in 2001, O'Neill recorded his two thousandth major-league hit on May 2. He became the oldest player to ever steal twenty bases and hit twenty homers in the same season. But a stress fracture in his left foot limited his playing time and production. O'Neill managed only twenty-six at bats after September 1 and ended the 2001 season with a .267 average, his lowest as a Yankee.

Thirty-eight years old, slowed by an injured left foot, number 21 called it quits after the 2001 World Series. The fan chants of "Paul-ie, Paul-ie" now belonged to history. His time as a Yankee ended after nine years and one day.

JOE PAGE

"Gay Reliever"

JOSEPH FRANCIS PAGE, a powerful left-handed hurler out of the coal-mining region of Pennsylvania, made his Yankee debut on April 19, 1944. That season he posted a 5–1 record and secured a place on the All-Star team.

Then a shoulder injury lessened his effectiveness and he drifted back and forth in mediocrity from starter to reliever. However, Bucky Harris saved Page's career in 1947 by putting him in the bullpen. A 14–8 record with seventeen saves and a 2.15 ERA in relief that season got Page a lot of attention. Those fourteen relief wins lasted as the AL record until Luis Arroyo snapped it in 1961.

Page followed up his regular-season heroics with outstanding hurling in the 1947 World Series, getting the save in game one and winning the clincher, holding the Dodgers to one hit in five scoreless innings. He was the first World Series Most Valuable Player.

In 1948, Page led the league with fifty-five appearances and became an All Star for the third time. Casey Stengel, the new manager in 1949, had an influence on Page, who was known as the Gay Reliever because of his fondness for the night life.

Under Casey, Page saved twenty-seven games and posted a 13–8 record. He closed out the Red Sox in the next-to-last game of the season, enabling the Yankees to win the pennant. In the World Series, Page won game three and held the Dodgers scoreless in game five from the seventh inning on.

Joe Page

Joe Page's final Yankee season was 1950. Perhaps it was the heavy workload through the years, perhaps it was just time. But after only seven seasons as a Yankee, he was done. Joe Page still ranks in seventh place in franchise history with seventy-six saves.

HERB PENNOCK

"Squire of Kennett Square"

JUST ANOTHER IN the long line of players stripped away from the Boston Red Sox, Herb Pennock came to the Yankees in 1923. Reborn in pinstripes, Pennock's first season saw him lead the league in winning percentage at .760, the first of four .700-plus seasons. There were also two wins for him in the 1923 World Series against the Giants.

He followed with a 21–9 record in 1924, and was 59–25 in 1926–1928. In 1926, he added two more victories in the World Series. In 1927, in game three of the World Series, he set down the first twenty-two Pirates he faced, ending with a three-hitter.

Dubbed the Squire of Kennett Square, Pennock was one of the classiest individuals in baseball during his time. He had attended the finest prep schools, was a horticulturist, and bred red silver foxes at his country home near Kennett Square, Pennsylvania.

On the mound he was grace and style personified with a flowing pitching motion. He did not overpower batters. He let them hit the ball, giving up more than a hit an inning in his career. Yet he won big with this approach, recording thirty-five lifetime shutouts.

Miller Huggins called Herb Pennock the greatest left-hander in the history of baseball and marveled at the way the Squire hurled at World Series time. Pennock was unbeaten in five World Series decisions and sported a glossy 1.95 lifetime ERA in the Fall Classic.

In eleven Yankee seasons, Pennock was 162–90 for a .643 winning percentage. He ranks fourth in complete games, all-time seventh in wins, eighth in innings pitched, eleventh in winning percentage, twelfth in shutouts and eighteenth in strikeouts. Pennock became general manager of the Philadelphia Phillies in 1944 and was on the scene until his death in 1948, the year he was admitted to the Baseball Hall of Fame. He was instrumental in the development of the 1950 team, the Whiz Kids.

LOU PINIELLA

"Part of me will always be a Yankee."

LOU PINIELLA WAS traded from Kansas City to the New York Yankees in 1973 for Lindy McDaniel. He played in 1,037 games for the Yankees over eleven seasons—batting .300 or better in five of those seasons. He played in one divisional playoff, five League Championship Series, and four World Series. He earned two World Series rings playing for the Yanks.

Lou Piniella claimed his most exciting season as a player was 1978. "We were the defending world champions, and we were determined to repeat. After we lost the first two to the Dodgers, we came back to win the next four in a row, and that had never been done before."

A Yankee scout, batting coach, manager, broadcaster, and executive, they called Piniella Sweet Lou. He was that for some and he was also the Lou of the terrible temper and feistiness for others.

One of the true Yankee professionals of the 1970s and 1980s, a fan favorite, Lou Piniella was consistent, solid in a clutch, competitive. Yankee Stadium would echo with the sound of the fans roaring for him: "Loooou."

A right-handed hitter, the native of Tampa, Florida, was more effective against lefties than righties, and platooned with Bobby Murcer and Oscar Gamble. Piniella posted a lifetime .319 World Series average for the Yankees.

After retirement in 1984, Sweet Lou stayed in the Yankee organization. First hired as a scout and batting coach, Piniella eventually became the team's manager in 1986. After hiring his former outfielder to replace Billy Martin, fired for the fourth time, George Steinbrenner said: "Lou was my kind of player—I think he'll be my kind of manager."

Steinbrenner's "kind of manager" lasted through 417 games. Then the Boss promoted him to GM and replaced him with Billy Martin as Yankee skipper. Midway into the 1988 season, Martin was fired again. Piniella returned as interim manager.

Public-address man extraordinaire Bob Sheppard remembers Piniella: "I liked Lou. He was a very tempestuous, highly volatile ballplayer, and a tempestuous and highly volatile manager."

WILLIE RANDOLPH

"I was there playing with guys I had grown up idolizing."

HIS MAJOR-LEAGUE debut was with Pittsburgh on July 29, 1975, but it is as a Yankee that second baseman Willie Randolph made his mark. He came to New York in a trade that year with the Pirates.

Playing thirteen seasons as a Yankee and appearing in more games at second base (1,688) than any other player in franchise history, Randolph also ranks second all-time in Yankee history in stolen bases with 251. A four-time Yankee All Star, he helped five teams reach postseason play. Randolph was also a key member of two world championship teams.

Born in South Carolina, Randolph grew up in Brooklyn. The slight and serious athlete was "Mr. Consistency." His batting average was in the high .270s to the mid .290s. He averaged around twenty doubles a year and a .380 on-base percentage. A steady, reliable, winning presence, Randolph was ready to play season after season as the Yankees went through thirty-two different shortstops in his time with the team.

One of his most memorable moments took place in 1977, at the All-Star Game at Yankee Stadium. "I was a young kid in front of my hometown fans, my family," Randolph recalled, "I played the whole game. I was there playing with guys I had grown up idolizing—Rod Carew, Reggie Jackson."

From March 4, 1986, to October 2, 1988, he was Yankee co-captain along with Ron Guidry. He has been the Yankees third-base coach since October 1993.

Willie Randolph

VIC RASCHI

"Springfield Rifle"

VICTOR JOHN ANGELO Raschi out of Springfield, Massachusetts, started late but made up for it, becoming a four-time All Star during his ten-year career. He was already twenty-eight years old in 1948 when he became a regular part of the Yankee pitching rotation.

Averaging twenty wins a season over the next five years, anchoring a pitching staff that won five straight world championships, the man they called the Springfield Rifle won five World Series games for the Yanks with a 2.24 ERA in 58⅔ innings. He was truly a big-game pitcher.

A constant five-o'clock shadow, scowling demeanor, blazing fastball, and a work ethic that saw him pitch through pain made him a main man on those great 1950s teams.

In 1949, Raschi won twenty-one games and pitched the pennant-clincher against the Red Sox on the last day of the season. In 1950, Raschi went 21–8 and pitched a two-hit 1–0 shutout in the World Series opener against the Phillies.

In 1951, Raschi again won twenty-one games as well as that year's final World Series game against the New York Giants. In 1952, Raschi's knees were starting to give way on him. But always the tough guy, Raschi toughed it out, winning sixteen games, posting a career-best ERA of 2.78. In the 1952 World Series, he won two more games.

Knee problems in 1953 forced Raschi to pitch less than two hundred innings, but he still managed to win thirteen games. In game three of the 1953 World Series against the Dodgers at Ebbets Field, he pitched a complete game but took a 3–2 loss. That was his final appearance as a Yankee.

Contract difficulties ended his time as a Yankee and he was sold to the Cardinals. On the all-time Yankee list, Vic Raschi still ranks fifteenth in strikeouts, thirteenth in innings pitched, eleventh in wins, and ninth in shutouts.

ALLIE REYNOLDS

"I always felt the pitcher had the advantage.
It's like serving in tennis."

ALLIE REYNOLDS RECORDED a no-hitter against Cleveland, a 1–0 gem with pitcher Bob Feller on the short end, on July 12, 1951. He threw another no-hitter against Boston, an 8–0 win on September 28, 1951. He earned five All-

Allie Reynolds

Star Game selections, and many rankings on the all-time Yankee list: fourth in winning percentage, fifth in shutouts, eighth in strikeouts, ninth in victories, a tie for twelfth in saves, fifteenth in complete games, sixteenth in games pitched, and twentieth in ERA.

And if not for injuries, there is no telling what Allie Pierce Reynolds might have accomplished. Through eight Yankee seasons, the power-pitching right-hander won 131 games and saved forty-one.

Coming to the Yankees in 1946 in a trade that sent Joe Gordon to the Indians, Reynolds became the first American Leaguer to record two no-hitters in a season in 1951.

In Reynolds's first couple of years as a Yankee, he was a thrower. Then in 1949, Casey Stengel took over as manager and utilized the big right-hander as a starter and a reliever. That move first paid big dividends in the 1950 World Series against the Phillies. He won game two. In game four, a young Whitey Ford was struggling. There were two outs but there were also men on base. Stengel waved in number 22. World championship, Yankees, again.

In 1952, the man they called Superchief (he was one-quarter Creek) had a career season with a 20–8 record and led the league in strikeouts, ERA, and shutouts. He even saved six games.

"Reynolds is two ways great," said Casey Stengel, "which is starting and relieving, which no one can do like him." Reynolds's skill as both a starter and a reliever was essential to the Yankees winning the 1952 World Series. After losing game one, Reynolds came back with a shutout victory in game four, saved game six, and relieved in game seven to get the win over the Dodgers and clinch the Yankee championship.

The Oklahoma native pitched for six Yankee championship teams, going 7–2 with four saves and a 2.79 ERA, striking out sixty-two in seventy-seven innings.

In a weird mishap, the team bus crashed into an overpass in Philadelphia, damaging Reynolds's back and forcing him to retire in 1954. That and starting and relieving pulled his win totals down and probably cost him a shot at the Baseball Hall of Fame.

"I knew that was going to happen," Reynolds said. "All the relief work I did was really a career shortener. But to me teamwork was more important than some kind of honor."

"He was a dominating pitcher," said Bobby Brown, who was there at third base so many times when Reynolds pitched. "He was as good as any pitcher who pitched during his time."

BOBBY RICHARDSON

"I played at the right time."

"WHEN I WAS fourteen years old playing American Legion baseball, they took our team to see a film, *Pride of the Yankees*, the story of Lou Gehrig," Bobby Richardson remembered. "And at that time, as a fourteen-year-old, I thought, 'Man, what a great organization.'"

One of the top second basemen of his time, Bobby Richardson was a fixture on seven Yankee pennant-winners from 1957 through 1964. A smooth fielder and a five-time Gold Glove award winner (1961–1965), Richardson had the respect of all, even though he played in the shadow of stars such as Roger Maris, Yogi Berra, and Mickey Mantle.

Casey Stengel platooned Richardson and never batted him more than 469 times a season. "He doesn't smoke," said Casey, who was very fond of Richardson, "he doesn't drink, and he still can't hit .250." Casey was doing a bit of exaggerating. Richardson was a lifetime .266 hitter, twice batting .300 and leading the American League with 209 hits in 1962.

Bobby Richardson (center) after hitting a grand slam in the 1960 World Series

Gifted with great range, particularly skilled at turning the double play, he matched perfectly with shortstop Tony Kubek. Together they led the AL in double plays four times.

When Ralph Houk became manager in 1961, he played the 170-pound singles hitter out of Sumter, South Carolina, every day and bumped him up to the top of the batting order. Richardson, a strong contact hitter, struck out just twenty-three times in 662 at bats in 1961. The combination of being the table setter for the best offense in the league and rarely walking saw Richardson leading the AL in at bats each year from 1962 through 1964, setting an AL record with 692 in 1962, collecting a league-high 209 hits and batting .302.

World Series time was Bobby Richardson time. The series MVP in 1960, Richardson was sensational. He batted .367 with eleven hits, a grand slam, and eight runs scored. He set records with twelve total RBIs and six RBIs in game three, though he had batted in just twenty-six runs during the regular season.

In 1961, Richardson tied records for a five-game series with nine hits and twenty-three at bats, for a .391 average. In 1962, he made the game-saving catch of a Willie McCovey liner that ended the World Series, defeating San Francisco and giving the Yankees the championship. In 1964, his final World Series appearance, he collected thirteen hits and batted .406.

After a dozen Yankee years, Richardson retired at age thirty-one. He played in his first Old Timers' game when he was thirty-two years old. Bobby Richardson Day was staged at Yankee Stadium on September 17, 1966. "I played at the right time," Richardson said. "Nine of the first ten years, we won the pennant."

DAVE RIGHETTI

"Rags"

IN THE TRADITION of Allie Reynolds, Dave Righetti out of San Jose, California, was a star Yankee pitcher who was both a starter and reliever. The all-time leader in saves (224) and games pitched (522), the man they called Rags was a fixture on the Yankee pitching staff for more than a decade. In 1986, he posted a then-record forty-six saves.

The handsome left-hander's fate and fortunes were wrapped up with two all-time Yankee great relief pitchers. Following the 1978 season, Righetti came to the Yanks in the Sparky Lyle trade to Texas, and later replaced Gossage as a closer.

The scouting report on the young Righetti read: "Dave Righetti, twenty-two, Yankees, P: Had 6–10 record with Columbus in International League in 1980. Posted 139 strikeouts in league, but also most walks, 101. Outstanding arm with above-average fastball and curve. Control will tell."

His major-league debut was on September 16, 1979, but it was not until the strike-shortened season of 1981 that Righetti came into his own. Starting fifteen games, posting an 8–4 record, a 2.06 ERA and going 3–1 in the postseason, he was Rookie of the Year.

In 1983, Rags compiled a 14–8 won-lost record. The highlight of that season was the no-hitter he hurled against the Red Sox at Yankee Stadium on the Fourth of July.

Following the 1983 season, manager Yogi Berra moved Righetti into the Yankee closer role, succeeding the departed Goose Gossage. Rags saved thirty-one games in 1984 and twenty-nine in 1985 while winning twelve games.

His career year as a closer was 1986. Converting twenty-nine of his final thirty save opportunities, including both ends of a season-ending doubleheader against the Red Sox, Righetti wound up with forty-six saves.

Over the next four seasons, the hard-throwing and highly popular southpaw saved 117 games. In eleven seasons with the Yankees, Righetti pitched in 522 games, breaking Whitey Ford's record of 498 career appearances, and finished as the Yanks career-saves record-holder with 224.

MARIANO RIVERA

"I'm not perfect."

THE SLIM RIGHT-HANDER with the smooth pitching motion made his debut with the Yankees on May 23, 1995. He was a starter but everyone soon realized that the best place for the quiet Panamanian was in the bullpen. In 1996, he was 8–3 in a setup role and set a Yankee reliever record for most strikeouts in a season with 130.

When John Wetteland departed for Texas in 1997, Rivera was given the closer role. There were those who knew that he had the stuff, but there were concerns about how much will he had. They would soon learn that he had plenty.

Slotting Rivera in as the Yankee closer was one of the smartest moves manager Joe Torre ever made. From 1997 through 1999, Rivera averaged forty-one saves and a 1.86 ERA, terrorizing batters and shattering pitching marks while rewriting the Yankee relief-pitcher record book.

One could mount a convincing argument that the 1997 and 1999 AL Fireman of the Year is the greatest postseason reliever in the history of baseball. Rivera said, "That's a blessing, just being in the playoffs. I just go out there and try my best."

His best has been unbelievable, incomparable. Rivera saved twenty-three postseason games in a row, and in nineteen of those games he pitched more than one inning.

Despite what happened in the 2001 World Series—the only blown save of his remarkable world-championship appearances—Rivera has been almost unhittable in postseason play, using a ninety-seven-mile-per-hour fastball and a cut fastball that moves as much as eight or nine inches to shatter bats.

He is the holder of the all-time record for postseason saves and also has the record for consecutive scoreless innings pitched in postseason play with 33⅓. A member of four world championship teams, Rivera was on the mound as the Yankees closed out titles in 1998, 1999 and 2000. He is just the third reliever in major-league baseball to be named World Series MVP (1999).

Mariano had thirty-six saves in 2000 to go along with a 7–4 record and 2.85 ERA. Since becoming the Yankees' closer in 1997, he has posted save totals of 43, 36, 45, and 36. His 50 in 2001 is the third-highest total in American League history.

Durable, intense, and highly competitive, Mariano Rivera became the highest-paid relief pitcher in baseball, signing a $39.99 million, four-year contract in 2001. George Steinbrenner also agreed to donate $100,000 to Rivera's church in Panama.

Early on in the 2002 season, Rivera broke Dave Righetti's all-time Yankee save mark. The man they call Mr. Automatic saved a team record 30 or more games (through 2001) for five straight seasons.

Rivera's postseason stats through 2001: fifty-two games, seventy-nine innings, 0.91 ERA and a 6–1 record. In eighteen World Series appearances he posted a 1.67 ERA, with a 2–1 record in twenty-seven innings pitched.

Off the mound, Mariano Rivera is a religious, quiet man. On the mound he is one of baseball's all-time best stoppers, a competitor par excellence who, before he retires, will have rewritten the relief-pitching record book.

PHIL RIZZUTO

"I'll go in even as a batboy."

AS A MINOR-LEAGUER, he was knocked down a couple of times by lightning, triggering some of his fears and superstitions, which included closing his eyes when passing a cemetery to insure getting a hit that day and keeping a large wad of gum on the top of his cap to keep a winning streak going.

Ed Barrow said of Phil Rizzuto: "His signing cost me fifteen cents: ten cents for postage and five cents for a cup of coffee we gave him the day he worked out at the stadium."

The first American Leaguer to wear a batting helmet, he was also among the first to bring his glove into the dugout between innings, but that created problems for him. He was afraid of things that crawled, and a lot of those things somehow wound up in his glove, by chance and otherwise.

Phil Rizzuto

Ty Cobb referred to the likable little guy as one of the best bunters of all time. Casey Stengel went even further: "He's the greatest shortstop I've ever seen. Honus Wagner was a better hitter, but I've seen this kid make plays Wagner never did."

Rizzuto is in the top-twenty Yankee list for games played, stolen bases, doubles, triples, at bats, and runs scored. Yet at the start of his career there were doubts, as he was rejected by both the Brooklyn Dodgers and the New York Giants. Too small was the rap on him.

In 1941, Philip Francis Rizzuto replaced Frank Crosetti at shortstop for the Yankees and hit .307. The following season he was an All Star, the first of five times.

He may have been a bit of a nervous wreck—always stepping out of bed on the same side, always avoiding stepping on the baselines, always on the lookout for insects—but Phil Rizzuto was durable, driven, an outstanding shortstop, a highly skilled bunter with a .273 lifetime batting average, and the anchor of those teams who won nine pennants and seven World Series during his thirteen Yankee seasons.

From 1949 to 1952, Rizzuto led the league in double plays and total chances three times, fielding and putouts two times, assists once, and sacrifice hits all those years—an all-time record.

The little shortstop's best years were 1949–1950, a time when he was moved from down in the batting order to the leadoff slot. Scoring 110 runs, batting .275, walking seventy-two times, Rizzuto finished second in the 1949 MVP voting behind Ted Williams.

In 1950, however, he won the league MVP, had a career-high two hundred hits and a .324 average, was third in the league in doubles, and second in runs scored. In 1951, Rizzuto was the World Series MVP.

After his brilliant playing career ended, Rizzuto spent forty years as a Yankee broadcaster (1957–1996). In his later years, Rizzuto would call only the first six innings, and before the seventh-inning stretch he was heading home over the GW Bridge.

At long last after twenty-eight years of eligibility and much frustration—"I'll go in even as a batboy"—Phil Rizzuto was finally elected to the Baseball Hall of Fame in 1994.

RED ROLFE

"The luckiest thing I ever did was sign with the Yankees."

HIS NAME WAS Robert Abial Rolfe, but everyone called him Red. The "Pride of Penacook," New Hampshire, where he was born in 1908, his career over-

Red Rolfe

lapped Babe Ruth's and Lou Gehrig's at the start and Joe DiMaggio's at the end.

A standout shortstop at Dartmouth College, he graduated in 1931 with a degree in English and was signed to a $5,000 bonus by scout Gene "White Ties" McCann. "The luckiest thing I ever did was sign with the Yankees," Rolfe said. "When you're with really great players, they pull you along."

In 1934, he began his Yankee decade as a skilled leadoff man and third baseman. In his seven years as a regular, there were six Yankee pennants and five world championships. Four times Rolfe hit .300 or better. His career best was .329 in 1939, a season when he led the American League in hits, doubles, and runs scored. He scored at least one hundred runs every year he was a regular. Twice he led AL third basemen in fielding. In six World Series, the left-handed hitter struck out just 9 times in 116 at bats.

"You know, they talk about all the other fellas on the Yankees, but I notice the man that hurts us is that third baseman," Philadelphia manager Connie Mack, who scouted Rolfe in college, pointed out. "There is a real team player. You might get him out three times, but then he'll come up where it means the ball game, and sure as anything, he's going to knock in those runs. Or, if the Yankees need that one big play in the field, they usually get it at third base."

A three-time All-Star third baseman, Rolfe's career batting average was .289. He retired in 1942 beset by medical problems. "Sick or well," manager Joe McCarthy said, "Rolfe was a real ballplayer."

Director of athletics at Dartmouth from 1954 to 1967, Rolfe had the baseball field named for him just before he died in 1969. That year he was named the all-time Yankee third baseman for the first one hundred years of the national pastime.

"Even when he was the best third baseman in the business, he was a sick man," columnist Red Smith wrote at the time of Rolfe's death. "Nobody will ever know how great he might have been if he had had his health."

RED RUFFING

"Run, run, run."

PAIN WAS A constant for Charles Herbert Ruffing, the result of the loss of four toes on his left foot from a mine accident. But he looked past the pain and pitched his way to the top in the 1930s, becoming one of the great hurlers in Yankee history.

Born May 3, 1905, in Granville, Illinois, the kid they called Red was already playing for the Nokomis mining-company team, piloted by his father, at age fifteen. Four years later Ruffing was on the Red Sox.

With Boston, Ruffing twice led the league in losses. Then in 1930, the Yankees acquired him for $50,000 and Cedric Durst. It was another case of a player coming to the Yankees and shining. Ruffing was a fifteen-game winner in his first New York season.

Utilizing a moving fastball with a sharp breaking curve, the powerfully built Ruffing went 231–124 in fifteen Yankee seasons. He had four consecutive twenty-victory seasons and won seven of nine World Series decisions for the Yankees. His three main rules of training were "Run, run, run."

A superb all-around athlete, Ruffing was one of the best fielding and hitting pitchers ever. Number 15 was so good with the bat (he hit .291 with five home runs in 1932) that manager Joe McCarthy liked to use him as a pinch hitter. He had more than two hundred career pinch-hit at bats. The all-time leader among Yankee pitchers in home runs, RBIs, and batting average for a season, Ruffing batted over .300 eight times.

Ruffing played on seven championship teams. First among all Yankee pitchers in complete games, Ruffing is second in innings pitched and wins, third in strikeouts and games pitched, and ninth in winning percentage.

Bill Dickey said of him: "If I were asked to choose the best pitcher I've ever caught, I would have to say Ruffing."

JACOB RUPPERT

"Yankee Stadium was a mistake,
not mine but the Giants'."

BORN IN NEW YORK City on August 5, 1867, Jacob Ruppert was the son and grandson of beer tycoons who founded the Ruppert Breweries. In his youth he tried out for the New York Giants but couldn't make the club.

His was a life of luxury filled with all that money could buy—including the New York Yankees. Heir to the family millions, Jake Ruppert used his money to get elected and serve as a four-time member of the House of Representatives from 1899 to 1906, representing the "Silk Stocking" district of Manhattan.

Aristocratic and arrogant, he lived in a fashionable twelve-room apartment on Fifth Avenue; five full-time servants catered to his every whim.

Colonel Jacob Ruppert, Miller Huggins, and Babe Ruth

As a bachelor, he seemed to always have one desirable woman or another with him as he made the rounds of New York's high society. His hobbies included collecting fine art and bric-a-brac. He had a passion for raising thoroughbred horses and pedigreed dogs.

His brewery occupied thirty-five red-brick buildings that stood like fortresses on four blocks from East 90th Street to East 94th Street in Yorkville between Second and Third Avenue. Ruppert, although he was born in New York, spoke with a heavy German accent. He was one of the richest men in the United States with a personal fortune of about $50 million, most of it coming from his beer business and real estate investments.

Everyone called him Colonel, but the title was an honorary one. It came from a stint served in the National Guard in the 1890s. He was an aide-de-camp to the governor of New York State.

Ruppert, a rabid baseball fan, rooted for the New York Giants. He had wanted to buy them but was told by his friend, manager John McGraw, that they were not for sale. "I think the Yankees might be," he said.

On January 11, 1915, Ruppert and Captain Tillinghast L'Hommedieu Huston became co-owners of the New York Yankees, a franchise that had a twelve-year record of 861–937 and an average attendance of just 345,000 each season.

Ruppert had said of the team he purchased: "I never saw such a mixed-up business in my life—contracts, liabilities, notes, obligations of all sorts. There were times when it looked so bad no man would want to put a penny into it." Ruppert and Huston, however, paid quite a few pennies: $460,000.

"It is an orphan ball club," Ruppert said, "without a home of its own, without players of outstanding ability, without prestige." At the time, all of that was true but things were about to change.

Ruppert started out with organizational changes, naming himself president of the team, appointing Harry Sparrow as business manager. "I want to win," Ruppert said. "Every day I want to win ten to nothing. Close games make me nervous."

The first couple of years he and Huston were very nervous as they lost almost as much money as they had paid to buy the Yankees. But they kept spending. Wally Pipp was purchased from Detroit for $7,500. Pitcher Bob Shawkey came from Philadelphia for $18,000. The Yankees finished the 1915 season in fifth place, then fourth place in 1916, their first time out of the second division since 1910.

Co-owner Til Huston had gone off to World War I and was stationed at an army base in France when Ruppert signed Miller Huggins as manager for 1918. Huston had wanted one of his cronies, Brooklyn's corpulent pilot Wilbert Robinson, to be Yankee manager. The hiring of Huggins enraged Huston and was the beginning of the end of his time as Yankee owner. It took a while, though.

On May 21, 1922, two weeks after construction of Yankee Stadium was begun, Ruppert bought out Huston for $1.5 million. The Yankees were in

Chicago. He fired off a telegram: "I am now the sole owner of the Yankees. Miller Huggins is my manager."

Decade after decade Ruppert, totally in power, worked in overdrive making the Yankees baseball's greatest franchise. He spent what it took, sometimes more, and he hired the best baseball people to run the show.

In 1939, Ruppert passed away.

Colonel Ruppert, whose idea of a wonderful day at the ballpark was any time the Yankees scored eleven runs in the first inning, and then slowly pulled away, was responsible for Yankee Stadium and for the foundations of the Yankee aura and successes. He truly earned his nickname, Master Builder in Baseball.

BABE RUTH

*"Never let the fear of striking out
get in your way."*

"NO ONE HIT home runs the way Babe did," teammate Lefty Gomez said. "They were something special. They were like homing pigeons. The ball would leave the bat, pause briefly, suddenly gain its bearings, then take off for the stands."

"I've seen them," Waite Hoyt, his friend and Yankee teammate, said, "kids, men, women, worshippers all, hoping to get his name on a torn, dirty piece of paper, or hoping for a grunt of recognition when they said, 'Hi-ya, Babe.' He never let them down; not once. He was the greatest crowd pleaser of them all."

Ruth homered once every 11.8 at bats. His home-run-to-hit ratio was 1 to 4.02. He won twelve home-run titles in a fourteen-year span and twelve slugging titles in thirteen seasons, slugging .847 in 1920 and .846 in 1921.

Born George Herman Ruth on February 6, 1895, in Baltimore, legend claims he was an orphan; the truth is his mother died when he was sixteen, his father when he was in the major leagues. His parents had placed him in St. Mary's Industrial School for Boys for his "incorrigible" behavior: stealing, truancy, chewing tobacco, and drinking whiskey. Ruth's entire youth was spent at St. Mary's, where his awesome baseball talent was developed.

In 1914, he began his storied major-league career with Boston, where he won eighty-nine games over six seasons before he was sold to the Yankees for $125,000 in 1920. His fifty-four home runs that year were more than the total number hit by any other team except the Phillies. His .847 slugging percentage stood as the all-time best until Barry Bonds came along in 2001.

Everything about the Babe was excessive: his bat, forty-four ounces; his frame, top playing weight of 254 pounds; his appetites, food and drink consumed in abundance; his salary, $75,000 in 1932–highest in the majors.

Just from a statistical point of view, what the man players called Jidge (short for George) accomplished is staggering stuff. Thirteen times he led the American League in home-run percentage. Twelve times he notched more than one hundred RBIs. Eleven times he was the league leader in walks. Six times he led the league in runs batted in.

During his fifteen seasons in New York, the Sultan of Swat powered the Yanks to four world championships. The six-feet-two, 215-pound Ruth revolutionized the game, changing it from a pitcher-dominated, scratch-out-a-run contest to a home-run-hitting, power-pays game.

The Babe was the first to reach 30 homers, then 40, 50, and 60. From 1920 to 1933, he slugged 637 homers, an average of 45.5 per season. From 1926 to 1931, when his age ranged from thirty-one to thirty-six and when he was supposed to be past his prime, he averaged 50 homers, 155 RBIs, 47 runs, and a .354 batting average.

The Yankees captured seven pennants and four World Series with Ruth en route to his 714 career home runs. He added 15 home runs in World Series competition. Ruth has the tenth-best average ever (.342), the second-most runs scored (2,174), second-most RBIs (2,211), highest slugging percentage (.690), and second-highest on-base percentage (.483). He ranks first in career walks with 2,056, one every fourth at bat.

When the 1923 season opened, the Sultan of Swat already had 197 career home runs—25 percent of what would be his lifetime total of 714. The 1924 season was even more successful, however, as Ruth finished the season at the top of the American League with a .378 batting average and 46 home runs. Ruth just missed winning the Triple Crown, coming in second in RBIs to Washington's Goose Goslin, 129–121.

The most celebrated sports figure of his time and perhaps of all time, the Babe hammered the first home run ever in Yankee Stadium. Number 3 said: "I could have had a lifetime .600 average, but I would have had to hit them singles. The people were paying to see me hit home runs."

GEORGE SELKIRK

"Twinkletoes"

HE PROBABLY HAD the most unpopular role in all of baseball, replacing Babe Ruth as the Yankees' right fielder in 1935, taking Ruth's number, 3. But after eight minor-league seasons, the Canadian-born George Selkirk had learned to take the criticism and boos in stride.

The very muscular outfielder was a skilled wrestler, a match even for the likes of Lou Gehrig. Selkirk batted .300 or better in five of his first six seasons and was a key member of six Yankee pennant winners and five world-championship teams from 1936 through 1942. He spent his entire major-league career with the Yankees and was a two-time All Star.

In 1936, he was one-third of an all-.300 Yankee outfield that included Joe DiMaggio and Jake Powell. The man they called Twinkletoes had a keen eye at the plate. Four times he drew two walks in an inning; in 1939 he walked 103 times.

His career year was 1939, when he drove in 101 runs and hit twenty-one home runs. That season Selkirk hit five home runs over four consecutive games. Ironically, the special season of 1939 was Selkirk's last as a regular. Tommy Henrich came along in 1940, and playing time began to wind down for Selkirk.

George Alexander Selkirk, one of the best baseball players to ever come out of Canada, averaged nearly a hit a game and recorded a .290 lifetime batting average. Not bad for a guy who heard a lot of boos when he started. In 1942, he called it a career after 846 games in Yankee pinstripes.

BOB SHAWKEY

"Sailor Bob"

IN 1923, HE pitched the first game at Yankee Stadium. He hit the second home run there—Babe Ruth crushed the first. In 1976, he threw out the first ball at the newly refurbished Yankee Stadium. Eye-catching resume items for Bob Shawkey, and there are more.

For thirteen seasons (1915–1927) Bob Shawkey pitched for New York; in eight of those years he was about as good a pitcher as the Yankees had. The wiry right-hander out of Sigel, Pennsylvania, was a very unassuming, some would say colorless, type. But he did sport a red-sleeved undershirt when he pitched.

Shawkey became a Yankee in mid-season, 1915, coming over from Philadelphia for cash. By 1916, the Yankees knew they had a steal as Shawkey won twenty-four games. Sailor Bob's success enabled the 1916 Yankees to post their first winning season in six years.

In 1919, Shawkey struck out fifteen Athletics in one game, a franchise record that stood for fifty-nine years. His seven 1–0 shutouts that year (he had thirty-seven career shutouts) are also a franchise record.

Four times Shawkey posted twenty-victory seasons as a Yankee. His last active season was 1927. When Miller Huggins died, Shawkey took over as manager for the rest of the 1929 season, and piloted the Yanks to a third-place finish in 1930.

Shawkey had various jobs in and around baseball, including a stint in the 1950s as Dartmouth College baseball coach. He still ranks fifth in wins, innings and games pitched, and complete games, and eighth in shutouts among all those who ever pitched for the New York Yankees.

BOB SHEPPARD

"Good evening, ladies and gentlemen,
and welcome to Yankee Stadium."

IT HAS BEEN said that "Every kid growing up has dreamed of lining up at Yankee Stadium and having Bob Sheppard announce his name." The New York Yankees public-address announcer has announced many names while working more than four thousand games.

On the New York scene as a speech professor at St. John's University, and a guy who knew his way around sports, Sheppard was hired as an announcer by the Yankees for the '51 season. He began work on April 17, 1951, Opening Day. The Yankee lineup that day was:

JACKIE JENSEN	LF
PHIL RIZZUTO	SS
MICKEY MANTLE	RF
JOE DIMAGGIO	CF
YOGI BERRA	C
JOHNNY MIZE	1B
BILLY JOHNSON	3B
JERRY COLEMAN	2B
VIC RASCHI	P

Favorite Yankee moments for the former St. John's quarterback and first baseman who works in a sound-proofed little glass booth include Larsen's perfect game, Maris hitting sixty-one home runs, Reggie's three home runs against the Dodgers, and Mantle's shot almost over the roof.

Joe DiMaggio and Mickey Mantle make Sheppard's all-time favorite list. "DiMaggio's name was symbolic of the early Yankees," Sheppard said, "and Mickey Mantle has a nice ring to it because the two *M*s make it alliterative.

"I just loved announcing his name. And one day, shortly before he died, we were both being interviewed on a television program. All of a sudden, he turned to me and said—right there on the air—that every time he heard me announce his name, he got goose bumps. And I felt the same way about announcing him."

Hundreds of eulogies have been written and delivered by Sheppard. "They ask me to do a eulogy. I try to tailor my remarks to the person I am eulogizing. Thurman Munson, Dick Howser, Billy Martin, Mickey Mantle.

Reggie Jackson claims that Sheppard's voice sounds like "the voice of God" as it reverberates through Yankee Stadium. Clay Bellinger made the point that "the first time I heard it, it was my realization of making the big leagues after ten years in the minor leagues. Just think of all the people he's announced."

"There are three things that are perfectly Yankee—the pinstripes, the logo, and Bob Sheppard's voice," comedian Billy Crystal said. "When I go to heaven, I want Bob Sheppard to announce me."

BILL SKOWRON

"I am first and foremost a Yankee."

BORN IN CHICAGO, a onetime kicker for Purdue, William Joseph Skowron signed to play baseball for the Yankees in 1951 for a $25,000 bonus. He won the Minor League Player of the Year award in 1952.

But the Yankees wanted him to get more seasoning and had him wait a year before they brought him up to the big show. Skowron's major-league debut was April 13, 1954.

Moose (the nickname came from his grandfather, who thought Skowron looked like Mussolini and contracted Mussolini's name) batted over .300 in his first four seasons with the New York Yankees, hit more than twenty home runs three straight seasons (1960–1962), and drove in eighty or more runs in five different years. A five-time All Star, number 14 was a Yankee anchor, a dependable

Bob Cerv and Bill Skowron

fielder at first base, a clutch hitter who helped the Yankees win seven pennants and four world championships.

Part of Skowron's hitting profile was powerful opposite-field home runs. He used one hand to slam shots when it seemed that he was fooled by outside curveballs. "I don't always swing at strikes," the Moose said. "I swing at the ball when it looks big."

It was Skowron who made the final out of the 1957 World Series as the Yankees lost to Milwaukee. The next year he became a hero in the World Series against the Braves, driving in the winning run in game six. His three-run homer in the eighth inning of game seven gave the Yankees a win and another world championship.

In 1962, Skowron was traded to the Los Angeles Dodgers. He played later for the Senators, White Sox, and Angels. But the affable Skowron, who five times as a Yankee batted over .300 and who had a .294 average in nine New York seasons, says: "I am first and foremost a Yankee."

GEORGE STEINBRENNER

*"You measure the value of a ballplayer
by how many fannies he puts in the seats."*

ON A RAINY morning in January of 1973, a young Cleveland industrialist
stood at the entrance to Manhattan's 21 Club. The new principal owner of the
Yankees said he would be too busy with his shipyard business to be that
involved in the day-to-day affairs of running the team.

Born July 4, 1930, in Rocky River, Ohio, George Michael Steinbrenner III
was a multi-sport athlete at Culver Military Academy, a Williams College graduate, an English major whose senior thesis was on the heroines in the novels
of Thomas Hardy. He went on to be an assistant football coach at
Northwestern and Purdue universities.

With the Yankees he was called "the Boss" almost from the start. In his first
seventeen years Steinbrenner changed managers seventeen times. And as the
years have gone on he's upped that stat–twenty-one managers and eleven GMs
moved in and out in twenty-seven years. Steinbrenner gave Billy Martin five
separate terms as manager.

Reggie Jackson and
George Steinbrenner

"Nothing is more limited," limited partner John
McMullen pointed out, "than being a limited partner of
George's." Center stage, top of the heap, pulling the
strings–all of these things have been Steinbrenner's way.

"I am dead-set against free agency," Steinbrenner said.
"It can ruin baseball." That is another part of his profile.
He says things he doesn't mean. Catfish Hunter, Reggie
Jackson, Dave Winfield, and many others have been
rewarded with millions and millions of George
Steinbrenner Yankee dollars. There have been times
when the Yankees were so stuffed with free-agent superstars that there was barely room in the lineup for all of
them.

Suspension for his dealings with small-time gamblers,
reinstatement, feuds with players–there have been
"issues" galore for the Yankee owner. But no one can
quarrel with his success, dedication, and pride. "Owning
the Yankees," the Yankee boss has said on many occasions, "is like owning the *Mona Lisa*."

As the 2002 season got under way, Steinbrenner's
tenure as Yankee owner–twenty-nine seasons–was the
all-time longest, five years more than Jake Ruppert.

YANKEE MANAGERS
Under George Steinbrenner

YEAR(S)	NAME	WINS-LOSSES
1973	RALPH HOUK	80–82
1974–1975	BILL VIRDON	142–124
1975–1978	BILLY MARTIN	279–192
1978	DICK HOWSER	0–1
1978–1979	BOB LEMON	82–51
1979	BILLY MARTIN	55–40
1980	DICK HOWSER	103–59
1981	GENE MICHAEL	48–34
1981–1982	BOB LEMON	17–22
1982	GENE MICHAEL	44–42
1982	CLYDE KING	29–33
1983	BILLY MARTIN	91–71
1984–1985	YOGI BERRA	93–85
1985	BILLY MARTIN	91–54
1986–1987	LOU PINIELLA	179–145
1988	BILLY MARTIN	40–28
1988	LOU PINIELLA	45–48
1989	DALLAS GREEN	56–65
1989–1990	BUCKY DENT	36–53
1990–1991	STUMP MERRILL	120–155
1992–1995	BUCK SHOWALTER	313–268
1996–	JOE TORRE	582–327 (THROUGH 2001)

MULTIPLE MANAGING STINTS

Billy Martin	5
Dick Howser	2
Bob Lemon	2
Gene Michael	2
Lou Piniella	2

CASEY STENGEL

*"I don't like them fellas who drive in
two runs and let in three."*

CHARLES DILLON STENGEL was born on July 30, 1890, in Kansas City,
Missouri. He died on September 29, 1975, in Glendale, California. "There
comes a time in every man's life," Casey said, "and I've had plenty of them."

His time as manager of the New York Yankees ranks way up there. Under
his leadership from 1949 to 1960, the Yankees won ten pennants and seven
World Series, including a record five straight world championships 1949–1953.
From 1949 through 1964, the team won fourteen pennants and nine world
championships. Only once in his dozen seasons did his teams win fewer than
ninety games; his Yankee career managing record was 1,149–696, a winning
percentage of .623.

He was something else. But at the start there were doubts.

"I didn't get the job through friendship," Casey said at his first press conference on October 12, 1948. "The Yankees represent an investment of millions
of dollars. They don't hand out jobs like this just because they like your company. I got the job because the people here think I can produce for them. I
know I can make people laugh. And some of you think I'm a damn fool."

"It was a shock," said pitcher Eddie Lopat. "We thought we got us a clown.
But we could see it was a treat for him to be with us after
all the donkey clubs he had been with."

In 1949, the string of five straight pennants and world
championships began. In the clubhouse celebration,
Stengel, who would be voted Manager of the Year,
announced: "I want to thank all these players for giving
me the greatest thrill of my life. And to think they pay
me for managing so great a bunch of boys."

Stengel's managerial method included riding players
when they were doing well, panning them at other times.
Platooning players became a Stengel managing trademark, as did using pinch hitters at unusual times.

Left-handed-hitting Gene Woodling and right-
handed-hitting Hank Bauer shared outfield duties. "We
didn't like it," Bauer said. "But you couldn't complain
too much—we walked into the bank every October."

In Casey's time, first base was held down at one time or
another by Tommy Henrich, Johnny Mize, Bill Skowron,
and Joe Collins. The second basemen included Jerry
Coleman, Billy Martin, Gil McDougald, and Bobby

Casey Stengel

Richardson. Third basemen included Gil McDougald, Billy Johnson, Bobby Brown, Hector Lopez, and Andy Carey. Shortstop belonged to Phil Rizzuto, but Billy Hunter, Tony Kubek, and Gil McDougald also had their time there.

Batting orders could be odd and were often changed. Hank Bauer batted everywhere from leadoff to seventh in the order. Starters like Allie Reynolds and Johnny Sain and others became relief pitchers.

"Sure he wasn't that young," Skowron said. "But he knew and we knew what we had to do. He'd leave us alone when we were winning. He'd holler 'butcher boy' and 'don't swing too hard at ground balls' and 'don't beat yourselves.' But when he saw us making mistakes, he'd get excited and do some yelling."

The Yankees took the 1958 pennant by ten games. The 1959 Yankees finished in third place, their low point in Stengel's time as manager. There were some who thought it was the beginning of the end. Nearing seventy, impatient, Casey made moves in games that seemed highly unorthodox even for him.

But in 1960 in a tough pennant race, the Ole Perfessor rallied the Yankees to another flag. But Bill Mazeroski's walk-off homer gave the world championship to Pittsburgh.

Yankee owners Dan Topping and Del Webb, anxious to get rid of Stengel, used the defeat by the Pirates as an excuse. Casey was fired.

"I commenced winning pennants when I got here," Stengel rasped, "but I didn't commence getting any younger. They told me my services were no longer desired because they wanted to put in a youth program as an advance way of keeping the club going. When a club gets to discharging a man on account of age, they can if they want to. The trick is growing up without growing old. Most guys are dead at my age anyway. You could look it up. I'll never make the mistake of being seventy years old again."

Inducted into the Baseball Hall of Fame in 1966, Casey Stengel was fittingly selected as Baseball's Greatest Manager during the sport's centennial.

"Casey was a great, great manager, probably the greatest of all," mused Jerry Coleman. "He understood his players, what they could do and what they couldn't do. He understood the front office—what they wanted from him. He understood the media and that was vital in New York. He understood the fans—he was a great communicator. You don't forget a man like Casey."

JOE TORRE

"Winning never gets old."

BUCK SHOWALTER LED the Yankees to a second-place finish in the AL East in 1995. Exit Showalter. Enter Joe Torre as manager for 1996.

"The media was against it," George Steinbrenner said. "He never won anywhere, they said. But he was a New Yorker, and mentally tough."

The fifty-five-year-old Torre, out of Marine Park in Brooklyn, out of St. Francis Prep, was the outsider. Prior to coming to the Yankees, the former All-Star catcher, National League MVP and batting champ had managed the Braves, Cardinals, and Mets.

He began the 1996 season with more than one thousand career losses, never finishing higher than fourth with the Mets from 1977 to 1981. His Braves were swept three straight by the Cardinals in the 1982 NLCS. In five years with St. Louis, his clubs never won more than eighty-seven games in any one season.

"When I first got the job," Torre said, "I felt a little strange putting on the Yankee uniform because of all the tradition that went with being a part of this organization."

His salary for 1996 was $500,000. He had earned more than that as a baseball broadcaster. It wasn't about money—it was about challenge. The man they called the Godfather didn't need the money, didn't even need the job. Perhaps that was part of the reason he was able to succeed where others had not. He was not intimidated by the domineering Steinbrenner or anyone else.

Joe Torre

Outwardly, Torre is affable, a communicator, able to get along well with all types of players. Inwardly, there is a steely resolve. If a player doesn't get it, Torre gives it to him. If a player does it Torre's way, he is given star treatment.

In 1996, the Yankees did it Torre's way, and he led them to a 92–70 finish. Surging through the playoffs, New York came up against favored Atlanta in the World Series. The Yankees dropped the first two games at Yankee Stadium, then won all three in Atlanta, and won game six at the stadium to record their first world championship since 1978.

Joseph Paul Torre, after 4,272 games as player and manager, after all the years of waiting, had a World Series ring.

In 1997, the Yankees won ninety-six games but lost in a hard-fought five-game series to Cleveland in the first round of the playoffs. The 1998 season was historic as the Yanks won a then-AL-record 114 games, sweeping the Padres in the World Series. In 1999, the man they call a players' manager overcame a battle with cancer and led his Yankees to their twenty-fifth World Series title, again in a sweep, this time over the Braves. They followed with another world championship in 2000, in five games against the Mets, and came within an eyelash of a fourth straight title in 2001, losing in seven games to the Diamondbacks.

All of these world championships and stunning managerial moves have made the reinvented Joe Torre seem like a genius. However, he also may have an extra edge through his sister, Sister Mary Marguerite Torre, who runs the show as principal at the Nativity of the Blessed Virgin Mary elementary school in Queens.

Torre's father was a New York City cop. He toyed with the idea of becoming a priest or a doctor. But instead he became the first Yankee manager to be born in the New York area, and the sixth manager in franchise history to reach the five-hundred-victory plateau.

After coming to the Yankees with a 894–1,003 managerial record (.471), Torre has gone 582–327 (.640) in six seasons in the Bronx.

Manager of the Year in 1996 and 1998, unflappable Joe Torre just loves being king of New York City and New York City wouldn't have it any other way. On December 11, 2001, Torre signed a new three-year contract with the Yankees for far more money than the $500,000 he settled for when he first began in 1996.

JIM TURNER

"It just happened."

JUST NINETEEN YEARS old when he began pitching in 1922 for Paris, Tennessee, for $150 a month, James Riley Turner was thirty-three years old when he finally reached the majors with the old Boston Bees. His major-league debut was April 30, 1937.

They called him the Milkman because of his off-season job delivering milk for his family's business. He was a relief pitcher for the Yankees from 1942 to 1945. At age forty-two, in his final season, he saved an AL-high ten games. "He knows all there is to know about pitching," said his manager, Joe McCarthy.

Turner, who had pitched for Casey Stengel in Boston, was hired by him in 1948 as a Yankee pitching coach. He was with the Yankees until 1959. After one year managing in the minors, the soft-spoken Turner became Cincinnati's pitching coach. Turner returned to the Yankees and served under Ralph Houk from 1966 to 1973. "Jim always talks sense," Houk said.

All told, Jim Turner spent a record fifty-one consecutive years in baseball and played or coached in thirteen World Series. "I'm mighty fortunate to have put in fifty-one complete seasons," Turner said. "But I do not think of it as a record or feat. It just happened."

On his eighty-fourth birthday, Turner commented: "If I live to be a hundred, I would never be able to repay baseball for what it has done for me." Turner passed away at the age of ninety-five in his hometown of Nashville in 1998.

GEORGE WEISS

"There is no such thing as second place. You're first or you're nothing."

"HE WAS THOROUGHLY Yankee all the way," Jerry Coleman recalled. "Very tough and cold, but brilliant. I worked in the front office for a couple of years. At five minutes to five the phone would ring. It was George—he wanted to make sure you were still working."

His first deal was acquiring Eddie Lopat for the Yankees and his last deal was getting Roger Maris. Warts and all, and there were many, George Weiss was the most respected figure in all of baseball in his time.

When it came to penny-pinching, George Weiss even outclassed Branch Rickey, whose farm-system concept he copied and surpassed. One of the most successful baseball executives ever, Weiss got an early start. While a student at Yale, he worked for a semipro team in New Haven that outdrew the local pro Eastern League entry. Always promotion-oriented, he even signed big-leaguers to game-to-game contracts.

In 1919, the twenty-four-year-old Weiss purchased the Eastern League New Haven team. By 1929, he was with Baltimore in the International League. Then Ed Barrow and Colonel Ruppert, in one of the best decisions the Yankees ever made, hired Weiss.

From the 1930s through the 1960s, the drab and detail-oriented George Weiss was the main man responsible for Yankee success. There were those who called him the Yankee inspector-general because he held sway over everything— the positions players were slotted for, the quality of toilet paper, the look of the players, and their uniforms. Everything.

"Weiss was a quiet man who did not like to get into crowds," said Jim Thomson, who was plant supervisor of Yankee Stadium under the Yankee GM. "But how he could pay attention to details."

"He didn't have a social relationship with anyone," noted Jerry Coleman. "They called him Lonesome George for good reason." Others had more earthy terms for the man who once said: "To hell with newspapermen, you can buy them with a steak." Shy, cold, colorless, and humorless, all Weiss really cared about were his wife, a tight circle of old friends, and the New York Yankees.

It was George Weiss who built the great farm system, which at one point boasted more than twenty teams. The Yankee minor-league clubs of the late 1930s were so talented that many claimed the second best team in baseball was their top farm team, the Newark Bears, who won their league's pennant in 1937 by twenty-five games. The Bears of the International League was the system's crown jewel; it sported talent that was a who's who of future major-league stars.

Weiss had an incredible knack for selecting the best personnel. Scouts like

(L to R): George Weiss, George Ruppert (Jacob's brother), and Joe McCarthy

Johnny Nee and Paul Krichell kept the Yankee talent pipeline flowing. After Ed Barrow retired, Weiss became Yankee general manager.

The Yankees finished third in 1948. Bucky Harris was fired as manager despite winning ninety-four games. Weiss convinced the owners to bring in Casey Stengel, whom he knew from time around the Oakland Oaks of the Pacific Coast League. It was Weiss's right touch on display again.

Frugality was almost a religion with Weiss, who believed in maximum profits at minimum cost. Taking a cue from his mentor Ed Barrow, he could be nasty in contract talks with players.

Weiss informed Mickey Mantle that he was cutting his pay $17,000 for the 1958 season. Mantle had batted twelve points higher in 1957 than in 1956 but hadn't won the batting title or the Triple Crown, as he had in 1956.

"Why the pay cut?" Mantle asked.

"It's what you're worth," Weiss responded. That ended that. Endings were Weiss's specialty. "You eat like a Yankee, but you don't perform like one on the field," he told a player he got rid of for running up extra-large room-service tabs. He ended Billy Martin's playing career as a Yankee after the Copa incident, trading him away. He cut Rizzuto from the roster at Old Timers' Day in 1956. He moved Vic Raschi after a salary dispute.

He was also a racist. That is now pretty much a matter of record. It took until 1955 for a black player (Elston Howard) to become a Yankee. That policy cost the Yankees when Weiss was no longer on the scene in the 1960s.

But while he was on the scene wheeling, dealing, tinkering with the roster, and planning ahead with personnel moves, pennants and world championships kept coming. After the Yankees finished second in 1954, ending the run of five consecutive championships, Weiss acquired young pitchers Bob Turley and Don Larsen, who had combined to go 17–36 that season. In pinstripes they shined. After the 1959 season, Weiss then traded Larsen and three others to Kansas City for Roger Maris.

In his twenty-nine seasons as general manager and mastermind of the Yankees, the team won nineteen pennants and fifteen world championships. Weiss was named Executive of the Year four times. In 1971, he was admitted to the Baseball Hall of Fame.

BERNIE WILLIAMS

"To me, it's an honor."

HE DIDN'T REALIZE it at first, he admits. "But through my third to fourth year," Bernie Williams said, "I started to be aware of all the tradition that came just from being a Yankee. And the type of responsibilities, if you will, were to me, to play in the same position that all those great players in the past played in Yankee Stadium, and to me it's an honor."

While he was growing up, playing baseball in Puerto Rico's Mickey Mantle League, Williams never dreamed that one day he would play center field for the Yankees and follow in the footsteps of the man his league was named for. Williams, a talented classical guitarist, even toyed with the idea of passing up a baseball career in favor of studying music.

The San Juan native was signed as a non-drafted free agent by the Yankees in 1985. Learning to switch-hit in the minor leagues, he reached the majors for the first time in the second half of the 1991 season. By 1993, the graceful Williams was a fixture in center field, using long, loping strides to track down balls.

"He's so fluid," David Cone said, "so graceful, so efficient. People often misread athletes like that."

From 1995 to 1997, Williams hit .313, averaging 103 runs scored, twenty-three homers and ninety-five RBIs. But 1998 was his career year. He became the first player to win a batting title, Gold Glove (the second of three in a row), and be on a World Series–winning team in the same season.

In 2000, Williams posted career highs in home runs (30), doubles (37), and RBIs (121), helping New York win its fourth World Series title in five years. Bernie scored more than 100 runs (108) for the fifth consecutive year and topped the .300 mark (.307) for the sixth year in a row. He also notched his fourth straight Gold Glove and played in his fourth All-Star Game.

Bernie Williams

The first player in major-league history to homer from both sides of the plate in a postseason game, holder of the record for the most career RBIs in a Division Series, the fifth Yankee to homer from both sides of the plate in the same game—Bernie Williams was well worth the seven-year, $87.5 million contract he signed after the 1998 season. He is a quiet Yankee superstar.

DAVE WINFIELD

"For a guy to be successful, you have to be like a clock spring—wound but loose at the same time."

BORN ON OCTOBER 3, 1951, in St. Paul, Minnesota, Dave Winfield never spent a day in the minor leagues. He attended the University of Minnesota on a baseball scholarship and was the MVP of the 1973 College World Series. Four teams in three different sports drafted him.

He chose baseball and San Diego, where he was the main man for eight seasons. In 1981, Dave Winfield was wearing pinstripes, signed to a ten-year contract that made him the highest-paid player in baseball.

A right-handed line-drive hitter, the six-feet-six-inch, 220-pound Winfield intimidated opposing pitchers by swinging a sledgehammer in the on-deck circle. His first home run for the Yankees was a game winner and set the tone for his time in New York. In seven full seasons with the Yanks, Winfield averaged over twenty-seven home runs per season, with four straight Gold Gloves.

Playing in just 105 games in his first season with the Yankees, Winfield batted .294 with thirteen home runs and sixty-eight RBIs and did well in divisional play. But a sickly .045 batting average in the World Series that the Yankees lost to the Dodgers prompted George Steinbrenner to call Winfield Mr. May. It was an unfortunate and undeserved nickname for a player who homered once every 23.7 at bats during his career and posted a home-run-to-hit ratio of 1 to 6.7.

Although the Yankees failed to get into postseason competition in the 1980s, it was not Winfield's fault. He drove in over one hundred runs each season from 1982 through 1986, becoming the first Yankee since Joe DiMaggio to do so in five consecutive seasons.

David Mark Winfield's time in New York was often fraught with controversy and misunderstandings. There was the "Seagull Incident" in 1983, when Winfield hit a bird with a ball. There was the acrimonious battle for the 1984 batting title with Don Mattingly. There were the lawsuits Steinbrenner and Winfield engaged in over the Dave Winfield Foundation. There were crippling injuries.

And finally, there was the trade in 1990 to the California Angels. All of that is why number 31 went into the Hall of Fame in 2001 as a Padre, not a Yankee.

HONORABLE MENTIONS

CLETE BOYER, RYNE Duren, Rickey Henderson, Gil McDougald, Bobby Murcer, Andy Pettitte, Jorge Posada, Mel Stottlemyre, Ralph Terry, Tom Tresh, Bob Turley, Roy White, Don Zimmer.

CHAPTER FIVE

THE *Teams*

BEST AND WORST

WITH TWENTY-SIX WORLD championships, thirty-eight pennants, and forty-one playoff appearances through the 2001 season, the New York Yankees have had a lot to brag about. The all-time franchise record through the 2001 season (including their two years in Baltimore before moving to New York) is 8,792 wins and 6,782 losses. Through the decades there have been so many extraordinary teams. There have also, however, been a few clunker clubs who have dimmed the luster of baseball's greatest franchise. What follows is a look at the best of the best and the worst of the worst.

◆

THE BEST

1927

◆ 110–44 (.714)

"BY GAME TIME the vast structure was packed solid," A *New York World* account related. "April 12, 1927, Opening Day at Yankee Stadium. Rows of men were standing in back of the seats and along the runways. Such a crowd had never seen a baseball game or any other kind of game in New York."

The Seventh Regiment Band played for the throng of 72,000, part of the 1,164,015 who came out during that 1927 season to cheer on the Yankees. Tiny Miller Huggins and tall Connie Mack posed for photographs. The Philadelphia Athletics and the Yankees marched in columns of four to the outfield. The national anthem was played, and New York City mayor Jimmy Walker presented Babe Ruth with a three-foot-high silver loving cup.

1927 New York Yankees

This was the Yankee Opening Day lineup:

EARLE COMBS	CF
MARK KOENIG	SS
BABE RUTH	RF
LOU GEHRIG	1B
BOB MEUSEL	LF
TONY LAZZERI	2B
JOE DUGAN	3B
JOHNNY GRABOWSKI	C
WAITE HOYT	P

The Yankees won that day, 8–3, settling into first place, where they remained throughout the season without a single change in a roster.

Switch-hitting Mark Koenig went 5 for 5 in the second game of the four-game series, a romp over the A's. The third game was tied 9–9 in the tenth inning but was then called because of darkness. The Yankees won the fourth game 6–3. Philadelphia, a team that would collectively bat .303 and win ninety-one games that year, was just delighted to get out of town. The powerful and versatile Yankee lineup was something to behold—unless you were on the opposing team.

Earle Combs and Mark Koenig served as table setters in the batting order. Combs batted .356 and led the league in hits, singles, and triples. Koenig, in his third Yankee season, batted .285 and fanned just 21 times in 586 at bats. But he was a self-deprecating kind of fellow. "Just putting on a Yankee uniform gave me a little confidence, I think. That club could carry you. You were better than you actually were. I was ordinary, very ordinary," the native Californian said. "I had small hands and made too many errors. But the Yankees could have carried a midget at shortstop. That's how good a club it was."

Locked into the third space in the powerful batting order was Babe Ruth, who hit .356 that year with 164 RBIs and a league best .772 slugging percentage. Scoring the most runs, drawing the most walks, recording the most total bases, and compiling the highest on-base percentage, Ruth by himself out-homered all major-league teams except the Giants, Cubs, and Cardinals.

The cleanup hitter was Lou Gehrig. He batted .373 (third in the American League), drove in a league best 175 runs, and smashed forty-seven home runs. His doubles total was tops in the American League and his slugging percentage of .765 was second only to Ruth. The Yankees were 33–7 (.825) in games when Gehrig homered. Almost 25 percent of all American League home runs in 1927 were hit by Gehrig and Ruth.

Bob Meusel batted fifth in the order. A .337 batter in 1927, he had 103 RBIs and twenty-four stolen bases. Tony Lazzeri, batting sixth, was in the second of what would be a dozen solid seasons as a Yankee second baseman. The quiet athlete finished third behind Ruth and Gehrig in home runs, notched a .309 average, and had 102 RBIs.

"Jumping Joe" Dugan, thirty, confidant of Babe Ruth, was peerless at third base. He did have a complaint, however: "It's always the same. Combs walks. Koenig singles. Ruth hits one out of the park. Gehrig doubles. Lazzeri triples. Then Dugan goes down on the dirt on his can."

Catching duties were shared by journeymen Johnny Grabowski and Pat Collins. Others on the roster included Walter Beall; third-string catcher Benny Bengough; outfielder Cedric Durst; Mike Gazella, who filled in for Joe Dugan in fifty-four games and batted .278; Joe Giard; Ray Morehart, who took over second base when Lazzeri was moved to short in place of Koenig; Ben Paschal; Myles Thomas; and Julie Wera.

"The secret of success as a pitcher lies in getting a job with the New York Yankees," was Waite Hoyt's famous quip, although it was as much a truism as a quip. The ace of the 1927 team, Hoyt paced the league in wins and winning percentage. But the Yankees had other winning arms, too.

Wilcy Moore's sidearm sinkerball helped him post a 19–7 record, 13–3 in relief, the lowest ERA and the most shutouts in the league. Urban Shocker, who suffered all through that 1927 season from a heart condition kept secret from his fellow Yankees, won 18 of 24 decisions. Walter Henry "Dutch" Reuther went 13–6 but was replaced in mid-season by the hard-throwing rookie George Pipgras, who went 10–3 (.769). Half a dozen pitchers won at least ten games. The 1927 Yankees had the three lowest ERAs in the league, with Moore (2.28), Hoyt (2.63), and Shocker (2.84), and four of the top seven.

Miller Huggins managed the collection of different personalities. Mark Koenig said of him: "He was a good manager, although he was a nervous little guy who moved his feet a lot in the dugout. But he didn't have to be much of a strategist with that club. Lots of times, we'd be down five, six runs, and then have a big inning to win the game."

By the end of May, the Yankees had won 23 of 33 games. By June 24, they had a 44–17 record. Heading into a Fourth of July doubleheader at Yankee Stadium, the Senators had won ten straight and D.C. was buzzing with talk that the Senators were making their push. The Yankees were disdainful of such banter.

In game one, the Yankees clubbed Washington 12–1. The nightcap was a 21–1 slaughter. Whacking competition was a trademark of the 1927 Yankees. Special victims were the St. Louis Browns, losers of twenty-one in a row to the New Yorkers.

Ruth at six feet two and Meusel at six feet three were the tallest players, and only two of the pitchers on the Yankees at that time were taller than six feet. But to the fans and players on other teams, it seemed that the 1927 Yankees were a collection of oversized giants.

"This isn't just a ball club!" sportswriter Arthur Robinson emoted. "This is Murderers' Row!"

1927
AMERICAN LEAGUE STANDINGS

TEAM	W	L	W-L%	GB
NEW YORK	110	44	.714	–
PHILADELPHIA	91	63	.591	19
WASHINGTON	85	69	.552	25
DETROIT	82	71	.536	27½
CHICAGO	70	83	.458	39½
CLEVELAND	66	87	.431	43½
ST. LOUIS	59	94	.386	50½
BOSTON	51	103	.331	59

"It was murder," Babe Ruth bragged justifiably. "We never even worried five or six runs behind. Wham! Wham! Wham! And wham! No matter who was pitching."

"When we were challenged," Waite Hoyt said, "when we had to win, we stuck together and played with a fury and determination that could only come from team spirit. We had a pride in our performance that was very real. It took on the form of snobbery. And I do believe we left a heritage that became a Yankee tradition."

Ritual and superstition were major elements of the makeup of the 1927 Yankees. Babe Ruth would warm up only with catcher Fred Hofman. After hitting a home run, the Babe would notch his bat. But when he hit his twenty-first home run, the new notch split his bat. That ritual stopped. Waite Hoyt warmed up only with his starting catcher. Infielder Joe Dugan always scratched out a mark at third base. Wilcy Moore threw his first warm-up pitch only to Eddie Bennett, Yankee batboy and good-luck charm. Manager Miller Huggins had messages delivered to the bullpen only by Mike Gazella.

The five-o'clock blowing of a factory whistle close by Yankee Stadium signaled the end of the workday. The Yankees were fond of the sound of the whistle; it underlined how they beat teams. They called it the end of their workday, Five O'clock Lightning.

By the end of July, a month in which the Yankees posted a 24–7 record, they led the AL by fifteen games and their winning percentage was a gaudy .730.

By August 31, the lead over the second-place Athletics was seventeen games. On September 13, the Yankees swept a doubleheader from Cleveland and clinched the pennant.

At Yankee Stadium on September 29, Ruth homered off two different

Washington pitchers in a 15–4 Yankee cakewalk, tying his record of fifty-nine in a single season.

Finishing with a 110–44 record, winning the pennant by nineteen games, the Yankees pounded 158 home runs, batted .307 as a team, recorded the all-time best slugging percentage of .489, averaged 6.5 runs a game, scored 975 runs, and held opponents to 599 runs.

Leading the league in every individual offensive category except for batting average, the Bronx Bombers had five regulars who batted .300 or better. Four of the eight American Leaguers who drove in one hundred or more runs were Yankees.

The pitching staff led the league in shutouts and its ERA was almost a run below the league average. The four best winning percentages in the league belonged to Yankee pitchers.

The 1927 Yankees were so free of injury that six of the eight position players logged more than five hundred at bats. Durability was a tremendous bonus for the team and masked a weakness of the Bronx Bombers, a thin bench.

The World Series competition was against the Pittsburgh Pirates. Babe Ruth said of that competition: "We won before it even got started. The first two games were scheduled for Forbes Field. Naturally we showed up a day early and worked out in the strange park—and we won the series during that workout.

"We really put on a show. Lou and I banged ball after ball into the right-field stands, and I finally knocked one out of the park in right center. Bob Meusel and Tony Lazzeri kept hammering balls into the left-field seats."

The Yanks took the Bucs in four, becoming the first American League team to sweep a World Series. "It all meshed for us," Mark Koenig said, "the personalities, the manager, the luck, everything that 1927 season."

Half a dozen Yankees from that fabled team, with an average age of twenty-seven, became Hall of Famers–Babe Ruth, Lou Gehrig, Herb Pennock, Waite Hoyt, Earle Combs, Tony Lazzeri–as did manager Miller Huggins.

1932
◆ 107–47 (.695)

IT HAD BEEN five years since the Yankees last won a world championship. Philadelphia had taken the last three pennants. The 1932 Yankees, with an average age of 28.2 years, were a little older than the 1927 team. The only prime-time players left from Murderers' Row were Ruth, Gehrig, Lazzeri, Combs, Pipgras, and Pennock.

In Meusel's place in left field was Ben Chapman, league leader in stolen bases from 1931 to 1933. The team included two rookies, pitcher Johnny Allen and shortstop Frank Crosetti.

With Crosetti and third baseman Joe Sewell—in his second season—playing next to each other, the left side of the Yankee infield was rock solid. At just five feet six and 155 pounds, Sewell swung a forty-ounce bat that he dubbed Black Betsy. Catcher Bill Dickey, in his third year as a Yankee, roomed with Gehrig on the road. "We were very good buddies," Dickey noted. "In fact, I'd say we were more like brothers." They read in the evenings and took up the challenge of Honeymoon Bridge.

On Opening Day, the Yankees hit five home runs at the stadium, winning the game 8–3. Babe Ruth, who had lost twelve pounds from a battle with the flu, clubbed one of the homers.

Slashing twenty home runs in their first eight games, winning ten of thirteen games in April, eighteen of twenty-six in May, and losing just five games in June, the Bronx Bombers were 48–19 heading into July, another big month of winning. August was swell, too, as the Yanks went 23–5.

The 1932 Yankees were a team of consistency and durability. Gehrig, Lazzeri, Combs, Sewell, and Chapman all tallied over five hundred at bats. Reserves were in short supply, but the Yankees made do with backup catcher Art Jorgens, Lyn Lary at shortstop, Doc Farrell at second and short, and outfielders Sammy Byrd and Myril Hoag, who performed as caddies for Babe Ruth.

Babe Ruth and Lou Gehrig

Gifted and durable, the six-man pitching staff featured three hurlers who logged more than two hundred innings each. Lefty Gomez won 24 of 31 decisions and was third in wins and second in strikeouts in the AL. Red Ruffing was 18–7, had the most strikeouts, and was second in AL ERA. George Pipgras went 16–9, Johnny Allen 17–4, and Herb Pennock 9–5, while Danny MacFayden, at 7–5, filled out the staff.

All the parts seemed to fit. Only Babe Ruth was out of place, out of time. A thirty-eight-year-old battler of demons, aches and pains, the great Ruth played in only 133 games in 1932, down a dozen from 1931.

Yet he was still Babe Ruth. His forty-one home runs led the list of half a dozen Yankees who popped at least ten home runs, even though for the first time in a decade the Yankees failed to lead the league in home runs.

Still, the 1932 Yankees were a wrecking crew. The team batting average was .286. Gehrig was third in the league in batting average, tied for second in RBIs, and fourth in home runs and runs scored. Ruth was second in homers, fifth in batting average, and fourth in RBIs.

Playing before a total attendance of 962,320 at home, the Yankees scored over a thousand runs, leading the league for the third year in a row in that category. No American League team drew more walks or had more RBIs. Joe McCarthy's club went through the entire season without being shut out once.

The Yankees finished thirteen games ahead of second-place Philly and copped their seventh pennant. McCarthy led his team up against the Chicago Cubs in the World Series, the team that had fired him in 1930. He wanted payback. He got payback. The Yankees swept the Cubs in four.

1932
AMERICAN LEAGUE FINAL STANDINGS

TEAM	W	L	W-L%	GB
NEW YORK	107	47	.695	–
PHILADELPHIA	94	60	.610	13
WASHINGTON	93	61	.604	14
CLEVELAND	87	65	.572	19
DETROIT	76	75	.503	29½
ST. LOUIS	63	91	.409	44
CHICAGO	49	102	.325	56½
BOSTON	43	111	.279	64

1936

◆ 102–51 (.667)

SEA CHANGES EXISTED for the Yankees as 1936 got under way. The last Yankee pennant was four years in the past. Babe Ruth was gone. Earle Combs had retired. Joe DiMaggio was in his rookie season. Lou Gehrig, the Pride of the Yankees, was now captain.

Going into the 1936 season, the Iron Horse had played in sixteen hundred straight games. His supporting cast included Red Rolfe, George Selkirk, Bill Dickey, Frank Crosetti, Tony Lazzeri, Red Ruffing, and Lefty Gomez.

The season began for the Yankees on April 14 in Washington. President Franklin Delano Roosevelt threw out the first ball. The start was muted for the Yankees, as the Senators won 1–0. But the New Yorkers would do better, much better.

They won ten of the fifteen games they played in April. One of those games at Yankee Stadium was attended by Eddie Brannick, the secretary of the New York Giants.

"What do you think of the Yankees?" Brannick was asked.

"Window breakers," was his response.

In spring training, the highly touted rookie Joe DiMaggio had rapped out a dozen hits in his first twenty at bats. Then he suffered the "hot foot" heard all over the Big Apple, burning his foot in a diathermy machine.

On May 3, 1936, DiMaggio, wearing number 9, played in his first major-league game, a 14–5 thumping of the Browns. Joe Dee was a major contributor to the pounding, tripling, singling twice, and scoring three times. Four days later DiMag threw out Pete Fox of Detroit at home preserving a 6–5 Yankee win. Three days later he hit the first of what would be 361 career home runs. The Yankees that day took over first place for the rest of the season.

Manager Joe McCarthy paired his prize rookie with the hyperactive Lefty Gomez. Roommates on the road, they were the original odd couple. "We were opposites," Gomez said. "I talked all the time and Joe never talked at all. He was always relaxed. And how that feller could sleep. The man I felt sorry for was Lou Gehrig. He had always played behind Ruth, and finally Ruth quit and he had it all to himself in 1935. Now Joe comes along. Lou had another big year, but Joe was the rookie sensation, so he got all the attention."

On May 24, Tony Lazzeri hit two grand-slam home runs, a bases-empty homer, and a triple—fifteen total bases in all—torquing a 25–2 ravaging of the Athletics in Shibe Park. The thirty-three-year-old Lazzeri batted eighth in the potent Yankee lineup.

The Yankees went 20–8 in May with DiMaggio playing left field. On June 14, the Yankees were in first place by a few games when they traded outfielder

Ben Chapman to Washington for outfielder Jake Powell. Chapman was a lifetime .300 hitter, but McCarthy disliked his often surly personality.

With Powell in place, McCarthy made the move he had in mind all season. "I started DiMaggio in left field," McCarthy explained, "and then I moved him to right field for a while. I wanted to make sure he was comfortable before I put him in center field." On August 8, the Yankee Clipper became the Yankee center fielder.

On June 17 the Yankees swept a doubleheader from Cleveland, pounding out nineteen hits in each game. The first game winner was Red Ruffing, who chipped in with two homers and a pair of singles.

On June 24, the *New York Times* reported on a game in Chicago: "With Colonel Jacob Ruppert in town for a brewer's convention viewing the spectacle and wearing at the same time the best smile . . . the Yankees today put on a gorgeous show for the edification of their employer."

The twenty-one-year-old Joe DiMaggio showed especially well, hitting his seventh and eighth home runs, crowning a ten-run fifth inning. He also collected two doubles (he would have a team-leading forty-four for the season) in the 18–11 Yankee bombing of the White Sox.

By the end of June, the Yankees had a 9½-game lead. The batting order boasted more overall power, more versatility, more talent than even the 1927 Murderers' Row.

This was the standard lineup (final season batting averages in parentheses):

CROSETTI	(.288)
ROLFE	(.291)
DIMAGGIO	(.323)
GEHRIG	(.354)
DICKEY	(.362)
SELKIRK	(.308)
POWELL	(.306)
LAZZERI	(.287)

Lou Gehrig was an offensive force unto himself. Lazzeri and Crosetti were a talented double-play combo. At third base in his third season, Robert "Red" Rolfe was highly skilled. With DiMaggio in center, Powell in left, and George Selkirk in right, the Yankees had a trio that hit, ran, and threw. Bill Dickey was like another manager on the field.

The Yankee pitching staff wasn't too shabby either that year, leading the league in saves, earned-run average, and strikeouts. Red Ruffing was 20–12. And for good measure he batted .291, with five home runs. Lefty Gomez won 13 of 20 decisions. Monte Pearson posted a 19–7 record for the top winning percentage in the league. Montgomery Marcellus "Bump" Hadley, the ex-Senator, was 14–4. Johnny Broaca won 12 of 19 decisions.

Pat Malone and Johnny Murphy gave the Yanks the top bullpen pair.

Malone led the league in saves (a stat not kept at the time) with nine, and was 12–4. "Fordham Johnny" Murphy, making his big curveball his "out" pitch, saved five and posted a 9–3 mark.

The Yankees won 21 of 19 games in August, scoring runs in bunches, "breaking windows." A doubleheader sweep of the Indians on September 9 clinched the pennant for the Yankees—the earliest date ever. Winning 102 games, the Yanks finished 19½ games ahead of second-place Detroit.

Five Yankees drove in more than one hundred runs and batted .300 or better, topped by Dickey's .362, the best ever for a catcher. The Yankees, who batted .300 as a team, hit more home runs (182) and scored more runs (1,065) than any other team in the American League.

The World Series matchup was against the New York Giants, the first Subway Series since 1923. It was the first Yankee World Series without Babe Ruth, but a young Joe DiMaggio was making his October debut.

On and off paper, the Yankees had bragging rights as one of the greatest teams of all time. They showed why, taking care of business and the Giants in six. The Bronx Bombers outscored the Giants 43–23 and batted .302 as a team.

"That club," said Giant manager Bill Terry, "has everything. They're the toughest club I've ever faced. I've always heard that one player could make the difference between a losing team and a winner, and I never believed it. Now I know it's true." That one player was Joe DiMaggio.

Joe McCarthy said: "Somebody came up to me and said my club was so good it don't look like anybody was going to beat us for a long time. I'll tell you, that fellow knew what he was talking about."

That 1936 season was the first of four straight pennants and world championships for the Yankees.

1936
AMERICAN LEAGUE FINAL STANDINGS

TEAM	W	L	W-L%	GB
NEW YORK	102	51	.667	–
DETROIT	83	71	.539	19½
CHICAGO	81	70	.536	20
WASHINGTON	82	71	.536	20
CLEVELAND	80	74	.519	22½
BOSTON	74	80	.481	28½
ST. LOUIS	57	95	.375	44½
PHILADELPHIA	53	100	.346	49

1939
◆ 106–45 (.702)

THE EARLY PART of the year had all kinds of bad news. Jacob Ruppert passed away in January. Lou Gehrig announced his retirement. Joe DiMaggio's leg injury forced him to miss most of the season's first month. Despite all of this, the 1939 New York Yankees had one of their most glorious seasons ever.

The very talented Yankees blended timely hitting, speed, power, top pitching, and defense. The usual batting order went this way:

FRANK CROSETTI	SS
RED ROLFE	3B
CHARLIE KELLER	RF
JOE DIMAGGIO	CF
BILL DICKEY	C
GEORGE SELKIRK	LF
BABE DAHLGREN	1B
JOE GORDON	2B

Charlie Keller,
Tommy Henrich,
Johnny Lindell,
and Joe DiMaggio

"We didn't have a weakness," said outfielder Tommy Henrich. "Leadoff man Joe Gordon was so darn good, right off the bat. Rolfe never made a mental error. Frank Crosetti was another smart guy. We had smart players who were very dedicated. Joe McCarthy had you indoctrinated in the total game. DiMaggio was the most complete player I've ever seen."

DiMaggio finished that season first in batting average, second in RBIs, and third in home runs. Rolfe was the league leader in runs scored and hits. Rookie Charlie Keller hit .324 and drove in eighty-three runs. And Dickey, left fielder George Selkirk, and second baseman Joe Gordon all joined DiMaggio in driving in one hundred-plus runs.

Reserves on the powerful Yankees could have played regularly on other teams, like catcher Buddy Rosar, who hit .276 in forty-three games, and Tommy Henrich, top pinch hitter and backup to Charlie Keller, who hit .277.

After the All-Star break, the Yanks won 35 of 49 games. The 1936 Yankees had talent spread thick, but its cornerstones were Joe DiMaggio and Red Ruffing. DiMag's MVP season saw him hit .381, with thirty homers and 126 runs scored. Red Ruffing was a twenty-game winner for the fourth straight time.

The remarkable pitching staff led the league in ERA (1.31 points lower than the league average), strikeouts, shutouts, and complete games. Eight different hurlers made at least eleven starts, showcasing the staff's balance. Seven pitchers had double-digit wins.

Twenty-eight-year-old rookie Johnny Allen was 17–4. Pipgras won 16 of 25 decisions. Herb Pennock, at age thirty-eight, was 9–5. Lefty Gomez, a twelve-game winner, was one of the seven Yankee pitchers to record double-figure victories. Johnny Murphy was the league leader in saves. Once-in-a-while relievers Steve Sundra and Oral Hildebrand won twenty-one games between them.

Domination was the theme of the 1939 New York Yankees. Sportswriters referred to the other seven American League teams as the Seven Dwarfs. Leading the league in home runs, RBIs, slugging percentage, walks, runs, and fielding percentage, allowing nearly 150 runs fewer than any other team in the league, the Yankees outscored their opponents by 411 runs, a greater run differential than any team in history, and won the pennant seventeen games ahead of second-place Boston.

"Everybody respected Joe McCarthy's judgment," Henrich said. "We thought like a team. And that was part of what made us what we were."

The Yankees then swept the Reds in four for their fourth consecutive World Series title, giving them a 28–3 record over their last thirty-one series games. Then the Bronx Bombers took the train back from Cincinnati to New York and a big celebration at the Commodore Hotel.

An oddity of that World Series was the fact that Tommy Henrich, starting right fielder on the 1938 team, didn't bat. "We had a guy named Charlie Keller come along," said Henrich. "And George Selkirk had a good streak going coming into the series, and it turned out we didn't need me to pinch-hit. I was disappointed, sure, but it was no embarrassment waiting to play on that team."

1939
AMERICAN LEAGUE FINAL STANDINGS

TEAM	W	L	W-L%	GB
NEW YORK	106	45	.702	–
BOSTON	89	62	.589	17
CLEVELAND	87	67	.565	20½
CHICAGO	85	69	.552	22½
DETROIT	81	73	.526	26½
WASHINGTON	65	87	.428	41½
PHILADELPHIA	55	97	.362	51½
ST. LOUIS	43	111	.279	64½

1956

◆ 97-57 (.680)

WITH MICKEY MANTLE the battering ram of the Yankee offense, and with Whitey Ford as the anchor of a young pitching staff that included Johnny Kucks, Tom Sturdivant, and Don Larsen, the Yankees won seven of their first eight games as the 1956 season got under way. They won and they just kept winning.

On May 18, in a ten-inning 8–7 Yankee win over Chicago, Mantle homered from both sides of the plate for the third time in his career. Six days later, the Yanks pounded the Tigers 11–4. Mantle, in the midst of a magical season, went 5 for 5.

The *New York Times* reported on June 20: "Mickey Mantle continued his one man reign of terror against American League pitchers with his 26th and 27th home runs." Both shots into the upper deck at Briggs Stadium in Detroit powered the Yankees to their seventh straight victory. Mantle was eighteen games ahead of Babe Ruth's sixty-home-run pace of 1927.

The Mick's power was the talk of the town, but Whitey Ford's masterful hurling was another reason the Yankees were on top of the world. For Whitey and Mickey and the rest of the Yankees in their primes, 1956 was their season of seasons. A half dozen of them were selected to the All-Star team—Yogi Berra, Johnny Kucks, Mickey Mantle, Billy Martin, Gil McDougald, and Whitey Ford.

Stengel called Ford "My banty rooster. He'd stick out his chest and walk out to the mound against any of those pitchers." Mantle, on the other hand, was Stengel's "big fella." On July 1, he homered right-handed and left-handed for

YANKEE STORIES
Andy Carey

I was signed by Joe Devine, the dean of Yankee scouts. He followed me and offered me a bonus of $60,000. The Yankees had just won three championships in a row, but it didn't occur to me that maybe it wasn't the smartest move on my part to join a team with all that talent.

In 1951, the Yankee spring-training site was in Phoenix. "How much can you eat?" I asked them.

"As much as you want."

I was running up bills like $80. "What the hell are you doing," Joe Devine said, "trying to eat yourself out of the league before you even get in?"

In those days there was no such thing as casual dress. Even when we were on the train, it was suits and ties like you were going on a big business trip. I didn't own a suit until I got with the Yankees.

Yankee Stadium was taller than any building in my hometown of Alameda. My first game I made two errors, both on high pop-ups. The sun over third can give you trouble there at certain times of the year. I didn't know how to use sunglasses, hadn't used them before. I was sent down to Triple A ball, where I learned how to use sunglasses and a lot of other things. But I'll never forget that first time at Yankee Stadium.

I remember going on the bus with the Yankees from the stadium to Brooklyn with an escort of about twenty policemen. Sirens were blaring. For a young kid in 1952, it was mind-boggling being part of this powerful team and legacy. It was some experience being on the same field with the likes of Phil Rizzuto, Joe DiMaggio, Yogi Berra. I actually sat at tables with these legends, and they made me feel very comfortable.

My Yankee career was eight and a half years. Moneywise I participated in all the World Series from 1952 on. In 1953, I batted .321 and didn't even get to play in the World Series. Stengel went with the veterans. It was frustrating, but the World Series checks were there.

the fourth time in his career. Against Chicago on August 23, he showed off the whole package: home run, triple, bunt single.

"On two legs Mickey Mantle would have been the greatest player who ever lived," Elston Howard noted. "The man hit all those home runs and did everything else on one leg."

There was a gathering of the clan at Yankee Stadium on August 25–Old Timers' Day at Yankee Stadium. Euphoria and Yankee pride were on parade. But there was a down moment. Phil Rizzuto, thirty-eight and past his time, was released. Enos Slaughter took his roster spot. Sentiment always took a backseat to adding another winning component.

With the old Cardinal on the Yankee roster, Stengel had even more maneuverability. Gil McDougald replaced Rizzuto at short. Billy Martin came out of two years of military service and took over at second base. With Andy Carey at third base and Moose Skowron at first base, the realigned infield turned a league-leading 214 double plays.

On September 11, Yogi Berra hammered his 236th career home run, tying him with Gabby Hartnett for most career home runs by a catcher. It was the 177th homer of the season for the Yankees.

Seven days later, on September 18, Mantle became only the eighth player ever to hit fifty home runs. His 171st career homer, a shot into the upper deck at Comiskey Park, sealed a 3–2 Yankee win over the White Sox. The team from the Bronx had its twenty-second pennant and Casey Stengel had his seventh.

On September 21, Mantle slugged another monster home run–this one traveled 480 feet, just a foot from the top of the bleachers at Fenway. His three

Billy Martin during the 1956
World Series against Dodgers

hits in that game put him neck and neck with Ted Williams in the battle for the batting title.

The season the twenty-four-year-old Mickey Mantle put together in 1956 was one of the greatest years any player ever had. The muscular center fielder's league-leading .353 average, fifty-two home runs, and 130 RBIs gave him the Triple Crown. He became the first Yankee since Gehrig in 1936 to win that award. The Mick also led the league in runs scored, slugging percentage, and total bases. Mantle's major-league-leading slugging percentage was the highest ever by a switch-hitter in a season, as were his 376 total bases and 130 runs batted in.

The Bronx Bombers scored more runs, hit more home runs, and slugged the ball at a higher percentage than any other American League team. Bill Skowron and Gil McDougald batted over .300, while Yogi Berra bagged thirty home runs and drove in 105 runs. Hank Bauer and Bill Skowron combined for forty-nine home runs.

The ace of the staff honors belonged to Whitey Ford, winner of nineteen games, loser of just six, for the league's best winning percentage. But the pitching staff had plenty of other talented arms. Johnny Kucks won eighteen games. Tom Sturdivant won sixteen games. Don Larsen was 11–5 and Bob Turley was 8–4. The Yankees won ninety-seven games and finished nine games ahead of Cleveland.

The fans of New York City baseball then took it for granted that there would be a Subway Series. In 1956, it was Dodgers versus Yankees–their fourth Fall Classic encounter in five years, their sixth since 1947. Only this time, it was the Yankees who sought revenge against "Dem Bums," who had won the world championship against the Yanks the year before. The Yankees had revenge. Casey Stengel had his sixth world championship. The Yankees had their seventeenth.

1956
AMERICAN LEAGUE FINAL STANDINGS

TEAM	W	L	W-L%	GB
NEW YORK	97	57	.630	–
CLEVELAND	88	66	.571	9
CHICAGO	85	69	.552	12
BOSTON	84	70	.545	13
DETROIT	82	72	.532	15
BALTIMORE	69	85	.448	28
WASHINGTON	59	95	.383	38
KANSAS CITY	52	102	.338	45

1961

◆ 109–53 (.673)

THERE WAS A lot that was brand-new about the 1961 baseball season for both the Yankees and the American League. The expansion Los Angeles Angels and the new Washington Senators joined the American League, and major-league baseball expanded its schedule to 162 games.

Casey Stengel was no longer Yankee manager, and George Weiss was out as general manager. It was common knowledge that the World Series defeat in 1960 to Pittsburgh triggered Casey Stengel's retirement/firing. In his place was Ralph Houk, hired to win the World Series. Roy Hamey replaced George Weiss as general manager.

The Yankees began the 1961 season slowly, a disappointing 9–19 in spring training, then a bland 18–15 to start the season. Only thirty-four home runs were hit by the Yankees in their first thirty-three games. Roger Maris did not hit his first home run until April 26. Batting seventh in the lineup during the first month of the season, Maris was wallowing about in a deep slump until the middle of May with just four home runs and a .210 average. Pitching was somewhat problematical. Al Ditmar was up and down, and Bob Turley had elbow problems.

But all was not bad news early on. Mickey Mantle had ten home runs. Elston Howard was hitting for a very high average, and Whitey Ford, starting every fourth day, was at the top of his game.

On May 30, the Yankees slammed seven homers in a 12–3 rout of Boston. Mantle, Maris, and Skowron each had a pair of homers. The victory snapped the Yanks out of their lethargy and kick-started the home-run race between Mantle and Maris.

It was like Babe Ruth and Lou Gehrig and 1927 all over again but better. At ballparks all over the American League fans ogled the new "home run twins." The 1961 Yankees would draw a total of 1,946,292 to their away games, a new road record, and 1,747,736 at Yankee Stadium.

Ralph Houk was a persuasive kind of man, and he was the same as a manager. Once he had decided what he thought worked best, that became team policy. Houk convinced Yogi Berra to move to left field and platoon with Hector Lopez. Defensively, the position became porous, a liability, but offensively there was more punch. The switch enabled Houk to give the starting catcher job to Elston Howard, who batted .348 with twenty-one homers.

Mickey Mantle had batted third his entire career; Houk convinced him that hitting cleanup would help him and the team. That move paid giant dividends, especially for Roger Maris. With Mantle batting behind him, Maris was not walked intentionally the entire 1961 season.

Houk played one set lineup and stayed with a set pitching rotation. The standard 1961 batting order:

BOBBY RICHARDSON	2B
TONY KUBEK	SS
ROGER MARIS	RF
MICKEY MANTLE	CF
YOGI BERRA	LF
ELSTON HOWARD	C
BILL SKOWRON	1B
CLETE BOYER	3B

Day after day, Houk, who had never hit a major-league home run, held sway over his thumpers, who would smash a record 240 home runs. Ten of those home runs were of the pinch-hit variety. Half a dozen Yankees hammered 20 or more home runs that year.

Bobby Richardson and Tony Kubek collectively manufactured 343 hits. As the keystone combination, they helped the infield turn most of its 180 double plays and anchored a Yankee defense that led the league in fielding percentage and double plays, and committed the fewest errors in the league. The infield of Skowron-Richardson-Kubek-Boyer had no equal defensively.

Back to back in the batting order, Maris and Mantle gave the Yankees the most potent one-two punch in baseball. They would hit a total of 115 home runs, a new record topping the mark of 107 set in 1927 by Babe Ruth and Lou Gehrig.

The fifth through eighth positions featured Yogi Berra, Elston Howard, Bill Skowron, and the fabulous-fielding Clete Boyer. "I used to watch how he crouched down," Tracy Nieporent said. "He almost dipped his glove against the dirt."

There were also reserves, like Hector Lopez, Bob Cerv, and Johnny Blanchard, who combined for a .305 average, 21 home runs, 54 RBIs, and a .613 slugging percentage, and who would have been starters for most other teams. Blanchard backed up Elston Howard and was a pinch hitter deluxe. Eight of Blanchard's home runs that season tied up games or were go-ahead runs.

The pitching rotation featured Whitey Ford, league leader in wins, winning percentage, and Cy Young Award winner (25–4, 209 strike-outs); Ralph Terry (16–3); Bill Stafford (14–9), the league leader in ERA (2.68), and Rollie Sheldon (11–5). Although Stafford and Sheldon had only hurled a combined sixty major-league innings prior to 1961, they were highly valuable number-three and -four starters. Jim Coates chipped in with double-digit wins. Little Louie Arroyo, thirty-four, pot-bellied, possessor of a multi-speed screwball, account-ed for a league-leading twenty-nine saves, fifteen wins, and an ERA of 2.19. He even batted .280.

Tony Kubek, Clete Boyer, and Bill Stafford lived at the Stadium Motor Lodge, a two-story motel just eight blocks from Yankee

Bill Skowron, Yanks vs. Red Sox

Stadium. The trio walked to work. After games, they often frequented the Dutchman, a steakhouse where steak was ordered by the ounce. In the doorway were two huge Dobermans on guard duty. Some of the veteran waiters remembered how Babe Ruth sometimes had slid head-first on the sawdust-covered floors after he had more than a few beers.

Another trio, Maris, Mantle, and Bob Cerv, lived quietly together in a Queens apartment. Cerv and Mantle often played a living room game of golf, trying to putt a golf ball on the carpet into a tin cup. Not a high-stakes game, just a nickel a shot, it relieved the pressure on the young men, as did their driving in Maris's convertible, top down.

After spending virtually the entire first half of the season in second place, the Yankees moved past Detroit following the All-Star break. On July 25, the Yankees swept a twi-night doubleheader at Yankee Stadium against Chicago. For most of July they had played musical chairs for first place in the standings with the Tigers—the double win put the Yankees into first place. But there was still a pennant race.

Although the Yankees played at a 22–9 clip in August, the Tigers hung around. The teams met on September 1. Playing before 170,000 and sweeping all three games, the Yankees took off on a thirteen-game winning streak and sent the Tigers into an eight-game losing streak.

The other race was Mickey Mantle pitted against Roger Maris for the home-run title. Maris spent much of his time in the clubhouse at a giant old oak table positioned in the middle of the room, a pack of Camels and a cup of coffee his props. Holding a box in his hands about one foot wide and three inches deep that contained forty holes on two platforms, Maris spent hours playing the game of manipulating a steel ball through the maze of holes. It was a way to retreat, to refine eye-hand coordination.

Roger Maris

By September 10, Mantle had fifty-three home runs. Maris had fifty-six. Maris was driven. Mantle was debilitated, in so much discomfort that Maris had to help him in and out of taxi cabs. The nagging mass of aches and pains—a pulled arm muscle, a bad head cold, an abscess from a flu shot—all ravaged the Mick.

On October 1, 1961, the Yankees played their final game of the season. Roger Maris, worn, frustrated, straining, hit number sixty-one off Tracy Stallard, a twenty-four-year-old Boston right-hander, a rookie.

"Maybe I wouldn't do it all over again if I had the chance," Maris said. "Sometimes I feel it wasn't worth the aggravation. But if I never hit another home run, this is the one they can never take away from me."

Overshadowed by the epic accomplishments of Roger Maris—who won his second straight MVP—were the amazing feats, individually and collectively, of the 1961 Yankees.

Winners of 109 games, the Bronx Bombers were something to behold, posting an incredible 65–16 record at Yankee Stadium, for a home winning percentage of .802. The Yanks were first in the league in fielding, made the fewest errors, and turned the most double plays. Professional was the word used to describe them—and professional they were.

Six Yankees ripped twenty or more homers. Ten pinch hitters homered. There were twenty-four times when two home runs were hit in a game. About the only thing the 1961 New York Yankees didn't do was steal bases. Only twenty-eight were pilfered, and all but seven of those were by Mantle (twelve) and Richardson (nine).

Lost in all the hoopla over Roger Maris were the fifty-four homers hit by Mantle, the most ever by a switch-hitter in a season, thirty of which were road home runs—also a record for a switch-hitter in a season. Coupled with the forty homers he hit in 1960, Mantle's two-season total of ninety-four was the most ever for a switch-hitter.

Finishing eight games ahead of the Detroit Tigers, the Yankees won their sixth pennant in seven years and went up against Cincinnati in the World Series.

Whitey Ford won game one, but Cincy won game two behind twenty-one-game winner Joey Jay. New York, however, was too much for the Reds. The Yankees went on to win three straight in Cincinnati. Another world championship.

1961
AMERICAN LEAGUE FINAL STANDINGS

TEAM	W	L	W-L%	GB
NEW YORK	109	53	.673	–
DETROIT	101	61	.623	8
BALTIMORE	95	67	.586	14
CHICAGO	86	76	.531	23
CLEVELAND	78	83	.484	30½
BOSTON	76	86	.469	33
MINNESOTA	70	90	.438	38
LOS ANGELES	70	91	.435	38½
KANSAS CITY	61	100	.379	47½
WASHINGTON	61	100	.379	47½

1977

◆ 100–62 (.617)

THERE WERE QUITE a few marker dates for the Yankees of the 1970s. One took place on New Year's Eve of 1974, when free-agent pitcher Jim "Catfish" Hunter signed on for five years. The big-time dollars paid triggered the cash flow for others, made for much criticism of George Steinbrenner, and earned the Yankees a reputation as "the best team money could buy."

In 1976, the remodeled Yankee Stadium was opened with a retooled team that included Willie Randolph at second base, Mickey Rivers in center field, Ed Figueroa and Dock Ellis on the mound. The Yanks posted a 97–62 record and finished first for the first time in a dozen years. Thurman Munson won the MVP award, Graig Nettles led the AL in homers, and Sparky Lyle emerged as the bullpen ace. A Chris Chambliss home run off KC's Mark Littell in game five of the Championship Series gave the Yankees their thirtieth pennant. But alas, the Yankees were swept in the World Series by the Big Red Machine of Cincinnati.

George Steinbrenner, ticked off by the defeat sweep, signed free-agent pitcher Don Gullett of Cincinnati for $2.09 million. Then he signed the most-prized free-agent of all, Reggie Jackson. Self-promoting (and self-deprecating of others), Reginald Martinez Jackson, in spring training of 1977, announced: "I didn't come to New York to be a star. I brought my star with me."

Manager Billy Martin, never consulted about the acquisition of Jackson, announced that Reggie would DH exclusively and bat sixth. That didn't sit too well with the egotistical Jackson; neither did the fact that Martin had him play every day in spring training.

With less than a month gone in the season, Billy Martin was under fire again. GM Gabe Paul—with Steinbrenner's blessings—claimed that Martin was making moves that defied explanation. The criticism vexed Billy Martin, always easy to vex.

Billy the Kid claimed that there was a conspiracy afoot, that his personal favorites were being traded away. His claims were correct. Oscar Gamble went to Chicago, along with pitcher LaMarr Hoyt and $400,000, for shortstop Bucky Dent, who took the place of another Martin favorite, Fred Stanley. Dock Ellis and his earring and attitude were dispatched to the Athletics for pitcher Mike Torrez. Cliff Johnson came over from Houston for three prospects.

No manager had a wrath like Martin and he took most of it out on Reggie Jackson, of whom he said: "Off the record, he's a piece of shit." But while the Jackson-Martin relationship was strained, the real tension was in Reggie's relationship with teammates. Most of them agreed with Martin's assessment.

The hot boil that was the 1977 Yankees finally came to a head June 17–19 in a three-game series against Don Zimmer's Red Sox before 103,910 at a windy and unfriendly Fenway. In the first game of the series Catfish Hunter was pounded for four first-inning home runs. Humiliating as that was, the most bizarre moment was still to come in the nationally televised middle game of the series.

Boston led 7–4. Jim Rice checked his swing. The ball landed in front of Reggie Jackson. "He jogged for the ball," Billy Martin exploded. "He fielded it on about the fiftieth hop, took his time throwing it in, and made a weak throw in the general direction of the pitcher's mound. I told my players if they ever embarrassed me on the field, I was going to embarrass them."

Martin embarrassed Jackson. He pulled him out of the game. Entering the Yankee dugout, Jackson yelled at Martin: "You showed me up on television!" Then he charged at his manager. It figured—lots of hot air, no punches thrown.

"The writers were never late that year," recalled Phil Rizzuto, "because something was always going on. A lot of egos were vying for the headlines."

The next day the Sox romped 11–1. In the three-game sweep, Boston hammered a record (for three games) sixteen home runs to none for the New Yorkers. It was called the Yankee Massacre.

Steinbrenner, furious, which was more or less his standard condition when the Yankees were humiliated, was ready to massacre someone. Then he calmed down, which was his way. But the on-the-edge Yankees would live with tumult and shouting for the rest of that memorable and manic season. The Bronx Zoo it was called, and it was.

Despite the boos and the catcalls, the negative and sometimes vitriolic press, and the screwed-up interpersonal relationships—the 1977 Yankees scored 831 runs while allowing just 651 runs. They were a team of great balance, character, talent, and depth. Five of them made the American League All-Star team: Reggie Jackson, Sparky Lyle, Thurman Munson, Graig Nettles, and Willie Randolph.

The infield of first baseman Chris Chambliss, second baseman Willie Randolph, shortstop Bucky Dent, and third baseman Graig Nettles (107 RBIs, thirty-seven home runs, most ever for a Yankee third baseman), blended intelligence, defense, power, and experience. The outfield of Roy White, Reggie Jackson (thirty-two home runs and 110 RBIs), and Mickey Rivers, the rabbit on a team of rackers, hit for average, power, and made the big defensive plays.

Bar none, the rough-and-gruff thirty-year-old Thurman Munson was baseball's best catcher. Roster versatility was provided by players like Lou Piniella (.330 with twelve homers) and Cliff Johnson.

Although a bad shoulder limited Catfish Hunter to a 9–9 mark that year, pitching was plentiful. Ed Figueroa and Ron Guidry each won sixteen games. Don Gullett was 14–4, while Mike Torrez and Dick Tidrow were 9–4. Sparky Lyle, having his greatest season (Cy Young Award, 26 saves 13 wins), was always pumped.

But into August the Yanks hovered about at the .500 level. The parts were all there, but the whole was out of order.

Then on August 7, Mike Torrez won his third straight, snapping a three-game Yankee losing streak. Three days later Reggie Jackson was in place as the regular cleanup hitter. The Yankees won forty of their final fifty-three games; Jackson hit thirteen home runs and drove in forty-nine runs during that time.

In mid-September, it was again showdown time—a three-game series with Boston at Yankee Stadium. On September 13, the middle game matched Ed Figueroa against Reggie Cleveland, winner of seven straight over the Yankees. The game was scoreless in the bottom of the ninth.

Munson singled. Then Reggie Jackson came to bat and homered into the deep part of the right-field bleachers.

"I hit the ball on the screws," Jackson said, "I knew it was gone."

The Sox were also gone. The Yankee victory pushed Boston 3½ games back. The Yankees went on to win the American League East and once again faced Kansas City in the League Championship Series.

And once again the Yanks eliminated Whitey Herzog's Royals—this time in the ninth inning of the fifth game on a Mickey Rivers game-winning hit. Working four of the five games, winning two of them, the mustached Sparky Lyle posted a glittery 0.96 ERA.

It was New York versus Los Angeles in the World Series. The first two games were played at Yankee Stadium. The Yankees were 4–3 victors in game one in twelve innings. The Dodgers came back to win game two 6–1 behind right-hander Burt Hooton. A three-run first inning iced game three; Mike Torrez gave up a three-run homer to Dusty Baker but stayed the distance as the Yanks won 5–3.

Game four was a 4–2 Yankee win highlighted by Reggie's homer and a double, and Ron Guidry's complete-game four hitter. Game five was a 10–4 Dodger romp behind Don Sutton.

1977
AMERICAN LEAGUE EAST DIVISION
FINAL STANDINGS

TEAM	W	L	W-L%	GB
NEW YORK	100	62	.617	—
BALTIMORE	97	64	.602	2½
BOSTON	97	64	.602	2½
DETROIT	74	88	.457	26
CLEVELAND	71	90	.441	28½
MILWAUKEE	67	95	.414	33
TORONTO	54	107	.335	45½

Back in the Big Apple, LA's Burt Hooton matched up against Mike Torrez in game six. That was the game they all talk about—Mr. October smashing three home runs on the first pitch off three different hurlers and the Yankees becoming world champions for the twenty-first time, the first time since 1962. It was the final, potent exclamation mark for the tumultuous season of one of the greatest Yankee teams.

1998

◆ 114–48 (.704)

"NO ONE IN my fifty-plus years in the game played like this," Don Zimmer said. "No one could stop us. Different teams tried different ways to do it, but we beat them all."

"Nothing was going to stop us," general manager Brian Cashman said. "It was an amazingly driven team, focused like you wouldn't believe."

The 1998 New York Yankees on paper did not look like one of the great teams in franchise history, much less one of the top teams ever. There was no real superstar, no impact player. But it was a team whose parts were greater than the whole, a team who knew how to win.

The 1998 Yankees month by month, wire to wire, were a piece of work in many ways. They took over first place in April, and despite a late-season slump, won 110 games—more than any other club in over ninety years.

On the first day of April, the season opener, Andy Pettitte lost 4–1 to the Angels. That started a Yankee three-game losing streak. On April 7, Joe Torre held a team meeting to discuss the team's 1–4 start. His no-panic-we-can-do-it-guys approach sunk in.

On April 22, Andy Pettitte pitched the team's first complete game of the season, a 9–1 rout of the Blue Jays. By April's end, the Yanks were 17–6, .739, in first place, a half game ahead of Boston.

May was a merry month for the Bronx Bombers. On May 2, Daryl Strawberry punched a ninth-inning pinch-hit grand-slam, punctuating a Yankee triumph over KC. Four days later, David Wells blew a nine-run lead, but Jorge Posada's tie-breaking RBI single gave the Yankees a 15–13 win. On May 17, Wells hurled a perfect game. The month ended with the Yankees at 37–13, .740, in first place, 7½ games ahead of the Red Sox.

Orlando Hernandez, making his major-league debut on June 3, trimmed the Devil Rays 7–1. Despite Bernie Williams being on the disabled list for thirty-one games, and despite a five-game suspension of Mike Stanton for throwing at Baltimore's Eric Davis, the Yankees kept on clicking. By June's end they were 56–20, .737, in first place, ten games ahead of the Red Sox.

Tino Martinez

1998
AMERICAN LEAGUE EAST DIVISION
FINAL STANDINGS

TEAM	W	L	W-L%	GB
NEW YORK	114	48	.704	–
BOSTON	92	70	.568	22
TORONTO	88	74	.543	26
BALTIMORE	79	83	.488	35
TAMPA BAY	63	99	.389	51

The lead at the end of July was fifteen games over the Red Sox. Bernie Williams was back in action and hitting. The Yankees entered August 76–27, .738, in first place.

On August 4, a 10–5 victory over the A's in the second game of a double-header sweep saw the Yankees at eighty wins in their 108th game, the earliest in club history. On the thirteenth, Hernandez fanned thirteen in a 2–0 win over the Rangers, a Yankee rookie record. Three days later a 6–5 victory over the Rangers tied the 1944 Cardinals, getting to ninety wins in 120 games, the fastest in major-league history. At August's end the Yankees were 98–37, .726, in first place, up eighteen games over the Red Sox.

On the first day of September, David Wells almost did it again. He pitched a perfect game into the seventh inning against Oakland, but a Jason Giambi single broke up the bid. In their 138th game, an 11–6 win over the White Sox on September 4, the Yankees gained their one hundredth victory, then the fastest pace in AL history.

Five days later the Yankees clinched their seventh AL East title. They finished the regular season at 114–48, .704, in first place, twenty-two games ahead of the Red Sox. The 1998 New York Yankees scored 965 runs, while holding the opposition to just 656.

They swept the Texas Rangers in the AL Division Series, took the AL Championship Series over the Indians four games to two, and then topped it all off with a World Series sweep over the Padres. That was the rock-and-roll end to the incredible 1998 season.

"The Yankees had no weaknesses whatsoever," San Diego manager Bruce Bochy said. "We had them on the ropes, and they came back against us. You come to a point where you have to just tip your cap and say they're one of the best of all time."

That may have been an overstatement, but the 1998 Yankees were one of the best Yankee teams ever. Bernie Williams won the batting title, hitting .339. Derek Jeter hit .324 and led the league with 127 runs scored. Tino Martinez and Paul O'Neill drove in 123 and 116 runs, respectively. The two Davids—Cone and Wells—led the pitching staff. Cone was 20–7 while Wells went 18–4, including a perfect game. Mariano Rivera saved thirty-six games and anchored the deep bullpen.

"I've never seen a team as good as this one in my lifetime," Joe Torre said. "And I won't ever again. That's why I enjoyed every minute of this season, because I recognized early on it was a once-in-a-lifetime experience."

THE WORST

1912

◆ 50-102 (.329)

BY 1912, NEWSPAPERS more and more were referring to the New York Highlanders as Yankees. On April 11, pinstripes first appeared on the uniforms of the Highlanders, a fashion statement that would become the most famous and celebrated uniform design in sports history. The *New York Times* reported: "The Yankees presented a natty appearance in their new uniforms of white with black pinstripes."

The 1912 baseball season of the New York Highlanders was one of all kinds of oddities and significant moments, a few positive, but mostly negatives.

A well-attended benefit game was played by the Highlanders and Giants to give aid to the survivors of the *Titanic* disaster.

On May 20, 1912, New York Giants owner John T. Brush invited the Highlanders to use the larger Polo Grounds for their Memorial Day doubleheader, underscoring the positive relationship between the two teams.

The Highlanders stole home eighteen times that year, a major-league record. Two of the steals were by outfielder Guy Zinn on August 15 in a 5–4 victory over the Tigers.

The Yankees/Highlanders played their final game ever in Hilltop Park on October 5, winning 8–6 over the Senators. Beginning in 1913, they would be tenants of the Giants at the Polo Grounds.

Those were a few of the positives. Unfortunately, for the 242,194 fans (second lowest attendance in the American League) who rooted for the home team that 1912 season at Hilltop Park, there were many more negatives than positives.

Committing the most errors, turning the fewest double plays, recording the worst ERA in the league, scoring 630 runs but having 842 runs scored against them, and posting the lowest fielding average in franchise history, the Highlanders were a shabby bunch.

Cigar-smoking rookie manager Harry Wolverton, who frequently used himself as a pinch hitter out of desperation, presided over a mostly inept collection of athletes who set the record for the lowest winning percentage (.329) and fewest wins (fifty) in franchise history.

The Highlanders, whose average age was 26.7, featured the brothers Homer and Tommy Thompson and players with unusual names like Hippo Vaughn, Klondike Smith, and pitcher Jack Warhop, who appeared in the most games and lost sixteen.

In addition to Warhop, there were three other hurlers with double-digit defeats: Ray Caldwell, a nineteen-game loser, George McConnell, a twelve-game loser, and Russ (not Whitey) Ford, whose twenty-one losses led the league. The Canadian-born hurler also had the most innings pitched, strikeouts, most hits allowed, walks, and complete games on the staff.

The Highlanders' porous defense featured Hal Chase, whose twenty-seven errors led all AL first basemen, and catcher Jay Sweeney, whose thirty-four errors did likewise for AL catchers.

Chase and outfielder Bert Daniels tied for the team lead in batting average at .274, while the talented Chase was the Highlander leader in RBIs, total bases, and hits. Guy Zinn, with six home runs, tied what was then the club record.

At season's end, manager Wolverton was fired. Zinn was sold off to the Braves in December. The next season, 1913, it was good riddance New York Highlanders. The name of the team was officially changed to New York Yankees.

1912
AMERICAN LEAGUE FINAL STANDINGS

TEAM	W	L	W-L%	GB
BOSTON	105	47	.691	–
WASHINGTON	91	61	.599	14
PHILADELPHIA	90	62	.592	15
CHICAGO	78	76	.506	28
CLEVELAND	75	78	.490	30½
DETROIT	69	84	.451	36½
ST. LOUIS	53	101	.344	53
NEW YORK	50	102	.329	55

1966
◆ 70–89 (.440)

"WHEN I WAS a kid," literary agent David Vigliano said, "the Yankees weren't any good, they stunk. It was CBS ownership time. There was always the big buildup–'we're going with speed or defense.' But they never really had anybody good. Anyone that had been good was broken down. It was very depressing."

Owned by CBS, the Yankees had their first losing season since 1925 in 1965. But the 1966 season seemed to be one of promise.

On March 8, it was announced that Casey Stengel was being inducted into the Hall of Fame. Later it was announced that the great poet Marianne Moore would throw out the first ball when the season began.

The team roster had a lot of prominent, or at least recognizable, names. Position players included Ruben Amaro, Ray Barker, Clete Boyer, Billy Bryan, Horace Clarke, Lu Clinton, Mike Ferraro, Jake Gibbs, Mike Hegan, Elston Howard, Hector Lopez, Mickey Mantle, Roger Maris, John Miller, Bobby Murcer, Joe Pepitone, Roger Repoz, Bobby Richardson, Dick Schofield, Tom Tresh, Steve Whitaker, and Roy White.

Pitchers included Stan Bahnsen, Jim Bouton, Jack Cullen, Al Downing, Whitey Ford, Bob Friend, Steve Hamilton, Bill Henry, Fritz Peterson, Pedro Ramos, Hal Reniff, Mel Stottlemyre, Fred Talbot, and Dooley Womack.

On paper, a team that still had Mickey Mantle, Roger Maris, Elston Howard, Bobby Richardson, and Clete Boyer should have been pretty good. But the big guns, Howard, Maris, and Mantle, were nearing the end of their careers. Of the three, Mantle, in one of his final and declining years, didn't do badly for an ordinary player—.288 with twenty-three home runs—but it wasn't good enough for the Mick.

On May 7, with the Yankees only winners of four of their first twenty games, GM Ralph Houk fired manager Johnny Keane and installed himself as manager for the rest of the season. He knew what he was getting himself into.

Johnny Keane and Ralph Houk

"Ralph came in when things weren't going good," the garrulous Pedro Ramos recalled. "He was there for the players. He was there to try and straighten things out." Unfortunately, Houk did not do much straightening.

What happened? The 1966 Yankees scored 611 runs but gave up 612 runs. The slow-footed team had Roy White as their leader in stolen bases with fourteen. Mel Stottlemyre went from being a twenty-game winner to leading the league in defeats, losing twenty games. But he also tied for the staff lead in wins with Fritz Peterson, at twelve.

There were some moments, a few good, but mostly bad.

On June 29, Bobby Richardson, Mickey Mantle, and Joe Pepitone all hit consecutive third-inning home runs at Fenway Park. Even with that home-run show the Yankees barely won the game, 6–5. That was good.

On August 25, Whitey Ford, with two wins and five losses, underwent surgery on his left shoulder for circulatory problems. That was bad. The next year, nearing forty-one, he would retire. Bobby Richardson could not wait for 1967— he called it a career at age thirty-one on August 31, 1966. That was bad. Hector Lopez also retired in 1966.

On September 19, Dan Topping sold his 10 percent stock interest in the Yankees to CBS. Mike Burke took over for him as president of the team. Six days later the smallest crowd in the history of the franchise showed up—413. The White Sox beat the Yankees 4–1. Red Barber, one of the greatest of all baseball broadcasters, was honest enough to point out the meager attendance. Tastelessness, as so often happens, ruled—Barber was fired.

Yankee home attendance dropped to its lowest level that season since World War II, 1.2 million. It was a mess.

One of the nice surprises for the Yanks was pitcher Dooley Womack, who went from a non-prospect to a must-use. In seventy-five innings, he was 7–3 with 4 saves and a 2.64 earned-run average.

One of the true bright spots on the team was "Pepi," Joe Pepitone. A team leader, he led all Yankees in slugging percentage, games played, runs scored, total bases, home runs, and RBIs. But he was not enough.

Horace Clarke became the symbol of that down Yankee era. Clarke, one of five different players who manned the shortstop position for the 1966 Yankees, played sixty-three games there, four games at third base, and sixteen at second base. Others who played shortstop that 1966 season included Clete Boyer, fifty-nine games; Dick Schofield, nineteen; Bobby Murcer, eighteen; and Ruben Amaro, fourteen.

Houk's 1966 Yankees won 66 games and lost 73, finishing 26½ games out of first, tenth in a ten-team league, the first last-place finish for a Yankee team since the 1912 Highlanders.

"It was unbelievable," Drew Nieporent recalled, "and it was before divisional play . . . for a team that was the most dominant team in sports. The sad part was that Michael Burke, a war hero and a very decent guy, presided over it."

A trivia note of little consolation: the .440 winning percentage was the highest for a last-place team in league history.

Pedro Ramos, superb as a stopper for two straight seasons, proud to be a Yankee, was traded off to the Phillies at the end of the season. Nothing was Yankee-like. Even Roger Maris was expendable. On December 8 he was dispatched to the Cardinals for third baseman Charlie Smith. Elston Howard, Johnny Blanchard, and Clete Boyer all were traded away. The general fire sale punctuated the sad fallout around one of the worst Yankee teams ever.

After the 1966 season, Yankee Stadium got a new paint job. In 1968, there was a rebound to an 83–79 fifth-place finish. There was Mickey Mantle Day in 1969. There was a second-place finish in 1970, but the Yankees were fifteen games back. Overall, the Yankees of 1965–1971 had few highlights and many low times. The 1966 team was a symbol of that period.

1966
AMERICAN LEAGUE FINAL STANDINGS

TEAM	W	L	W-L%	GB
BALTIMORE	97	63	.606	–
MINNESOTA	89	73	.549	9
DETROIT	88	74	.543	10
CHICAGO	83	79	.512	15
CLEVELAND	81	81	.500	17
CALIFORNIA	80	82	.494	18
KANSAS CITY	74	86	.463	23
WASHINGTON	71	88	.447	25½
BOSTON	72	90	.444	26
NEW YORK	70	89	.440	26½

1990
♦ 67–95 (.414)

THE YANKEES, WHOSE average age was twenty-nine years and one month, began their 1990 season in New York. Billy Martin's son threw out the first ball to the cheers of 50,114. By day's end the Yanks had a 6–4 win over the Indians. It was Luis Polonia's hit that broke a tie to put the Yankees ahead. No gratitude, though. Two weeks later he was traded to the Angels for Claudell Washington. There was a message there.

Bucky Dent had been on the scene as manager from August 18, 1989. On June 6, 1990, with the Yankees in seventh place at 18–31, Dent got the axe. Stump Merrill was brought up from the Columbus farm team.

"Here we have a fellow who doesn't come with a whole lot of glamour." George Steinbrenner smiled as he said it. "For the first five years I knew him, I kept calling him 'Lump.' He was madder than hell."

There were lots of times through the 1990 season, and also 1991–Stump's last as a Yankee pilot–that he was "madder than hell."

The 1990 Yankees scored 603 runs but allowed 749 runs. Their pitchers didn't lead the league in any category, except for Tim Leary, who had the most losses–nineteen.

The hitters were even worse. As a team the Yankees batted an American League low .241. Bragging rights for the team's best player belonged to thirty-year-old Jesse Barfield, with a .246 average and twenty-five homers. He also struck out 150 times, becoming the first Yankee to earn that dishonor. It was partly due to Jesse that the Yankees came within sixteen strikeouts of their worst-ever total, set in 1967, of 1,043. Roberto Kelly, who never saw a pitch he didn't like and would not walk, had the best batting average (.285). But he fanned 148 times.

The catching situation was woeful. The full-time catcher was Bob Geren. He had a .213 average and was never a full-time catcher again. His backup was Matt Nokes (eight home runs, .238). His backup was Brian Dorsett, who had five hits in thirty-five at bats.

The best Yankee starting lineup most of that woeful season featured Geren at backstop. Don Mattingly played first base, sometimes. He complained of a bad back, got into only eighty-nine games, and batted .256 with just five homers and forty-two RBIs. Second baseman Steve Sax (the only player from the club to make the All-Star team) wound up with a .260 average and forty-three stolen bases. Randy Velarde, with a .210 average, was at third base a lot. Shortstop Alvaro Espinoza finished the season with two home runs and twenty RBIs.

The starting outfield was Mel Hall (twelve homers, forty-six RBIs), team batting champ Roberto Kelly (.285, forty-two stolen bases), and Jesse Barfield. Oscar Azocar also played the outfield, and in 214 at bats walked twice. He, too, never saw a pitch he didn't like. He batted .248.

Other non-pitchers taking up roster space and clubhouse room included rookie utility man Jimmy Leyritz (.257, five home runs) and Dave Winfield, who hit .213 in thirty-eight games before he was traded on May 11 to the Angels for Mike Witt. The lanky and controversial outfielder at first balked at the trade. Then he realized the Yankees were doing him a favor; he reported five days later to the Angels.

1990
AMERICAN LEAGUE EASTERN DIVISION FINAL STANDINGS

TEAM	W	L	W-L%	GB
BOSTON	88	74	.543	–
TORONTO	86	76	.531	2
DETROIT	79	83	.488	9
CLEVELAND	77	85	.475	11
BALTIMORE	76	85	.472	11½
MILWAUKEE	74	88	.457	14
NEW YORK	67	95	.414	21

On August 2, rookie first baseman Kevin Maas hammered his tenth home run in just seventy-seven at bats. It was the quickest any player had reached that mark. But predictably, the Yankees lost another tough game, 6–5 in eleven to the Tigers. Maas wound up with twenty-one round-trippers in 254 at bats, and writers raved about his sweet lefty swing, just made for Yankee Stadium's short right-field porch. He fizzled, but at least he flamed for a while, which could not be said about a lot of the other 1990 Yanks.

That 1990 roster also included Steve "Bye Bye" Balboni (seventeen homers but only a .192 batting average), Matt Nokes, Rick Cerone, Mike Blowers, Deion Sanders, Hensley Meulens, Claudell Washington, Wayne Tolleson, Luis Polonia, and Jim Walewander.

The only Yankee starting pitcher to win more than seven games was nine-game winner Tim Leary. But he also lost nineteen before Stump Merrill showed some pity and took him out of the rotation.

Other starters were Dave Lapoint (7–10); Chuck Cary (6–12); Andy Hawkins (5–12), who got everyone both excited and dejected on July 1, 1990, when he pitched and lost a no-hitter 4–0 against the White Sox; and Mike Witt (5–6).

Steve Adkins made his debut on September 12, 1990. He didn't allow a hit, but he walked eight batters in just 1⅓ innings. The twenty-five-year-old rookie was 1–2 with a 6.38 ERA in five starts. He never pitched again in the major leagues after that 1990 season.

Others who took the ball to the hill with little success for the Bombers included Greg Cadaret, Eric Plunk, Jimmy Jones, Alan Mills, Dave Eiland,

Mark Leiter, Clay Parker, Lance McCullers, Pascual Perez, John Habyan, Rich Monteleone, and Jeff Robinson. One of the few bright spots on the pitching staff was closer Dave Righetti, with thirty-six saves. Lee Guetterman went 11–7.

On June 30, George Steinbrenner was banned by commissioner Fay Vincent from the day-to-day operations of the Yankees because of his alleged dealings with a known gambler. The Boss became the first American League owner ever to be removed by disciplinary action. Then Steinbrenner resigned as managing general partner of the Yankees and watched from the sidelines as the miserable season finally came to an end.

The hapless New Yorkers finished twenty-one games behind Boston in the AL East, the first time during the Steinbrenner era that the Yankees finished in last place.

3

CHAPTER SIX

TALKIN'
Yankees

ON THE YANKEES

"I would rather beat the Yankees regularly than pitch a no-hit game."
—Bob Feller

"It was a death struggle every day being a Yankee—you either won or you lost. There was no second place. Half of us were nuts by the end of a season." —Jerry Coleman

"When I was a player and we would play the Yankees in spring training, even though the game didn't mean anything, it was a special day."
—Joe Torre

"I wish I'd never see them again. I wish they'd disappear from the league."
—Pedro Martinez, Boston Red Sox

"Hating the Yankees is as American as pizza pie and cheating on your income tax." —COLUMNIST MIKE ROYKO

"Hating the Yankees isn't part of my act. It is one of those exquisite times when life and art are in perfect conjunction." —BILL VEECK

"Going north from spring training, we'd pass through small towns and people would be out there early in the morning as the train went by, waving to us. I don't know how they got the word—but we'd be having our breakfast in the diner and they'd be there." —JERRY COLEMAN

"You kind of took it for granted around the Yankees that there was always going to be baseball in October." —WHITEY FORD

"This isn't just a ball club! This is Murderers' Row!"
—SPORTSWRITER ARTHUR ROBINSON

"There has never been anything like it. Even as these lines are batted out on the office typewriter, youths dash out of the AP and UP ticker room every two or three minutes shouting, 'Ruth hit one! Gehrig hit another one!'" —SPORTSWRITER PAUL GALLICO

"I was known as a Yankee killer. My best year against them was 1953. I beat them five times and shut them out four times. You just played a little harder against them." —BOSTON RED SOX PITCHER MEL PARNELL

"Rooting for the Yankees is like rooting for U.S. Steel."
—COMEDIAN JOE E. LEWIS

"Rooting for the Yankees is like owning a yacht."
—SPORTSWRITER JIMMY CANNON

"The majority of American males put themselves to sleep by striking out the batting order of the New York Yankees." —JAMES THURBER

"They have, what, twenty-six World Series titles? But that doesn't mean they are going to beat us. We deserve to be here as much as they do. I'm not trying to get Babe Ruth or Lou Gehrig or Mickey Mantle out. I'm trying to get the Yankees' lineup out today." —CURT SCHILLING, ARIZONA DIAMONDBACKS PITCHER, BEFORE GAME ONE, 2001 WORLD SERIES

"Somebody told me that we beat the Yankees in the bottom of the ninth! I still don't believe it!" —MARK GRACE, DIAMONDBACKS FIRST BASEMAN, 2001 WORLD SERIES

"When my Yankee career is over I'll play anywhere, but I'm positive that I'll never find a team quite like the Yankees." —BERNIE WILLIAMS

"These are your Yankees. They leave their hearts on the field for you." —JOE TORRE

ON YANKEE STADIUM

"When I come here, it's like standing on hallowed ground." —CAL RIPKEN

"It was so large and the fans there were so rabid. It was amazing for me to go out there and stand on the mound and look around and realize that was the place that Ruth built." —CLEVELAND PITCHER BOB FELLER

"Most guys won't admit it, but it can be an intimidating thing your first few times there. All the lore of the stadium and the mystique can be difficult to deal with." —PITCHER AL LEITER

Yankee Stadium —Yanks vs. Oakland on July 29, 1997

"It is the most magical ballpark ever built. Playing there as a Yankee was like being in the Marines, the feeling that you were in a special ballpark, special town, special uniform, special history." —PHIL LINZ

"When I went to the American League as an umpire, I had never been to a major-league ballpark. This was 1963. You went out of the umpires' dressing room and down the hallway and up the ramp and stepped out onto the field. Here's this kid from Little Rock, Arkansas, standing in New York City in Yankee Stadium. It was a pretty incredible thing."
—BILL VALENTINE

"I loved Yankee Stadium because I was left-handed. I usually faced mostly right-handed-hitting teams there. The fence in center field was 461 feet away, and left center field was 457 feet. As long as you kept the hitters from hitting the ball down the line, it was a great park to pitch in."
—WHITEY FORD

"Being from New York, it meant a lot for me to play in my hometown. I knew every nook and cranny there, and we had the fans behind us. Back then, you had the monuments in the outfield and that was unbelievable."
—PHIL RIZZUTO

"The cathedral of baseball." —DAVID CONE

"Baseball heaven." —RANDY JOHNSON

"The stadium is a part of the Yankees and the Yankees are a part of the stadium. That will never change." —CHUCK KNOBLAUCH

ED BARROW

"You ought to know that you're making a mistake."
—TO RED SOX OWNER HARRY FRAZEE ON THE SALE OF BABE RUTH TO THE YANKEES

YOGI BERRA

"Congratulations on breaking my record last night. I always thought the record would stand until it was broken." —TO JOHNNY BENCH, WHO BROKE HIS RECORD FOR CAREER HOME RUNS BY A CATCHER

"I didn't say the things I said."

"The other teams could make trouble for us if they win."

"If you don't know where you are going, you will wind up somewhere else."

"If you come to a fork in the road, take it."

"He must have made that before he died." —ON A STEVE MCQUEEN MOVIE, 1982

"A nickel ain't worth a dime anymore."

"It's tough to make predictions, especially about the future."

"The future ain't what it used to be."

"A home opener is always exciting, no matter if it's home or on the road."

"I take a two-hour nap between 1 P.M. and 3 P.M."

"Baseball is ninety percent mental. The other half is physical."

"You have to give one hundred percent in the first half of the game. If that isn't enough, in the second half, you have to give what is left."

"It gets late out there early." —REFERRING TO THE BAD SUN CONDITIONS IN LEFT FIELD AT THE STADIUM

"He is a big clog in their machine."

"I've been with the Yankees seventeen years, watching games and learning. You can see a lot by observing."

"Baseball is the champ of them all. Like somebody said, the pay is good and the hours are short."

"All pitchers are liars and crybabies."

"Bill Dickey learned me all his experience."

"I want to thank you for making this day necessary." —TO FANS IN HOMETOWN ST. LOUIS FOR GIVING HIM A DAY IN 1947 AT SPORTSMAN'S PARK

Yogi Berra

"I've known this guy so long. Can't he spell my name right?" —AFTER RECEIVING A CHECK THAT READ "PAY TO THE ORDER OF BEARER"

"I think Little League is wonderful. It keeps the kids out of the house."

"If the people don't want to come out to the ballpark, nobody's going to stop them."

"Pair off in threes."

"We have very deep depth!"

"We made too many wrong mistakes." —WHEN ASKED WHY THE YANKEES LOST THE 1960 SERIES TO PITTSBURGH

"Think? How the hell are you gonna think and hit at the same time?" —WHEN TOLD BY YANKEE MANAGER BUCKY HARRIS TO THINK ABOUT WHAT WAS BEING PITCHED TO HIM

"Yeah, for what paper?" —WHEN TOLD ERNEST HEMINGWAY WAS A GREAT WRITER

"I don't know, I'm not in shape." —WHEN ASKED WHAT HIS CAP SIZE WAS AT THE BEGINNING OF SPRING TRAINING

"It's déjà vu all over again."

"It ain't over till it's over."

ON YOGI BERRA

"You can't compare me to my father, our similarities are different." —DALE BERRA

"They say he's funny. Well, he has a lovely wife and family, a beautiful home, money in the bank, and he plays golf with millionaires. What's funny about that?" —CASEY STENGEL

"He'd fall in a sewer and come up with a gold watch." —CASEY STENGEL

"Where he was especially dangerous was in the final two innings. You couldn't pitch to him. He had no weaknesses. He was the most dangerous hitter ever." —JERRY COLEMAN

"Not only was he lucky, he was never wrong." —WHITEY FORD

"Yogi's face is his fortune." —MIKE STANLEY

ROGER CLEMENS

"I thought it was the ball."
—ON THROWING A SPLINTERED BAT AT MIKE PIAZZA

"I don't worry about New York being my town. I definitely enjoy representing the city for sure, from the point of view of the history, the tradition, the pride that goes with it."

BILL DICKEY

"A catcher must want to catch. He must make up his mind that it isn't the terrible job it is painted, and that he isn't going to say every day, 'Why, oh why with so many other positions in baseball did I take up this one?'"

"I loved to make a great defensive play. I'd rather do that than hit a home run."

"I don't recall your name but you sure were a sucker for a high inside curve."

JOE DIMAGGIO

"I'd like to thank the Good Lord for making me a Yankee."

"A ballplayer has to be kept hungry to become a big-leaguer. That's why no boy from a rich family has ever made the big leagues."

"If anyone wants to know why three kids in one family made it to the big leagues they just had to know how we helped each other and how much we practiced back then. We did it every minute we could."

"I can remember a reporter asking me for a quote, and I didn't know what a quote was. I thought it was some kind of soft drink."

"You always get a special kick on opening day, no matter how many you go through. You look forward to it like a birthday party when you're a kid. You think something wonderful is going to happen."

"I'm just a ballplayer with one ambition, and that is to give all I've got to help my ball club win. I've never played any other way."

"The phrase 'off with the crack of the bat,' while romantic, is really meaningless since the outfielder should be in motion long before he hears the sound of the ball meeting the bat."

"The test of an outfielder's skill comes when he has to go against the fence to make a catch."

Bill Dickey

"There is always some kid who may be seeing me for the first or last time, I owe him my best."

"You start chasing a ball and your brain immediately commands your body to 'Run forward, bend, scoop up the ball, peg it to the infield,' then your body says, 'Who me?'"

"I'm a ballplayer, not an actor." —WHEN ASKED WHY HE HAD A SERIOUS LOOK AFTER HITTING A HOME RUN

"It's got to be better than rooming with Joe Page." —WHEN ASKED WHETHER MARRIAGE TO MARILYN MONROE WAS GOOD FOR HIM

"I feel like I have reached the stage where I can no longer produce for my club, my manager, and my teammates. I had a poor year, but even if I had hit .350, this would have been my last year. I was full of aches and pains and it had become a chore for me to play. When baseball is no longer fun, it's no longer a game."

"Now I've had everything except for the thrill of watching Babe Ruth play."

ON JOE DIMAGGIO

"You've bought yourself a cripple." —BILL TERRY OF THE GIANTS TO THE YANKEES ON THEIR PURCHASE OF JOE DIMAGGIO IN 1936

"I can describe Joe in one word: class. He was the most perfect ballplayer I ever saw, but, he was a shy fellow. I'll tell you something else though, when Joe DiMaggio walks into the clubhouse, the lights flicker. He's the star." —PETE SHEEHY, FORMER YANKEE CLUBHOUSE MANAGER

"There was an aura about him. He walked like no one else walked. He did things so easily. He was immaculate in everything he did. Kings of State wanted to meet him and be with him. He could fit in any place in the world." —PHIL RIZZUTO

"Joe did everything so naturally that half the time he gave the impression he wasn't trying. He made the rest of them look like plumbers." —CASEY STENGEL

"DiMaggio seldom showed emotion. One day after striking out, he came into the dugout and kicked the ball bag. It really hurt. He sat down and the sweat popped out on his forehead and he clenched his fists without ever saying a word. Everybody wanted to howl, but he was a god. You don't laugh at gods." –JERRY COLEMAN

"Joe's a man who was meant to play ball on hot afternoons on the grass of big cities. He never belonged in the rain."
–SPORTSWRITER JIMMY CANNON

"'I would like to take the great DiMaggio fishing,' the old man said. 'They say his father was a fisherman. Maybe he was as poor as we are and would understand.'" –ERNEST HEMINGWAY, *The Old Man and the Sea*

"Where have you gone, Joe DiMaggio? A nation turns its lonely eyes to you." –PAUL SIMON AND ART GARFUNKLE, *Mrs. Robinson*

WHITEY FORD

"Army life was rough. Would you believe it, they actually wanted me to pitch three times a week."

Whitey Ford
and Luis Arroyo, 1961

"Hell, if I didn't drink or smoke, I'd win twenty games every year."

"I didn't begin cheating until late in my career, when I needed something to help me survive. I didn't cheat when I won the twenty-five games in 1961. I don't want anybody to get any ideas and take my Cy Young Award away. And I didn't cheat in 1963 when I won twenty-four games. Well, maybe a little."

"I know Koufax's weakness. He can't hit."

"I never threw the spitter, well, maybe once or twice when I really needed to get a guy out real bad."

"Sooner or later the arm goes bad. It has too. . . . Sooner or later you have to start pitching in pain."

"The way to make coaches think you're in shape in the spring is to get a tan."

"You would be amazed how many important outs you can get by working the count down to where the hitter is sure you're going to throw to his weakness, and then throw to his power instead."

ON WHITEY FORD

"If the World Series was on the line and I could pick one pitcher, I'd choose Whitey Ford every time." —MICKEY MANTLE

"If you had one game to win and your life depended on it, you'd want him to pitch it." —CASEY STENGEL

"When Ford was on the mound, Ford pitched. He didn't come off the mound, or beg or cry. But when he was on the bench—not the day he was pitching—then he would yell and cuss." —UMPIRE BILL VALENTINE

LOU GEHRIG

"The Babe is one fellow, and I'm another, and I could never be exactly like him. I don't try, I just go on as I am in my own right."

"What do you think of the nerve of that big monkey [Babe Ruth]? Imagine the guy calling his shot and getting away with it?"

"I'm not a headline guy. I know that as long as I was following Ruth to the plate I could have stood on my head and no one would have known the difference."

"The ballplayer who loses his head, who can't keep his cool, is worse than no ballplayer at all."

"In the beginning I used to make one terrible play a game. Then I got so I'd make one a week and finally I'd pull a bad one about once a month. Now, I'm trying to keep it down to one a season."

"Joe [McCarthy], I'm not helping this team any. I know I look terrible out there. This string of mine doesn't mean a thing to me. It isn't fair to the boys for me to stay in there. Joe, I want you to take me out of the lineup today."

"There is no room in baseball for discrimination. It is our national pastime and a game for all."

ON LOU GEHRIG

"A huge man and a small child combined in one runaway personality."
—ELEANOR GEHRIG, LOU GEHRIG'S WIFE

"I had him for over eight years and he never gave me a moment's trouble.
I guess you might say he was kind of my favorite." —JOE MCCARTHY

"Lou was the kind of boy that if you had a son, he's the kind of person
you'd like your son to be." —PITCHER SAM JONES

"There was absolutely no reason to dislike him, and nobody did."
—SPORTSWRITER FRED LIEB

"It has been aptly said that while Ruth was the Home Run King, Gehrig was
the Crown Prince. Joe DiMaggio must therefore have been heir apparent."
—CONNIE MACK

"Lou Gehrig was a guy who could really hit the ball, was dependable and
seemed so durable that many of us thought he could have played forever."
—YANKEE OUTFIELDER GEORGE SELKIRK

"What visions burn, what dreams possess him, seeker of the night. The
packed stands of the stadium, the bleachers sweltering with their unshaded
hordes, the faultless velvet of the diamond. The mounting roar of 80,000
voices and Gehrig coming to bat."
—THOMAS WOLFE, *You Can't Go Home Again*

"This Iron Man stuff is just baloney. I think he's making one of the worst
mistakes a ballplayer can make. The guy ought to learn to sit on the bench
and rest." —BABE RUTH

LEFTY GOMEZ

"I'd rather be lucky than good."

"I talked to the ball a lot of times in my career. I yelled, 'Go foul. Go foul.' "

"One rule I had was make your best pitch and back up third base. That
relay might get away and you've got another shot at him."

"When I first signed with the Yankees, the regulars wouldn't talk to you until you were with the team three or four years. Nowadays the rookies get $100,000 to sign and they don't talk to the regulars."

"You keep the salary, I'll take the cut."
—TO COLONEL JACOB RUPPERT WHEN THE YANKEE OWNER WANTED TO REDUCE HIS $20,000 SALARY TO $7,500.

"I don't wanna throw him nothing. Maybe he'll just get tired of waitin' and leave."

"A lot of things run through your head when you're going in to relieve in a tight spot. One of them was, 'Should I spike myself?'"

"I was the worst hitter ever. I never even broke a bat until last year when I was backing out of the garage."

"The secret of my success was clean living and a fast outfield."

"I'm throwing twice as hard, but the ball is getting there half as fast."

"When Neil Armstrong first set foot on the moon, he and all the space scientists were puzzled by an unidentifiable white object. I knew immediately what it was. That was a home-run ball hit off me in 1933 by Jimmie Foxx."

ON GOOSE GOSSAGE

"The Goose should do more pitching and less quacking." —GEORGE STEINBRENNER

"There's smoke coming out of his nose and his cap is down over his eyes, and he's so big and hulking. You need a cape to face Gossage, not a baseball bat." —TOM PACIOREK

MARK GRACE

"It's like winning in the bottom of the ninth off of God!" —A REFERENCE TO ARIZONA'S COME-FROM-BEHIND SEVENTH-GAME WIN IN THE 2001 WORLD SERIES

RICKEY HENDERSON

"This shit don't count. This shit don't go on the bubble gum card."
—ON SPRING TRAINING

ORLANDO HERNANDEZ

"Sometimes the hitter gets a hit, sometimes I strike them out, but in neither case does anyone die."

ON ORLANDO HERNANDEZ

"If we sign him, he's twenty-eight. If he signs somewhere else, he's forty-five." —YANKEE GM BRIAN CASHMAN, BEFORE SIGNING HERNANDEZ IN 2000

ON ELSTON HOWARD

"He was always griping and groaning for his pitcher. Close pitch, Yankees leading 7–1, top of the ninth. He was always saying, 'Oh, I've got to have that.' He never knew there was a time to argue and a time to ask."
—BILL VALENTINE

MILLER HUGGINS

"A good catcher is the quarterback, the carburetor, the lead dog, the pulse taker, the traffic cop and sometimes a lot of unprintable things, but no team gets very far without one."

"Coive him! Coive the busher!"

"Any ballplayer that played for me could come to me if he were in need and I would give him a helping hand. I made only two exceptions, Carl Mays and Joe Bush. If they were in a gutter, I'd kick them."

ON MILLER HUGGINS

"Miller Huggins was a good manager, although he was a nervous little guy who moved his feet a lot in the dugout. But he didn't have to be much of a strategist with that club. Lots of times, we'd be down five, six runs, and then have a big inning to win the game." —MARK KOENIG

CATFISH HUNTER

"The sun don't shine on the same dog's ass all the time."

"If I had done everything I was supposed to, I'd be leading the league in homers, have the highest batting average, have given $100,000 to the Cancer Fund and be married to Marie Osmond."

"Winning isn't everything. Wanting to is."

REGGIE JACKSON

"I didn't come to New York to be a star, I brought my star with me."

"To walk out and feel your spikes in the grass is a good feeling."

"Some people call October a time of pressure. I call it a time of character."

"The only difference between me and the other great Yankees is my skin color."

"I go to pieces in turmoil, but I thrive on pressure."

"Billy Martin is not an intellectual, but there is a cunningness to him that is something to behold."

"You know this team . . . it all flows from me. I've got to keep it going. I'm the straw that stirs the drink."

"When you've played this game for ten years, gone to bat seven thousand times, and gotten two thousand hits, do you know what this really means? It means you've gone zero for five thousand."

"The only reason I don't like playing in the World Series is I can't watch myself play."

"Fans don't boo nobodies."

"For a certain amount of money, you'll eat Alpo."

"He [Claudell Washington] plays the outfield like he's trying to catch grenades."

"I'd like to be able to light the fire a little bit."

"I don't mind getting beaten, but I hate to lose."

"If I was playing in New York, they'd name a candy bar after me."

"I have a hard time believing athletes are overpriced. If an owner is losing money, give it up. It's a business. I have trouble figuring out why owners would stay in if they're losing money."

"It's a fickle town [New York], a tough town. They getcha, boy. They don't let you escape with minor scratches and bruises. They put scars on you here."

"I was reminded [by Jim Bouton] that when we lose and I strike out, a billion people in China don't care."

"October, that's when they pay off for playing ball."

"Please God, let me hit one. I'll tell everybody you did it."

"So many ideas come to you [when slumping] and you want to try them all but you can't. You're like a mosquito in a nudist camp. You don't know where to start."

"The only way I'm going to win a Gold Glove is with a can of spray paint."

"After Jackie Robinson the most important black in baseball history is Reggie Jackson. I really mean that."

"Hitting is better than sex."

"I am the best in baseball."

"In the building I live in on Park Avenue, there are ten people who could buy the Yankees. But none of them could hit the ball out of Yankee Stadium."

"God, do I love to hit that little round sum-bitch out of the park and make 'em say 'Wow!'"

ON REGGIE JACKSON

"Out of what . . . a thousand?" —OUTFIELDER MICKEY RIVERS ON REGGIE JACKSON'S CLAIM TO HAVING AN I.Q. OF 160

"I must admit, when Reggie hit his third home run and I was sure nobody was looking, I applauded in my glove." —STEVE GARVEY, DODGER FIRST BASEMAN AFTER THE THREE CONSECUTIVE HOME RUNS IN GAME SIX OF THE 1977 WORLD SERIES

"No wonder you're all mixed up. You got a white man's first name, a Spanish man's second name and a black man's third name." —MICKEY RIVERS

"He'd give you the shirt off his back. Of course, he'd call a press conference to announce it." —CATFISH HUNTER

"Championship teams keep following Reggie around." —EARL WEAVER

"When you unwrap a Reggie Bar, it tells you how good it is." —CATFISH HUNTER

"Off the record, he's a piece of shit." —BILLY MARTIN

DEREK JETER

"To have the chance to play at Yankee Stadium and be on their team, I must be one of the lucky ones."

"My heroes, my dreams, and my future lie in Yankee Stadium and they can't take that from me."

"I didn't make this game, this game made me."

"I still get excited about the game. There's nothing better than the postseason in New York."

ON DEREK JETER

"There are some things that cannot be defined by batting average, home runs and runs batted in. Equally important are an athlete's heart and desire." —GEORGE STEINBRENNER

"He's a natural. Young. Handsome. He can play his ass off, playing shortstop for the Yankees. What more do you want? The fact that he's here in the greatest sports town—greatest city in the world—makes it that much better." —SPIKE LEE

"The guy's amazing, man. That's the guy everybody's chasing. When people come to Yankee Stadium, they don't come to see Luis Sojo. They come to see Derek Jeter. If I was a fan, that's the guy I'd come watch play." —LUIS SOJO

"With Derek, you can just see on his face how much he loves to play and loves to compete. He brings that to the ballpark every day." —JOE TORRE

"Being Derek Jeter in New York now is about as good as it gets." —DAVID CONE

"Derek Jeter is the kind of player, who one day I will get to say, 'I played with him.'" —PAUL O'NEILL

"When I come back, I want to come back as Derek Jeter."
—GEORGE STEINBRENNER

Derek Jeter
and Chuck Knoblauch

WEE WILLIE KEELER

"I keep my eyes clear and I hit 'em where they ain't."

"Learn what pitch you can hit good; then wait for that pitch."

ON WEE WILLIE KEELER

"He may have been small in size but he was huge with the bat." —TED WILLIAMS

DON LARSEN

"I still find it hard to believe I really pitched the perfect game. It's almost like a dream, like something that happened to somebody else."

"They can never break my record. The best they can do is tie it."

ON DON LARSEN

"If Nolan Ryan had done it, if Sandy Koufax had done it, if Don Drysdale had done it, I would have nodded and said, 'Well, it could happen.' But Don Larsen?" —BOB SHEPPARD

ON TONY LAZZERI

"I've seen a few better second basemen, but not many. He has a phenomenal pair of hands, a great throwing arm and he covers acres of ground." —MILLER HUGGINS

PHIL LINZ

"You can't get rich sitting on the bench, but it's worth a try."

SPARKY LYLE

"Why pitch nine innings when you can get just as famous pitching two?"

"I wanted to find out if the diamond was for real, so I cut the glass on my coffee table with it. Then I found out that the coffee table was worth more than the ring." —ON HIS YANKEE WORLD SERIES RING

"When you start thinkin' is when you get your ass beat."

JOE MCCARTHY

"Let me do the worrying." —TO SPORTSWRITERS

"I never challenged an umpire except on rules. I never went to the mound to take out a pitcher. I never roamed the dugout. I was there, seated in the middle, the command post."

"So I eat, drink and sleep baseball twenty-four hours a day. What's wrong with that? The idea of this game is to win and keep winning."

"You have to improve your club if it means letting your own brother go."

MICKEY MANTLE

Mickey Mantle, Yanks vs.
Orioles at Municipal Stadium,
Miami, during spring
training

"If I'd known I was going to live so long I'd have taken better care of myself."

"Don't do as I did. I'm living proof of how not to live."

"After I hit a home run I had a habit of running the bases with my head down. I figured the pitcher already felt bad enough without me showing him up rounding the bases."

"I've heard about you, too." —MICKEY RESPONDING TO THE DUKE OF WINDSOR WHEN THEY MET FOR THE FIRST TIME

"I figure I got all the breaks. Otherwise I'd have been in the mines."

"To play eighteen years in Yankee Stadium is the best thing that could ever happen to a ballplayer."

"Ever since I retired, I keep having these dreams. The worse one is I go to the ballpark late, jump out of a cab, and I hear 'em calling my name on the public-address system. I try and get in and all the gates are locked. Then I see a hole under the fence and I can see Casey looking for me, and Yogi and Billy Martin and Whitey Ford. I try to crawl through the hole and I get stuck at the hips. And that's when I wake up, sweating."

"Yet even as the years grew lean, I became aware that my place in the game, the image people had of me, had taken on a kind of permanence."

"I've often wondered how a man who knew he was going to die could stand here and say he was the luckiest man on the face of the earth, but now I guess I know how he felt."

Mickey Mantle

ON MICKEY MANTLE

"The body of a god. Only Mantle's legs are mortal."
—JERRY COLEMAN

"There isn't any more that I can teach him."
—TOMMY HENRICH ON ROOKIE MICKEY, SPRING TRAINING IN 1951

"There've been a lot of fast men but none as big and strong as Mantle. He's gonna be around a long time, if he can stay well, that fella of mine." —CASEY STENGEL

"With his combination of speed and power he should win the triple batting crown every year. In fact, he should do anything he wants to do." —CASEY STENGEL

"You guys got to see this kid we have in camp. Out of class C ball, hits 'em both ways—five hundred feet both ways! You've got to see him." —BILL DICKEY

"We know you can bunt, Mick. You're not down here to bunt. You're here to get some hits and get your swing back." —KANSAS CITY BLUES MANAGER GEORGE SELKIRK TO MICKEY AFTER HE BUNTED SAFELY HIS FIRST AT BAT AFTER BEING SENT DOWN BY THE YANKEES IN 1951

"I thought he had been shot." —JOE DiMAGGIO WHEN MANTLE WAS INJURED IN THE 1951 WORLD SERIES

"I'd say Mantle is the greatest player in either league." —BOSTON RED SOX OUTFIELDER CARL YASTRZEMSKI

"Let's see—uh, yes. There's one thing he can't do very well. He can't throw left-handed. When he goes in for that we'll have the perfect ballplayer." —ST. LOUIS BROWN'S MANAGER MARTY MARION WHEN ASKED IF MANTLE HAD A WEAKNESS

"The thing I really liked about Mickey was the way he treated everyone the same." —RED SOX PITCHER BILL MONBOUQUETTE

"They ought to create a new league for that guy." —WHITE SOX PITCHER JACK HARSHMAN

"With his one good leg, he could outrun everyone." —GENE WOODLING

"When he took BP [batting practice] everybody would kind of stop what they were doing and watch." —PITCHER JIM KAAT

"If I could run like Mantle I'd hit .400 every year!" —TED WILLIAMS AFTER LOSING THE 1956 BATTING RACE TO MICKEY ON THE LAST DAY OF THE SEASON

"We never thought we could lose as long as Mickey was playing. The point was, we had Mickey and the other team didn't."
—Yankee outfielder Tom Tresh

"One of these days he'll hit the ball so hard, it'll burst and all he'll get for his efforts will be a single." —Casey Stengel

"I never saw anybody hit the ball so hard. When he swings the bat, you just have to stop and watch." —Phil Rizzuto

"That's what Mickey was all about—winning. Nobody cared more about winning, and nobody took losing harder." —Whitey Ford

"He kept a smile on his face, his head on straight and became a leader of one of the greatest teams ever assembled." —Mel Allen

"Mickey had everything going for him. He had the good looks and innocence we wanted to see in our heroes. He had outstanding strength. He even had that billboard name. Mickey was exceptional and the world loved him." —Bobby Murcer

ROGER MARIS

"Maybe I'm not a great man. But I damn well want to break the record."

"As a ballplayer, I would be delighted to do it again. As an individual, I doubt if I could possibly go through it again."

"Every day I went to the ballpark—in Yankee Stadium as well as on the road—people were on my back. The last six years in the American League were mental hell for me."

"I think the most privacy I had was when the game was going on."

"I never wanted all this hoopla. All I wanted is to be a good ballplayer and hit twenty-five or thirty homers, drive in a hundred runs, hit .280 and help my club win pennants. I just wanted to be one of the guys, an average player having a good season."

"If all I am entitled to is an asterisk—that will be all right with me."

ON ROGER MARIS

"It would be a shame if Ruth's record is broken by a .270 hitter."
—ROGERS HORNSBY

"I don't know why Roger isn't in the Hall of Fame. To me, he was as good as there ever was." —MICKEY MANTLE

"Maris broke the wrong record." —JERRY COLEMAN

"That Maris. You'd tell him something, and he'd stare at you for a week before answering." —CASEY STENGEL

BILLY MARTIN

"The rules are made by me, but I don't have to follow them."

"A ballplayer could go to college and be a sportswriter. But what writer could be a ballplayer?"

Billy Martin

"When I get through managing, I'm going to open a kindergarten."

"When you're a professional, you come back, no matter what happened the day before."

"I don't want to fight you. Little kids fight. Men don't fight." —JUST PRIOR TO HITTING A RENO SPORTSWRITER, 1978

"If they try to knock you over, hit the motherfucker right in the mouth with the ball." —TO A ROOKIE CATCHER, 1978

"All I know is I pass people on the street these days, and they don't know whether to say hello or good-bye."

"The two of them deserve each other. One is a confirmed liar [Jackson] and the other is a convicted felon [Steinbrenner]."

ON BILLY MARTIN

"He's a smart-assed kid who's always sassin' people and gettin' away with it." —CASEY STENGEL OF BILLY MARTIN IN 1977

"Billy copied Casey to a 'T.'" —MICKEY MANTLE

TINO MARTINEZ

"That's just playing in New York. Obituaries are written every day if you have a bad day, so you just learn to not pay attention to it."

DON MATTINGLY

"Honestly, at one time I thought Babe Ruth was a cartoon character. I really did, I mean I wasn't born until 1961 and I grew up in Indiana."

"The players get no respect around here. They [the Yankees] give you money, that's it, not respect. That's why nobody wants to play here."

"This guy is working all week and he brings his son to this show, has to pay two dollars to get in, maybe five dollars for a picture and then six dollars for an autograph. These guys have to think you're a real ass with your head down all the time signing."

"We still played hard every day." —ON THE 1990 YANKEES

ON DON MATTINGLY

"I'm glad I don't have to face him every day. He has that look that few hitters have. I don't know if it's his stance, his eyes, or what. But you can tell he means business." —DWIGHT GOODEN

ON BOB MEUSEL

"Meusel's arm was the best I ever saw. And I'm talking about strong arms, not merely accurate ones. Meusel threw strikes to any base from the outfield." —BOB QUINN, FORMER PRESIDENT OF THE RED SOX AND BRAVES

"He's learning to say hello when it's time to say good-bye."
—WRITER FRANK GRAHAM, JR., ON MEUSEL'S MELLOWING AS HE
REACHED THE END OF HIS CAREER

GRAIG NETTLES

"Growing up I always wanted to play baseball or join the circus. With the Yankees I've done both."

"People recognize me wherever I go, where it used to be just New York. I guess people who aren't even baseball fans watch the World Series. I was driving down the freeway in Los Angeles over the winter and a guy pulled up next to me and gave me the finger."

"Since it's a two-team town, I preferred to think that many of the people who were booing me were Mets fans."

PAUL O'NEILL

"I hit the jackpot. I came here at the right time. I played with the right people. I was a little part of the right team. You expect to win but not the way we won."

WALLY PIPP

"I took the two most expensive aspirins in history."

VIC RASCHI

"Give me the goddamn ball and get the hell out of here." —TO YOGI BERRA IN A TIGHT MOMENT IN THE 1949 WORLD SERIES

MARIANO RIVERA

"I left everything on the mound. I'm not going to second-guess myself. I was feeling good. I couldn't finish it up. I threw the pitches that I wanted to throw. They hit it." —AFTER HIS GAME SEVEN WORLD SERIES DEFEAT, 2001

ON MARIANO RIVERA

"He's as automatic as anybody ever has been." —MIKE STANTON

MICKEY RIVERS

"We'll do all right if we can capitalize on our mistakes."

"The wind was blowin' about a hundred degrees."

"I don't get upset over things I can't control, because if I can't control them there's no use getting upset. And I don't get upset over the things I can control, because if I can control them there's no use in getting upset."

"Me and George [Steinbrenner] and Billy [Martin] are two of a kind."

"My goals are to hit three hundred, score one hundred runs, and stay injury-prone."

"Pitching is eighty percent of the game and the other half is hitting and fielding."

"You can't improve what's bad, you can only build up what's good."

PHIL RIZZUTO

"I started my career being naïve and finished my career the same way."

"They still can't steal first base."

"Holy cow!"

"That huckleberry!"

"I like radio better than television because if you make a mistake on radio, they don't know. You can make up anything on the radio."

"I'll never forget September 6, 1950. I got a letter threatening me, Hank Bauer, Yogi Berra and Johnny Mize. It said if I showed up in uniform against the Red Sox I'd be shot. I turned the letter over to the FBI and told Casey Stengel about it. You know what Casey did? He gave me a different uniform and gave mine to Billy Martin."

"I'll take any way to get into the Hall of Fame. If they want a batboy, I'll go in as a batboy."

"Well that kind of puts the damper on even a Yankee win." —ON THE PASSING OF POPE PAUL VI

"You played for the love of the game and for just enough money so that you might not have to work in the winter. I was lucky because with the Yankees we'd be in the World Series almost every year. There were two years when I made more money from World Series cuts than I did from my salary."

"The first game that I played was one of my great thrills because I saw my first real, live president. Now some of you people don't remember him, but it was Franklin Delano Roosevelt who was president in 1941. He threw out the first ball when we played in Washington and I'd never been in Washington, D.C. Joe DiMaggio told me, 'Don't try to get the ball because when he throws it everyone dives for it. People have gotten spiked and broken hands.' I didn't come close to getting it, but I saw the president and that was a big thrill."

"The writers were never late in 1977."

"I was sick when they dug the first hunk of dirt out of the infield. I spent half my life in this stadium." —ON THE REMODELING OF THE OLD YANKEE STADIUM

ON PHIL RIZZUTO

"I heard doctors revived a man who had been dead for four and a half minutes. When they asked him what it was like being dead, he said it was like listening to Yankees announcer Phil Rizzuto during a rain delay." —DAVID LETTERMAN

COLONEL JACOB RUPPERT

"I found out a long time ago that there is no charity in baseball and that every club owner must make his own fight for existence."

"Close games make me nervous."

"What's the matter with you? Other pitchers win their games nine to three, ten to two. You win yours two to one, two to nothing. Why don't you win your games like the others?" —TO PITCHER WAITE HOYT

BABE RUTH

"Cobb is a prick but he sure can hit. God Almighty, that man can hit."

"I suppose you were in the war." —WHEN INTRODUCED TO MARSHALL FOCH, THE GREAT WAR HERO

"They're coming out in groves." —IN REFERENCE TO THE CROWDS HE ATTRACTED

"Scallions are the greatest cure for a batting slump ever invented."

"Reading isn't good for a ballplayer. Not good for his eyes. If my eyes went bad, even a little bit, I couldn't hit home runs. So I gave up reading."

"You got ten years ahead of you in the big leagues, Lou [Gehrig]. Save your dough. Start one of those trust funds. Every dollar you save will be one more laugh when your home run days are over."

Babe Ruth and Lou Gehrig fishing, December 12, 1933

"All the parks are good except the stadium. There is no background there at all. I cried when they took me out of the Polo Grounds."

"When I am out after a home run, I try to make mush out of this solid ash handle. The bat overcomes all the resistance of the ball and keeps right on moving after it has struck."

"The way a team plays as a whole determines its success. You may have the greatest bunch of individual stars in the world, but if they don't play together, the club won't be worth a dime."

"Just one. Whenever I hit a home run, I make certain I touch all four bases." —WHEN ASKED IF HE HAD ANY SUPERSTITIONS

"Never let the fear of striking out get in your way."

"I've never heard a crowd boo a homer, but I've heard plenty of boos after a strikeout."

"All I can tell them is pick a good one and sock it. I get back to the dugout and they ask me what it was I hit and I tell them I don't know except it looked good."

"Every strike brings me closer to the next home run."

"I swing as hard as I can, and I try to swing right through the ball. The harder you grip the bat, the more you can swing it through the ball, and the farther the ball will go. I swing big, with everything I've got. I hit big or I miss big. I like to live as big as I can."

"I coulda hit a four-hundred lifetime average easy. But I woulda had to hit them singles. The people were payin' to see me hit them home runs."

"Pitchers began pitching to me because if they passed me they still had Lou to contend with."

"All ballplayers should quit when it starts to feel as if all the baselines run uphill."

"It's hell to get older."

"The only real game, I think, in the world is baseball."

Babe Ruth and Lou Gehrig
signing autographs

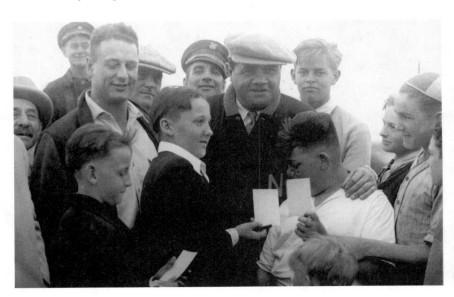

ON BABE RUTH

"I don't room with him. I room with his suitcase." —PING BODIE

"He was a parade all by himself. A burst of dazzle and jingle, Santa Claus drinking his whiskey straight." —JIMMY CANNON

"A rabbit didn't have to think to know what to do to dodge a dog. The same kind of instinct told Babe Ruth what to do and where to be." —SAMMY VICK

"I've seen them: kids, men, women, worshippers all, hoping to get his name on a torn, dirty piece of paper, or hoping for a grunt of recognition when they said, 'Hi-ya, Babe.' He never let them down; not once. He was the greatest crowd pleaser of them all." —WAITE HOYT

"When he hit one, he just dropped the bat and started that little trot. He didn't just stand there and show the pitcher up, like sometimes you see certain players today. He knew it was gone. He hit it out of sight. And every once in a while he would bunt the ball because they'd put the shift on, and there'd be no third baseman, and he'd bunt it, and he'd get down to first base, and he'd chuckle like a big elephant. Just laugh. In other words, he was a great, great man." —RED SCHOENDIENST

"It's a pretty big shadow [Babe Ruth's]—it gives me lots of room to spread myself." —LOU GEHRIG

"No one hit home runs the way Babe did. They were like homing pigeons. The ball would leave the bat, pause briefly, suddenly gain its bearings, then take off for the stands." —LEFTY GOMEZ

"There will never be another guy like the Babe. I get more kick from seeing him hit one than I do from hitting one myself." —LOU GEHRIG

"Babe Ruth struck out 1,330 times." —GRAFFITI SCRAWLED ON A WALL SOMEWHERE IN NEW YORK CITY

"Babe would often sit by the phone waiting for the call [for work] that never came. Sometimes when he couldn't take it any longer, he'd break down, put his head in his hands, and weep." —CLAIRE RUTH ON RUTH AFTER HE RETIRED

GABE PAUL

"The great thing about baseball is there's a crisis every day."

"There is no such thing as second place. Either you're first or you're nothing."

LUIS SOJO

"I've always said that I wanted to retire as a Yankee. I could play one or two more years if I wanted to, but I don't want to go play anywhere else."

GEORGE STEINBRENNER

"Owning the Yankees is like owning the *Mona Lisa*; it's something that you'd never sell."

"I won't be active in the day-to-day operations of the ball club at all."

"I am dead-set against free agency. It can ruin baseball."

"I'm not a good loser. I believe in what Ernest Hemingway said: 'The way you get to be a good loser is practice and I don't want to practice.' "

"The Mets gave us everything we could want. It was great for the city of New York. I hope we don't have to go through this again for another forty-four years."–2000 WORLD SERIES

"We'll be back. Mark that down. We'll be back." —RIGHT AFTER WORLD SERIES 2001 LOSS TO ARIZONA

ON GEORGE STEINBRENNER

"It's a good thing Babe Ruth isn't still here. George would have him bat seventh and say he's overweight." –GRAIG NETTLES

"What does George know about Yankee pride? When did he ever play for the Yankees?" –BILLY MARTIN

"I was happy for George because George wanted it so bad. I said to myself, 'Now he can really have fun at the 21 Club. He'll go around and give rings to his friends and he'll be able to talk about this one as long as he lives." —Reggie Jackson on winning the 1977 World Series

"I tell George what I think, and then I do what he says." —Bob Lemon, manager, 1982

CASEY STENGEL

A STENGELESE MONOLOGUE
SPRING TRAINING, 1955

"And now we come to Collins which may be an outfielder. He played centerfield at Newark and also played right field for me in the World Series. You can look it up, but he had Novikoff on one side of him and someone else whose name I have forgotten on the other but you can look it up. That should prove he's a great outfielder in order to do it with them guys on either side of him.

"There's a kid infielder named Richardson who was in our rookie camp which he doesn't look like he can play because he's as stiff as a stick—but whoosh—and the ball's there and he does it so fast it would take some of them Sunshine Park handicappers with the field glasses on to see him do it so fast does he do it. He never misses. As soon as he misses a ball, we'll send him back home.

"We started out to get us a shortstop and now we got eight of them. We don't fool, we don't. I ain't yet found a way to play more than one man in each position although we can shift them around and make them maybe outfielders outa them or put 'em all at ketch like we done with Howard."

At the Congressional hearings on baseball's Reserve Clause, July 19, 1958:

"In Kankakee, Illinois or someplace like that, I tore my suit sitting in the stands . . . now they've got good seats.

"I got a little concern yesterday in the first three innings when I saw the three players I had gotten rid of, and I said when I lost nine what am I going to do and when I had a couple of my players I thought so great of that did not do so good up to the sixth inning I was more confused but I finally had to go and call on a young man in Baltimore that we don't own and the Yankees don't own him, and he is doing pretty good, and I would actually have to tell you that we are more the Greta Garbo type now from success.

"We are being hated, I mean from the ownership and all, we are being hated. Every sport that gets too great or one individual—but if we made 27 cents and it pays to have a winner at home, why would you have a good winner in your own park if you were an owner?

"That is the result of baseball. An owner get most of the money at home and it's up to him and his staff to do better or they ought to be discharged."

"I broke in with four hits and the writers promptly decided they had seen the new Ty Cobb. It took me only a few days to correct that impression."

"I was such a dangerous hitter I even got intentional walks during batting practice."

"What I learned from McGraw [whom he played for in the 1920s], I used with all of them. They are still using a round ball, a round bat and nine guys on a side."

"I got players with bad watches—they can't tell midnight from noon."

"Mickey [Mantle] has it in his body to be great."

"Kid [Phil Rizzuto], you're too small. You ought to go out and shine shoes."

"Look at him [Bobby Richardson]—he doesn't drink, he doesn't smoke, he doesn't chew, he doesn't stay out late, and he still can't hit .250."

"Johnny Sain don't say much, but that don't matter much, because when you're out there on the mound, you got nobody to talk to."

"Bobby Brown reminds me of a fellow who's been hitting for twelve years and fielding one."

"Jerry Lumpe looks like the best hitter in the world until you put him in the lineup."

"Ryne Duren takes a drink or ten, comes in with them Coke bottles [eyeglasses], throws one on the screen, and scares the shit out of them. And when he starts pitching, people stop eating their popcorn."

"Ed Lopat looks like he is throwing wads of tissue paper. Every time he wins a game, fans come down out of the stands asking for contracts."

"Son, we'd like to keep you around this season, but we're trying to win the pennant."—to a Yankee rookie

"Managing is getting paid for home runs someone else hits."

"You ask me what kind of ball club I want, one with power or one with speed, well a lot of power but not too much, and a lot of speed but not too much. The best club is the versatile club, the one that has a homer hitter here and a bunter there, a fastball pitcher here and a change-of-pace pitcher here. That way, the other team never knows what's going to hit it next."

"The secret of managing is to keep the guys who hate you away from the guys who are undecided."

"What the hell is baseball but telling the umpire who's gonna play and then watching them play."

"Now there's three things you can do in a baseball game: You can win or you can lose or it can rain."

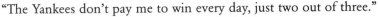

"The Yankees don't pay me to win every day, just two out of three."

"You got to get twenty-seven outs to win."

"You gotta lose 'em some of the time. When you do, lose 'em right."

"The best thing to do is to have players who can hit right-handed and left-handed and hit farther one way and farther sometimes the other way and run like the wind."

"Nobody ever had too many of them [pitchers]."

"It's high time something was done for the pitchers. They put up the stands and take down fences to make more home runs and plague the pitchers. Let them revive the spitter and help the pitchers make a living."

"Good pitching will always stop good hitting and vice-versa."

"Left-handers have more enthusiasm for life. They sleep on the wrong side of the bed and their head gets more stagnant on that side."

"These old-timers' games, they're like airplane landings. If you can walk away from them, they're successful."

"About the autograph business—once somebody sent up a picture to me and I write: 'Do good in school.' I look up to see who was gettin' the picture. This guy is seventy-eight years old."

"It's wonderful to meet so many friends that I didn't used to like."

"There comes a time in every man's life and I've had plenty of them."

"Don't drink in the hotel bar, that's where I do my drinking."

"I came in here and a fella asked me to have a drink. I said I don't drink. Then another fella said, 'I hear you and Joe DiMaggio aren't speaking,' and I said, 'I'll take that drink.'"

"They say some of my stars drink whiskey, but I have found that ones who drink milkshakes don't win many ballgames."

"The trouble is not that players have sex the night before a game. It's that they stay out all night looking for it."

"Don't cut my throat, I may want to do that later myself."

"Anyone comes looking for me, tell 'em I'm being embalmed."

"Most people my age are dead at the present time and you can look it up."

"I'd want to thank all my players for giving me the honor of what I was."

"They told me my services were no longer desired because they wanted to put in a youth program as an advance way of keeping the club going. I'll never make the mistake of being seventy again."

"I couldn'a done it without my players."

A Dictionary of
STENGELESE

- BUTCHER BOY = *a chopped ground ball*
- EMBALMED = *sleeping*
- GREEN PEA = *rookie or unseasoned player*
- HE COULD SQUEEZE YOUR EARBROWS OFF = *a tough player*
- HOLD THE GUN = *I want to change pitchers*
- NED IN THE THIRD READER = *naiveté*
- PLUMBER = *a good fielder*
- ROAD APPLE = *a bum*
- WHISKEY SLICK = *a playboy*
- WORM KILLERS = *low balls*

(L to R): Johnny Neun, Frank Crosetti, Casey Stengel, Jim Turner, and Bill Dickey

ON CASEY STENGEL

"I never saw a man who juggled his lineup so much and who played so many hunches so successfully." –CONNIE MACK

"There were things that would irritate Casey, but trying too hard or getting mad at sitting on the bench weren't among them." –MICKEY MANTLE

"Watch the old man. Watch how the old man keeps the guys who aren't playing happy." –BILLY MARTIN TO MICKEY MANTLE

"After a play in the field Casey would turn [to the players on the bench] and say, 'What did he do wrong?' or 'You're better than that guy.' Either way, he'd keep them from getting stale."

"It's the first role I've done in a foreign language." –ACTOR CHARLES DURNING ON PORTRAYING STENGEL IN THE 1981 ONE-MAN SHOW *Casey Stengel*

JOE TORRE

"I've never been so happy. I never thought this would happen to me." –AFTER WINNING HIS FIRST WORLD CHAMPIONSHIP IN 1996

"I don't play names." –TO WADE BOGGS

"I think we should rank up there with any of them. To get to the World Series four years in a row, five out of six years with all the layers of playoffs we have to go through. Years ago when I first came to the big leagues, you won your league and went to the World Series." –2001

ON JOE TORRE

"He's one of the steadiest men I've ever known. Sometimes I couldn't believe how calm he was. I thought, is this a mask? To this day, I don't know." –JOHN WETTELAND ON THE 1996 SEASON

JIM TURNER

"Watch out for the writers. Don't tell them sons-o-bitches nothing."

George Weiss and Casey Stengel

GEORGE WEISS

"You made an easy play look hard." —TO BILLY MARTIN ON HIS CATCH IN GAME SEVEN OF THE 1952 WORLD SERIES

DAVID WELLS

"The shutout doesn't matter. It's the 'W.' You want to have the 'W' instead of the 'L.'"

ON DAVID WELLS

"At nighttime, you just try to keep him out of jail." —DAVID CONE

BERNIE WILLIAMS

"When it comes down to it, there's only one day a year when we allow ourselves to get giddy—the parade."

DAVE WINFIELD

"Good hitters don't just go up and swing. They always have a plan. Call it an educated deduction. You visualize. You're like a good negotiator. You know what you have, you know what he has, then you try to work it out."

Dave Winfield and
George Steinbrenner

"I never had to cheat, I get them with what I got."

"These days baseball is different. You come to spring training, you get your legs ready, your arms loose, your agents ready, your lawyer lined up."

"Tom Cruise only makes one or two film appearances a year. A baseball player can be the hero or the goat one hundred and sixty-two times a year."

"All good balls to hit are strikes, though not all strikes are good balls to hit."

DON ZIMMER

"I want to make sure no one is in my uniform." —ON ALWAYS ARRIVING EARLY TO THE BALLPARK

"Now after fifty years, I am still in baseball. It's my life."

ON DON ZIMMER

"Zimmer's face looks like a blocked kick." —JOE GARAGIOLA

CHAPTER SEVEN

WHAT'S IN A
Name

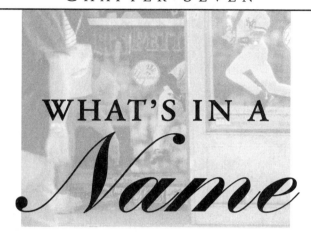

Noms de plume, aliases, sobriquets, catchwords—nicknames, all time, all ways for Yankees. Through the decades, sporting scribes, fans, friends and relatives, opponents and teammates have come up with nicknames for Yankees.

These have run the gamut, from apt to asinine, from complimentary to embarrassing, from hero worshipping to amusing to silly to on-target. Herewith, a sampler.

◆

"THE BABE": George Herman Ruth leads off the list and pads it for most nicknames acquired. He got the nickname Babe from his teammates on the Baltimore Orioles, his first professional team, because of his youth. Yankee teammates called G. H. Ruth Jidge, short for George. Opponents called him the Big Monk and Monkey and a lot of unmentionables.

Many of Babe Ruth's nicknames came from overreaching sportswriters stretching to pay tribute to his slugging prowess:

The Bambino, the Wali of Wallop, the Rajah of Rap, the Caliph of Clout, the Wazir of Wham, the Sultan of Swat, the Colossus of Clout, Maharajah of Mash, the Behemoth of Bust, and the King of Clout were just a few of the hype names tossed his way.

Ruth, however, was also known for giving out nicknames—or, rather, a nickname. He called most players Kid because he couldn't remember the names of even his closest friends.

But enough of George Herman Ruth. Now on to the bon mots, aliases, and expressions for all matter of Yankees.

"ALL-AMERICAN OUT": What Babe Ruth called Leo Durocher because of his limited hitting ability.

"ALMIGHTY TIRED MAN": Mickey Rivers, for his slouching demeanor.

"BABE RUTH'S LEGS": Sammy Byrd, used as a pinch runner for Ruth.

"BAM-BAM": Hensley Meulens, who could speak about five languages and had a difficult name to pronounce.

"BANTY ROOSTER": Casey Stengel's nickname for Whitey Ford because of his style and attitude.

"BARROWS": Jacob Ruppert's mangling of Ed Barrow's name.

"BATTLE OF THE BILTMORE": At the 1947 series celebration in Manhattan's Biltmore Hotel, Larry MacPhail drunkenly fought with everyone, ending his Yankee ownership time.

"BILLY BALL": Aggressive style of play utilized by Billy Martin.

"BISCUIT PANTS": A reference to the well-filled-out trousers of Lou Gehrig.

"BLIND RYNE": Pitcher Ryne Duren, for his very poor vision and thick glasses. Uncorrected, his eyesight was 20/70 and 20/200.

Lou Gehrig

"BLOODY ANGLE": During the 1923 season the space between the bleachers and right-field foul line at Yankee Stadium was very asymmetrical, causing crazy bounces. It was eliminated in 1924.

"BOB THE GOB": Bob Shawkey spent most of 1918 in the navy as a yeoman petty officer aboard the battleship *Arkansas*. Also called "Sailor Bob."

"BOOMER": David Wells, for his in-your-face personality.

"THE BOSS": George Steinbrenner.

"THE BOSTON MASSACRE": Describes the Red Sox collapse in 1978, specifically the Yankee sweep of a four-game series that September.

"BROADWAY": Shortstop Lyn Lary, married to Broadway star Mary Lawler.

"BRONX BOMBERS": For the borough that houses Yankee stadium and home-run power.

"BRONX ZOO": A derogatory reference to off-color Yankee behavior on and off the playing field through the years, but especially in the 1970s.

"BROOKLYN SCHOOLBOY": Waite Hoyt, for his time as a star pitcher at Erasmus High School.

"BRUISER": Outfielder Hank Bauer, for his burly ways.

"BULLDOG": Pitcher Jim Bouton, for his tenacity.

"BULLET BOB": Bob Turley, for the pop on his fastball.

"BULLET JOE": Joe Bush, also for the pop he could put on his fastball.

"BYE-BYE": Steve Balboni, the primary DH of the 1990 Yankees, had seventeen homers but hit just .192.

"CARNESVILLE PLOWBOY": Pitcher Spud Chandler, raised on a farm near Carnesville, Georgia.

"THE CAT-A-LYST": Name given to Mickey Rivers by Howard Cosell for his ability to trigger Yankee team offense.

"GEORGIA CATFISH": Name given to Jim Hunter by Oakland owner Charles Finley to give the young pitcher more of an identity; he was known primarily as just Catfish.

"CHAIRMAN OF THE BOARD": Elston Howard's phrase in tribute to Whitey Ford and his commanding manner on the mound.

"COLUMBIA LOU": Lou Gehrig, for his collegiate roots.

"COMMERCE COMET": Mickey Mantle, for his hometown of Commerce, Oklahoma, and his speed.

"THE COUNT": Pitcher Sparky Lyle, for his handlebar mustache and lordly ways.

"THE CROW": Shortstop Frank Crosetti, for his loud voice and chirpy ways.

"THE CURSE OF THE BAMBINO": Since 1920 and the selling of Babe Ruth to the Yankees by Boston owner Harry Frazee in 1920, the Yankees have won twenty-six championships. The Red Sox have won none.

"DADDY LONGLEGS": Outfielder Dave Winfield, for his size and long legs.

"DANISH VIKING": Pitcher George Pipgras, for his size and roots.

"DEACON": Shortstop Everett Scott, for his not-too-friendly look.

"DEATH VALLEY": The old deep left center field in Yankee Stadium, where a home run was a mighty poke.

"DIAL-A-DEAL": Former general manager Gabe Paul, for his telephone trading habits.

"DONNIE BASEBALL": Don Mattingly, the only player in any sport to have a nickname with the actual name of his or her sport in it. Some say it was coined by Yankee broadcaster Michael Kay; others say it came from Kirby Pucket. Kay takes the credit; Mattingly gives the credit to Puckett.

"EL DUQUE": Pitcher Orlando Hernandez, for his lordly ways.

"EL DUQUECITO": Adrian Hernandez, because of a pitching style similar to Orlando "El Duque" Hernandez.

Don Mattingly

"ELLIE": Affectionate abbreviation of Elston Howard's first name.

"FATHER OF THE EMORY BALL": Right-hander Russ Ford, who had a legitimate claim to that distinction.

"FIGGY": Pitcher Ed Figueroa, short for his surname, which was tough, for some, to pronounce.

"FIREMAN": Johnny Murphy was the first to have this nickname for his great relief pitching; Joe Page later picked it up because of his own top relief work.

"FIVE O'CLOCK LIGHTNING": The five o'clock blowing of a factory whistle near Yankee Stadium signaled the end of the workday in the 1930s; this also describes the Yankees' performance on the field.

"FLASH": Joe Gordon, for his fast, slick fielding and hot line drives, and the play on his last name.

"FORDHAM JOHNNY": Pitcher Johnny Murphy, for the college he attended.

"FOUR HOUR MANAGER": Bucky Harris, for coming to the park with little time to spare before a game and leaving quickly after a game was over.

"FRIDAY NIGHT MASSACRE": April 26, 1974, Yankees Fritz Patterson, Steve Kline, Fred Beene, Tom Buskey, and half the pitching staff were traded to Cleveland for Chris Chambliss, Dick Tidrow, and Cecil Upshaw.

"GATOR": Pitcher Ron Guidry, for his hailing from Louisiana alligator country.

"GAY RELIEVER": Joe Page, for his night-owl activity.

"GEHRIGVILLE": Bleachers in right center at Yankee Stadium.

"THE GODFATHER": Manager Joe Torre, for his Italian roots and his leadership skills on the baseball field.

"GOOFY" OR "EL GOOFO": Pitcher Lefty Gomez, for his wild antics.

"GOONEYBIRD": Pitcher Don Larsen, for his late-night behavior.

"GOOSE": Pitcher Richard Michael Gossage, for his loose and lively style. Gossage was also often called the "White Gorilla" for the way he looked.

"GRANDMA": Johnny Murphy, for his rocking-chair-style pitching motion. Another explanation has it that fellow Yankee Pat Malone gave him the name because of his frequent complaining, especially about food and lodgings.

"THE GREAT AGITATOR": Billy Martin—no explanation necessary.

"HAPPY JACK": Jack Chesbro, the nick-name derived for his time as an attendant at the state mental hospital in Middletown, New York, where he pitched for the hospital team and showed off a very pleasant disposition.

"HOLY COW": One of Phil Rizzuto's ways of expressing awe.

"HOME RUN": Shortstop Frank Baker, for the two game-winning homers he hit in the 1911 World Series.

"HOME RUN TWINS": Mickey Mantle and Roger Maris, phrase coined in 1961.

"HORSE NOSE": Catcher Pat Collins, for his nose. The nickname was given to him by Babe Ruth.

"HORSEWHIPS SAM": Sam Jones, for his sharp-breaking curveball.

"HOUSE THAT RUTH BUILT": Ruth's immense popularity propelled the Yankees into their new home, Yankee Stadium.

"IRON HORSE": Lou Gehrig, for his power and steadiness.

"JOLTIN' JOE": Joe DiMaggio, for the jolting power shots he hit.

"JUMPING JOE": Third baseman Joe Dugan, for being AWOL from his first big-league club.

"JUNK MAN": Eddie Lopat, for frustrating hitters and keeping them off stride with an assortment of slow breaking pitches thrown with cunning and accuracy.

"KENTUCKY COLONEL": Outfielder Earl Combs, for his Kentucky roots and elegant hearing.

"THE KING AND THE CROWN PRINCE": Babe Ruth and Lou Gehrig.

"KING KONG": Outfielder Charlie Keller, for his muscular body type and black bushy brows.

"KNIGHT OF KENNETT SQUARE": Pitcher Herb Pennock, for his raising of thoroughbreds and hosting of fox hunts in his hometown of Kennett Square, Pennsylvania. Also sometimes called the "Squire of Kennett Square."

"KNUCKSIE": Phil Niekro, for his knuckleball.

"LARRUPIN' LOU": Lou Gehrig, for his powerful ways.

"THE LIP": Infielder Leo Durocher, for his mouth.

"LONESOME GEORGE": George Weiss, for his aloof ways.

"LOUISIANA LIGHTNING": Pitcher Ron Guidry, for his fastball and the state he came from.

"M&M BOYS": Mickey Mantle and Roger Maris.

"MAIL CARRIER": Outfielder Earle Combs, for his speed and base-stealing skills.

"MAJOR": Catcher and manager Ralph Houk, for rank held in the armed forces and his demeanor.

"MAN IN THE IRON HAT": Captain Tillinghast L'Hommedieu Huston, for the same squashed derby hat he wore over and over again.

"MAN NOBODY KNOWS": Bill Dickey, for his blandness.

"MAN OF A THOUSAND CURVES": Johnny Sain, hyperbolic reference to his assortment of curveballs.

"MARSE JOE": Manager Joe McCarthy, for his commanding style.

"MASTER BUILDER IN BASEBALL": Jacob Ruppert, and that he was.

"THE MERRY MORTICIAN": Pitcher Waite Hoyt, for his cheery soul and off-season work as a mortician.

"THE MICK": Short for Mickey (Mantle).

"MICK THE QUICK": Mickey Rivers, for his speed.

"MICKEY MOUTH": Mickey Rivers, for his motor mouth.

"MIGHTY MITE": Miller Huggins, for his size and power.

"MILKMAN": Jim Turner, for an off-season job delivering milk.

"MR. AUTOMATIC": Mariano Rivera, for his virtually unflappable behavior and special skills as a Yankee stopper.

"MR. CANDY": Reggie Jackson, for his candy bar.

"MR. MAY": George Steinbrenner's sarcastic jibe at Dave Winfield because of his postseason struggles, as compared to Reggie Jackson's successes and "Mr. October" nickname.

"MR. NOVEMBER": Derek Jeter, for his World Series home run on the first of November 2001.

"MR. OCTOBER": In game five of the 1977 ALCS, Billy Martin benched Reggie Jackson. In a comeback win against Kansas City, Jackson returned to slap a single. Thurman Munson sarcastically called Jackson "Mr. October." The nickname would have taken on a negative meaning, but Jackson fitted the nickname to his persona.

"MOOSE": Bill Skowron's grandfather called him Mussolini because of a resemblance to the Italian leader. As the story goes, the family shortened the nickname to Moose.

"MOOSE": Mike Mussina, for his size, also a shortening of his surname.

"MURDERERS' ROW": In the standard version, this refers to the powerful batters of the 1927 lineup of Tony Lazzeri, Lou Gehrig, Babe Ruth, Earle Combs, and Bob Meusel. A less-prominent version refers to the 1919 line-up of Ping Bodie, Roger Peckinpaugh, Duffy Lewis, and Home Run Baker.

"MY WRITERS": Casey Stengel's phrase for journalists he was close to.

"NICKEL SERIES": When New York City teams played against each other and the subway fare was five cents.

"NIGHTRIDER": Don Larsen called himself that because it reminded him of comic-book heroes he read about, and it fit with his late-night bar wanderings.

"OKLAHOMA KID": The young Mickey Mantle, for the state he came from.

"OLD FOX": Clark Griffith of the old Highlanders, for his cunning ways.

"OLD RELIABLE": Mel Allen gave Tommy Henrich that nickname after a train that ran from Cincinnati through Allen's home state of Alabama and was always dependably on time. Henrich was also called the Great Debater for his sometimes loquacious and argumentative ways.

"OLE PERFESSOR": Casey Stengel, for the time in 1914 when he had a spring-training baseball coaching stint at the University of Mississippi.

"THE ONE AND ONLY": Babe Ruth.

"PEPI": Shortened version of Joe Pepitone's surname.

"THE PEERLESS LEADER": Manager Frank Chance, for his keen baseball mind.

"PLOWBOY": Pitcher Tom Morgan, for the way he moved about.

"POOSH 'EM UP, TONY": Tony Lazzeri was a magnet for Italian fans at Yankee Stadium, who would scream out this phrase, urging him to hit home runs.

"PORKY": Pitcher Hal Reniff, for his physical appearance.

"PRIDE OF PENACOOK": Red Rolfe, for the little town he hailed from in New Hampshire.

"THE PRIDE OF THE YANKEES": Lou Gehrig.

"PRINCE HAL": First baseman Hal Chase, for his charismatic, elegant, royal quality.

"THE PRINCE OF BEER": Jacob Ruppert, brewery owner with a royal manner.

"THE PRINCE OF THE CITY": Shortstop Derek Jeter, for his good looks, charisma, and class.

"THE PRINCIPAL OWNER": George Steinbrenner.

"PUSH BUTTON MANAGER": Joe McCarthy, for his by-the-book ways.

"RAGIN' CAJUN": Ron Guidry, for his Louisiana roots and fire.

"RAGS": Dave Righetti, variation on an abbreviation of his surname.

"REG-GER-OO": Reggie Jackson, an endearing reference coined by Howard Cosell.

"ROCKET": Roger Clemens, for the speed and power of his fastball.

"ROOT": Jake Ruppert's corruption of Babe Ruth's name.

"RUBBERARM": Alan Russell, a starter and reliever 1915–1919, a hurler who never turned his back on a chance to pitch.

"RUPPERT RIFLES": The Yankees during Jake Ruppert's tenure.

"RUTHVILLE": Bleachers in right center where Babe Ruth hit home runs.

"SAD SAM": Sam Jones, for his downcast look on the playing field.

"SCHOOLBOY" AND "SCHOOLBOY WONDER": Waite Hoyt, for his major-league debut in 1918 when he was a teenager

"SCOOTER": "I guess it was when I was down south," Rizzuto explained. "You know, southerners have a very quaint, unusual way of saying things. Well, Billy Hitchcock was on the team with me down in spring training. You know my legs are short (I'm short all over but my legs are very short), and when he saw me run, he said: 'Man, you are not running, you're scootin'.' And from scootin' I got Scooter." Nickname for Phil Rizzuto also coined by Mel Allen, as another explanation goes.

"SECOND PLACE JOE": Joe McCarthy's three straight second-place finishes prompted this tag in the three seasons before the Yanks won four consecutive world championships, 1936–1939. The name was also used when he was manager of the Cubs, where more disappointing second-place finishes followed.

"SHORT PORCH": The right-field stands in Yankee Stadium.

"SILENT BOB": Bob Meusel, for his aloofness.

"SILENT ONE": Chris Chambliss, a name given by Howard Cosell for his taciturn manner.

"SLICK": Whitey Ford used a spitball to strike out Willie Mays in the 1964 All-Star Game. That was just one of the reasons for the Yankee star's nickname.

"SLOW": Joe Doyle, for his time-consuming pace.

"SMASH": Gil McDougald, for the verve of his personality.

"SOLID CITIZENS": Name Joe McCarthy gave to players he relied on.

"SPRINGFIELD RIFLE": Vic Raschi, after his birthplace in Springfield, Massachusetts.

Whitey Ford, Ed Lopat,
Allie Reynolds, and Vic Raschi—
star pitchers all

"SPUD": Spurgeon Ferdinand Chandler was called that, a painless shortening of his given names.

"STEADY EDDIE": Eddie Lopat, for his consistency year after year as a Yankee pitcher; the nickname originated with Mel Allen.

"STICK": Gene Michael, for his lean and long appearance.

"SUPERCHIEF": Allie Reynolds, for his one-quarter Creek Indian ancestry and winning ways on the mound.

"SUPER-SUB": Johnny Blanchard, a pinch hitter extraordinaire with many home runs.

"THE SWITCHER": Mickey Mantle, for switch-hitting par excellence.

"T. J.": Tommy John

"THE TABASCO KID": Norman Arthur Elberfeld, for his liking of the stuff and his personality.

"TANGLEFOOT LOU": Lou Gehrig, for his early days and fielding trials as a player.

"THREE MILLION DOLLAR MAN": Nickname given to Catfish Hunter when he signed with the Yankees as a free agent for that sum in 1974.

"TWINKLETOES": George Selkirk, who ran with his weight on the balls of his feet; the nickname was given to him by teammates at Newark in the International League.

"TWO HEAD": A negative nickname used by opponents to describe the size of Babe Ruth's head, which seemed gigantic to some.

"THE UNHOLY TRIO": Billy Martin, Mickey Mantle, and Whitey Ford, for their devilish ways.

"THE WARRIOR": Outfielder Paul O'Neill, name pinned on him by George Steinbrenner for the outfielder's pugnacious ways.

"THE WEATHERMAN": Outfielder Mickey Rivers, for his knack for predicting weather.

"WHITEY": Pitcher Edward "Whitey" Ford, for the towhead blonde hair he sported as a 1950s hurler.

"WINDOW BREAKERS": Name given to the 1936 Yankees for their slugging power.

"WINNY": Outfielder Dave Winfield, affectionate shortening of his surname.

"THE YANKEE CLIPPER": Joe DiMaggio, for the way he glided about center field at Yankee Stadium.

"THE YANKEE CLIPPER": A slap at George Steinbrenner, who longed to see all his players clean-shaven.

"THE YANKEE EMPIRE BUILDER": Ed Barrow was all of that.

"YANKEE KILLER": Boston pitcher Willard Nixon, known for his mastery of the Yankees during the 1950s, beating New York six games in a row during 1954 and 1955.

"THE YANKEE MASSACRE": A three-game sweep of the Yankees by Don Zimmer's Red Sox July 17–19, 1977.

"YOGI": Catcher Lawrence Berra's nickname.

"YO-YO": Pitcher Luis Arroyo, for his small size and hyperactivity.

CHAPTER EIGHT

BY THE
Numbers

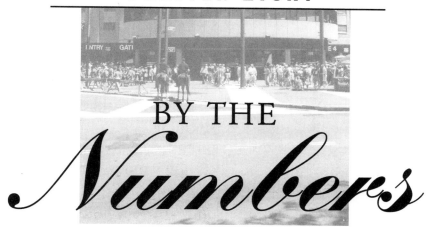

"All I ever wanted to be was a Yankee. When I was a kid, I was always hoping there'd be a jersey left for me to wear with a single digit."
—DEREK JETER (NUMBER 2)

◆

NUMBERS, NUMBERS, NUMBERS. Yankee baseball has always been about numbers. Salary numbers, uniform numbers, record numbers—all making for fascinating history and trivia. In 1929, the New York Yankees introduced identifying numbers sewn on the backs of player jerseys, the first time that uniform numbers were used on a full-time basis.

The "original" ten Yankee uniform numbers were:

Number 1, EARLE COMBS

Number 2, MARK KOENIG

Number 3, BABE RUTH

Number 4, LOU GEHRIG

Number 5, BOB MEUSEL

Number 6, TONY LAZZERI

Number 7, LEO DUROCHER

Number 8, JOHNNY GRABOWSKI

Number 9, BENNY BENGOUGH

Number 10, BILL DICKEY

Bill Dickey

Beginning with Lou Gehrig's number 4 in 1939, the Yankees have retired fifteen uniform numbers honoring sixteen players and managers. Only two single-digit numbers have yet to be retired: number 2 (worn by Derek Jeter) and number 6 (worn by Joe Torre). Torre had originally requested thirteen, but it belonged to utility man Jim Leyritz.

In two different tours of duty with the Yankees, Charlie Keller wore four different numbers. From 1939 to 1943, and then again in 1949, he wore number 9. From 1945 to 1948 he wore number 12. In 1952, his final year as a player, the man they called King Kong alternated between number 28 and 99 in the two games he played.

Jim Bouton was given number 56 in spring training in 1962. When it was obvious that the hyper hurler was going to make the team, he was given number 27. But Bouton wanted to keep 56 to "remind me of how close I was to not making the team."

The following list has all kinds of numbers associated with Yankee players, streaks, and feats.

0

Fewest passed balls allowed by catching staff in a season: 1931.

The 1932 Yankees were the first team to go through an entire season without being shut out.

The number of days Dave Winfield spent in minor-league baseball before reaching the majors.

The number of grand slams that were part of Roger Maris's sixty-one homers in 1961.

.00009

The difference between the batting average of Yankee outfielder George "Snuffy" Stirnweiss (.30854) and White Sox player Tony Cuccinello (.30854) in the closest batting race in major-league history, 1945.

1

The number of times Babe Ruth was pinch-hit for. (Bobby Veach on August 9, 1925.)

Joe DiMaggio is the only player to get at least one hit in All-Star Games at Yankee Stadium, the Polo Grounds, and Ebbets Field.

During Joe DiMaggio's record fifty-six-game hitting streak, he had one hit per game, in thirty-four of them.

Billy Martin's number, which was retired August 10, 1986.

When he appeared in the 2001 playoffs, reliever Mike Stanton became one of only three players to play in all of the past ten postseasons.

1.10

The major-league rule banning a sticky substance, such as pine tar, on a bat beyond eighteen inches from the bottom. That rule led to the "pine tar incident" in a Yankees-Royals game in 1983.

1.64

The best Yankee-earned run average in a season: Spud Chandler, 1943.

1.95

The career earned-run average of Herb Pennock in World Series competition.

2

The number of times Babe Ruth hit grand-slam homers on consecutive days.

The number of managerial tours of duty of Dick Howser, Bob Lemon, Gene Michael, and Lou Piniella.

The fewest shutouts by a pitching staff in a season, 1994.

The fewest times in a season grounding into a double play: Mickey Mantle, 1961; Mickey Rivers, 1977.

Most grand slams in a game: Tony Lazzeri, May 24, 1936, at Philadelphia.

The number of times a pitcher gave up home runs to the same batter in All-Star competition. Willie Mays homered off Whitey Ford in 1956 and then again in 1960.

2.57

Lowest earned-run average by a Yankee pitching staff, 1904.

3

The number of times Lou Gehrig batted .373 or better without winning the batting crown.

Babe Ruth's uniform number, retired June 13, 1948. Before it was retired, right fielder George Selkirk wore it and occupied the Babe's third spot in the lineup.

The number of times Bob Meusel hit for the cycle. He's the only American League player ever to do so.

The number of times Phil Rizzuto led the American League in double plays and total chances.

The number of times Joe DiMaggio, Mickey Mantle, and Yogi Berra were MVPs. (Roger Maris was a two-time winner.) Yogi Berra is the only catcher to win three AL MVP awards and is the only catcher in baseball history to win consecutive MVP awards.

The number of times Joe Torre managed in the World Series against a team that fired him. The Braves canned him in 1984, then lost the 1996 and 1999 series to Torre's Yanks. The Mets fired him in 1981 and lost to the Yankees in 2000.

Phil Rizzuto

The highest number of perfect games by one team: Don Larsen (1956), David Wells (1998), and David Cone (1999). The Yankees are the only team to enjoy this distinction. Mike Mussina came within one strike of a perfect game in 2001.

4

The most consecutive losing seasons in Yankee history (1912–1915, 1989–1992).

Joe DiMaggio is the only player to win a World Series ring in each of his first four seasons (1936–1939).

Lou Gehrig's number, which was retired on July 4, 1939. Gehrig was the first athlete in any sport to have his number retired. He is the only Yankee to have worn number 4.

The highest number of consecutive titles won: 1936–1939 and 1949–1953. The Yankees are the only team that has ever won four or more straight titles.

The most balks in a game: Pitcher Vic Raschi, May 3, 1950, against Chicago.

The most consecutive years managing losing All-Star teams: Casey Stengel with American League teams in 1950, 1951, 1952, and 1953.

Most consecutive years managing losing All Star teams, Casey Stengel with American League teams in 1950, 1951, 1952, 1953. It was one of the few negative stats Stengel had in his time as Yankee manager.

The number of Yankees who have hit four consecutive home runs: Lou Gehrig, July 3, 1932; Johnny Blanchard, July 21–26, 1961; Mickey Mantle, July 4–6, 1961; and Bobby Murcer, July 24, 1970.

The number of managers who have managed both the Yankees and the Mets: Casey Stengel, Yogi Berra, Dallas Green, and Joe Torre.

In 2001, Joe Torre joined John McGraw (New York Giants, 1921–1924), Joe McCarthy (Yankees, 1936–1939), and Casey Stengel (Yankees, 1949–1953 and 1955–1958) as the only managers to win four straight pennants.

4.02

The stat for Lou Gehrig's career RBIs per at bat, second all-time only to Babe Ruth.

4.88

The highest earned-run average by a Yankee pitching staff, 1930.

5

The number of times a shot from Mickey Mantle reached the gothic iron façade that hung from the old stadium's roof.

The Yankees are the only franchise to win five consecutive World Series (1949–1953).

Joe DiMaggio's uniform number, retired in 1952.

The record Lou Gehrig set for consecutive bases on balls (1928 World Series).

Roger Clemens is the only pitcher to garner five Cy Young Awards.

6.

The record set by Red Ruffing for most home runs by a pitcher in a season. He had 31 overall in his career.

The number of times Billy Martin had a tour of duty as manager of the Yankees.

The number of Yankee starters in the 1939 All-Star Game at Yankee Stadium. Bill Dickey, Joe DiMaggio, Joe Gordon, Red Rolfe, Red Ruffing, and George Selkirk.

Mickey Mantle's rookie uniform number.

7

Mickey Mantle's major-league number, retired June 8, 1969. He wore it from 1951 on.

The record set by Mariano Rivera for World Series saves (two were in the 2000 World Series).

8

The number of consecutive seasons Babe Ruth had one hundred or more RBIs: 1926–1933.

The record set by Lou Gehrig for the most seasons leading the league in games played.

Mickey Mantle

Yogi Berra

The number of times Lou Gehrig was pinch-hit for in his career—but that happened only twice after 1925: Earle Combs in 1932 and Myril Hoag in 1935.

Bill Dickey's number, retired in 1972. Ironically, Dickey didn't wear that number at the start or the end of his Yankee career 1929–1941. When Dickey first came up, Benny Bengough wore number 8.

Yogi Berra's number worn 1946–1963 and retired 1972.

The number of batters walked by Steve Adkins in 1⅓ innings in his major-league debut, September 12, 1990.

First eight Yankee batters hit safely on September 25, 1990, in a 15–3 New York win over Baltimore. The Yankees tied a major-league record.

The most home runs by the Yankees in one game: June 28, 1939, in a 23–2 romp over Philadelphia.

The age of famed Metropolitan Opera Star Robert Merrill when he became a Yankee fan and saw Babe Ruth play. Merrill went on to sing the national anthem at Yankee Stadium many, many times.

9

Myril Hoag's uniform number.

Charlie Keller's uniform number from 1939 to 1943 and in 1949. From 1945 to 1948 he wore number 12. In his final year, 1952, Keller played in two games wearing number 28 and 99.

Joe DiMaggio's rookie number.

Roger Maris's number, retired July 21, 1984.

The most .300 hitters in a season: 1930.

The most shutouts in a season: Ron Guidry, 1978.

10

Phil Rizzuto's number, retired August 4, 1985.

The highest number all time for home runs by pinch hitters in a season, 1961.

The highest number of all-time World Series pinch-hitting appearances: Johnny Blanchard who played for the Yankees in 1960–1964.

The record for the most double-digit home-run hitters: 1998.

The number of Whitey Ford World Series wins.

The number of World Series rings won by Yogi Berra.

11

The record for at bats in one game: Bobby Richardson, June 24, 1962, at Detroit, twenty-two innings.

The record for most consecutive games with an RBI: Babe Ruth, 1931.

The highest number of walks gotten in one inning: third inning against the Washington Senators, September 11, 1949.

12

The number of ballparks Babe Ruth hit at least one home run in.

The number of times Babe Ruth led the American League in homers.

Billy Martin's rookie uniform number.

Tom Zachary's pitching record: 12–0, the best 1.000 percent pitching record ever, 1929. Two years before, he gave up Babe Ruth's sixtieth home run of the season.

13

The fewest home runs allowed by a Yankee pitching staff, 1907.

The number of years Joe DiMaggio played for the Yankees.

The number of games lost in the longest losing streak (including one tie) by a Yankee team, 1913.

The most home runs Roger Maris hit in one season against a team, 1961, against the Chicago White Sox.

14

The number of players the Yankees lost in the 1918 season to military service.

The record for the most consecutive years playing in one hundred games or more: Lou Gehrig.

The team record for runs scored in an inning: fifth inning, Yankees against Washington, July 6, 1920.

The record for the fewest batters hit by a pitch in a season: 1969.

Derek Jeter hit in fourteen straight World Series games. His streak was stopped in game one of the 2001 series. The record for longest World

Series hitting streak belongs to Hank Bauer, 17.

Lou Gehrig, career home base steals.

15

Babe Ruth three times had fifteen homers in one month; DiMaggio and Maris accomplished that feat only once.

The number of Yankee retired numbers, the most for any team.

Babe Ruth's total World Series home runs, second place all-time.

Thurman Munson's uniform number, retired September 20, 1980.

Number of times the Yankees have won more than one hundred games a season (through 2001), a record.

Most runs allowed by the Yankees in postseason competition (15), game six, 2001 World Series.

The number of games won by a pitcher in the longest winning streak in Yankee history. The record was set by Roger Clemens, who passed Jack Chesbro and Whitey Ford, winning his fifteenth straight on September 5, 2001. Chesbro won fourteen straight in 1904, and Ford won fourteen straight in 1961.

16

Whitey Ford's uniform number, retired 1974.

The number of Hall of Famers who have a Yankee logo on their plaque in Cooperstown.

Dallas Green was fired on August 16, 1989, becoming the sixteenth manager fired by Steinbrenner. The Boss also disposed of four coaches that day for good measure.

Highest number of home runs Mickey Mantle hit in one month, May 1956.

17

Highest number of home runs Babe Ruth hit in one month, September 1927.

Mickey Mantle struck out a record seventeen times in sixteen All-Star at bats.

Roy White set the franchise record of seventeen sacrifice flies in a season, 1971.

The number of years Bill Dickey played for the Yankees, all as a catcher.

The trade that brought Don Larsen to the Yankees was the largest in history. Completed in two stages, it involved seventeen players. On November 18, 1954, Larsen, Bob Turley, and Billy Hunter came to the Yankees, while Harry Byrd, Jim McDonald, Hal Smith, Gus Triandos, Gene Woodling, and Willie Miranda went to Baltimore.

The deal, however, wasn't, finalized until December 1, with Mike Blyzka, Darrell Johnson, Jim Fridley, and Dick Kryhoski also coming to New York for Bill Miller, Kal Segrist, Don Leppert, and minor-leaguer Ted DelGuercio.

Thurman Munson

In August 1989, Bucky Dent replaced Dallas Green as manager—the seventeenth managerial shift since 1973, when George Steinbrenner bought the Yankees.

Late in his career, Gehrig's hands were x-rayed and doctors spotted seventeen fractures that had "healed" while he continued to play.

On his seventeenth birthday on September 13, 1985, in his native Puerto Rico, Bernie Williams signed a contract to play professional baseball for the Yankees. Williams was a non-drafted free agent. He had won four gold medals at the age of fifteen in an international track meet.

18

Most years with the Yankees: Yogi Berra (1946–1963) and Mickey Mantle (1951–1968).

Most World Series home runs, Mickey Mantle.

19

Babe Ruth and Lou Gehrig in a decade of playing together homered in the same inning nineteen times.

Number of consecutive games won by the 1947 Yankees, the longest winning streak in the team's history.

Total number of managerial changes Steinbrenner made in eighteen years, before Buck Showalter came along and lasted four years as manager.

Whitey Ford's rookie uniform number.

Roger Maris

Derek Jeter set a five-game World Series record with nineteen total bases in 2000.

21

Babe Ruth hit twenty-one of his sixty homers in 1927 with the same bat. He used to carve a notch around the trademark each time he homered.

22

Most hits ever in a World Series game, game six, 2001. The final score of that game was 15–2.

23

Most intentional walks in a season, Mickey Mantle, 1957.

Most career grand slams, Lou Gehrig.

Most triples in a season, Earle Combs, 1927.

Most times caught stealing in a season, Ben Chapman, 1931.

Don Mattingly's number, retired August 31, 1997.

24

Fewest stolen bases by a Yankee team, 1948.

Most shutouts by a Yankee pitching staff, 1951.

Most times hit by a pitch in a season, Don Baylor, 1985.

25

Fewest total players used in a season, 1923 and 1927.

Most consecutive games by the Yankee team with a home run, 1941.

Don Zimmer's age in 1956 when his Brooklyn Dodgers played the Yankees in the World Series. A broken cheekbone kept Zimmer from playing.

Uniform number selected by Jason Giambi when he signed with the Yankees in December 2001. The 2 and 5 added up to 7, the retired number of Mickey Mantle, who Jason's father idolized growing up. The new Yankee would have preferred number 16, but that was Whitey Ford's number, long retired.

27

Reggie Jackson played in twenty-seven World Series games.

28

Joe DiMaggio hit safely against twenty-eight left-handed pitchers during his fifty-six-game hitting streak in 1941.

Thurman Munson's rookie uniform number.

29

Most home runs by a rookie, Joe DiMaggio, 1939.

Of the sixty-one home runs hit by Roger Maris in 1961, twenty-nine were hit in New York.

30

Most home runs by a catcher in a season, Yogi Berra, 1952 and 1956.

Most homers by a second baseman in a season, Joe Gordon, 1940.

Dave Winfield hit into the highest number of double plays in a season, 1983.

The Yankees had thirty hits against the Boston Red Sox on September 28, 1923, a team record.

The length in inches of Wee Willie Keeler's bat, the shortest in major-league history.

31

Total number of Yankee managers, including Joe Torre, since the team was started in 1903.

Elston Howard

32

Most passed balls, 1913.

Caught stealing most times in a season, Doc Cook, 1914.

Uniform number of catcher and designated hitter Charlie Sands.

Elston Howard's uniform number, retired July 21, 1984.

33

Hal Chase hit in thirty-three straight games in 1907, the second longest Yankee hitting streak.

33 1/3

Longest scoreless innings streak, consecutive innings, in postseason play, Mariano Rivera.

36

Reggie Jackson was the thirty-sixth Yankee elected to the Baseball Hall of Fame.

Frank Crosetti wore Yankee pinstripes for a record 36 years.

37

Of the thirty-seven players who performed for the 1949 Yankees, only Yogi Berra still played for them in 1960.

Casey Stengel's number, retired in 1970.

38

Homers hit by Phil Rizzuto in thirteen Yankee seasons.

In 1961, Tony Kubek had thirty-eight doubles, a Yankees shortstop record.

Yankees won their record thirty-eighth American League pennant in 2001.

39

Most consecutive Yankee winning seasons, 1926–1964.

Yogi Berra, second all-time in most World Series RBIs.

Joe DiMaggio attempted only thirty-nine career steals and was safe thirty times.

40

The male Mantles frequently died before age forty. Mickey's father and two uncles passed away before they were forty. There was a family history of Hodgkin's disease.

Most World Series home runs, Mickey Mantle.

41

Major-league record most wins in a season for a pitcher since 1900, Jack Chesbro, 1904.

42

Most sacrifice hits in a season, Willie Keeler, 1905.

Jackie Robinson's number, retired April 15, 1997.

43

Alfonso Soriano stole forty-three bases in 2001, a rookie Yankee record.

44

Fewest losses in a season, 1927 Yankees.

Reggie Jackson's number, retired in 1993.

45

Forty-five different players wore the Yankee uniform in 1913, including seven catchers.

Reggie Jackson played in forty-five league championship games.

47

Forty-seven different players wore Yankee pinstripes in 1979, a team record.

Roger Clemens set an ALCS record on October 21, 2001, with his forty-seventh career strikeout.

Most losses at home, 1908 and 1913 Yankees.

48

Most complete games pitched in a season, Jack Chesbro, 1904.

Reggie Jackson, second most career postseason RBIs.

49

Most home runs in a season by a Yankee first baseman, Lou Gehrig, 1934 and 1936.

50

The bat that Babe Ruth hit his fiftieth home run with in 1920 was auctioned off to raise money to help starving Armenians in Turkey.

Fewest wins in a season by a Yankee team, 1912.

Most players used in a season by a Yankee team, 1989.

Mariano Rivera saved fifty games in 2001, setting a new team record and recording the third-highest total in AL history.

53

Most total bases in one game, June 28, 1939, against Philadelphia.

Most doubles in one season, Don Mattingly, 1986.

Most Yankee batters hit by a pitch in a season, 1990.

54

2002 marked Don Zimmer's fifty-fourth season in professional baseball.

Mickey Mantle hit fifty-four home runs in 1961, a career best and most ever for a switch-hitter.

Most road wins in a season, 1939.

56

Joe DiMaggio's fifty-six-game hitting streak included fifty-six singles and fifty-six runs scored. It covered fifty-three day games and three night games with twenty-nine played at Yankee Stadium, and twenty-seven road games. He had 223 official at bats, a batting average of .408, ninety-one hits, sixteen doubles, four triples, fifteen home runs, and fifty-five RBIs. DiMag struck out seven times, walked twenty-one times, and was hit by a pitch twice.

57

Joe DiMaggio lost $10,000 when his hitting streak was stopped at fifty-six games. He had a contract pending with Heinz 57 for that amount of money for an endorsement.

58.4%

About the only thing the 1927 Yankees couldn't do well was steal bases. They finished tied for fifth in the league with a success rate of only 58.4%.

60

When Babe Ruth hit sixty home runs in 1927, nineteen were off left-handers, two were grand slams. The sixty homers produced one hundred RBIs.

62

Allie Reynolds struck out sixty-two batters in fifteen World Series games, the third-highest number in baseball history.

63

Joe DiMaggio hit safely against sixty-three right-handed pitchers during his fifty-six-game hitting streak in 1941.

Original number of Bernabe Figueroa "Bernie" Williams in 1991.

65

Most home wins in a season, 1961.

Mickey Mantle played in a dozen World Series, sixty-five games in total, second most all-time.

71

Most career hits in World Series, Yogi Berra.

72

Babe Ruth homered twice in a game seventy-two times, a major-league record.

Babe Ruth and Lou Gehrig homered in the same game seventy-two times. Only sixteen times did they homer back-to-back.

Charlie Keller, Tommy Henrich, Johnny Lindell, and Joe DiMaggio

Number of games the Highlanders won in 1903, their first season.

74

Club record for stolen bases set by Fritz Maisel in 1914; broken by Rickey Henderson in 1985.

75

Yogi Berra played in seventy-five World Series games, the most of any player.

80

On August 4, 1998, a 10–5 victory over Oakland in the nightcap of a doubleheader sweep gave the Yankees 80 wins in their 108th game, the earliest point in club history.

82

Franchise record, most times caught stealing in a season, 1920.

88

Number of pitches David Cone threw in his perfect game, July 19, 1999.

89

The Yankees and the Orioles played to a 1-1 tie in 15 innings, the 89th tie in franchise history. It was Cal Ripken's last game at Yankee Stadium.

91

Fewest errors in a season, 1996 Yankees.

93

Most stolen bases in a season, Rickey Henderson, 1988.

94

Whitey Ford, World Series strikeout leader in twenty-two games and 146 innings pitched.

100

Only two Yankee teams have lost more than one hundred games: 1912, 50–102, and 1908, 51–103.

At Yankee Stadium, on September 24, 1920, Babe Ruth hit his one hundredth career home run off of Washington's Jim Shaw.

104

Bill Virdon, Manager of the Year award winner in 1974, was fired after 104 games in 1975.

112

The best base-stealing combo in Yankee history was Fritz Maisel and Roger Peckinpaugh in 1914. Maisel stole seventy-four bases and Peckinpaugh added thirty-eight.

114

Most wins in a season, American League, 1998, all-time record until 2001, when the Seattle Mariners won 116.

115

In 1961, Mantle and Maris hit a combined number of 115 home runs, the most of any teammates in a season.

119

Most extra-base hits in a season, Babe Ruth, 1921: forty-four doubles, sixteen triples and fifty-nine homers.

123

Most complete games by a Yankee staff, 1904.

126

Cal Ripken, most games played at Yankee Stadium by an opposing player June 18, 1982–September 30, 2001.

129

His 129th time at bat, Jack Reed homered in the 22nd inning to give the Yankees a 9–7 win over Detroit on June 24, 1962. It was Reed's only home run in 199 at bats in a three-year career.

134

Number of home runs Yankees hit at Hilltop Park, 1903–1912.

156

Most strikeouts in a season, Danny Tartabull, 1993. He played in just 133 games.

162

Most games played in a season, Bobby Richardson (1961), Roy White (1970 and 1973), Chris Chambliss (1978), Don Mattingly (1986), and Roberto Kelly (1990).

163

Most career triples; Lou Gehrig had 163 triples during his fifteen-year career—a major-league record.

Of Mickey Mantle's 536 career home runs, 163 were hit from the right side.

170

Most walks in a season, Babe Ruth, 1923.

177

Most runs scored in a season, Babe Ruth, 1921.

179

Most home runs allowed in a season by a Yankee pitching staff, 1987.

.183

Team batting average in 2001 World Series is the lowest for a team in a World Series that went seven or eight games. The previous lowest average was .185 by the 1985 St. Louis Cardinals.

184

Most runs batted in during one season, Lou Gehrig, an American League record.

200

Babe Ruth recorded his two hundredth home run on May 12, 1923, at Detroit, off Tiger pitcher Herman Pillette.

201

Over nine years (1948–1956) catcher Charlie Silvera played in a total of 201 games and batted .291.

236

Career wins by Whitey Ford, a franchise record.

238

The number of hits Don Mattingly had in 1986.

The Yankees hit 238 home runs at the Polo Grounds, 1913–1922.

240

Most home runs by a Yankee team in a season, 1961.

245

Fewest walks allowed by a Yankee pitching staff, 1903.

248

Most strikeouts in a season, Ron Guidry, 1978, a team record. The previous record of 239 strikeouts in a season was set by Jack Chesboro in 1904.

252

The 1914 Yankees stole a total of 252 bases.

259

Yogi Berra recorded 259 World Series at bats during his career, the highest number in major-league history.

261

Most career complete games by a Yankee pitcher, Red Ruffing.

266

Most home runs hit at Yankee Stadium, Mickey Mantle.

284

Number of working days it took to build Yankee Stadium in 1922–1923.

289

Most stolen bases in a season by a Yankee team, 1910.

300

On September 8, 1925, Babe Ruth hit home run number three hundred at Fenway Park off Buster Ross of Boston.

.309

Highest team batting average for a season, 1930, six regulars batted over .300, topped by Lou Gehrig's .379 average.

321

The number of games Casey Stengel's Oakland Oaks team in the Pacific Coast League won in the three seasons before the "Ol' Professor" came up to manage the Yankees in 1949.

326

Rickey Henderson's franchise-leading stolen-base total.

332

Home runs by Yankees from 1913–1922 at their home park, the Polo Grounds.

.349

Babe Ruth, highest Yankee career batting average, 1920–1934.

.361

Lifetime average Lou Gehrig compiled in 34 World Series games, spread over seven seasons.

.362

Bill Dickey's batting average in 1936, the best ever in a season for a catcher.

373

Number of career home runs Mickey Mantle hit left-handed. Mantle hit a total of 163 home runs when batting right-handed.

382

Most errors in a season, Yankees 1912. The team also had the fewest double plays (77).

.393

Highest batting average in a season, Babe Ruth, 1923.

394

Fewest earned runs allowed by a Yankee staff, 1904, paced by Jack Chesbro's 1.82 E.R.A.

400

On September 12, 1927, Babe Ruth hit his four hundredth home run in Philadelphia off Rube Walberg.

$400

The amount Mickey Mantle was paid in 1949 to finish out a minor-league season.

407

Yogi Berra and his son Dale held the record for most home runs by a father-son tandem until Bobby Bonds and Barry Bonds shattered it.

413

Smallest home attendance for a game, September 25, 1966.

420

Fewest strikeouts in a season, 1924 Yankees.

.439

Highest World Series batting average, Bobby Brown. Brown played in the 1947, 1949, 1950, and 1951 World Series.

454 2/3

Number of innings Jack Chesbro pitched for Highlanders, 1904.

457

Babe Ruth, all-time major-league season leader in total bases—1921: 101 singles, 44 doubles, 16 triples, 59 home runs.

459

Fewest runs scored by a team in a season, 1908.

.471

Joe Torre's career winning percentage as a manager prior to coming to the Yankees in 1996.

493

Career home runs by Lou Gehrig, most by any first baseman ever.

.498

Slugging percentage of 1927 Yankees, all-time record.

500

On August 11, 1929, at Cleveland, Babe Ruth hit his five hundredth career home run.

$500

Amount posted by Dave Winfield as bond to the Ontario Provincial Police after being charged with cruelty to animals for accidentally killing a seagull with a thrown ball, August 4, 1983, in Toronto.

514

Most outs in a season, Horace Clark, 1970.

520

Third most hits ever for a pitcher, Red Ruffing. He batted .269 in 22 major-league seasons.

522

Number of games Dave Righetti pitched in, a franchise record.

535

Most career doubles, Lou Gehrig.

536

Career home runs by Mickey Mantle, most ever by a switch-hitter.

.545

Babe Ruth, record on base percentage, 1923.

548

The number of regular-season games third baseman Bobby Brown played for the Yankees. He played in seventeen World Series games.

600

Babe Ruth hit his six hundredth home run on August 21, 1931, in St. Louis, off George Blaeholder.

692

Most at bats in one season, Bobby Richardson, 1962.

700

Babe Ruth hit career home run number seven hundred on July 13, 1934, at Detroit, off Tommy Bridges.

.704

1998 team winning percentage based on a record of 111 wins and 48 losses.

Red Ruffing

714

Babe Ruth's record career home-run total; broken by Hank Aaron, 1974.

757

Most plate appearances in a season, Frank Crosetti, 1938.

766

Most walks in a season, 1932 Yankees led by Babe Ruth with 130 and Lou Gehrig with 108.

783

Babe Ruth (434) and Lou Gehrig (349) playing together hit 783 homers, an all-time record.

.800

The 1939 Yankees posted a 44–11 record in their first fifty-five games.

.847

Slugging percentage of Babe Ruth, 1927, an all-time mark until Barry Bonds slugged .863 in 2001.

.862

Record winning percentage for a month, July 1941, 25-4. The Yankees finished the season with a 101-53 won-lost record.

.891

Reggie Jackson's slugging percentage in three World Series as a Yankee.

.893

Top winning percentage of any twenty-game winner in history, Ron Guidry, 1978.

955

Number of wins Casey Stengel presided over as manager.

996

Most hits in majors, 1996–2000, Derek Jeter.

1,043

Most strikeouts in a season by a Yankee team, 1967. In contrast, Yankee pitchers struck out just 898 batters, third lowest in the league.

1,067

Most runs scored in a season, 1931 Yankees.

1,137

Fewest hits by a team in a season, 1968.

1,172

The number of games Dave Winfield played in as a Yankee; he played in 2,973 games overall in a 22-year major-league career.

1,507

Most innings pitched by a Yankee staff in one season, 1984.

1,677

Mickey Mantle, third all-time leader behind Babe Ruth and Lou Gehrig in runs scored.

1,683

Most hits by a Yankee team in a season, 1930, including league leading amount of triples, home runs and runs scored.

1,710

Mickey Mantle, career strikeouts.

1921

In the 1921 World Series, it was brother versus brother—Bob Meusel of the Yankees against Emil Meusel of the Giants. It was also the first time in baseball history that the World Series was played at one stadium, the Polo Grounds. It was the final best-of-nine-games World Series.

1956

The numbers Mickey Mantle put up in 1956 are still mind-boggling: second in on-base percentage (.464), first in slugging (.705), first in runs scored (132), first in RBIs (130). He led both leagues with fifty-two home runs, stole ten bases in eleven attempts, and grounded into only four double plays.

1,959

Most runs scored, Babe Ruth, 1920–1934, franchise record.

1,995

Most Yankee career RBIs, Lou Gehrig.

2010

Derek Jeter's contract expiration year. He signed the contract on February 9, 2001.

2,120

Number of games Babe Ruth played for the Yankees, 1920–1934.

2,130

The number of consecutive games Lou Gehrig played in.

2,401

Most games played in by a Yankee, Mickey Mantle, 1951–1968.

2,597

The record number of career strikeouts by Reggie Jackson.

2,721

Yankee record number of hits recorded by Lou Gehrig.

3,654

The number of home runs the Yankees hit at the old Yankee Stadium, 1923–1973.

5,705

Most at bats by a Yankee team in a season, 1964.

8,102

Mickey Mantle, all-time leader in at bats.

$6,595.38

The amount payable in 1927 in biweekly checks to Babe Ruth that added up to the record salary he earned of $70,000.

7,000

Parking spaces at Yankee Stadium.

$7,500

Mickey Mantle's 1951 rookie salary.

$8,000

Joe DiMaggio's rookie season salary, 1936.

$18,000

Cost of purchasing the franchise of Baltimore and transferring it to New York City in 1903.

$50,000

The New York Giants offered that unheard-of amount to the Yankees for Yogi Berra at the start of his career.

57,545

Seating capacity of Yankee Stadium as of 2002.

64,519

The number of people in attendance at Yankee Stadium in 1956 when Don Larsen pitched the perfect game. Those who claim they were there push the attendance much beyond that figure.

$65,000

Gillette and Ford paid this amount for the exclusive sponsorship rights to the first televised World Series, shown only in New York City, 1947. Liebmann Brewery had offered $100,000 for the rights, but baseball commissioner Chandler rejected the offer, claiming it wouldn't be appropriate having the series sponsored by the producer of an alcoholic beverage.

$451,541

In 1999, the uniform Gehrig wore during his farewell speech sold for this amount in an auction. The winning bid came from a man in South Florida. In 1991, Gehrig's 1938 road uniform sold for $220,000, and an autographed bat went for $47,500.

Bernie Williams

2,561,123

Shea Stadium attendance for the Yankees 1974–1975.

3,451,542

Hilltop Park attendance 1903–1912.

6,220,031

Yankee Polo Grounds attendance 1913–1922.

$10,000,000

Amount George Steinbrenner and his group paid to purchase the Yankees from CBS on January 3, 1973.

$12,357,143

Annual salary of Bernie Williams in 2001, a sum greater than that paid to the entire division playoff opposition Oakland infield and two of its outfielders.

$39.99 million

The amount of Mariano Rivera's four-year contract signed in 2001.

60,010,531

Yankee Stadium total attendance 1976–2001.

64,188,862

Yankee Stadium total attendance 1923–1973.

$88,500,000

The amount of Mike Mussina's seven-year contract, signed November 2000.

$120,000,000

Postseason payroll in 2001.

$189,000,000

The amount of Derek Jeter's ten-year deal, signed in 2001. Under this deal, Jeter's annual salary is $12.6 million.

CHAPTER NINE

100 *Question* YANKEE QUIZ

D IEHARD FANS AND casual fans, serious pinstripe followers or once-in-a-while guys, all have one thing in common—Yankee knowledge. Some of it is deep. Some of it is scant. Let's go to the Yankee quiz and see what you know.

Admittedly, the questions here range from the ridiculous to the sublime. Some truly test your Yankee knowledge—others test your patience. Whatever—here is the scoring breakdown:

75-100 CORRECT	HALL OF FAMER
50-74 CORRECT	ALL STAR
25-49 CORRECT	MAJOR-LEAGUER
10-24 CORRECT	MINOR-LEAGUER
9 OR FEWER CORRECT	ROOT FOR ANOTHER TEAM

1. What number did Don Mattingly wear when he first played for the Yankees?

    A. 16   **B.** 26   **C.** 36   **D.** 46

2. When David Wells joined the Yankees for his first tour of duty, what uniform number did he request and why?

3. Name the four managers who have piloted both the Yankees and the New York Mets.

4. In 1977, who nicknamed Reggie Jackson Mr. October?

    A. Willie Randolph   **B.** Thurman Munson   **C.** Goose Gossage   **D.** Mickey Rivers

5. What Yankee hit two homers in one inning in 1977?

    A. Cliff Johnson   **B.** Graig Nettles   **C.** Reggie Jackson   **D.** Chris Chambliss

6. Who did Derek Jeter replace in 1996 to become the regular shortstop?

    A. Andy Fox   **B.** Pat Kelly   **C.** Alvaro Espinoza   **D.** Tony Fernandez

7. What former Yankee was the first pitching coach for the New York Mets in 1962?

    A. Joe Page   **B.** Red Ruffing   **C.** Vic Raschi   **D.** Johnny Sain

8. Who was nicknamed Bulldog?

    A. Jim Bouton   **B.** Ron Guidry   **C.** Joe Page   **D.** Monte Pearson

9. Who pitched the first no-hitter against the Yankees?

    A. George Foster   **B.** Cy Young   **C.** Bob Feller   **D.** Hoyt Wilhelm

10. What was the biggest deficit the Yankees ever came back from in a regular-season game?

    A. Eleven runs   **B.** Fourteen runs   **C.** Nine runs   **D.** Sixteen runs

11. The Yankees won forty-one games during Joe DiMaggio's fifty-six-game hitting streak. How many did they lose?

    A. Ten   **B.** Twelve   **C.** Thirteen   **D.** Five

12. How many played third base for the Yankees after Clete Boyer left at the end of the 1966 season and before Graig Nettles started in 1973?

   A. Two   **B.** Three   **C.** Five   **D.** Eleven

13. Who caught Dave Righetti's no-hitter on July 4, 1983?

14. Who caught Don Larsen's perfect game in the 1956 World Series?

15. Who was the player Don Larsen struck out for the final out in his perfect game?

   A. Gil Hodges   **B.** Roy Campanella   **C.** Dale Mitchell
   D. Carl Furillo

16. Who was the first major-leaguer to hit two grand slams in one game?

   A. Babe Ruth   **B.** Lou Gehrig   **C.** Mickey Mantle   **D.** Tony Lazzeri

17. What is Don Mattingly's middle name?

18. Elston Howard was the first black player on the Yankees, in 1955. Name the second. (Fifty bonus points for the year he first played.)

19. Who was the last Yankee to hit a grand slam in the old Yankee Stadium?

20. What former Yankee did Earl Weaver replace as Baltimore manager on July 11, 1968?

21. Who played the most games for the Yankees?

   A. Mickey Mantle   **B.** Yogi Berra   **C.** Lou Gehrig   **D.** Joe DiMaggio

22. How many games did he play?

   A. 3,011   **B.** 2,107   **C.** 1,777   **D.** 2,401

23. How many no-hitters have been thrown against the Yankees?

   A. Two   **B.** Four   **C.** Six   **D.** Nine

24. Name the pitchers who threw them.

25. How many players wore number 7 before Mickey Mantle?

   A. Twenty-seven   **B.** Two   **C.** Zero   **D.** Fourteen

26. Reggie Jackson hit three homers in game six of the 1977 World Series. This feat was accomplished two other times in Yankee history. Name the player or players who did it.

27. Name the National Football League coaching legend who played briefly for the Yankees.

    A. Tom Landry **B.** George Halas **C.** Jim Thorpe
    D. Curly Lambeau

28. Whose number was retired by both the Mets and Yankees?

29. What Yankee pitcher has the most World Series victories?

    A. David Cone **B.** Allie Reynolds **C.** Whitey Ford
    D. Lefty Gomez

30. What uniform number was retired by the Yankees to honor a player who was never on the team?

    A. Jackie Robinson **B.** Bob Feller **C.** Dom DiMaggio **D.** Pee Wee Reese

31. First baseman Wally Pipp has gone down in history for being the player Lou Gehrig replaced. What other distinction belongs to Pipp?

    A. He was a baseball manager. **B.** He came from the same neighborhood Gehrig grew up in. **C.** He was a home-run champ. **D.** He made money endorsing aspirin.

32. Who had the second-longest hitting streak in American League history?

33. Who remains the only Yankee to hit four home runs in one game?

    A. Lou Gehrig **B.** Reggie Jackson **C.** Babe Ruth **D.** Yogi Berra

34. What former Yankee Star managed Kansas City, Baltimore and Oakland?

    A. Billy Martin **B.** Andy Carey **C.** Hank Bauer **D.** Bucky Dent

35. Who backed up Willie Randolph at second base for the 1976 New York Yankees?

36. In defeating the Oakland A's in the 2001 American League Division playoffs, what did the Yankees accomplish that no team had ever done before in a three-of-five-game series?

A. They limited their opponents to a total of two runs. **B.** They had a perfect fielding percentage. **C.** They won three straight after losing two games at home. **D.** They hit at least one home run in every game.

37. What Yankee MVP appeared in the fewest games in the year in which he won the award?

38. Reggie Jackson was inducted into the Hall of Fame as a member of what team?

A. A's **B.** Orioles **C.** Yankees **D.** Angels

39. Reggie Jackson hit three home runs in game six of the 1977 World Series against the Los Angeles Dodgers, each off a different pitcher. What pitcher gave up Jackson's third home run?

A. Burt Hooton **B.** Charlie Hough **C.** Elias Sosa **D.** Don Sutton

40. Which of the following was not a Babe Ruth nickname?

A. "Bambino" **B.** "Wali of Wallop" **C.** "Rajah of Rap" **D.** "Caliph of Clout"

41. When Babe Ruth retired in 1935 with 714 home runs, only two other players had hit 300 or more home runs. Who were they? Hint: One played for the Yankees, the other mostly for the St. Louis Cardinals.

42. Mickey Mantle made his big-league debut on April 17, 1951, but it was a different New York Yankee who came away with Rookie of the Year honors. Who was that player?

A. Gene Woodling **B.** Hank Bauer **C.** Gil McDougald **D.** Andy Carey

43. Who was the only Yankee to play on four World Championship teams in his first four years as a major-leaguer?

A. Derek Jeter **B.** Yogi Berra **C.** Lou Gehrig **D.** Joe DiMaggio

44. What Yankee hit safely in seventeen straight World Series games?

45. Who was the only Yankee to steal two bases in the same inning in a World Series game?

A. Joe Gordon **B.** Derek Jeter **C.** Babe Ruth **D.** Rickey Henderson

46. Two Yankees went straight to the majors having never played in the minors. Who were they?

47. Joe DiMaggio retired in 1951, having played his entire career with the Yankees. What team did he go on to coach for?

A. Yankees B. A's C. Padres D. Dodgers

48. The Yankees have appeared in the most World Series. What team has appeared in the second-most World Series?

49. Name the pitcher from New Hampshire brought up by the Yankees in 1986.

A. Bob Tewksbury B. Bob Shirley C. Dennis Rasmussen
D. Doug Drabek

50. Who was the only player to be elected to the Baseball Hall of Fame in the same year he was playing in the majors?

51. What pitcher won his first eight postseason decisions?

A. Whitey Ford B. Ron Guidry C. Orlando Hernandez
D. David Wells

(52–55: Match the Yankee with his jersey number)

52. Reggie Jackson A. 25 B. 44 C. 49 D. 50

53. Billy Martin A. 17 B. 16 C. 1 D. 11

54. Casey Stengel A. 30 B. 37 C. 47 D. 49

55. Jason Giambi A. 12 B. 22 C. 25 D. 40

56. Don Mattingly had 145 RBIs in 1985. Name the teammate he drove in for fifty-six of those RBIs.

57. Who managed in the most World Series?

58. How many World Series did he manage?

59. Name the Yankee great who participated in the D-day landing at Omaha Beach on June 6, 1944.

A. Yogi Berra B. Ralph Houk C. Jerry Coleman D. Hank Bauer

60. Who was the last switch-hitter to win the American League MVP award?

61. Name the two Yankees who led the AL in homers since Roger Maris's sixty-one in 1961.

A. Roger Maris and Graig Nettles **B.** Graig Nettles and Reggie Jackson **C.** Reggie Jackson and Mickey Mantle **D.** Mickey Mantle and Roger Maris

62. At the opening of Yankees Stadium in 1923, which event did not take place?

A. Babe Ruth homered. **B.** Composer John Philip Sousa and the United States Marine Corps marching band entertained the fans. **C.** Aviator Charles Lindbergh landed his plane in the outfield during pregame ceremonies. **D.** The Yankees won the game.

63. Who wore Number 26½?

64. Name three current Yankees who have roots in Brooklyn, New York.

65. From 1961 to 1963, three different Yankees won the American League MVP award. Two of the MVPs were Roger Maris in 1961 and Mickey Mantle in 1962. Who was the third?

66. Name the first rookie to play in an All-Star Game.

67. Bob Sheppard has the nickname the "Voice of God." Who gave it to him?

A. Mel Allen **B.** Red Barber **C.** Reggie Jackson **D.** Derek Jeter

68. Derek Jeter was the last Yankee Rookie of the Year in 1996. Who was the Yankee Rookie of the Year before him?

A. Tom Tresh **B.** Tony Kubek **C.** Thurman Munson **D.** Dave Righetti

69. Who was the manager of the Yankees before Joe Torre?

70. Who was the first Yankee admitted to the Hall of Fame?

A. Wee Willie Keeler **B.** Babe Ruth **C.** Lou Gehrig **D.** Herb Pennock

71. Who was the first Yankee Cy Young Award Winner?

    A. Red Ruffing **B.** Allie Reynolds **C.** Bob Turley **D.** Whitey Ford

72. What year was Billy Martin named Yankee manager for the first time?

73. How many World Series games did Casey Stengel manage?

    A. Fifty **B.** Fifty-five **C.** Sixty-three **D.** Sixty-seven

74. Joe Torre's father was a:

    A. firefighter **B.** police officer **C.** priest **D.** baseball player

75. Who created the Yankee Stadium "Stadium Club"?

    A. Colonel Jake Ruppert **B.** Casey Stengel **C.** Dan Topping
    D. Larry MacPhail

76. Through 2002, how many managers have there been in the George Steinbrenner era?

    A. Eleven **B.** Twenty-one **C.** Thirty-one **D.** Forty-one

77. Everyone knew him as "Casey," but what was Stengel's full given name?

78. Bobby Murcer announced his first game the day after he retired as a player. What year was that?

    A. 1980 **B.** 1981 **C.** 1982 **D.** 1983

79. Name the only Yankee pitcher to hurl two no-hitters in the same season.

    A. Allie Reynolds **B.** Lefty Gomez **C.** Dave Righetti
    D. George Mogridge

80. Who was the first Yankee to be named captain since Lou Gehrig?

    A. Willie Randolph **B.** Mickey Mantle **C.** Thurman Munson
    D. Phil Rizzuto

81. Who has the most career steals in Yankee history?

82. Which one of the following was not a Yankee manager?

    A. Hal Chase **B.** Harry Wolverton **C.** Joe McCarthy **D.** Red Rolfe

83. What years did the Yankees play at Shea Stadium?

84. What Yankee was the first relief pitcher to win the Cy Young Award?

    A. Sparky Lyle **B.** Dave Righetti **C.** Goose Gossage
    D. Mariano Rivera

85. The first designated hitter was a Yankee. Who was he?

86. Which Yankees won the first and the last to date MVP awards?

87. What Yankee had the most career at bats?

    A. Joe DiMaggio **B.** Mickey Mantle **C.** Lou Gehrig
    D. Frank Crosetti

88. The Yankees were the first team to train outside of the United States. Where did they train?

    A. Cuba **B.** Dominican Republic **C.** Jamaica **D.** Bermuda

89. Who has the highest winning percentage of any manager in Yankee history?

    A. Joe McCarthy **B.** Joe Torre **C.** Buck Showalter
    D. Casey Stengel

Phil Rizzuto, Casey Stengel,
Billy Martin, and Yogi Berra

90. What was the cost of building the original Yankee Stadium?

   A. $1.7 million   **B.** $2.5 million   **C.** $5 million   **D.** $7 million

91. What is the significance of Tom Zachary and Tracy Stallard to Yankee history?

92. All of the following played for the Mets and Yankees except for one. Who was he?

   A. Gene Woodling   **B.** Lee Mazzilli   **C.** Rusty Staub   **D.** Phil Linz

93. Whose nickname was King Kong?

94. What was Babe Ruth's uniform number?

95. Who owned the Yankees before George Steinbrenner and company?

96. Who was the first Yankee World Series MVP?

97. Who was the last Yankee World Series MVP as of 2001?

98. Who replaced Babe Ruth in the Yankee lineup?

99. Who replaced Lou Gehrig in the Yankee lineup?

100. What Yankee has the most career steals of home?

   A. Babe Ruth   **B.** Roy White   **C.** Lou Gehrig   **D.** Mickey Mantle

ANSWERS

1. **D.** From 1982 to 1983–Don Mattingly's first two seasons with the Yankees–he wore number 46, while appearing in only ninety-eight games. After that, Mattingly wore number 23 for the rest of his fourteen-year career with the Yankees.

2. Wells has always admired Babe Ruth and requested number 3.

3. Yogi Berra, Dallas Green, Casey Stengel, and Joe Torre.

4. **B.** Thurman Munson

5. **A.** Cliff Johnson

6. **D.** Tony Fernandez

7. **B.** Red Ruffing

8. **A.** Jim Bouton

9. **B.** Cy Young

10. **C.** The New York Yankees have overcome a nine-run deficit three times. The most recent time was on June 26, 1987, against the Boston Red Sox. Roger Clemens blew a 9–0, second-inning lead to the Yankees, who won 12–11 in ten innings.

11. **C.** Thirteen; they tied two games

12. **C.** Clete Boyer was a Yankee from 1959 to 1966, and Nettles played for the team from 1973 to 1983. In between, five players played the "hot corner" for New York: 1967, Charley Smith; 1968, Bobby Cox; 1969–1971, Jerry Kenney; 1972, Celerino Sanchez and Bernie Allen.

13. Butch Wynegar

14. Yogi Berra

15. **C.** Dale Mitchell

16. **D.** Tony Lazzeri, in 1936

17. Arthur

18. Harry Simpson, in 1957

19. Fred Stanley, on September 8, 1973

20. Hank Bauer

21. **A.** Mickey Mantle

22. **D.** 2,401

23. **C.** Six

24. The pitchers in those games were Cy Young, Rube Foster, Ray Caldwell, Bob Feller, Virgil Trucks, and Hoyt Wilhelm.

25. **D.** Mickey Mantle was the last Yankee ever to don the number 7, wearing it from 1951 until he retired. Fourteen other Yankees wore the number in their careers, the last two being Bob Cerv and Cliff Mapes, who wore the number at times during Mantle's rookie season.

26. It was accomplished by Babe Ruth, twice.

27. **B.** George "Papa Bear" Halas played six games for the 1919 Yankees.

28. Casey Stengel's number 37. Stengel was an outfielder for the Mets, 1922–1923, and then was their manager from 1962 to 1965. During

the twelve years Stengel managed the Yankees, he brought the team to the World Series ten times, winning the series seven times.

29. C. Whitey Ford, ten. He started twenty-two World Series games.

30. A. Jackie Robinson, number 42. The number was retired on April 15, 1997, on the fiftieth anniversary of the breaking of baseball's color line. Mariano Rivera is the last Yankee to wear the number.

31. C. Pipp was the AL home-run champion, 1916–1917.

32. George Sisler. Before Joe DiMaggio set the record in 1941, the St. Louis Browns' first baseman George Sisler held the American League record by hitting in forty-one consecutive games in 1922.

33. A. Lou Gehrig

34. C. Hank Bauer managed a total of 1139 games with these teams.

35. Sandy Alomar. Willie Randolph played 124 games at second base. His backup was Sandy Alomar, who played in 38 games.

36. C. They won three straight after losing two games at home.

Babe Ruth

37. Pitcher Spud Chandler appeared in thirty games when he won the American League MVP award in 1943.

38. C. Yankees

39. B. Charlie Hough

40. Sorry about that—trick question. All of the choices were nicknames for the Babe.

41. Lou Gehrig, 378; Rogers Hornsby, 300.

42. C. Gil McDougald. McDougald played the majority of his games in 1951 at third base but occasionally covered second as well. Later in his career, McDougald also spent some time playing shortstop.

43. D. Joe DiMaggio: 1936–1939 Yankees

44. Hank Bauer hit safely in seventeen consecutive World Series games spanning 1956 to 1958.

45. C. Babe Ruth

46. Catfish Hunter and Dave Winfield

47. B. A's. DiMaggio was a batting coach and executive vice-president for the A's from 1967 to 1989.

48. The Dodgers

49. (A) Bob Tewksbury

50. Lou Gehrig

51. C. Orlando Hernandez

52. B. 44

53. C. 1

54. B. 37

55. C. 25

56. Rickey Henderson

57. Casey Stengel.

58. There were ten World Series that Stengel managed in. He won seven of them.

59. A. Yogi Berra

60. Mickey Mantle was the last switch-hitter to win the AL MVP award. The year was 1962. Mantle hit .321 with thirty home runs and eighty-nine RBIs.

61. **B.** Graig Nettles hit thirty-two in 1976 and Reggie Jackson hit forty-one in 1980.

62. **C.** Neither "Lucky Lindy" nor any other pilot has ever landed a plane at the stadium.

63. The number was worn by pitcher Orlando Hernandez on rehab assignment at Staten Island in 2001. His regular number is 26.

64. Joe Torre, Willie Randolph, Lee Mazzilli.

65. Elston Howard in 1963

66. Joe DiMaggio

67. **C.** Reggie Jackson

68. **D.** Dave Righetti

69. Buck Showalter

70. **B.** Babe Ruth

71. **C.** Bob Turley

72. 1975

73. **C.** 63

74. **B.** Police officer

75. **D.** Larry MacPhail

76. **B.** 21

77. Charles Dillon Stengel

78. **D.** 1983

79. **A.** Allie Reynolds. On July 12, 1951, Reynolds threw a no-hitter against Cleveland. He pitched his next no-hitter on September 28, 1951, against the Boston Red Sox.

80. **C.** Thurman Munson

81. Rickey Henderson, 326.

82. **D.** Red Rolfe

83. 1974–1975

Rickey Henderson

84. **A.** Sparky Lyle. Southpaw Lyle won the award in 1977. He was credited for twenty-six saves that year and led the AL in the number of games he pitched in, seventy-two in total.

85. Ron Blomberg in 1973

86. Babe Ruth, 1923, and Don Mattingly, 1985

87. **B.** Mickey Mantle, 8,102

88. **D.** Bermuda, 1913

89. **A.** Joe McCarthy, .614, the highest in history

90. **B.** $2.5 million, built in less than nine months, completed in 1923.

91. Pitcher Tom Zachary gave up Babe Ruth's sixtieth home run in 1927 and Tracy Stallard yielded the sixty-first homer hit by Roger Maris in 1961.

92. **C.** Rusty Staub. Over the course of his twenty-three-year career, Staub played for the Houston Astros, the Montreal Expos, the New York Mets, the Detroit Tigers, and the Texas Rangers—but never the Yankees

93. Charlie Keller

94. 3

95. CBS

96. Don Larsen, who pitched a perfect game in the 1956 World Series

97. Derek Jeter, who batted .409 in the 2000 World Series

98. George Selkirk

99. Babe Dahlgren

100. **C.** Lou Gehrig stole home fifteen times.

CHAPTER TEN

FOR THE
Record

LONGEST YANKEE
WINNING STREAKS

1947: **19**

1953: **18**

1926: **16**

1906, 1960: **15**

1941: **14**

1954, 1961: **13**

◆

LONGEST YANKEE
LOSING STREAKS

1913: **13** (and one tie)

1908: **12**

1926: **9** (twice)

1916, 1945, 1953, and 1982: **9**

◆

TWO HOME RUNS
IN ONE INNING

JOE DIMAGGIO	June 24, 1936 at Chicago
JOE PEPITONE	May 23, 1962 vs. KC
CLIFF JOHNSON	June 30, 1977 at Toronto
ROY SMALLEY	September 5, 1982 at KC
BERNIE WILLIAMS	4 times: June 6, 1994 at Tex; October 6, 1995 at Sea; September 12, 1996 at Detroit; October 5, 1996 at Tex

◆

THREE HOME RUNS
IN ONE GAME

TONY LAZZERI	June 8, 1927 vs. Chicago; May 24, 1936 at Philadelphia
LOU GEHRIG	June 23, 1927 at Boston; May 4, 1929 at Chicago; May 22, 1930 at Philadelphia
BABE RUTH	May 21, 1930 at Philadelphia
BEN CHAPMAN	July 6, 1932 vs. Detroit
JOE DIMAGGIO	June 13, 1937 at St Louis; May 23, 1948 at Cleveland; September 10, 1950 at Washington
BILL DICKEY	July 26, 1939 vs. St Louis
CHARLIE KELLER	July 28, 1940 at Chicago
JOHNNY MIZE	September 15, 1950 at Detroit
MICKEY MANTLE	May 15, 1955 vs. Detroit
TOM TRESH	June 6, 1965 vs. Chicago

BOBBY MURCER	June 24, 1970 vs. Cleveland; July 13, 1973 vs. Kansas City
CLIFF JOHNSON	June 30, 1977 at Toronto
MIKE STANLEY	August 10, 1995 vs. Cleveland
PAUL O'NEILL	August 31, 1995 vs. California
DARYL STRAWBERRY	August 6, 1996 vs. Chicago
TINO MARTINEZ	April 2, 1997 at Seattle

◆

Yankee Home Run Champions

YEAR	NAME	NUMBER OF HOME RUNS
1916	WALLY PIPP	12
1917	WALLY PIPP	9
1920	BABE RUTH	54
1921	BABE RUTH	59
1923	BABE RUTH	41
1924	BABE RUTH	46
1925	BOB MEUSEL	33
1926	BABE RUTH	47
1927	BABE RUTH	60
1928	BABE RUTH	54
1929	BABE RUTH	46
1930	BABE RUTH	49
1931	LOU GEHRIG	46
	BABE RUTH	46
1934	LOU GEHRIG	49
1936	LOU GEHRIG	49
1937	JOE DIMAGGIO	46
1944	NICK ETTEN	22
1948	JOE DIMAGGIO	39
1955	MICKEY MANTLE	37
1956	MICKEY MANTLE	52
1958	MICKEY MANTLE	42
1960	MICKEY MANTLE	40
1961	ROGER MARIS	61
1976	GRAIG NETTLES	32
1980	REGGIE JACKSON	41

YANKEE BATTING CHAMPIONS

Bob Turley

YEAR	NAME	BATTING AVERAGE
1924	BABE RUTH	.378
1934	LOU GEHRIG	.363
1939	JOE DIMAGGIO	.381
1940	JOE DIMAGGIO	.352
1945	SNUFFY STIRNWEISS	.309
1956	MICKEY MANTLE	.353
1984	DON MATTINGLY	.343
1994	PAUL O'NEILL	.359
1998	BERNIE WILLIAMS	.339

CY YOUNG WINNERS

BOB TURLEY	1958
WHITEY FORD	1961
SPARKY LYLE	1977
RON GUIDRY	1978
ROGER CLEMENS	2001

STRIKEOUT LEADERS

YEAR	NAME	NUMBER OF STRIKEOUTS
1932	RED RUFFING	190
1933	LEFTY GOMEZ	163
1934	LEFTY GOMEZ	158
1937	LEFTY GOMEZ	194
1951	VIC RASCHI	164
1952	ALLIE REYNOLDS	160
1964	AL DOWNING	217

ERA Leaders

YEAR	NAME	ERA
1920	BOB SHAWKEY	2.45
1927	WILCY MOORE	2.28
1934	LEFTY GOMEZ	2.33
1937	LEFTY GOMEZ	2.33
1943	SPUD CHANDLER	1.64
1947	SPUD CHANDLER	2.46
1952	ALLIE REYNOLDS	2.06
1953	EDDIE LOPAT	2.42
1956	WHITEY FORD	2.47
1957	BOBBY SHANTZ	2.45
1958	WHITEY FORD	2.01
1978	RON GUIDRY	1.74
1979	RON GUIDRY	2.78
1980	RUDY MAY	2.46

All-Time Saves Leaders

MARIANO RIVERA	225+
DAVE RIGHETTI	224
GOOSE GOSSAGE	151
SPARKY LYLE	141
JOHNNY MURPHY	104

No-Hitters

GEORGE MOGRIDGE (at Boston), April 24, 1917

SAM JONES (at Philadelphia), September 4, 1923

MONTE PEARSON (vs. Cleveland), August 27, 1938

ALLIE REYNOLDS (vs. Cleveland), July 12, 1951

ALLIE REYNOLDS (vs. Boston), September 28, 1951

DON LARSEN (vs. Brooklyn), October 8, 1956 (perfect game, World Series)

DAVE RIGHETTI (vs. Boston), July 4, 1983

JIM ABBOTT (vs. Cleveland), September 4, 1993

DWIGHT GOODEN (vs. Seattle), May 14, 1996

DAVID WELLS (vs. Minnesota), May 17, 1998 (perfect game)

DAVID CONE (vs. Montreal), July 18, 1999 (perfect game)

No-Hitters
Pitched Against the Yankees

CY YOUNG (Boston), June 30, 1908

RUBE FOSTER (Boston), June 21, 1916

RAY CALDWELL (Cleveland), September 10, 1919, the first game of a doubleheader

BOB FELLER (Cleveland), April 30, 1946

VIRGIL TRUCKS (Detroit), August 25, 1952

HOYT WILHELM (Baltimore), September 20, 1958

Twenty-Game Winners

YEAR	PITCHER	W	L
2001	ROGER CLEMENS	20	3
1998	DAVID CONE	20	7
1996	ANDY PETTITTE	21	8
1985	RON GUIDRY	22	6
1983	RON GUIDRY	21	9
1980	TOMMY JOHN	22	9
1979	TOMMY JOHN	21	9
1978	ED FIGUEROA	20	9
1978	RON GUIDRY	25	3
1975	CATFISH HUNTER	23	14
1970	FRITZ PETERSON	20	11
1969	MEL STOTTLEMYRE	20	14
1968	MEL STOTTLEMYRE	21	12
1965	MEL STOTTLEMYRE	20	9
1963	JIM BOUTON	21	7
1963	WHITEY FORD	24	7
1962	RALPH TERRY	23	12
1961	WHITEY FORD	25	4
1958	BOB TURLEY	21	7
1954	BON GRIM	20	6
1952	ALLIE REYNOLDS	20	8
1951	VIC RASCHI	21	10
1951	EDDIE LOPAT	21	9
1950	VIC RASCHI	21	8
1949	VIC RASCHI	21	10
1946	SPUD CHANDLER	20	8
1943	SPUD CHANDLER	20	4
1942	ERNIE BONHAM	21	5
1939	RED RUFFING	21	7
1938	RED RUFFING	21	7
1937	RED RUFFING	20	7
1937	LEFTY GOMEZ	21	11
1936	RED RUFFING	20	12
1934	LEFTY GOMEZ	26	5
1932	LEFTY GOMEZ	24	7
1931	LEFTY GOMEZ	21	9
1928	WAITE HOYT	23	7
1928	GEORGE PIPGRAS	24	13
1927	WAITE HOYT	22	7
1926	HERB PENNOCK	23	11

TWENTY-GAME WINNERS *(continued)*

YEAR	PITCHER	W	L
1924	HERB PENNOCK	21	9
1923	SAD SAM JONES	21	8
1922	BOB SHAWKEY	20	12
1922	JOE BUSH	26	7
1921	CARL MAYS	27	9
1920	BOB SHAWKEY	20	13
1920	CARL MAYS	26	11
1919	BOB SHAWKEY	20	11
1916	BOB SHAWKEY	24	14
1911	RUSSELL FORD	22	11
1910	RUSSELL FORD	26	6
1906	JACK CHESBRO	24	16
1906	ALBERT ORTH	27	17
1904	JACK POWELL	23	19
1904	JACK CHESBRO	41	12
1903	JACK CHESBRO	21	15

ROOKIES OF THE YEAR

GIL MCDOUGALD, third baseman, 1951
BOB GRIM, pitcher, 1954
TONY KUBEK, shortstop, 1957
TOM TRESH, outfielder/shortstop, 1962
STAN BAHNSEN, pitcher, 1968
THURMAN MUNSON, catcher, 1970
DAVE RIGHETTI, pitcher, 1981
DEREK JETER, shortstop, 1996

YANKEE MVPs

LOU GEHRIG, first baseman, 1936

JOE DIMAGGIO, outfielder, 1939, 1941, 1947

JOE GORDON, second baseman, 1940

SPUD CHANDLER, pitcher, 1943

PHIL RIZZUTO, shortstop, 1950

YOGI BERRA, catcher, 1951, 1954, 1955

MICKEY MANTLE, outfielder, 1956, 1957, 1962

ROGER MARIS, outfielder, 1960, 1961

ELSTON HOWARD, catcher, 1963

THURMAN MUNSON, catcher, 1976

DON MATTINGLY, first baseman, 1985

GRAND SLAMS IN WORLD SERIES

TINO MARTINEZ, October 17, 1998, seventh inning
JOE PEPITONE, October 14, 1964, eighth inning
BOBBY RICHARDSON, October 8, 1960, first inning
BILL SKOWRON, October 19, 1956, seventh inning
YOGI BERRA, October 5, 1956, second inning
MICKEY MANTLE, October 4, 1953, third inning
GIL MCDOUGALD, October 9, 1951, third inning
TONY LAZZERI, October 2, 1936, third inning

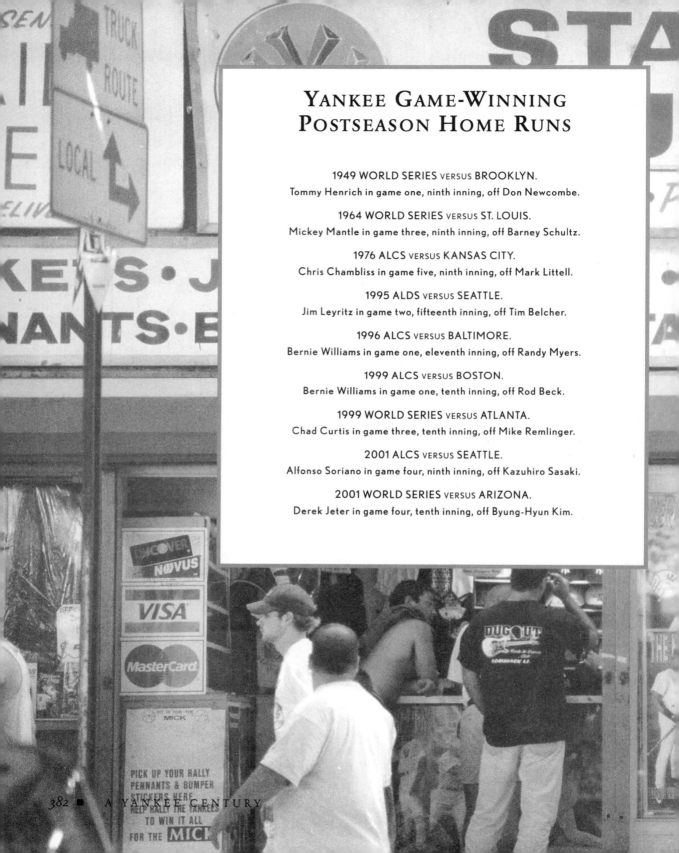

YANKEE GAME-WINNING POSTSEASON HOME RUNS

1949 WORLD SERIES VERSUS **BROOKLYN.**
Tommy Henrich in game one, ninth inning, off Don Newcombe.

1964 WORLD SERIES VERSUS **ST. LOUIS.**
Mickey Mantle in game three, ninth inning, off Barney Schultz.

1976 ALCS VERSUS **KANSAS CITY.**
Chris Chambliss in game five, ninth inning, off Mark Littell.

1995 ALDS VERSUS **SEATTLE.**
Jim Leyritz in game two, fifteenth inning, off Tim Belcher.

1996 ALCS VERSUS **BALTIMORE.**
Bernie Williams in game one, eleventh inning, off Randy Myers.

1999 ALCS VERSUS **BOSTON.**
Bernie Williams in game one, tenth inning, off Rod Beck.

1999 WORLD SERIES VERSUS **ATLANTA.**
Chad Curtis in game three, tenth inning, off Mike Remlinger.

2001 ALCS VERSUS **SEATTLE.**
Alfonso Soriano in game four, ninth inning, off Kazuhiro Sasaki.

2001 WORLD SERIES VERSUS **ARIZONA.**
Derek Jeter in game four, tenth inning, off Byung-Hyun Kim.

Consecutive Home Runs in a World Series Game

REGGIE JACKSON, October 18, 1977, (3 consecutive)

BABE RUTH, October 9, 1928 (2 consecutive)

BABE RUTH, October 6, 1926 (2 consecutive)

◆

Home Run First World Series At-Bat

BOB WATSON, 1981

JIM MASON, 1976

ROGER MARIS, 1960

ELSTON HOWARD, 1955

GEORGE SELKIRK, 1936

◆

World Series MVPs

1956 DON LARSEN (PERFECT GAME)

1958 BOB TURLEY

1960 BOBBY RICHARDSON

1961 WHITEY FORD

1962 RALPH TERRY

1977 REGGIE JACKSON

1978 BUCKY DENT

1998 SCOTT BROSIUS

1999 MARIANO RIVERA

2000 DEREK JETER

◆

Yankee Hall of Famers

BABE RUTH 1936

LOU GEHRIG 1939

WILLIE KEELER 1945

CLARK GRIFFITH 1946

FRANK CHANCE, JACK CHESBRO 1948

HERB PENNOCK 1952

PAUL WANER 1953

EDWARD G. BARROW 1954

BILL DICKEY 1955

"HOME RUN" BAKER, JOE DIMAGGIO, DAZZY VANCE 1957

JOE MCCARTHY 1962

BILL MCKECHNIE 1964

BURLEIGH GRIMES, MILLER HUGGINS 1966

CASEY STENGEL 1967

BRANCH RICKEY, RED RUFFING, STAN COVELESKI 1969

WAITE HOYT 1970

EARLE COMBS, GEORGE M. WEISS 1971

YOGI BERRA 1972

LEFTY GOMEZ 1974

MICKEY MANTLE, WHITEY FORD 1975

BUCKY HARRIS 1977

JOE SEWELL 1978

MEL ALLEN 1978

RED BARBER 1978

LARRY MACPHAIL 1981

JOHNNY MIZE 1985

ENOS SLAUGHTER 1987

JIM "CATFISH" HUNTER 1991

GAYLORD PERRY, TONY LAZZERI 1993

REGGIE JACKSON 1994

PHIL RIZZUTO 1997

DAVE WINFIELD 2001

RETIRED NUMBERS

1 BILLY MARTIN

3 BABE RUTH

4 LOU GEHRIG

5 JOE DIMAGGIO

7 MICKEY MANTLE

8 YOGI BERRA

8 BILL DICKEY

9 ROGER MARIS

10 PHIL RIZZUTO

15 THURMAN MUNSON

16 WHITEY FORD

23 DON MATTINGLY

32 ELSTON HOWARD

37 CASEY STENGEL

42 JACKIE ROBINSON

44 REGGIE JACKSON

◆

YANKEE CAPTAINS

HAL CHASE	1912
ROGER PECKINPAUGH	1914–1921
BABE RUTH	MAY 20, 1922–MAY 25, 1922
EVERETT SCOTT	1922–1925
LOU GEHRIG	APRIL 21, 1935–JUNE 2, 1941
THURMAN MUNSON	APRIL 17, 1976–AUGUST 2, 1979
GRAIG NETTLES	JANUARY 29, 1982–MARCH 30, 1984
WILLIE RANDOLPH	MARCH 4, 1986–OCTOBER 2, 1988
RON GUIDRY	MARCH 4, 1986–JULY 12, 1989
DON MATTINGLY	FEBRUARY 28, 1991–1995

Yankee Managers

CLARK GRIFFITH 1903–1908
KID ELBERFELD 1908
GEORGE STALLINGS 1909–1910
HAL CHASE 1910–1911
HARRY WOLVERTON 1912
FRANK CHANCE 1913–1914
ROGER PECKINPAUGH 1914
BILL DONOVAN 1915–1917
MILLER HUGGINS 1918–1929
ART FLETCHER 1929
BOB SHAWKEY 1930
JOE McCARTHY 1931–1946
BILL DICKEY 1946
JOHNNY NEUN 1946
BUCKY HARRIS 1947–1948
CASEY STENGEL 1949–1960
RALPH HOUK 1961–1963
YOGI BERRA 1964
JOHNNY KEANE 1965–1966
RALPH HOUK 1966–1973
BILL VIRDON 1974–1975
BILLY MARTIN 1975–1976
DICK HOWSER 1978
BOB LEMON 1978–1979
BILLY MARTIN 1979
DICK HOWSER 1980
GENE MICHAEL 1981
BOB LEMON 1981–1982
GENE MICHAEL 1982
CLYDE KING 1982
BILLY MARTIN 1983
YOGI BERRA 1984–1985
BILLY MARTIN 1985
LOU PINIELLA 1986–1987
BILLY MARTIN 1988
LOU PINIELLA 1988
DALLAS GREEN 1989
BUCKY DENT 1989–1990
STUMP MERRILL 1990–1991
BUCK SHOWALTER 1992–1995
JOE TORRE 1996–PRESENT

TEAM PRESIDENTS

1901	SIDNEY W. FRANK
1902	JOHN J. MAHON
1903–1906	JOSEPH W. GORDON
1907–1914	FRANK J. FARRELL
1915–1938	JACOB RUPPERT
1939–1944	EDWARD G. BARROW
1945–1947	LELAND S. MACPHAIL
1948–1966	DANIEL R. TOPPING
1966–1973	MICHAEL BURKE
1973–1977	GABRIEL H. PAUL
1978–1980	ALBERT L. ROSEN
1980–1990	GEORGE M. STEINBRENNER
1990–1991	ROBERT NEDERLANDER
1992	DANIEL MCCARTHY
1993–PRESENT	GEORGE M. STEINBRENNER

THE SPORTING NEWS
MAJOR LEAGUE
EXECUTIVE OF THE YEAR AWARD
TO YANKEES

ED BARROW 1937

ED BARROW 1941

GEORGE WEISS 1950

GEORGE WEISS 1951

GEORGE WEISS 1952

GEORGE WEISS 1960

DAN TOPPING 1961

GABE PAUL 1974

THE YANKEE UNIFORM

THE INTERLOCKING "NY" first appeared on the uniforms of the New York Highlanders in 1909. It was a design created in 1877 by Louis B. Tiffany for a medal to the New York City Police Department for Officer John McDowell, the first NYC policeman shot in the line of duty.

It first was placed on the cap and jersey's left sleeve, replacing the separated "N" and "Y."

Their last season at Hilltop Park, the Yankees debuted on April 11, with their traditional white uniforms now trimmed with black pinstripes. The uniform would remain virtually unchanged through the decades.

The Yankees tried various cap designs—including pinstripes—from 1903 until 1922, when they finally settled on a solid navy cap with the interlocking "NY" insignia. In 1917, the "NY" monogram was removed from the jersey and replaced by a plain, pinstripes-only look. The "NY" remained off the uniform—except for the cap—for the next two decades. In 1936, it was used again. With the exception of minor alterations, the uniform has not changed in more than sixty years.

THE NAME

THEY WERE CALLED "Yankees" first by sportswriters Mark Roth of the *New York Globe* and Sam Crane of the *New York Journal*. The name first appeared in print on June 21, 1904, in the *Boston Herald*.

By 1912, the Highlanders were frequently being referred to as Yankees in newspapers. The *New York Times* noted: "The Yankees presented a natty appearance in their new uniforms of white with black pinstripes."

YEARLY FINISHES

YEAR	W	L	POS	PCT	GB
1903	72	62	4	.537	17½
1904	92	59	2	.609	1
1905	71	78	6	.477	21½
1906	90	61	2	.596	3
1907	70	78	5	.473	21
1908	51	103	8	.331	39½
1909	74	77	5	.490	23½
1910	88	63	2	.583	14½
1911	76	76	6	.500	25½
1912	50	102	8	.329	55
1913	57	94	7	.377	38
1914	70	84	6	.455	30
1915	69	83	5	.454	32½
1916	80	74	4	.519	11
1917	71	82	6	.464	28½
1918	60	63	4	.488	13½
1919	80	59	3	.576	7½
1920	95	59	3	.617	3
1921	98	55	1	.641	0
1922	94	60	1	.610	0
1923	98	54	1	.645	0
1924	89	63	2	.586	2
1925	69	85	7	.448	28½
1926	91	63	1	.591	0
1927	110	44	1	.714	0
1928	101	53	1	.656	0
1929	88	66	2	.571	18
1930	86	68	3	.558	16
1931	94	59	2	.614	13½
1932	107	47	1	.695	0
1933	91	59	2	.607	7
1934	94	60	2	.610	7
1935	89	60	2	.597	3
1936	102	51	1	.667	0
1937	102	52	1	.662	0
1938	99	53	1	.651	0
1939	106	45	1	.702	0
1940	88	66	3	.571	2
1941	101	53	1	.656	0
1942	103	51	1	.669	0

YEARLY FINISHES *(continued)*

YEAR	W	L	POS	PCT	GB
1943	98	56	1	.636	0
1944	83	71	3	.539	6
1945	81	71	4	.533	6½
1946	87	67	3	.565	17
1947	97	57	1	.630	0
1948	94	60	3	.610	2½
1949	97	57	1	.630	0
1950	98	56	1	.636	0
1951	98	56	1	.636	0
1952	95	59	1	.617	0
1953	99	52	1	.656	0
1954	103	51	2	.669	8
1955	96	58	1	.623	0
1956	97	57	1	.630	0
1957	98	56	1	.636	0
1958	92	62	1	.597	0
1959	79	75	3	.513	15
1960	97	57	1	.630	0
1961	109	53	1	.673	0
1962	96	66	1	.593	0
1963	104	57	1	.646	0
1964	99	63	1	.611	0
1965	77	85	6	.475	25
1966	70	89	10	.440	26½
1967	72	90	9	.444	20
1968	83	79	5	.512	20
1969	80	81	5	.497	28½
1970	93	69	2	.574	15
1971	82	80	4	.506	21
1972	79	76	4	.510	6½
1973	80	82	4	.494	17
1974	89	73	2	.549	2
1975	83	77	3	.519	12
1976	97	62	1	.610	0
1977	100	62	1	.617	0
1978	100	63	1	.613	0
1979	89	71	4	.556	13½
1980	103	59	1	.636	0
1981	59	48	3	.551	2

YEARLY FINISHES *(continued)*

YEAR	W	L	POS	PCT	GB
1982	79	83	5	.488	16
1983	91	71	3	.562	7
1984	87	75	3	.537	17
1985	97	64	2	.602	2
1986	90	72	2	.556	5
1987	89	73	4	.549	9
1988	85	76	5	.528	3
1989	74	87	5	.460	14½
1990	67	95	7	.414	21
1991	71	91	5	.438	20
1992	76	86	4	.469	20
1993	88	74	2	.543	7
1994	70	43	1	.619	0
1995	79	65	2	.549	7
1996	92	70	1	.568	0
1997	96	66	2	.593	2
1998	114	48	1	.704	0
1999	98	64	1	.605	0
2000	87	74	1	.540	0
2001	95	65	1	.594	0

Through ten Yankee decades there have been all types of marker moments, firsts and lasts, oddities, rituals, misconceptions and superstitions. What follows is a selective sampling.

YANKEE FIRSTS

- First home run, John Ganzel in Detroit against the Tigers, May 11, 1903

- First Yankee pitcher to hit a home run, Clark Griffith, July 14, 1903

- First spring-training site, Atlanta, Georgia, 1903–1904

- First hitter to hit for the cycle, Bert Daniels, July 25, 1912

- First team to train outside of the United States, Bermuda, 1913

- First Sunday home game, June 17, 1917, 3–0 win over the Giants at the Polo Grounds

- First home run in the 1920s, Wally Pipp, April 14, 1920, first inning, Philadelphia

- First World Series game broadcast, 1921, New York Giants versus the Yankees. Grantland Rice handled the microphone on KDKA Pittsburgh for game one, the only game that was broadcast.

- First regular-season game at Yankee Stadium, April 18, 1923, a 4–1 win over Boston

- First pitch thrown in Yankee Stadium, Bob Shawkey, Yankees, April 18, 1923

- First batter at Yankee Stadium, Chick Fewster, Boston Red Sox, April 18, 1923

- First hit at Yankee Stadium, George Burns, Boston Red Sox, April 18, 1923, second-inning single

- First Yankee hit at Yankee Stadium, Aaron Ward, April 18, 1923, third-inning single

- First error, Babe Ruth, April 18, 1923, dropped fly ball in fifth inning

- First home run in Yankee Stadium, Babe Ruth, a two-run shot in the third inning off Boston's Howard Ehmke in a 4–1 Yankee victory, April 18, 1923

- First loss at Yankee Stadium, 4–3 to Washington, April 22, 1923

- First World Series game in Yankee Stadium, and first one heard on a nationwide radio network, October 10, 1923

- First World Series home run at Yankee Stadium, Casey Stengel of the New York Giants, an inside-the-park shot in game one of the 1923 World Series

- First World Series to generate $1 million in gate receipts, 1923

- First Yankee winning pitcher in World Series, Joe Bush, October 14, 1923

- First major-league team to lead wire to wire in the standings, 1927

- First team to have top four pitchers in winning percentage and top three in ERA in the same season, 1927

- First pennant winner in major-league history to have four regulars hit .333 or more, 1927

- First American League team with four players recording one hundred or more RBIs in the same season, 1927

- First team in major-league history to reach triple figures in doubles, triples, and home runs, 1927

- First team in American League history to sweep a World Series, 1927

- First team to permanently add numbers to their jerseys, April 16, 1929

- First AL player to hit four home runs in a game, Lou Gehrig, June 3, 1932. Gehrig hit three homers off George Earnshaw of the Philadelphia A's and another off reliever Roy Mahaffey.

- First Sunday game played at Fenway Park, July 3, 1932, Yankees beat the Red Sox 13–2. For three previous years, Boston played Sunday games at Braves Field because Fenway was thought to be too close to a church.

- First manager to win a pennant in both leagues, Joe McCarthy, 1932

- First five players elected to the Hall of Fame in 1936 included Babe Ruth, Ty Cobb, Honus Wagner, Christy Mathewson, and Walter Johnson.

- First rookie to play in an All-Star Game, Joe DiMaggio, went 0 for 5 and was charged with an error, 1936

Mickey Mantle

- First time in 2,131 games Lou Gehrig's name was not on a lineup card, May 2, 1939

- First game Yankees played at night, June 26, 1939, at Philadelphia

- First player to have his number retired, Lou Gehrig, number 4, on Lou Gehrig Appreciation Day, July 4, 1939

- First time four different pitchers each won a game in a World Series, 1939 Yankees

- First regular relief pitcher, Johnny Murphy (1934–1943); also the first used fifty or sixty times a season in relief roles

- First plaque placed on the center field wall in 1940 in Yankee Stadium honored Jacob Ruppert.

- First issue of *Sport* magazine featured Joe DiMaggio and his son on the cover, 1946.

- First Yankee player representative, Johnny Murphy, 1946

- First time Yankees travel by air, United Airlines, 1946

- First night game at Yankee Stadium, May 28, 1946, a 2–1 loss to Washington

- First World Series on television, Yankees versus Dodgers, shown only in New York City area, 1947

- First World Series pinch-hit home run, Yogi Berra, against the Brooklyn Dodgers, game three of the 1947 World Series

- First $100,000 ballplayer, Joe DiMaggio, Feb. 7, 1949

- First World Series Most Valuable Player, Joe Page. In the 1949 World Series he made three appearances, recorded a win and a save and a 2.00 ERA.

- First manager to win five consecutive World Series: Casey Stengel, 1949–1953. He was also the first manager to win nine pennants in ten seasons.

- First rookie to get two hits in one inning, Billy Martin, in a nine-run Yankee eighth inning at Fenway Park, April 18, 1950

- First Yankee Stadium day game completed with lights, August 29, 1950

- First time Joe DiMaggio was benched, after he had gone 4 for 30, August 11, 1950

- First major-league home run by Mickey Mantle, off Chicago's Randy Gumpert, May 1, 1951

- First rookie to hit a grand slam in a World Series game, Gil McDougald, October 9, 1951

- First black New York Yankee player, Elston Howard, April 14, 1955

- First black to be a World Series MVP, Elston Howard, 1958

- First message scoreboard unveiled at Yankee Stadium, April 1959

- First time in 35 years Pittsburgh won World Series. Bill Mazeroski homers in game seven against Yankees, 1960.

- First home run in a domed stadium, Mickey Mantle, April 9, 1965

- First major league at bat, home run, John Miller on September 11, 1966, against Boston

- First designated hitter, Ron Blomberg, April 6, 1973, at Fenway Park

- First home game outside of Yankee Stadium since 1922, the Yanks begin playing the first of two seasons at Shea Stadium April 6, 1974

- First home run at refurbished Yankee Stadium, April 15, 1976

- First Yankee American League Championship Series game, October 9, 1976, at Kansas City, a 4–1 Yankee win

- First American League Championship Series game at Yankee Stadium, October 12, 1976, at Kansas City, a 5–3 win over Kansas City

- First World Series game played by Yankees at night, October 17, 1976, at Cincinnati, a 4–3 loss to the Reds

- First night World Series game at Yankee Stadium, October 19, 1976, a 6–2 loss to Cincinnati

- First reliever to win the Cy Young Award, Sparky Lyle, 1977

- First team to host both the All-Star Game and World Series in the same season, New York Yankees, 1977

- First designated hitter to bat in a World Series game, Lou Piniella, 1976, Yankees versus Reds

- First two major-league games, home run, Joe Lefebvre, May 22–23, 1980

- First Yankee to drive in one hundred or more runs in five consecutive seasons, Dave Winfield, 1982–1986

- First payroll to have average player salary in excess of two million dollars, 1995

Billy Martin and
George Steinbrenner

- First father-son tandem to be elected to the Baseball Hall of Fame, Larry and Lee MacPhail, 1978 and 1998
- First time in postseason history that a team had three straight home runs, game one of the division series against Cleveland, Tim Raines, Derek Jeter, and Paul O'Neill, 1997
- First to pitch a regular-season perfect game at Yankee Stadium, David Wells, May 17, 1998
- First AL player to hit two pinch-hit grand slams in the same season, Daryl Strawberry, 1998
- First player to win a batting title, Gold Glove, and be on a World Series championship team in the same season, Bernie Williams, 1998
- First time switch-hitters homered in the same game from both sides of the plate, Bernie Williams and Jorge Posada, April 23, 2000
- First "Subway Series" in forty-four years, Yankees versus Mets, 2000
- First to win All-Star Game MVP award and World Series MVP award in same season, Derek Jeter, 2000
- First major-league pitcher to go 20–1, Roger Clemens, September 19, 2001, as the Yankees beat the Chicago White Sox 6–3
- First rookie to hit a walk-off playoff home run, Alfonso Soriano, October 22, 2001, against Seattle
- First time a president of the United States visited Yankee Stadium during the World Series, George W. Bush threw out the first ball, game three, October 30, 2001
- First November World Series game, November 1, 2001, Yankees versus Diamondbacks at Yankee Stadium
- First team in postseason history to win two straight games when trailing after eight innings, 2001 World Series, games four and five

YANKEE LASTS

- Last man cut by the Yankees in spring training in 1948 was Jerry Coleman: "Bucky Harris was the manager. The thing I remember most coming up from Florida was that they dumped us at Penn Station, which was like a zoo. I didn't know where I was or what I was doing, I spotted one of the players and followed him and got to the hotel."

- Last Yankee to have three triples in one game, Joe DiMaggio, August 28, 1938, against St. Louis

- Last triple play by the Yankees, June 3, 1968, against Minnesota (Womack–Cox–Mantle)

- Last home run by Mickey Mantle, September 20, 1968, off Boston's Jim Lonborg

- Last Yankee pitcher to hit a home run, Lindy McDaniel, off Mickey Lolich, September 28, 1972

- Last game at original Yankee Stadium, September 30, 1973, an 8–5 loss to the Detroit Tigers before 32,869

- Last batter at original Yankee Stadium, September 30, 1973, Mike Hegan, who flew out to center field

- Last home run at original Yankee Stadium, September 30, 1973, Duke Sims off Fred Holdsworth

- Last pitch at original Yankee Stadium, September 30, 1973, John Hiller

- Last Yankee victory at original Yankee Stadium, September 29, 1973, 3–0 over Detroit Tigers

- Last Yankee winning pitcher at original Yankee Stadium, Doc Medich, September 29, 1973, a 3–0 complete-game win over Detroit.

- Last player to score 100 or more runs in a season, Rickey Henderson, 118 in 1988.

- Last of the 1927 Yankee starters to die, Mark Koenig, April 25, 1993

YANKEE LONGEST

- The Yankees have gone the longest time without being no-hit of any existing team. The last time the Yankees were victimized by a no-hitter was on September 20, 1958, by Hoyt Wilhelm of the Orioles.

- Longest running promotion, Bat Day, started in 1965

- Longest game in World Series history, four hours and fifty-one minutes, in a thirteen-inning, 4–3 victory over the New York Mets in game one of the World Series on Saturday, October 21, 2000.

YANKEE OLDEST

◆ Phil Niekro became the oldest pitcher in major-league history to throw a shutout. The forty-seven-year-old Yankee pitcher blanked the Blue Jays on the final day of the 1985 season.

◆ David Cone, thirty-six, became the oldest pitcher to throw a perfect game since Cy Young in 1904.

◆ Paul O'Neill, thirty-eight, became the oldest player to steal twenty-plus bases and hit twenty-plus home runs in one season, 2001.

ODDITIES

◆ In 1993, a memorial plaque was placed in the Presbyterian Hospital Medical Center Garden, whose entrance is on Ft. Washington Avenue next to the Harkness Pavilion and behind where home plate had once existed at Hilltop Park. Former Yankee Chester Hoff, 102 years old, was there for the dedication. He had come all the way from Florida and said he wouldn't have missed the occasion for anything.

◆ Manager George Stallings allegedly paid the rent for an apartment just outside of Hilltop Park, where he stationed a "spy" with binoculars to pick up the opposition's signals. A mirror was employed to relay the signs to Yankee batters. The cloak-and-dagger work notwithstanding, Stallings was gone as manager in 1910.

◆ Yankee Stadium was built almost on the same spot where baseball originated in the Bronx. The Unions of Morrisania, who called themselves the champions of the world around 1866, played near the spot where the old Melrose Station of the Harlem Railroad was located.

◆ Hal Chase, who played first base for the Yankees from 1905 to 1912, had the bizarre habit of chewing on his bats.

◆ Jake Ruppert wanted to name his team the Knickerbockers after his best-selling beer. It was an advertising ploy that did not work. The name was too long for newspaper headlines.

◆ The Baby Ruth candy bar first debuted in 1921. It was actually named after President Grover Cleveland's first daughter, Ruth Cleveland, who died at the age of twelve, not Babe Ruth. There was also "Babe Ruth's Home Run Candy," brand of chocolate bar that went out of business due to a patent fight.

◆ Technically, the first two all-NYC series, in 1921 and 1922, were not Subway Series because the Yankees and Giants shared the same ballpark, the Polo Grounds.

- Eddie Bennett, the Yankee mascot throughout the 1920s and early 1930s, was as well known by fans as the Yankee stars they idolized. He was there to shake hands whenever a Yankee hit a home run. Whenever the Babe was in the on-deck circle awaiting his time to bat, Bennett was right next to Ruth. Bennett's growth was stunted when he fell out of a baby carriage. He grew to a height of just four and a half feet and was a hunchback. A mascot batboy with the White Sox and Dodgers, Bennett was signed on by the Yankees in 1921. New York won the pennant that year and the next two with Bennett on the scene. He became a good-luck charm for the team. Most team photographs feature him in the the center of the front row. Most Yankees would allow only the little mascot-batboy to handle their bats. On the road he roomed with pitcher Urban Shocker.

Kate Smith and Babe Ruth

- When Ruth hit sixty home runs in 1927, he hit 14 percent of all home runs in his league that year. Today for a player to hit 14 percent of all home runs he would have to hit over three hundred home runs in one season.

- Before he signed with the Yankees in 1923, Gehrig was a feared college slugger known as Columbia Lou. He also was an outstanding pitcher. On the day that Yankee Stadium opened in 1923, with Ruth hitting the first home run, Gehrig, still in college, struck out seventeen Williams College batters.

- In early 1925 the Yankees offered to trade Lou Gehrig to the Red Sox for first baseman Phil Todt to make up to Boston for the Babe Ruth trade. The deal was turned down by the Sox.

- Babe Ruth is the only player to end a World Series by being thrown out on a base-stealing attempt, game seven, 1926.

- Joe McCarthy managed the 1943 American League All-Star team and did not use any of the six Yankees picked for the game. The American League won 8–5. McCarthy proved his point that he could beat the National League without his Yankees even playing.

- Joe DiMaggio is the only player to get at least one hit in All-Star Games at Yankee Stadium, the Polo Grounds, and Ebbets Field.

- Joe DiMaggio was never thrown out going from first to third in his entire major-league career. He had that innate sense of knowing how fast he could go, how good a jump he got, and the speed of the outfielder's throw.

- Joe DiMaggio was the batting coach for Oakland in 1967 when Reggie Jackson was a rookie, and he tried to convince the youngster to reduce his swing. Jackson said he would do it his way.

- On September 23, 1955, the Yankees clinched the pennant with a 3–2 win over the Red Sox—and the winning pitcher wasn't even there to see it. Relieved in the eighth inning by Whitey Ford, Don Larsen turned on all the showers in the visiting clubhouse to drown out the crowd noise and the clubhouse radio, and hid in an adjacent utility room. His teammates found him still in his uniform, sitting on a block of ice, with his fingers in his ears, drinking a beer.

- Dave Winfield accidentally killed a seagull with a between-innings throw at Toronto's Exhibition Stadium on August 4, 1983. When the game was over, Winfield was met by several plainclothes officers and taken to a Toronto station and charged with cruelty to animals. Winfield posted $500 bond, and the charges eventually were dropped.

- Point Loma High School in San Diego is the only one to produce two pitchers who threw perfect games in the majors, Don Larsen and David Wells.

- When Columbo was a kid, his heroes were Joe DiMaggio and Phil Rizzuto.

- Part of the Yankee legacy of Sparky Lyle is that he worked with Ron Guidry and was instrumental in the development of his wicked slider.

- Ron Guidry was a fairly skilled amateur drummer who kept a trap set at Yankee Stadium and once played with the Beach Boys during a post-game concert.

- Tommy James was the first artist to feature the synthesizer in the production of his classic LP *Cellophane Symphony* in 1968. The instrument was owned by Hall of Famer Whitey Ford.

- David Wells grew up a Yankee fan in Southern California, a devotee of Babe Ruth. His first son was born February 6, the same day Ruth was born. The Babe wore number 3, and Wells's second son was born at 3:33 P.M. in March, the third month.

RITUALS

- Whenever Wilcy Moore got up to loosen his arm in late innings, mascot Eddie Bennett caught the first warm-up toss.

- Roger Clemens always pats the Babe Ruth monument for good luck before coming in to pitch.

- Jorge Posada, before every home game, goes out to Monument Park to touch the Thurman Munson monument.

- Roger Clemens and Andy Pettitte don't shave the day before pitching.

- Pitcher Randy Choate enters a dugout only through the same entrance he used the first time he entered that dugout.

- Orlando Hernandez jumps over the baseline to and from the mound.

- George Steinbrenner, sporting a turtleneck and blazer, always sits in the same lucky spot in a game's crucial moments.

- After the Yankees lost the first two games of the division series to Oakland in 2001, Joe Torre noticed a hat that bore the words of Yogi Berra: "It ain't over till it's over." Torre threw the hat into his bag and had a clubhouse attendant sew a Port Authority Police logo onto the right side. The Yankees won game three in Oakland and advanced to the World Series, and Torre wore the hat before and after each game.

MISCONCEPTIONS

◆ Many people believe that the day Lou Gehrig replaced Wally Pipp at first base was the day the 2,130-game streak began. It actually began the day before when the man they would call the Iron Horse pinch-hit for Pee-Wee Wanninger, who replaced shortstop Everett Scott, who had the record for consecutive games played (1,307) until Wanninger took his place.

◆ That Billy Martin punched St. Louis catcher Clint Courtney at St. Louis's Sportsman's Park on April 28, 1953. The game between the Yanks and the Browns was a close one that day, but in the top of the tenth, Gil McDougald broke the 6–6 tie by barreling into Courtney at home plate and jarring the ball loose. "I'm going to cut the first guy I reach," Courtney announced when he came to the plate in the bottom of the inning. Yankee hurler Allie Reynolds heard the declaration and tried to go up and in on Courtney but missed. The St. Louis catcher lined the ball into right field and raced around the bases in search of a double. Scrap Iron Courtney came through on his promise and slid into second with his spikes high. Phil Rizzuto was covering second on the play and was cut badly. Reynolds, McDougald, and first baseman Joe Collins were immediately on top of Courtney, swinging wildly. Both benches cleared. After a lot of flying dust and a lot of flying punches, the melee cleared. Umpire John Stevens had a separated shoulder. The fines handed out totaled $850–Courtney was docked $250. But the most mysterious fine was the $150 fine given to Billy Martin, who never threw a punch.

INDEX

Page numbers in *italic* indicate photographs; those in **bold** indicate tables.

American League Most Valuable
    Players (MVP)
    Greatest Yankees, 136, 140, 151,
        155, 158, 161, 165, 171, 185,
        194, 197, 212
    numbers and, 331
    Quiz, 363, 365
    records, **381**
    teams (best and worst), 254, 256
    timeline, 14, 15, 18, 21, 22, 23, 31
American League wins, xv, xvi, xvii
Amoros, Sandy, 88, 89, **138**
Amyotrophic lateral sclerosis (ALS,
    Lou Gehrig's disease), 13, 37,
    70, 157, 168
Anderson, Sparky, 31
Andrews, Mike, 102
Andrews, Shane, **124**
Appling, Luke, 72
Arroyo, Luis (Yo-Yo), 253, *283*
Astor, William Waldorf, 42
Attendance at Yankee Stadium, 43,
    46, 356
Avila, Bobby, 84
Azocar, Oscar, 268

b

Babe, The. *See* Ruth, George
    Herman
Babe Ruth's Legs. *See* Byrd, Sammy
Babich, Johnny, 13
Baby Ruth (candy bar), 398
Baerga, Carlos, **117**
Bahnsen, Stan, 24, 265, **381**
Baker, Dusty, 105, **384**
Baker, Frank (Home Run), 320
Balboni, Steve (Bye-Bye), **114,** 269
Bam-Bam. *See* Meulens, Hensley
Banty Rooster. *See* Ford, Edward
    Charles (Whitey)
Barber, Red, 20, 77, 78, 132, 165,
    384
Barfield, Jesse, 268
Barker, Ray, 265
Barnes, Frank, 17
Barrow, Edward Grant (The Yankee
    Empire Builder)
    Greatest Yankees, 134–35, 210,
        230
    memorable moments, 70

records, **384, 387**
talkin' Yankees, 276
timeline, 7, 10, 13, 17
Yankee Stadium and, 52
Baseball Hall of Fame
    (Cooperstown)
    Greatest Yankees, 132, 137, 146,
        148, 151, 155, 156, 158, 166,
        167, 168, 169, 172, 175, 180,
        182, 202, 212, 226, 231
    inductees, xvi
    numbers and, 336
    Quiz, 362, 363
    records, **384**
    teams (best and worst), 240, 265
    timeline, 13, 20, 23, 25, 33, 35,
        39
Baseball original spot in Bronx and
    Yankee Stadium, 398
Batista, Miguel, 128
Batting champions, **376**
Batting title, Don Mattingly vs.
    Dave Winfield (1984), *115,*
    115–16
Battle of the Baltimore, 314
Bauer, Henry Albert (Hank,
    Bruiser)
    Greatest Yankees, 135–36,
        135–36, 190, 225, 226
    memorable moments, 90, 91,
        92
    numbers and, 336
    photographs of, *135–36*
    Quiz, 359, 360, 361
    teams (best and worst), 251
    timeline, xviii, 22
Baylor, Don, 30, 108, **114,** 193,
    338
Beall, Walter, 238
Beattie, Jim, 108
Beautiful Bella (Babe Ruth's bat),
    62
Beck, Rod, **382**
Beene, Fred, 319
Behemoth of Bust. *See* Ruth,
    George Herman (Babe)
Belcher, Tim, **382**
Belle, Albert, **117**
Bellinger, Clay, 125, 221
Bench, Johnny, 276

Bengough, Benny, 70, 238, 328,
    334
Benitez, Armando, 120
Bennett, Eddie, 399
Berra, Dale, 279
Berra, Lawrence Peter (Yogi)
    Greatest Yankees, 136–37, *137,*
        138, 163, 165, 182, 192, 194,
        209, **224**
    memorable moments, 82, 84, 86,
        87, 88, 90, 91, 92, 93, 99, 100,
        123
    numbers and, 331, 332, 334, *334,*
        335, 337, 339, 340, 343, 344,
        347, 349, 354
    photographs of, *51, 137, 278,*
        334, 365
    Quiz, 358, 359, 362
    records, **381, 384, 385, 386,**
        394, 401
    talkin' Yankees, 276–80, *278*
    teams (best and worst), 248, 249,
        250, 252, 253
    timeline, xvi, xviii, 15, 18, 20,
        22, 23, 25, 31, 37
    Yankee Stadium and, 47, *51,* 52
Bertoia, Reno, 49
Best teams, 236–62
Bevens, Bill, *77,* 77–78, 79, **138**
Beville, Monte, 57
Big Bertha (Babe Ruth's bat), 62
Billy Ball. *See* Martin, Billy
Biscuit Pants. *See* Gehrig, Heinrich
    Ludwig (Lou)
Black Betsy (Babe Ruth's bat), 62
Black Yankees of Negro National
    League, 48
Blaeholder, George, 351
Blair, Paul, 104–5
Blanchard, Johnny (Super-Sub), 93,
    162, 253, 267, 332, 334
Blind Ryne. *See* Duren, Ryne
Bliss, Elmer, 57
Blomberg, Ron, 24, 25, 101–2,
    103, 365, 395
Bloody Angle of Yankee Stadium,
    316
Blowers, Mike, 116, 269
Blue, Vida, 27
Blyzka, Mike, 20, 337

Turley, Bob (continued)
Quiz, 364
records, *376*, **379, 383**
teams (best and worst), 251,
252
timeline, 20
Turner, James Riley (Jim,
Milkman), *147,* 228, 310
Twain, Mark, 200
Twelfth-inning single by Paul Blair
(1977), 104–5
Twenty-game winners, **379–80**
Twinkletoes. *See* Selkirk, George
Alexander
Two Head. *See* Ruth, George
Herman (Babe)

u

Unholy Trio, The. *See* Ford, Edward
Charles (Whitey); Mantle,
Mickey; Martin, Billy
Uniforms, 5, 10, *328,* 328–29, **385,**
388
Unions of Morrisania, 398
Unitas, Johnny, 42
Upper-grandstand seats of Yankee
Stadium, 43
Upshaw, Cecil, 319

v

Valentin, Javier, 122, **122**
Valentine, Bill, 154–55, 183, 276,
284, 287
Vance, Dazzy, **384**
Vaughn, Hippo, 263
Vault underneath second base of
Yankee Stadium, 43
Veeck, Bill, 274
Velarde, Randy, **117,** 268
Ventura, Robin, 39, 116
timeline, 40
Vick, Sammy, 303
Vidro, Jose, 123, **124**
Vigliano, David, 52, 197, 264
Vincent, Fay, 34, 270
Virdon, Bill, 25, **224,** 345, **386**
Vizquel, Omar, 200
"Voice of the Yankees." *See* Allen,
Melvin
Vollmer, Clyde, 82

w

Wagner, Honus, 393
Walewander, Jim, 269
Wali of Wallop. *See* Ruth, George
Herman (Babe)
Walker, Jimmy, 236
Walsh, Ed, 142
Waner, Lloyd, 60
Waner, Paul, 60, **384**
Wanninger, Pee-Wee, 8, 67, 155, 402
Ward, Aaron, 392
Warhop, Jack, 6, 263
Warrior, The. *See* O'Neill, Paul
Andrew
Washington, Claudell, 32, 268, 269
Washington, U.L., 111, **114**
Wathan, John, **114**
Watson, Bob, **383**
Wazir of Wham. *See* Ruth, George
Herman (Babe)
Weatherman, The. *See* Rivers,
Mickey
Weaver, Earl, 290, 359
Webb, Del, 15, 22, 134, 179, 180,
226
Weiss, George (Lonesome George)
Greatest Yankees, 134, 149, 175,
191, 229–31, *230*
memorable moments, 92
photographs of, *230*
records, **384, 387**
talkin' Yankees, 311
teams (best and worst), 252
timeline, 11
Wells, David Lee (Boomer)
Greatest Yankees, 142
memorable moments, 55
numbers and, 331
perfect game (1998), 120–23,
121, **122**
photographs of, *36*
Quiz, 358
records, **378,** 396, 400
talkin' Yankees, 311
teams (best and worst), 259, 261,
262
timeline, 36, *36,* 37, 40
Welteroth, Dick, 82
Wera, Julie, 238
Wetteland, John, 36, 199, 209, 310

Whitaker, Steve, 265
White, Bill, 110
White, Frank, **114**
White, Rondell, **124**
White, Roy, 234
memorable moments, **103,** 110
numbers and, 337, 346
teams (best and worst), 257, 265,
266
timeline, xviii
White Construction Company, 42
White Gorilla. *See* Gossage, Richard
Michael
Whitey Pitcher. *See* Ford, Edward
Charles (Whitey)
Whiz Kids, 202
Who's Who. *See* Greatest Yankees
Widger, Chris, **124**
Wild pitch of Jack Chesbro (1904),
57–58
Wilhelm, Hoyt, 21, 359, **378,** 397
Williams, Bernie
Greatest Yankees, 231–33, *232*
memorable moments, **117,** 119,
120, **122, 124,** 126
numbers and, 337, 343, 355, *355*
photographs of, *232, 355*
records, **374, 376, 382,** 396
talkin' Yankees, 275, 311
teams (best and worst), 259, 261,
262
timeline, xviii, 31, 34, 36, 39
Williams, Gerald, **117**
Williams, Jimmy, 57
Williams, Ted
Greatest Yankees, 151, 212
memorable moments, 81, 84
talkin' Yankees, 291, 294
teams (best and worst), 251
timeline, 14, 15, 21
Williamson, Ned, 7
Wilson, Enrique, 125
Wilson, Jim, 21
Wilson, Willie, 111, **114**
Wiltse, Snake, 57
Window Breakers, 326
Winfield, Dave (Daddy Longlegs,
Mr. May, Winny)
batting title vs. Don Mattingly
(1984), 115–16

World Series at, 44, 53
Yankee Stadium II, **54**
Yastrzemski, Carl, 109, 110, 294
Year finishes, **389–91**
Yost, Eddie, 82
Young, Cy, 358, 359, **378**
Yo-Yo. *See* Arroyo, Luis

z

Zachary, Tom, 62, 63, 335, 366
Zalusky, Jack, 57
Zimmer, Don
 Greatest Yankees, 192, 234
 memorable moments, 109
 numbers and, 338, 342

talkin' Yankees, 312
teams (best and worst), 256, 259
Zinn, Guy, 263, 264
Zuvella, Paul, 32

ABOUT THE AUTHOR

Harvey Frommer, celebrated author of more than thirty sports books, including the classics *Shoeless Joe and Ragtime Baseball, New York City Baseball,* and *The New York Yankee Encyclopedia,* was honored by the New York State Legislature and cited in the Congressional Record as a sports historian and journalist. Together with his wife, Myrna Katz Frommer, he authored the critically acclaimed oral histories *It Happened in Manhattan, It Happened in Brooklyn, It Happened in the Catskills, It Happened on Broadway,* and *Growing Up Jewish in America.* Frommer is a professor in the Master of Arts in Liberal Studies program at Dartmouth College and a longtime Yankee fan. He wrote for *Yankees Magazine* for 16 years.

BOOKS BY HARVEY FROMMER

HARDBACK BOOKS

A Yankee Century, Berkley 2002
It Happened in Manhattan with Myrna Katz Frommer, Berkley 2001
Growing Up Baseball with Frederic J. Frommer, Taylor 2001
It Happened on Broadway with Myrna Katz Frommer, Harcourt Brace 1998
The New York Yankee Encyclopedia, Macmillan 1997
Growing Up Jewish in America with Myrna Katz Frommer, Harcourt Brace 1995
Big Apple Baseball, Taylor 1995
It Happened in Brooklyn with Myrna Katz Frommer, Harcourt Brace 1993
Shoeless Joe and Ragtime Baseball, Taylor 1992
It Happened in the Catskills with Myrna Katz Frommer, Harcourt Brace 1991
Holzman on Hoops with Red Holzman, Taylor 1991
Behind the Lines: The Autobiography of Don Strock, Pharos 1991
Running Tough: The Autobiography of Tony Dorsett, Doubleday 1989
Growing Up at Bat: 50th Anniversary Book of Little League Baseball, Pharos 1989
Throwing Heat: The Autobiography of Nolan Ryan, Doubleday 1988
Primitive Baseball, Atheneum 1988
150th Anniversary Album of Baseball, Franklin Watts 1988
Red on Red: The Autobiography of Red Holzman, Bantam 1987
Olympic Controversies, Franklin Watts 1985
Baseball's Greatest Managers, Franklin Watts 1985
National Baseball Hall of Fame, Franklin Watts 1985

Games of the XXIIIrd Olympiad, International Sport Publications 1984
Jackie Robinson, Franklin Watts 1984
Baseball's Greatest Records, Streaks and Feats, Atheneum 1982
Baseball's Greatest Rivalry, Atheneum 1982
Rickey and Robinson, Macmillan 1982
Basketball My Way: Nancy Lieberman with Myrna Frommer, Scribners 1982
New York City Baseball, Macmillan 1980
The Great American Soccer Book, Atheneum 1980
Sports Roots, Atheneum 1980
Sports Lingo, Atheneum 1979
The Martial Arts: Judo and Karate, Atheneum 1978
A Sailing Primer with Ron Weinmann, Atheneum 1978
A Baseball Century, Macmillan 1976

PAPERBACK BOOKS

Growing Up Jewish in America with Myrna Katz Frommer, University of
    Nebraska Press, 1999
It Happened in the Catskills with Myrna Katz Frommer, Harcourt Brace 1996
It Happened in Brooklyn with Myrna Katz Frommer, Harcourt Brace 1995
Shoeless Joe and Ragtime Baseball, Taylor 1993
New York City Baseball, Harcourt Brace 1992
Running Tough: The Autobiography of Tony Dorsett, Berkley 1992
Throwing Heat: The Autobiography of Nolan Ryan, Avon 1989
Red on Red: The Autobiography of Red Holzman, Bantam 1988
New York City Baseball, Atheneum 1985
Baseball's Greatest Rivalry, Atheneum 1984
Basketball My Way: Nancy Lieberman with Myrna Katz Frommer, Scribners
    1984
Sports Lingo, Atheneum 1983
Sports Genes with Myrna Katz Frommer, Ace 1982
The Sports Date Book with Myrna Katz Frommer, Ace 1981

BOOKS IN TRANSLATION

Throwing Heat: The Autobiography of Nolan Ryan, Kaoru Takeda (Japan), 1993